Argentine Jewish Theatre

Jacket cover for *On the Argentine Pampas* by Mordechai Maidanik.

Argentine Jewish Theatre

A Critical Anthology

Edited and Translated by

Nora Glickman and Gloria F. Waldman

Lewisburg
Bucknell University Press
London: Associated University Presses

Associated University Presses
440 Forsgate Drive
Cranbury, NJ 08512

Associated University Presses
16 Barter Street
London WC1A 2AH, England

Associated University Presses
P.O. Box 338, Port Credit
Mississauga, Ontario
Canada L5G 4L8

The paper used in this publication meets the requirements of the American National Standard for Permanence of Paper for Printed Library Materials Z39.48-1984.

Library of Congress Cataloging-in-Publication Data

Argentine Jewish theatre : a critical anthology / edited and translated by Nora Glickman and Gloria F. Waldman.
   p. cm.
  Includes bibliographical references (p.   ).
  Contents: Aarón the Jew / Samuel Eichelbaum—Petroff's junkshop / Alberto Novión—The tithe / César Tiempo—Simón Brumelstein, knight of the Indies / Germán Rozenmacher—Krinsky / Jorge Goldenberg—A thousand years, one day / Ricardo Halac—Onward, Corazón! / Osvaldo Dragún—Lost belongings / Diana Raznovich.
  ISBN 0-8387-5287-X (alk. paper)
  1. Argentine drama—Jewish authors Translations into English.
2. Argentine drama 20th century—Translations into English.
3. Jews—Argentina Drama. I. Glickman, Nora. II. Waldman, Gloria.
PQ7737.E5A74   1996
862–dc20
                                     95-10883
                                       CIP

Contents

Acknowledgments

In the course of the eight years work on this project we often changed our minds as to what were the most representative plays to be included in this collection. We recognize that the eight we finally chose are a small sampling of the wealth of material available in the field of Argentine Jewish theatre. At the same time we are confident that the plays selected do capture the essential aspects of the Jewish presence in Argentina in the twentieth century. We hope that this anthology will encourage other scholars to make more works available to English-speaking readers.

During the course of our work on the book we made many calls to many people regarding its contents, at all hours of the day and night. To all we say . . ¡gracias! To Nora's ever helpful mother, a devoted Yiddishist from the Pampas, Rosalía Rosembuj; to Gloria's ever helpful father, Harry Feiman. To Nora's husband Henry, for providing the right word when needed. To Gloria's amigo, Sandy Berger, for his Yiddish expertise during the final editing process; to professors Gonzalo Sobejano, Joseph Landis, Angela Dellepiane, and Sarah Blacher Cohen; Richard Carlow and Dina Abramowicz, from the YIVO Institute for Jewish Research; Jacob Kovadloff, from the Latin American Division of the American Jewish Committee; Ana E. Weinstein, from the Mark Turkow Center of Documentation on Argentine Judaism; our careful readers, Petra Hall, David Berger and Ellen Marson; Michael Koy, Managing Editor of Associated University Presses, for his patience and useful advice; Gloria's generous colleagues at York College: Bonnie Grossman, fairy godsister and secretary; Liz Hamilton, Director of Mail Services; Bill Warren, Director of Printing Services; Robert Machelow, Chief Librarian; Regina Caulfield, extremely resourceful grants advisor at Queens College; and Nora's City University of New York PSC/CUNY grant for the writing of this book.

Introduction

Argentina has the largest Jewish population in Latin America and has produced the richest dramatic repertory. Its literature illustrates the problems of acculturation that immigrants faced when they first settled in the country and the effects their adaptation had on later generations. For religious, cultural, and linguistic reasons the transition was easier and less violent for the Catholic majority of Italians and Spaniards than for the Jews.

While influenced by European masters of realism and symbolism—Ibsen, Strindberg, Chekhov—Argentine theatre closely relates to the social realities of the periods it describes. It evokes the clashes between natives and immigrants and the nostalgia for a world that was left behind.

One of the earliest manifestations of Jewish culture in Argentina was the Yiddish theatre, most popular from the 1900s to the 1930s. The plays presented since 1901 under the leadership of actor Bernardo Vaisman were biblical, folkloric, and traditionalist by nature.[1] The first Yiddish performances were operettas presented by foreign companies, since the new immigrant could not afford to mount expensive shows. Ironically, some of the financial backers of the theatre companies were the *temeyim,* the pimps who were responsible for organizing the traffic of Jewish women from Eastern Europe to Argentina for prostitution. Until 1926, when a public scandal caused the expulsion of the *temeyim,* they were the most generous and enthusiastic public for Yiddish theatre in Argentina.[2]

When Boris Tomachevsky, the founder of Yiddish theatre in the United States, came to Argentina on tour with *Dos Pintale Yid* (That little spark of Jewishness), he was extraordinarily successful. From 1930 to 1946 many prestigious actors from Europe performed throughout the Jewish colonies in the provinces of La Pampa, Entre Ríos, and Buenos Aires, which increased the production and success of the local Yiddish theatre. The content of the plays expanded to include universal themes and social issues related to the lives of Argentine Jews. Comedies, operettas, and melodramas were staged not only by local groups but by international repertory companies. International actors like Maurice Schwartz and Yosef Buloff were contracted to perform.

Popular Jewish theatre saw its beginnings in 1932 with the *Prolet Bine,* or Proletarian Stage. It later changed its name and became known as the IFT, the Yiddish Folk Theater. The IFT, a collective company, presented the Yiddish versions of plays by Berthold Brecht, Arthur Miller, and the original work of the Yiddish authors Abraham Goldfaden, Shalom Asch, Shalom Aleichem, S. An-Ski, I. L. Peretz, and others.

By 1930 Jewish dramatists began to make the language transition from Yiddish to Spanish. Actors like Berta and Paulina Singerman, Cipe Lincovsky, and Fanny Brener began their careers as Yiddish actors and then devoted themselves exclusively to Argentine theatre; several of them moved from the theatre to the cinema. This gave rise to the flourishing of the newly formed *teatro independiente,* an innovative cultural movement that spanned three decades from 1930 to 1960. In 1952, with the assassination of Jewish writers and doctors in the Soviet Union, the IFT members were divided among those who still sympathized with the Soviet regime and those who tended towards a Jewish, Zionist identity. Since 1957, with the presentation of *The Diary of Anne Frank,* the IFT undertook the decision to do theatre in Spanish. This "independent theatre" responded to the repressive era that began with the coup d'etat that put Irigoyen in power in the 1930s. The demand for Yiddish theatre decreased as the newcomers adapted to the country, as a new generation was born, and as the immigrants became involved in national issues.

Since its early stages the Independent Theatre included many dramatists, directors, and actors of European origin: its Italian founder, Leónidas Barletta, Roberto Arlt, César Tiempo, and Samuel Eichelbaum, among others. Critic David W. Foster suggests that Argentine Jewish artists became part of the mainstream in their attempt to represent Jewish culture with eloquence in the face of indifference or aggressive anti-Semitism in the society at large.[3]

Ashkenazi or Eastern European Jews were generally known as *rusos* and were set apart because of their religion, language, and peculiar way of dressing; the Sephardic Jews—generally called *turcos*—arriving from Turkey and Morocco, spoke Ladino or Judeo-Spanish, which is very close to Spanish, and therefore had less difficulty integrating into the society. In Argentine drama the Jew did not appear as a central character until the turn of the twentieth century. Only then, when large waves of Italian and

Spanish immigrants flooded the country, did the Jew become a visible presence as part of an ethnic minority.

Dramatists found inspiration in the Jew as a real flesh-and-blood immigrant only when they came to settle the land, or to peddle in the streets of the big city. Still, the Jew is portrayed as a peculiar and idiosyncratic subject, caricatured in one-act plays written during the first three decades of Argentine popular drama called *sainetes*. The authors, non-Jews and mostly first generation Argentines of Italian and Spanish background, had the intention of providing large immigrant audiences with entertainment. The caricatures that emerged from the *sainete* incorporated the prejudices held against each immigrant group. The action of the *sainete* usually took place in the *conventillo* or tenement house, where immigrants of all ethnic origins converged. While maintaining a jovial tone, the *sainete* revealed the prejudices prevalent in the society.

Given that thousands of *sainetes* were written, and that the figure of the immigrant is the most important one, there are relatively few such plays where the Jew is a central character. *El barrio de los judíos* (The Jewish neighborhood) (1919), by Alberto Vacarezza; *El cambalache de Petroff (Petroff's Junkshop)* (1937), by Alberto Novión; *Ropa vieja* (Old clothes), by Carlos María Pacheco; *La librería de Abramoff* (Abramoff's bookshop) (1920), by Rafael Di Yorio, are among the most popular *sainetes* dealing with Jews. In these dramas Jews usually appear dressed in their particular garb, faithfully following the precepts of their religion. The typical plot of the *sainete* goes through the stages of elopement, secret wedding, and reconciliation. The daughter of a Jewish immigrant elopes with her creole boyfriend in order to marry him. In so doing, she defies the authority of a fanatical and recalcitrant old father. Finally the father concedes, and the two generations reconcile. This solution represents the victory of the melting pot.

In Argentina the portrait of the Jew was based primarily on cultural and religious prejudices. It took on the characteristics of the Wandering Jew and of Judas, both inspired by the teachings of the conservative Catholic religion practiced by the majority. Carlos Schaeffer Gallo's play *El gaucho judío* (The Jewish gaucho) (1920) is a representative model. From the European literary tradition the most important influence is perhaps that of Ivo Pelay's play *Judío* (The Jew) (1916), directly inspired by the figure of Shylock in Shakespeare's *The Merchant of Venice*.

While most playwrights presented an optimistic outlook on the advantages of immigration and a view of the "happy" fusion of the races, Jewish authors—the sons of Eastern European immigrants who spoke Yiddish as their first language—tended to express themselves in a literature that more accurately reflected the prevailing social tensions of the times. They portrayed the Jew more seriously in full-length dramas in which they invested large amounts of personal experience and favored a background of Jewish folklore and traditions. Within the framework of a "type," only the authors of Jewish origin sought to correct the distorted vision of the immigrant presented by non-Jewish authors. Thus they enriched the theatrical repertoire with more complex dramas and compensated for the stereotype of Jews by throwing light on the moral aspects of their personalities. They also clarified ambiguities regarding the Jewish religion. We see these features in César Tiempo's *La alfarda (The Tithe)* (1937), *El teatro soy yo* (I am the theatre) (1933), *Pan Criollo* (Creole bread) (1935), and in Samuel Eichelbaum's *El judío Aarón (Aarón the Jew)* (1926). These plays present the perspective of Jews in conflict with their social milieu. Two decades later, toward the 1960s, Jewish playwrights would delve deeper into these themes. In *Réquiem para un viernes a la noche* (Réquiem for a Friday night) (1935) and in *Simón, Caballero de Indias (Simón Brumelstein, Knight of the Indies)*, Germán Rozenmacher portrays assimilated Jews who are tormented by their conscience. In *Krinsky* (1977), by Jorge Goldenberg, the Jew is preoccupied with memories of the pogroms.

With very few exceptions Argentine Jewish dramatists wrote exclusively in Spanish and directed their plays towards a large population of gentile spectators. They sought to present the viewpoint of the "enlightened author." In so doing they challenged traditional Jewish values, particularly the preoccupation with Jewish exclusiveness and separation.

The authors included in this anthology analyze the process of change and examine the dilemmas that Jewish immigrants faced as they adapted to a foreign culture. The authors also observe the dichotomies that the immigrants' descendants encountered when choosing to depart from their traditional values. The characters in the plays portray three generations of men and women who made the physical voyage from Eastern Europe to the Americas and struggled for acceptance in their adopted countries while maintaining a close affiliation with Europe. Their main concern was to relate intimate experiences that had to do with generational conflicts and with problems of identity, intermarriage, integration, and assimilation. The issue of ethnic identity in particular, rather than becoming outdated or exhausted, continues to occupy Jewish writers in Argentina. Over the past decades a number of dramatists have concerned themselves with questions regarding their origins and their traditions, among them, José Rabinovich, Hebe Serebrinsky, Elio Brailovsky, and Aída Bortnik.

We have chosen these eight plays as representative of the seminal themes elaborated in Argentine Jewish drama over the century. Our intention in including a *sainete,* written by an acclaimed Argentine dramatist who is not Jewish, was to present a different perspective on the figure of the Jew. The caricaturesque depiction provided by Alberto Novión in *Petroff's Junkshop* is one of thousands of superficial portrayals of immigrants written in the early 1900s when Argentina was growing in population at a vertiginous speed. Novión's simplistic solution to the highly emotional issue of intermarriage is treated with more pathos and intensity by the Jewish authors included here—Eichelbaum, Rozenmacher, and Halac. In contrast with Novión, the Jewish portrayals seem far more profound, as these dramatists counteract unidimensional stereotypes and present their own views to the rest of their contemporaries.

The publication dates of the plays included in this anthology span five decades. The plays have been organized in chronological order, reflecting the date when they were originally written. It is remarkable that certain features remain constant: the motifs of alienation and "foreignness"; the singular characteristics of Jewish immigrants accosted by the ghosts of the past; the need for a land to call their own, and the need for freedom of expression. Interestingly enough, all the characters in the eight plays we have selected could be relatives. They share a nostalgia for the past, a need to reject and at the same time embrace their culture, while engaged in the eternal process of assimilating into the national culture. The dramatists as well as their characters are part of this national reality, yet always remain on its periphery since they are indeed the current embodiment of the Wandering Jews of the past. Their creative strength derives from these conflicting and opposing forces. This existential condition, often charged with *angst,* creates many of the thematic similarities found in the plays, notably the terrible isolation and loneliness of the characters trapped in a world that oscillates between hostile and dehumanizing to overtly threatening.

For Samuel Eichelbaum *(Aarón the Jew)* the Jewish immigrant is represented as a progressive Russian pioneer who arrives in the Pampas equipped to teach liberalism and equality. Four decades later Osvaldo Dragún *(Onward, Corazón!)* recreates similar situations and characters, but uses expressionist techniques and arrives at a very different outcome. Jorge Goldenberg's striking character Krinsky *(Krinsky),* with his colorful speech interspersed with Yiddish phrases and colloquialisms, can be considered a tragic hero or madman, evoking his former glory as a participant in the Russian Revolution. Germán Rozenmacher's antihero *(Simón Brumelstein, Knight of the Indies)* is a spiritual younger brother to Krinsky, seeking refuge from the dissatisfactions of petit bourgeois life in the splendid mythical kingdom of Chantania that he, the sixteenth-century Jewish conquistador, has created for love and justice to reign. Halac's Queen Isabel and her Jewish lover, Doctor Isaac Levy *(A Thousand Years, One Day),* heatedly discuss the expulsion of the Jews from Spain in 1492 to no avail, and thus set the stage for the life and death struggles between Jews and non-Jews for the next five hundred years. And Diana Raznovich's modern protagonist, Casalia Beltrop *(Lost Belongings),* is as much a Wandering Jew lost in the theatre of the absurd, as Dragún's antihero Corazón is lost in a metaphorical exploration of repressive Argentine history.

This anthology is a sampler of Jewish voices of anger, protest, reconciliation, self-criticism, loyalty, defensiveness, madness, biting sarcasm, black humor, and sometimes gentle humor—all with a distinct Latin American flavor due to the singular circumstance of the Jewish migration to Argentina in the past century.

Notes

1. Myrtha Schalom, "Teatro judío en la Argentina," in *Judíos argentinos: Homenaje al centenario de la inmigración judía a la Argentina 1889–1989* (Buenos Aires: M. Zago Ediciones, 1988), 88–96.

2. "Argentina," in *Enciclopedia Judaica Castellana* (México: Editorial Enciclopedia Judaica Castellana, 1961), 472.

3. David W. Foster, "César Tiempo y el teatro argentino-judío," in *El Cono Sur: Dinámica y dimensiones de su literatura,* ed. Rose S. Minc (Montclair: Montclair State College Publication, 1985), 43–48.

Argentine Jewish Theatre

The Plays

Samuel Eichelbaum: *Aarón the Jew*

SAMUEL EICHELBAUM (ENTRE RÍOS, 1894–
BUENOS AIRES, 1967)

Samuel Eichelbaum inherited from his father, a Russian immigrant, his interest in politics and his involvement in defending the rights of the working class, as seen in *El judío Aarón* (*Aarón the Jew*, 1926). Along with Alberto Gerchunoff—the leading Jewish writer in Argentina at the time—Eichelbaum contributed articles to journals and newspapers. He was also a prolific short-story writer who called himself "a maniac for introspection." He strove to go beyond the mediocrity of contemporary drama in Argentina, examining inner psychological clashes and crises, and attempting to understand the reasons why people act the way they do. His drama *Aarón the Jew* reflects these concerns.

Eichelbaum's first creative period reveals a strong interest in universal issues. He follows the European tradition with plays like *La mala sed* (Evil thirst), *Un hogar* (A home), and *La hermana terca* (The stubborn sister). Critics today praise the foreign influence on Eichelbaum's work: Ibsen, O'Neill, Pirandello, and Dostoyevsky. Yet Eichelbaum felt the need to defend himself against the accusation of national critics that he was a "foreignizer." His insistence on giving his universal themes a Latin American, localistic focus, probably derives from this pressure. Coincidentally, this marks the most successful period of his dramatic career with plays like *Un guapo del 900* (A big shot from the 1900s) (1940) and *Un tal Servando Gómez* (A certain Servando Gómez) (1942). Both offer a profound analysis of the Argentine mentality. Eichelbaum's last, more mature period shows technical growth, richer texture, and more innovative ideas in plays like *Dos brasas* (Two live coals), *Las aguas del mundo* (The waters of the world), and *Subsuelo* (Underground).

Some recurrent aspects in Eichelbaum's plays are affective bonds, religious and racial tensions, the lack of spirituality in human relationships, and the loneliness of individuals who adhere to

SAMUEL EICHELBAUM

Un tal
SERVANDO GÓMEZ
VERGÜENZA DE QUERER
DIVORCIO NUPCIAL

Samuel Eichelbaum

their own convictions. Although he sees society as an artist and not as a social reformer, Eichelbaum's foremost interest is in the individual. His outlook on life, although somewhat pessimistic, strives towards hope for a better world.

Eichelbaum's theatre is discursive. External action is limited to what is absolutely indispensable. His language, while folkloric, gradually becomes more spontaneous and natural. He believes in the strength engendered by noble ideas and trusts in the power of pure sentiments. Don Aarón embodies these ideas and feelings as he tries to find the way to lighten human misery and to resolve social, economic, and even racial conflicts.

When Eichelbaum wrote *Nadie la conoció nunca* (No one ever knew her) (1923), the Jewish press reviewed it mostly in terms of the image it projected to the Argentine public at large. The criticism was biased, since the play dealt with the taboo theme of prostitution. When the Yiddish play "Regeneration," exposing the notorious White Slave Trade, was presented in Buenos Aires in 1927, it provoked such a turmoil among the Jewish public that the author, Leib Malach, had to flee to Paris, where he died a short time later. In his play "Two Live Coals," Eichelbaum touches upon the subject of prejudice and attempts to create a mood of tolerance in a biased society. Like César Tiempo's "I Am the Theatre," "Two Live Coals" develops the author's views on human integrity and idealism as it traces the relationship between two persecuted ethnic groups: Blacks and Jews.

The action of *Aarón the Jew* takes place in a colony of immigrants in Entre Ríos—a colony like the one Eichelbaum came from. What distinguishes Aarón from other colonists is his conviction that everything should be for the common good. Aarón strives for social justice based on solidarity, honest work, and the proportional distribution of the profits from crops among Jewish *colonos* and native *criollo* peasants. Aarón's liberal, integrationalist ideas antagonize the rich settlers who object to his demands, partly for economic considerations, and partly because of their traditionally ingrained mistrust of the *goy* (the non-Jew). Aarón's ideas clash with the selfishness of his coreligionists to such a degree that they end up isolating him. Although Aarón is not a revolutionary, he does perceive money as the "enemy" and preaches the advantages of doing away with it. For this reason he is singled out by the authorities as an extreme leftist.

In a larger sense the play centers upon the conflict between Eastern European immigrants and the rural peasants in the Pampas.[1] The characters discuss issues that affect their daily lives with the local farmers and workers in the new agricultural settlements. Some of the immigrants' innovative ideas that derived from Russian socialism, like the establishment of cooperative farms, are met with suspicion by the local Argentines.

On the personal level, the relationship between Don Aarón and Tomasa, the native Argentine peasant, reveals the dramatist's desire to demonstrate that true understanding between men and women can transcend the barriers of race and religion. Aarón identifies with Argentina and the *criollos*. His love for Tomasa integrates both:

¡Qué linde! ¡Qué linde! Cómo mi gusta cante criolle. . . . Mi le guste mate, mi le guste sandíe y vos mi le guste más qui todes. . . .

[How nice, how nice! I like these *criollo* songs so much. . . . I like *mate,* I like watermelon, but most of all, I like you. . . .] (pp. 36 and 45–46)

Goyito, Aarón's son, follows in his father's footsteps as he also goes against convention and rejects material gain. In love with Cecilia Kohen, the daughter of his father's rival, Goyito and Cecilia elope and marry in spite of Kohen's objections. Don Aarón may be financially defeated by his opponent, but he cannot hide his pleasure as the couple refuses to accept Kohen's money even after he is reconciled with them.

Eichelbaum's political types are represented in the figures of the urban *criollo* and of the *guapo*. Like Ecuménico, the hero of "A Big Shot from the 1900s," Aarón has high moral standards that he defends notwithstanding the adverse consequences they might have. When Goyito asks Aarón to keep his ideas secret so as not to jeopardize his plans involving Cecilia's father, Aarón replies:

Ese nu poide ser. Yo precise dicir tudes las coses, la verdad, la verdad. . . . Ese está la primer cose en la vide. La verdad precisa decirla siempre. Quien nu dice la verdad que sabe, nu merece pisar la tierra qui pise . . .

[That's out of the question. I need to say everything. The truth, the truth. That's the first thing in life. You must always tell the truth. Whoever doesn't tell the truth when he knows it, doesn't deserve to walk this earth.] (p. 27)

Aarón, a lonely character, insists on speaking his mind even if it makes him unpopular. When his friends abandon him, he reflects that some behavior is beyond his comprehension, yet he accepts it with resignation:

> Boine, boine, boine. Ya cumprende bien tode; ustedes están boina gente. Palabre di honor que yo nu comprende cume astán hombre de ideies. . . . así, la cumesarie también poide astar hombre boine. Hablar nu coiste plate.

> [Well, well, well. I understand everything. You're all good people. I swear, I don't understand how you're all considered thinking men. So, a policeman can also be a good man? Talk is cheap.] (p. 32)

Don Aarón's pride in his defense of human solidarity and social justice connects him with the essence of Mosaic Law and with the teachings of the Hebrew prophets. That is why when he sees injustice around him he cries out and takes his own share of the blame as a "judío verdadero" [a true Jew]:

> El Talmud, noistre Biblie, qui dice tantes coses lindes, dice qui es mejor sembrar qui hacer sembrar. Nosotros hacemes sembrar y guardamos fruto. Tampoco estamos boinos judíos. Yu nu astoy loco. . . . Un gran rabino . . . dijo qui más vale recebir el auxilio de un préstamo, que el de una lemosna. Aarón no hace lemosna.

> [The Talmud, our Bible, that says so many beautiful things, says it's better to sow than to make others sow. We make others sow and we keep the fruit. We are not very good Jews either. I am not crazy. . . . A great Rabbi . . . said that it's better to receive help from a loan than from charity. Aarón does not give charity.] (p. 42)

Almost a decade before César Tiempo's "Creole Bread," Eichelbaum's thesis of the integration of Jews and non-Jews, immigrants and natives, rich and poor represents the voice of his generation of Argentine Jewish intellectuals. While Eichelbaum addresses this issue from the farmers' perspective in a rural setting, César Tiempo approaches it from the mixed couple's point of view and moves its stage to an urban setting.

NOTE

1. It should be noted that in Argentina, and to a lesser extent in Brazil and Uruguay, a great number of Jews were rural, rather than urban dwellers.

Aarón the Jew

List of Characters
Don Aarón
Kohen
Police Chief
Dr. Gorovich
Efraín
Roter
Goyito
Singer
Faerman
Dinerstein
Tape Elías
Tomasa
Petronila
Cecilia
Palmira
Guri
Sindicato
Dr. Bachini
Tapes 1, 2, 3 and 4
Tapes and Colonos

The action takes place in the province of Entre Ríos, 1925.

A Play in Two Acts

Act I

Farming Development. On the left the house is prominently seen. It is low and painted pink. Sloping thatched roof with three double doors. Around the house, high spreading trees. In the back from side to side, a well-tended plot with a wide selection of plants and vegetables. On the right, a windmill with a water tank and a trough.

As the curtain rises DON AARÓN, *dressed in overalls and boots, is on the stage, busy with his garden. After a long pause, during which* DON AARÓN *works with his shovel,* TAPE[1] ELÍAS *the worker appears from the direction of the windmill.*

Tape. Don Aarón! . . . Don Aarón! I came to show you what's hurting me, Don Aarón!

Don Aarón. (*Only now, aware of* TAPE ELÍAS'S *presence*) Come over here. (*They approach each other. They meet halfway.*)

Tape. (*Showing him the wound in his foot*) Do you see? It's an ingrown toenail. It's dug deep into my skin and it's a mess.

Don Aarón. (*Laughing*) You're right. It's a real mess. Okay, Elías, you'd better go home. Tell your woman to put the creamy part of the milk on it. The thick part. Tomorrow it will be all gone.

Tape. But Don Aarón, what I wanted was for you to take me to Doctor Bachini. It really hurts a lot.

Don Aarón. Yes, yes, yes. Of course I will. If that's what you want, I'll do it! But I'm telling you, the doctor is not in Domínguez. He's away. Just put some thick cream on it and tomorrow I'll send you to the doctor.

Tape. All right, Don Aarón. As soon as I finish my work. When the sun goes down.

Don Aarón. No, no, no. That's no good. Now, you have to go home right now. You don't have to work anymore.

Tape. All right, Don Aarón. . . . Whatever you say. . . . Thank you. Goodbye now. (*Leaves from where he entered*)

Don Aarón. So long! (*Returns to his work. After a brief pause he shouts.*) Toca! Toca! Toca! (*The dogs bark and he shouts louder.*) Venero! Venero! Venero! The cow's all the way near the haystack. Get her out of there! Toca! Toca! Toca! . . . Venero! (GOYITO *appears through one of the three doors of the house.*)

Goyito. (*To* DON AARÓN) Papá, Papá. Come over here.

Don Aarón. (*Stops working and approaches* GOYITO) What's the matter, Goyito?

Goyito. Are they still going to have that meeting tomorrow at the Communal Trust?

Don Aarón. Yes, yes, yes. Tomorrow. No time to waste. It has to be done right away. Why do you ask?

Goyito. I wanted to know, Papá, because I wanted to ask you not to make a big deal about your project.

Don Aarón. Goyito, tell me what's really on your mind. Your father knows you too well. Say what you mean. Do you understand? What are you trying to say?

Goyito. Nothing, Papá; I don't want you to make a scene. You're not going to make people understand if they don't want you to. If they don't understand your project, leave them alone. Too bad for them.

Don Aarón. I'm going to tell it to you straight. (*Counting on his fingers*) First, I don't need them to understand the project. They're dumb. If they don't say anything, they don't bother me.

Let the ones who know speak. . . . Second, I'll make as much trouble as I can. Third, you're still a kid *(getting angrier by the second)* who doesn't know how to respect his father, who knows nothing, nothing, nothing. Enough. Now I'm mad at you. *(He walks hurriedly towards the garden.)*

Goyito. But listen to me, Papá. Wait. Come back.

Don Aarón. You're stupid. Just like all the shopkeepers in town. That's enough.

Goyito. Just listen to me first. Then if you want, get mad.

Don Aarón. (Turning around) What is it?

Goyito. Do you know why I'm asking you this?

Don Aarón. I don't know! But I think it's because I have money and you want me to have more. And then later it will all be yours, of course!

Goyito. No, no, Papá! What do you mean mine? You know why I'm saying this? I'm in love with Cecilia, Papá!

Don Aarón. (Trying to remember) Cecilia . . . Cecilia! Who's Cecilia?

Goyito. Don't you know? Don Isaac Kohen's daughter.

Don Aarón. The biggest businessman in town? You're in love with her?

Goyito. It's the truth. And since she loves me too, I spoke to her father. And Don Isaac said that he couldn't give his daughter to the son of his worst enemy. He says that you, with your ideas and those projects at the Communal Trust, directly hurt him. He says you are the mortal enemy of all the business people. That's why I asked you not to insist too much. For my sake, so he doesn't stop me from marrying Cecilia. If you go on like this, of course he won't give his consent.

Don Aarón. What am I going to tell you? This Isaac is not as foolish as he seems when he makes jokes. He's realized I'm the enemy of all businessmen. True, true. I'm their worst enemy. But apart from that, he's a big fool. What is it to him if I'm the way I am? But you're not the enemy. Is Cecilia going to marry me?

Goyito. He says that in these matters children always turn out like their parents. That later on I'll end up thinking just like you.

Don Aarón. I doubt it very much.

Goyito. What's your answer, Papá?

Don Aarón. (Thoughtful) Are you in love with Cecilia? What nonsense, what nonsense. Cecilia is a very pretty young girl, I don't say she's not. She's certainly nice. But she's not for you. She likes the young people from Buenos Aires. She likes dancing the tango. I saw her at the party the other day. You saw her too. She wasn't dancing the way a good girl should. She was dancing close, too close to the young man. It's not right, not right, Goyito. *(Pause)* It's true she plays the piano, true . . . I like that, but. . . .

Goyito. I love her anyway, Papá, just the way she is.

Don Aarón. Then that's it. You like her? That's good enough for me. You're going to have to live with her three hundred and sixty five days a year.

Goyito. *(After a pause)* Well? Are you going to do what I ask?

Don Aarón. What? Let the project go, just like that?

Goyito. I'm not asking for that much. What I'm saying is that you don't get too stubborn and don't become too aggressive with the business people who don't accept you.

Don Aarón. That's out of the question. I need to say everything. The truth, the truth. That's the first thing in life. You must always tell the truth. Whoever doesn't tell the truth when he knows it, doesn't deserve to walk this earth. My father taught that to me when I was a young boy and I learnt it well. I also taught that to you, but you didn't learn anything. You went to school in Buenos Aires, you even went from one grade to the next, but you're not a man!

Goyito. *(Upset)* All right, all right! Do what you want! *(Exits towards the house.* DON AARÓN *approaches the windmill and turns it off. Then he walks slowly towards the house and disappears. Stage right,* TOMASA *appears. She is a pleasant looking* criolla.[2] *She is dressed in mourning and is accompanied by a ten-year-old boy.)*

Guri. And from there, Mamá? Should I tell Don Seba to ride it for me to the corral?

Tomasa. Do you have Don Aarón's permission?

Guri. You ask him.

Tomasa. Me? That's just what I need.

Guri. Then I'll bring El Casero. I have to race with the Martínez kid.

Tomasa. No, no, son. Don't even mention El Casero. He's very wild and clever. Wherever they leave him he takes off his bridle and runs back home. You should see him fly, my son. Not even last night's wind could catch up with him!

Guri. If you don't ask Don Aarón for the bay, I'm going to ride El Casero. You know Mamá, that if I say that I'll ride it, I'll ride it even if I know it will throw me later.

Don Aarón. (From the house) How are we doing, how are we doing, little *gaucho*?

Guri. Okay, I guess.

Don Aarón. Didn't you go to the races?

Guri. I don't have a horse, Don Aarón!

Don Aarón. And your bay?

Guri. There's something wrong with his leg. I don't want to ride him because he's going to get worse on me. . . .

Don Aarón. Do you want me to lend you one?

Guri. You bet!

Don Aarón. Tell Seba to bring you a horse. Do you want the highstepper?

Guri. Well, if the bay is being used. . . .

Don Aarón. Do you like the little bay? Then just tell Seba to bring it to you.

Guri. (Exits quickly and as he leaves, he stops.) Thanks, Don Aarón! *(Leaves)*

Don Aarón. (After a long pause, during which both are about to talk, but inexplicably, don't) I have big watermelons in the garden. . . . This big! *(Gestures)* Tomorrow we'll eat them.

Tomasa. For all I care, you can eat them all yourself.

Don Aarón. Are you angry, Tomasa?

Tomasa. Me? Why? Me angry? What a question! Why should I be angry? Ahh! Has anyone done anything to me? Why should I be angry?

Don Aarón. (Laughing) What a woman you are, Tomasa. You don't even know how to deceive men! I know you well, I do. You are angry with me. And I know why, too.

Tomasa. I'm not angry. The truth is I waited for you with hot water and the *mate*[3] ready. If you didn't show up, too bad for you, not for me. It's also true that I was mad because I waited for you all night long 'til the candle went out. But if you didn't come, too bad for you, not for me.

Don Aarón. Of course, too bad for me. If I don't eat, too bad for me; if I don't smoke when I like to, of course too bad for me. If I don't drink *mate* with the *criolla* who makes such good *mate*, sure, it's too bad for me. I know! But you're a little angry, too. I see it in your eyes. I like it when you get angry. I really like it. If you get angry I know that you like to drink *mate* with *gringos*[4] like me. *(Pause, smooth talking)* You're angry, right?

Tomasa. (Gently) A little. And I have a right, you know? I waited for you 'til the wick began to smoke.

Don Aarón. I couldn't, I couldn't come, Tomasa. Goyito was at the house, you know? He came and hasn't budged. I was very mad, very mad, and the worst is that I had to pretend, imagine, to pretend, you know? Then I made jokes. I was even funny, me, funny!

Tomasa. What a pity, Don Aarón! Oh, well, it's over and done with. You see, Don Aarón, there's nothing worse then waiting desperately for something you want very much and you know it won't come.

Don Aarón. Of course it won't come. That's why it's best not to wait for things. I never wait. When I like something very special that I don't think I'll get, I don't expect it, and then it comes all by itself, just like the rain. When my land needs water, I say to myself, "I need water and there isn't any? Patience." Then I go to sleep, calmly, calmly, one night, two nights, three, ten nights. When I finally wake up, you can bet that it's raining.

Tomasa. Sure! It has to rain some time.

Don Aarón. It's the same with other things. You waited for me. I didn't come yesterday? Patience. Today, tomorrow, or even after that, I'll come. And if I don't, too bad for me. You said it.

Tomasa. You're right, Don Aarón, you'll come some day. But if you take too long, you may not be so welcome.

Don Aarón. Why do you say that? Do you mean it?

Tomasa. No, Don Aarón, don't pay any attention to me. I said it just to tease you. Don't pay any attention to me.

Don Aarón. The buggy is coming.

Tomasa. (*Turning*) Yes, it's the Singer's buggy. I'm leaving. See you later, right?

Don Aarón. Don't wait for me. If you wait, I'm not coming.

Tomasa. I won't wait for you. But you're coming later, right?

Don Aarón. Yes, yes, of course I'm coming! (TOMASA *leaves from left and disappears behind the house. From right,* SINGER, FAERMAN *and* DINERSTEIN *show up in a buggy.*) At last the company is here.

Singer. What's doing? (*The four men greet each other warmly.*)

Don Aarón. Come in, come in! (*He leads them to the house.*) What do you like better, inside or out?

Singer. We're fine here, friend. (DON AARÓN *goes into the house, comes out with chairs which he offers his guests. They all sit down.*)

Faerman. How's the threshing season going?

Don Aarón. My harvest will be ready pretty soon. A very good harvest, this year. Nice, really nice. Have you seen my wheat this season? Thick like this. (*Gestures*) Thicker than the beard of our own Communal Fund president. It has yielded me fourteen bushels an acre.

Faerman. I'm very happy for you.

Singer. And I congratulate you, Aarón, my friend. As for my crop, I don't believe it'll yield more than eight bushels. The head of the wheat is too small. On the other hand, it may not even yield a single bushel.

Dinerstein. The size of the head is not important at all.

Singer. I'm not saying it because of that. I was referring to the boycott that the owners of the threshing machines called against me.

Don Aarón. (Interested) Boycott! Why? Why?

Singer. What do you mean why? Don't you know they believe that you and I are the instigators of unionism? They can't do anything to you, but as for me, it seems revenge is easy for them.

Don Aarón. What people! My God! They are idiots, rich idiots! I swear unionism is older than all of them, older than the Bible. When there were just three men in the world, the idea was already there. Two fought against one. That was unionism too.

Singer. That's true. But go make them understand that.

Don Aarón. So how will your harvest turn out?

Singer. I don't know. The workers decided to finish the harvest even during the strike. Let's see how they'll do it, and with what machines.

Don Aarón. Then it's all right. Don't worry, I have a thresher, I have an engine. Your harvest won't be lost.

Singer. Thanks for your offer. I'll speak to the workers. They'll be coming soon to get started.

Faerman. What did you want to talk to us about, Don Aarón?

Singer. Right. What about that project of yours that's causing so much talk?

Don Aarón. They talk, they talk! They're such big mouths. That's why they talk. Sure. They know I'm not going to come up with any projects for our organization so that merchants earn more money. They know I'm going to clip the wings of all of them. I called you because you are good people. Let's see, how much money does our organization have?

Singer. I don't know the exact amount, but in cash it must have at the very least between three hundred and four hundred thousand pesos.

Don Aarón. Very good. Let's say it has two hundred thousand pesos. What's the cash flow of Kohen's shop?

Singer. I don't know either. But it can't be more than one hundred thousand pesos.

Faerman. That's a high figure. Maybe it isn't even eighty thousand.

Don Aarón. It doesn't matter. Let's say he works with one hundred thousand pesos. I want my project to help the Communal Fund to set up a better business than Kohen's.

Faerman. Very well thought out. And for the farmers to have what they need at a lower price.

Singer. Sure! I fully approve, Don Aarón!

Faerman. You have my unconditional support.

Singer. And mine.

Dinerstein. And mine, of course.

Don Aarón. It seems to me you're telling me about my own project. Are you in a great hurry?

Singer. No, no, speak Don Aarón.

Don Aarón. That's not the issue. It's not a question of selling cheaper or dearer. That's all nonsense, trifles. Ten cents less for slippers, ten more for a pound of sugar. These are dust, nonsense. I'll say it again. Do you know why I want the Communal Fund to set up a business? *(Drawing his listeners nearer with gesture)* To do away with money. *(Raising his voice, in contrast with the last sentence he will have uttered in a low voice)* Enough with money. We *colonos*[5] don't need money. We need to work well, to eat well; we need a good school for our children. We'll have all that when there is no money.

Singer. But I don't understand you, Don Aarón! How are you going to do away with money?

Don Aarón. My plan is very simple. The *colonos* will buy all they need at the Communal Fund and instead of paying with money, they'll pay with grain. Our organization will set up a price for each crop, and that price will hold for the whole year. Apart from that, the settlers will be able to pay with cheese, eggs, and fruit. When the *colonos* realize they can pay with fruit, they'll grow their own. Now—if the truth must be told—the Jewish farmers, myself included and you too, don't know how to work the land. Land is something that you have to love dearly. Our *colonos* believe that the land yields only wheat, corn, flax, oats, and that's it. They are wrong. It yields a lot more. . . . I have everything on my farm. I have a vegetable plot, flowers, and grain too. When the Communal Fund turns out the way I want it to, watermelon, melon, cucumber, cauliflower, cabbage, tomatoes, potatoes, will all be like hard money and even better. *(Pause)* What do you think of my project?

Singer. (After observing FAERMAN *and* DINERSTEIN *questioningly)*
I'm convinced that applying your plan would not be beneficial
now. The idea would fail because it's premature to apply it.

Faerman. As for myself, Don Aarón. I feel exactly the same.

Don Aarón. And you, Mr. Singer, are you a man who looks for
everybody's happiness?

Singer. Of course I am.

Don Aarón. And how about you, Mr. Dinerstein? Are you also a
man who wants everybody's happiness?

Dinerstein. Yes I do, Don Aarón.

Don Aarón. And Mr. Faerman too, and am I not that way too?
Well, well, well. I understand everything. You're all good people.
I swear, I don't understand how you're all considered thinking
men. So a policeman can also be a good man? Talk is cheap.

Singer. You offend us, Don Aarón. Just because we don't agree
with your project doesn't mean we're bad people. We're noble
people. We advocate the common good through the slow evolu-
tion of institutions. We don't believe in violence as a means, nor
in the radical implementation of absolute reforms. We believe in
democracy and we're democrats.

Don Aarón. Nice, nice speech. It's a pity that I haven't understood
a word of it. Doctrine, democracy, all lies, lies. I'm very happy
that I've never been a democrat.

Faerman. I won't allow you, Don Aarón.

Don Aarón. You won't allow me? What do you mean by that?
*(*GOYITO's *voice from within)*

Goyito. Papá, Papá! *(Comes from behind the house. Left inside.
Upon seeing the guests, he hides his excitement.)* How are you,
Mr. Singer? *(Greets everybody)*

Don Aarón. What's the matter? *(Gradually it becomes darker. In
a while the scene is only lit by the bright reflection of the moon.)*

Goyito. Nothing, nothing.

Tomasa. (Also coming from stage left) We'll see if I'm some kind
of peon here! What does he think!

Don Aarón. (Going towards TOMASA*)* What's the matter?

Goyito. (Following his father) But tell me, Papá, just what is Tomasa's role here?

Tomasa. That's just what I'd like to know.

Goyito. She gives more orders around here than I do. She gives
counter orders. I say one thing and she contradicts me on
purpose.

Tomasa. Don't pay any attention to him, Don Aarón. He's the one
who made *gurisa*[6] Palmira think that she's the boss, not me.

Who knows why, Don Aarón! Palmira doesn't even listen to me! It's obvious, Goyito gets along with her.

Goyito. But, do you see, do you see her, Papá? She butts into everything. Even if it were true. What does it matter to her? She's a servant around here and that's all. If she doesn't like it, let her leave.

Tomasa. (Whimpering) You see? This is the way he treats me after fifteen years of work in this house. After I've taken care of him for so long.

Don Aarón. Poor Aarón! Poor Aarón! He always has to put up with you two fighting like small, silly children! *(To* GOYITO*)* Are you the boss around here? *(To* TOMASA*)* Are you the boss in this house too? Does Palmira give orders too? And I'm the only one who listens to you all! What a fool I am. Poor Aarón! *(From the stage right,* TAPE 1, 2, 3, 4 *enter)*

Tape 1. Hello.

Don Aarón. (Goes to greet them) Come in, come in. *(After greeting them one by one)* How are you? How's the strike going?

Tape 1. No news, Don Aarón.

Don Aarón. What do the bosses say? Poor things!

Tape 2. They don't say anything, Don Aarón. They won't budge!

Don Aarón. And the *colonos?*

Tape 2. They're against us.

Tape 1. They believe that if they charge them $2.10 it's because of our strike.

Don Aarón. Are there many men working?

Tape 1. Quite a few, Don Aarón. Three hundred sixty of us are on strike, and there are more than eight hundred altogether.

Don Aarón. It doesn't look good, then. Not at all. You won't win. You don't have a chance.

Tape 2. That's what it looks like. We *criollos* are very weak when it comes to these matters, Don Aarón.

Don Aarón. Weak? Worse than women.

Tape 2. I came to ask you a favor, Don Aarón. My wife is sick in bed. She's very sick. She's about to give birth. She felt very bad last night. I went for Doctor Gorovich, who is the police doctor, and it seems he didn't want to come. He sent word that he was feeling sick.

Tape 1. That's not true. I saw him this morning in his buggy. He was going to his farm. A little too polite and not wanting to talk too much. It's just not true. He didn't go because this man here is one of the strikers. That's why, Don Aarón.

Tape 2. I wanted you to talk to Doctor Bachini and ask him to come right away.

Don Aarón. Doctor Bachini is not in the village just now. Elías is also sick and the doctor has not seen him yet. If he comes tonight, let me know. I'll send him on right away.

Tape 2. Thanks a lot, Don Aarón. I'll let you know then.

Don Aarón. (*After a long pause*) Do you know my engine and my thresher?

Tape 1. I know it well, Don Aarón. I was second machinist the first year you used it. Do you remember, Don Aarón?

Don Aarón. That's right, of course. Okay, then you're going to take my machine and my thresher and you're going to work like a cooperative. Cheaper than anywhere else. One fifty for the wheat. You can pay me later. You can work for the farmers who don't have the men to do the job. What do you say?

Tape 2. All right, Don Aarón!

Tape 1. Thank you, Don Aarón.

Tape 2. So you're putting it at the service of the union?

Don Aarón. Of course I am. Tomorrow I'll be done with my threshing. You can send for it the next day. (SINGER, DINERSTEIN *and* FAERMAN *get up at the same time.*)

Singer. We're leaving, Don Aarón! (*Shaking his hand*) Till next time, Don Aarón. I'm only sorry I don't agree with certain things.

Don Aarón. With everything, it seems.

Dinerstein. See you tomorrow.

Faerman. Have a good day.

Don Aarón. Thanks, thanks. (*The three men climb into the buggy and leave from stage right.*) We have agreed. The day after tomorrow you'll form a cooperative with my machine.

Tape 2. And how much are you renting us the machine for?

Don Aarón. That doesn't matter. We'll settle it later. First you work, then we'll talk about the price. I don't want to make a profit from you. (TOMASA *crosses the stage from left to right, humming a song. She exits back right. Immediately a loud shout from* TOMASA *is heard as if she had been scared. The voice of* SINDICATO *is also heard.*)

Sindicato. Hey! Whoa! Don't be scared, old girl. It's the old nag that was frightened by a piece of paper. (*He appears stage right riding a horse without a saddle.*) Hello, Don Aarón!

Tape 2. What are you doing, Sindicato?

Don Aarón. Where are you coming from? Your horse looks tired.

Sindicato. I've galloped from Domínguez.

Tape 2. Where did you stretch your legs?

Sindicato. At Pineyro's. I had a fight there. A Jewish *gringo* said that we union men were all just a bunch of lazy bums and drunks. They're such fools. What does that have to do with my drinking? Everyone can do what the hell he pleases. I was drinking before the union too. I drink because I like to, and so what? I don't have a wife or kids. I had a wife and she left me because I had no money. Why? Because I worked for umpteen years on the Vélez farm for fifteen a month. Sure! How could I have money! Now when I work I earn more, but now I don't have any wife, or shack, or kids any longer. . . . I don't need to. I don't get drunk because I'm in the union. I get drunk because I like to, and I like to because when I'm high I don't remember anyone. I don't need anyone and I'm not even afraid of the police.

Don Aarón. Go to sleep, go to sleep. . . .

Sindicato. Don't you agree, Don Aarón?

Don Aarón. Right, right, go to sleep. . . . (SINDICATO *moves across the stage and exits behind the house.)*

Tape 2. We're going too, Don Aarón. *(The four of them say good-bye to* DON AARÓN.) Don't forget about the doctor, Don Aarón.

Don Aarón. Don't *you* forget. . . .

Tape 2. Not me, Don Aarón! *(The four men exit stage right,* DON AARÓN *remains a moment observing the night. Then he walks slowly towards the second door of the house.)*

Palmira. (Appears from rear left) Don Aarón!

Don Aarón. They already told me. I already know that you've been fighting with Tomasa. Nonsense, plain nonsense.

Palmira. That's not what I had to tell you, Don Aarón.

Don Aarón. Another piece of news?

Palmira. What I wanted to tell you is that I'm leaving.

Don Aarón. You're leaving? To Villaguay?

Palmira. That's right!

Don Aarón. Why?

Palmira. I miss my aunt a lot. . . . *(Sniffling)* I love my aunt a lot.

Don Aarón. All right, all right, all right, Don't cry. Early tomorrow we'll hitch up the sulky[7] and you can leave.

Palmira. Sorry, Don. I love my aunt a lot but she deceived me. When I was coming here to the settlement, my aunt told me that here everything was very happy and that here there were lots of young people. And there aren't any young people here.

Don Aarón. Young people? That's nice, very nice. Just look at her. Youth she needs. You're very funny, you are. The only young person here is Goyito! After January my nephews are coming and some students from Buenos Aires, but I didn't know that.

Palmira. Now the only one is Goyito. But there might as well be no one because Tomasa doesn't let anyone out of her sight. Wherever you go, there she is. She acts like she's your mother.

Don Aarón. You've said enough. Enough, enough talking! Tomorrow they'll take you to Villaguay.

Palmira. Good. . . .(*After a brief pause*) But if later on things get more lively around here, I'll stay.

Don Aarón. You're staying? Fine, fine. You need young people. How honest you are. (GOYITO *crosses the stage from right to left carrying a guitar.* PALMIRA *exits left. Soon* GOYITO's *voice is heard accompanied by the guitar. He sings in a moving* criollo *style.* DON AARÓN *listens to him, totally absorbed.*)

Don Aarón. How nice, how nice! I love these *criollo* songs so much! Goyito is in love. For sure he's in love. That's why he sings so well. When a man is in love, he sings better than a lark.

Act II

Large zinc plated barn. Two sliding doors in the rear. Inside right, sacks of grain in piles. On the left, close to the wall, a large table put together with two or three boards and a few other pieces of wood. Wherever there is room, old straw chairs arranged for a meeting. When the curtain goes up, there is a group of people next to each door. On the left side KOHEN, DR. GOROVICH, LEVINOFF, GRINMAN, *the* POLICE CHIEF. *The group on the right is made up of six or seven young workers and* TAPE ELÍAS.

Kohen. You see, Chief, I can't say yes and I can't say no. But I know that that man has no head. He thinks we don't know what nonsense he has planned for the society. We know, we know very well.

Gorovich. Let me tell you, Chief, don't doubt for a moment that he's a dangerous fellow.

Kohen. (*Interrupting him*) Precisely.

Gorovich. I met him one afternoon when I was going to the station to wait for the Buenos Aires train to bring some weekly magazines that, by the way, I always buy. I read a lot. I spend my life reading. Well, that day he was introduced to me. We spoke about a number of things, and whatever we talked about, the man had to bring up his idea about the land belonging to everyone.

Kohen. That's the problem.

Gorovich. The fact is I understood right away that I was dealing with a Jew who could get very carried away with lies.

Kohen. Too much so, if you ask me.

Police Chief. And how come Don Aarón is so respected?

Tape Elías. (To TAPE 3*)* Who's going to take him on?

Tape 1. Why not the police chief?

Tape Elías. (To TAPE 3*)* There's the doctor. Didn't you say that wherever you saw him he would pay what he owed you?

Tape 1. What for? I'll always be the loser anyway. Look how he hangs out with the police chief. He acts as if he's the boss.

Gorovich. If I were the government, I would round them all up and make them sleep on the ice all winter.

Kohen. And that's not even enough.

Police Chief. That depends on your own feelings. I feel sorry for them, I can't punish them that much. I just put them in the stocks and leave them without any food until hunger turns them yellow. Then I let them go. *(Little by little both groups increase in number. All kinds of people start arriving, from the aggressive merchant who parades around the village in* alpargatas[8] *to the young and presumptuous grain collector, who in a vague and unsettling way represents city elegance to the town. The first group is mostly made up of settlers. They are all foreign types, with coarse features and long, unkempt beards. They gesticulate and speak timidly.* DON AARÓN *joins the group of* tapes. *He is wearing a wide-brimmed straw hat, a long cotton jacket that has evidently never been touched by an iron.* DON AARÓN *is animatedly speaking with the* tapes. *His words can't be heard, but the effect they have on his audience indicates that* DON AARÓN *is in a splendid mood.)*

Gorovich. He's with them already. He deserves to have his head chopped off. Have you ever seen such nerve? He gets together with all the scum, and afterwards he's capable of getting angry if someone tells him that he's just like them. *(*EFRAÍN *and* ROTER, *the president and the secretary of the Communal Fund, enter from the front door. The former is over sixty years old, of very frail appearance, with a long white beard. His speech is blurred and laborious. The latter is the opposite: young and energetic, and speaks Spanish correctly in spite of being Jewish. Both men leave their hats on the table.)*

Efraín. We can't start yet. There aren't enough members.

Roter. What do you mean, Señor Efraín? I think there are enough. I believe we should begin the meeting because it's going to be a long one.

Efraín. All right, if you think so. *(He pounds the table with his hands.)*

Roter. (He also pounds the table, but much louder. The groups disband and the men take their seats. DON AARÓN *sits down on the first chair in front. The laborers who form the majority, sit on the sacks or lean on piles of stacked grain. The* POLICE CHIEF *stays near the door nervously shifting from one side to the other, constantly stroking his heavy, drooping moustache. So many different kinds of people cannot naturally remain silent. The chatting among them consequently produces an annoying murmuring which hurries the opening of the assembly.* EFRAÍN *takes the presidential post, and* ROTER *that of secretary.* EFRAÍN *insistently rings a bell for order. When it becomes quiet, the president stands up. Whispering to the president)* Dear members . . .

Efraín. Dear members . . .

Roter. The assembly is now open . . .

Efraín. The assembly is now open . . .

Roter. . . . for which

Efraín. . . . for which

Roter. you have been . . .

Efraín. you have been . . .

Roter. called—called—

Efraín. called—called—

Roter. Get up, get up. You haven't finished yet.

Efraín. (Obeying) Today's topic is . . .

Roter. No, no, no. The member . . .

Efraín. The member . . .

Roter. Aarón Leibovich . . .

Efraín. Aarón Leibovich . . .

Roter. is going to give us information about the project that we will vote on . . .

Efraín. is going to give us information about the project that we will vote on . . .

Roter. To be discussed next.

Efraín. To be discussed immediately. *(Tries to sit down)*

Roter. (Stopping him) Don't be in a rush. The member has the floor.

Efraín. Member Leibovich has the floor . . . *(They all immediately look at* DON AARÓN. TOMASA *appears stage left. The commotion starts up again.)*

Don Aarón. (After a pause) Mr. President, I'm requesting silence! *(*EFRAÍN *rings the bell until it is quiet. Dries his sweat with a handkerchief)* Good. First of all I have to say this. I'm a simple

man. Everyone in the assembly knows me. I can't speak as well
as the deputies. I speak like all the *colonos*. I ask that you listen
well with your ears and that you think with your heads. Those
of us who are here, who live in this settlement, know that there
is no peace, no quiet. There is nothing but fighting every day,
there's a lot of anger, a lot of anger. The *colono* who lives in
front of me says that I'm a thief, the *colono* who lives behind
me doesn't say that I'm a thief, he says that I'm a murderer.
And I say that they're all thieves and murderers too.

Various Voices. Lies! Slander!

Don Aarón. Quiet, quiet! There are still worse things. *(Pause)* I
ask, why, why do my dear neighbors speak that way, and why
am I talking about them like this? Do you know why? It's not
their fault, or mine either. There is one thing in the world that
can turn all men into tigers. There is one thing that brings a
sadness that breaks up families, that makes children hate their
parents. That thing is called money. *(Murmur of astonishment)*
Money is worse than a cannon, worse than poison, worse than
any sickness. *(Pointing as he names people)* Mr. Kohen, every
time he sees me he murders me with his eyes. Why? Because
he has money and he wants to have mine too. Mr. Efraín, our
president, cannot stand the secretary, and why? . . .

Efraín. Lies! I don't need you to talk about me.

Voices. Talk about the project.

Don Aarón. He can't stand him because both of them have a lot
of money and both of them think they have a little money. Mr.
Haimovich is always angry with the *tapes*. Why? Because the
tapes don't have any money, they're just poor devils, and he
thinks that whoever doesn't have money is not a man. None of
the *tapes* like Mr. Kohen, or the president, or the secretary, or
me, or the governor, or the rancher who grills his meat with the
skin on. They don't like him and they're right not to. We all
deserve it. Why? Because we have money and they don't. It's
unjust. It means that money is the enemy of all men and of all
women, too. Our youth, the boys who study in Buenos Aires, in
Uruguay, study for money. All the students want to marry rich
girls, and all the parents of rich girls want their daughters to
marry rich young men, doctors, lawyers. From all the things I've
said, it means that money is a big misery.

Gorovich. Enough talk.

Grain Collector. That's it. To the point.

Don Aarón. Mr. Grain Collector, we are not doing business now.

Kohen. All right, all right. What is it you want?

Don Aarón. I say we have to do away with money. I realize we can't eliminate it because we're not the government. That's why I want our society at the Communal Fund to do away with money. That's my plan.

Kohen. You're crazy, Mr. Leibovich. You're an ignoramus.

Don Aarón. Right, Mr. Kohen. I know nothing, I don't say I do. But by learning I can become wise, while Mr. Kohen can't. Our Talmud, the Jewish Bible, says that merchants will never be wise or just. *(Short pause)* To do away with money I propose that the Communal Fund sets up a large warehouse with a clothing store including a shoeshop, with everything that's necessary for life in the settlement.

Voices. What will that do for us?

Don Aarón. The Communal Fund will sell to its members at cost and the settlers will not pay with money, they'll pay with the produce from the harvest. Wheat, flax, a little corn, oats, and all the rest. This way the *colonos* will have everything cheap. The Communal Fund will determine a fixed price for each bushel of grain each year. This way the members can have cheap bread. Remember what happened in 1919. The *colonos* sold the wheat during harvest time to the buyers at fourteen dollars a bushel, that means, fourteen cents a kilo, and then, who ended up paying thirty-eight cents a kilo of flour in order to be able to eat bread at home? If the Communal Fund goes along with my project, this sad, unfair nightmare will not happen again. The *colonos* will have cheap bread and it will be the same with other things. With this out of the way the neighbors might become less selfish, egotistical, and jealous. *(The* TAPES *applaud enthusiastically. One of them shouts, "Long Live Don Aarón!" and is immediately arrested by the* POLICE CHIEF.*)*

Kohen. I'll say it again. Don Aarón is crazy. I also say he's dangerous.

Gorovich. Very well put. It's the truth. We are dealing with a crazy man, a real madman.

Colono 1. We don't have to do away with money.

Colono 2. It would be a big mistake.

Colono 3. He should have his head examined.

Gorovich. I won't do it. I refuse to examine such an obtuse skull. *(A tremendous clatter is heard. Everyone is talking. The* PRESIDENT *insistently rings the bell, which is as old and ineffective as the old man himself. The* SECRETARY *tires himself out shouting.)*

Roter. Fellow members, fellow members, I'm asking for a little silence . . . silence. . . .

Don Aarón. (*Standing up and showing his fists in defiance*) Cowards! Cowards! (*Gradually, order is restored.*)

Efraín. Mr. Leibovich still has the floor.

Don Aarón. (*Sitting down again*) I'm very pleased with the protests. Since the businessmen in our society don't want the projects, that must mean that it's a very good idea.

Some Colonos. Don't let him go on.

Kohen. Shut him up.

Gorovich. Have the *china*[9]-loving lecherous Jew shut up! (*Gasps of astonishment*)

Tomasa. They're lying! They're lying! Scoundrels! (*Everyone turns towards* TOMASA *who continues.*) They're lying! They're lying! And even if he were, he's more honest than any of you henpecked bastards. And what's going on at home, Doctor? Let the *criollo* girls who live at your eucalyptus ranch tell us! (DON AARÓN, ROTER, *and* EFRAÍN *all try to quiet* TOMASA *down. The* POLICE CHIEF *gets close to her and strongly rebukes her, but* TOMASA *only listens to* DON AARÓN, *with whom she starts talking in Yiddish. Everyone becomes silent as they hear their own language being spoken by the* criolla. *Some phrases that* TOMASA *uses provoke angered responses from the* COLONOS, *a clear indication that she's not exactly praising them. Later on, when* TOMASA *and* DON AARÓN *finish talking, order is slowly reestablished, or at least a relative order, the only kind that can reign in that hall. In a muffled voice*) Aladios[10]! Bad Christians! (*Some participants laugh between the teeth at* TOMASA'S *latest utterance. Others can barely hide the anger and intolerance, uttering rude Yiddish or* criollo *exclamations.*)

Some Colonos. How shameful! It's a big disgrace! (*The* PRESIDENT'S *bell rings again.*)

Don Aarón. I'm sixty years old and I'm strong enough for everyone. Strong enough to fight with you and strong enough for anything a man needs. I'm happy and I'm proud of it. I believe that *criolla* women—the *chinas*—are as good as any woman and even better. They don't need pretty dresses. They don't have to make up their faces. If they're not pretty, they are good. If they are pretty, they are pretty and good too. I'm very sorry if our president and Mr. Kohen and Mr. Grinman and Doctor Gorovich can't do what I do. I eat the nuts I crack myself. It looks like Doctor Gorovich doesn't like nuts because he doesn't have the strength to crack them or the teeth to eat them. (GOYITO *and* CECILIA *enter stage right and stand near the* TAPES.)

Efraín. Has Mr. Leibovich anything else to say?

Don Aarón. Who said that I was finished? I still have to present the second part of my project.

Gorovich. Still?

Don Aarón. The statutes of our society need changes. We have to make all the *criollos* our partners. We don't live alone here.

A Settler. This is a *colono* society.

Gorovich. Naturally.

Kohen. We don't have anything to do with the *tapes.*

Another Colono. I also want to speak.

Don Aarón. I'm asking you not to interrupt me.

Efraín. (*After shaking the little bell to no avail*) Shh! . . . Shhh! . . .

Don Aarón. I repeat: we don't live alone in the settlement. If it weren't for the *tapes,* none of us could harvest our crops. True, we do work, but we work feeling more secure than they do, we earn more than they do. Of course our interests are against theirs. We *colonos* want to become the owners of the land we work. The *tapes* don't have any land. They work our land. We don't want to work other people's land. That's fine. That's the way it should be. But they don't have land to work. That's why we have to help them to live better. We, the Israelites, the Jewish *colonos,* have to give them a part of our farms instead of paying them a miserable salary!

Kohen. The man is sick.

Don Aarón. The Talmud, our Bible, that says so many beautiful things, says it's better to sow than to make others sow. We make others sow and we keep the fruit. We are not very good Jews either. I am not crazy. I'm speaking as a good Jew, as a true Jew.

Gorovich. He's a cynic.

Kohen. You, a good Jew? Listen, you better shut up. You're an anti-Semite. You're always like this with the *tapes* (*joining his index fingers to show chumminess*). You're a *goy* just like them.

Don Aarón. Sure, sure. That's why I'm a good Jew. When the *tapes* are on strike because the rich Jewish settlers refuse to pay an extra fifty cents for bread, Aarón Leibovich loans them his engine and his harvester so they can work like a cooperative.

Gorovich. You're lying! You loaned them the engine and the harvester. You haven't given away anything.

Don Aarón. True, you're right. A great Rabbi who Doctor Gorovich doesn't know, said that it's better to receive help from a loan than from charity. Aarón doesn't give charity. (*The* TAPES *applaud. The* POLICE CHIEF *goes over to them and prevents them from saying another word.*) I have something else to say, fellow

members, now you know my plan. Think well with your heads
as I did before I came to you. I know the project does not benefit
all the businessmen in town, or the grain collectors, or Doctor
Gorovich who lives off the *tapes'* work. But it is good for the
farmers who sow the land to be able to eat. It is good for the
poor folks who live on the farms, in ugly houses, like shacks. It
is good for the *criollos* who eat bread and rabbit once a month;
for the *tapes* who get drunk on cheap gin because the thirty
pesos they earn a month are not enough for anything else. If we
do away with money at the Communal Fund, we'll all have an
easy conscience. Without money hidden away, people are
stronger, they are freer. The Bible says, "Happy is the man who
can die in the innocent state in which he was born." It's true,
word of honor. I want to die like that. We should all want to die
like that. That is why we need to do away with money. Enough
whispering. (EFRAÍN *stands up.*)

Roter. (*Prompting him*) The debate is open. . . .
Efraín. The debate is open. . . .
Roter. Regarding the project . . .
Efraín. Regarding the project . . .
Roter. of fellow member . . .
Efraín. of fellow member Aarón Leibovich.
Gorovich. I have heard Mr. Leibovich's speech. Everything he
said seems to have come out of those sick minds for which there
are special places. There is no point arguing against him. This
declaration should suffice: if I were the authorities, I'd give him
a swift kick for the ideas he left out. (*Long pause*)
Singer. I'm asking for the floor.
Efraín. You have it.
Singer. It seems to me that some of the ideas in Leibovich's project
are too daring. But there are others which are not only accept-
able but really worth using, indeed, worth carrying out as soon
as possible. I refer especially to the idea of the wheat in the
Communal Fund for consumption by those members who de-
posit it, a measure which, as fellow member Leibovich pointed
out so well, offers the great advantage of supplying bread for the
whole year round at the same price that the settler sells the kilo
of wheat to the grain buyers. I find this proposition both plausible
and possible. I vote in favor.
Dr. Bachini. (*Who will enter hurriedly stage left a few seconds
before* SINGER *finishes his brief speech. He stands next to*
SINGER.) Has my colleague spoken yet?
Singer. Doctor Gorovich?

Dr. Bachini. Yes.

Singer. Of course he spoke.

Dr. Bachini. Which way did he go?

Singer. Against. What sort of question is that?

Dr. Bachini. I want the floor Mr. President. . . .

Efraín. Doctor Bachini has the floor.

Dr. Bachini. I vote for it. I don't know every detail of the project but from what I know about it, it makes good sense to vote in favor .

Kohen. I voted against it.

Don Aarón. I can explain why Mr. Kohen voted against it.

Gorovich. Don't let him talk any more. He is making fun of us. He's a cynic.

Don Aarón. (To DOCTOR GOROVICH*)* You're very unfair, Doctor Gorovich. It's not my fault if I was never sick. You shouldn't be angry with me because of that. The *tape* who got sick didn't go to see you because there's another doctor he can go to. Do you understand?

Efraín. (With sudden and fleeting energy) The project will be voted on. . . .

Gorovich. (Indignantly) I move that the project be rejected without a vote, because it's incongruous and absurd.

Everyone. (Except DON AARÓN, SINGER, DOCTOR BACHINI, PRESI-DENT, *and* SECRETARY.*)* Very good! Very good! *(Applause)*

A Colono's Voice. Bravo! Bravo!

Don Aarón. It doesn't matter. My idea is not dead. (DOCTOR GORO-VICH *approaches the* POLICE CHIEF *and speaks to him with obvious fear of being overheard. The* COLONOS *get up and leave, arguing among themselves.* EFRAÍN *and* ROTER *leave their seats. The* TAPES *leave, some in silence, others angry, but all with the impression of having been defeated by* DON AARÓN'S *defeat.* TOMASA *remains motionless.)*

Police Chief. May I have a few words with you, Don Aarón?

Don Aarón. Of course! Of course!

Police. I wanted to tell you, Don Aarón, that you've been spreading dangerous ideas. There are a lot of people who say so. And do you know what kind of crime that is? It's very serious. I don't want to take steps against you because I believe you're a good person, but I'm warning you to watch it.

Don Aarón. Look here, Chief. I don't steal from anyone, I don't kill anyone, I'm no criminal, I'm no thief.

Police Chief. I'm not saying you are. There are other crimes. I'm doing my duty by warning you, that's all. So long, Don Aarón. *(Exits)*

Tomasa. (While the POLICE CHIEF *was talking to* DON AARÓN *she came closer to listen. When the* POLICE CHIEF *left she observed* DON AARÓN *with increasing interest and saw how upset* DON AARÓN *was by the weight of his defeat.* DON AARÓN *sits in the same chair where he sat during the assembly and he seems to remove himself from the world. He is evidently thinking about his own ideas. He gesticulates as if he were still giving his speech.* TOMASA *speaks to him softly.)* Don Aarón, don't pay any attention. *(*AARÓN *looks at* TOMASA *and moves his head as if to express the disaster that his dreams led him to.)* Don't pay any attention. They're a bunch of wild men, Don Aarón.

Don Aarón. I know. But they're many and they do what they want.

Tomasa. Can I tell you something, Don Aarón?

Don Aarón. Go ahead, Tomasa. You might as well speak too. You speak better than they do.

Tomasa. It's a good thing they didn't listen to you. It's better that there's money. And it would be good if you had it in heaps, in bushels, to fill up as many sacks of money as wheat.

Don Aarón. What do you need money for?

Tomasa. Not for me, Don Aarón, for you. While you have it, I don't need it. Not me, nor all the good people wandering around without bread, without a roof over their head. All those *criollos* and *gringos* who always go to your farm, since it's the favorite haven of all the poor folks around here. For that reason it's right for you to have plenty of money, to be even better. *(In a low voice)* And also, Don Aarón, for the boy. Don't you remember the boy? Goyito has to be taught to be good like you. They all should be Aaróns. Your house should always be the Aaróns' house, so that when you leave forever, you'll be remembered a thousand miles away. How lovely, Don Aarón! People will always call it "The Aaróns' Farm." *(Moved by* TOMASA's *words,* AARÓN *dries his eyes. Suddenly, in a burst of affectionate energy,* TOMASA *says)* Now get up. Enough. We have to drink some *mate.* Tomasa is going to make us even more delicious *mate* than the watermelons you ate by yourself.

Don Aarón. (Reacting, with sudden vigor) Let's eat the watermelon now! At your place. Would you like that?

Tomasa. How could I not like it!

Don Aarón. I'd like it too. I like *mate,* I like watermelon, but most

of all, I like you. You are sweeter than the sweetest watermelon.
(They walk towards the rear of the stage.)
Curtain

Act III

*Interior facade of a ranch. Narrow corridor with a zinc roof. In
the yard, a rather low well with a waterpump. A great many car-
tons, bottles of beer, and other drinks strewn about. In the hallway,
two kerosene lamps. Three doors, stage rear. To the left an entrance that opens onto the patio, from the street. It is nighttime.
When the curtain goes up various voices of the villagers are heard
at the general store.* KOHEN's *voice is heard intermingled with the
rest.* GOYITO *appears at the gate, looks around with interest, then
withdraws, afraid to be seen. This happens two or three times.*
CECILIA *does the same from rear door on the right. She peers in,
looking for someone, and hides right before she is seen. The fourth
time they surprise each other.*

Goyito. Shh . . . Shh . . . Shhh . . . (CECILIA *approaches* GOYITO
and remains near the gate. In a hushed voice.) Are you ready?
(Cecilia does not answer.) Well, did you prepare everything?

Cecilia. I'm afraid, Goyito. I'm sorry. If we go ahead with it,
Mamá is going to die when she finds out, and Papá too.

Goyito. That would happen to your father if you took his money.
Don't be silly, my love. Neither of them is going to die. What
makes you think that we're so lucky?

Cecilia. Don't talk like that, Goyito. You frighten me.

Goyito. But Cecilia, there's no time to lose. We have half an hour
before the train leaves.

Cecilia. No, I'm not eloping. I really believe that if you insisted,
Papá would finally agree to our marriage.

Goyito. Don't even dream about it, Cecilia. Your father is like a
wild animal, against all the Leiboviches of the present and the
future. Since that famous meeting nothing and no one will ever
reconcile your father and mine. Several centuries of bourgeois
thinking separate them. I know what I'm talking about.

Cecilia. But tell me, Goyito. Do you think it's right that we elope?
It's not decent, it's not moral, as my father would like things
to be.

Goyito. Don't exaggerate, Cecilia. We're doing it decently. Remember, you're not taking a penny of your father's. Besides, I know
that what we're going to do is not immoral. It depends on who

is judging us. For my dad, it's a very reasonable form of independence. I'm sure of it.

Cecilia. Then why are you hiding it from him?

Goyito. (*At a loss for words*) Well . . . because. . . .

Cecilia. Why? Why?

Goyito. Well . . . because my father didn't want me to do it so that
it wouldn't upset your parents.

Cecilia. Well, I don't want to elope. Talk to him again.

Goyito. All right. Not another word. I'm leaving for Buenos Aires
alone. You'll never see me again. And you will forever be
haunted for having betrayed me at the last moment. Besides,
you already made up your mind to run away with me. In your
last letter you were hurrying me to do it. So from the ethical
point of view, which is what worries you, it's as if you had already done it. Your repentance is only a hypocritical attitude
that you're assuming out of fear and weakness. You love me and
you want to leave with me, too. The only thing that stops you is
your stupid fear of upsetting your parents and the only effect that
can cause is reducing their fortune. That's enough. I'm leaving.
Goodbye and remember my words. (*He extends his hand to her.
At that moment a woman comes out from the right side door
and disappears through the middle door, interrupting the pre-
dictably sad farewell between* GOYITO *and* CECILIA, *making them
tremble with fear and hide behind the fence, until they assume
she has left. Lowering his voice even more*) Goodbye! . . .

Cecilia. (*Whimpering*) Don't leave, Goyito. I love you. I can't live
without you.

Goyito. You know what you're doing. And don't stop me, because
it will be in vain.

Cecilia. All right, I'm going with you, whatever happens. I'm going
to get my clothes. (*She leaves from the right side door. The same
woman as in the previous scene comes through the second door,
moves to the well, fills a kerosene can with water and leaves by
the same door. In a little while* CECILIA *appears with a medium
size suitcase, dressed in travelling clothes.*)

Goyito. You haven't forgotten anything?

Cecilia. There's so little anyway, and I have it all.

Goyito. Come, let's leave right away. (*They disappear, holding
each other very close, almost embracing, leaving the scene in a
silence that seems to have intensified after the lovers' flight. After
a long silence,* KOHEN *and* GOROVICH *appear through the second
door and sit down in the corridor.*)

Gorovich. I've been saying it for a long time, our police chief has

no guts. That Aarón the Jew is a dangerous man, and in spite of
it, the chief doesn't make a move. The chief doesn't think he's
dangerous! Of course he wouldn't! A great reason not to do
anything and let the danger spread.

Kohen. I don't know where we'll end up with these things. Leibovich is ruining us all. He's like this *(putting his index fingers
together)* with the strikers. He laughs with them, he talks with
them, and he gives them advice too.

Gorovich. It's obvious that he's the real instigator of the latest
strike. What a shameless *gringo*! I don't know what the chief
is waiting for before he teaches him a lesson, like he taught
the others.

Kohen. The sheriff is no good, Doctor. To be a sheriff, you need
to be strong, and he's not strong.

Gorovich. I have an idea. What if we collect signatures to ask the
police chief for a change of sheriff?

Kohen. That's a good idea. A very good idea, Doctor.

Gorovich. We would have to speak to Efraín and Roter. If they
agree, we'll make our request immediately.

Kohen. We can speak to Efraín and Roter now. They're nearby.
Let's go right away.

Gorovich. Right. No time to lose. What a little trick we're going
to play on our sheriff for being such a weakling. This will teach
him to keep order. *(At the same time as* KOHEN *and* GOROVICH
*leave through the middle door, the same woman who appeared
twice before, reenters. She is* PETRONILA, *the maid, a rather self-
indulgent person. She sits down and sings as she sews.)*

Petronila. You see that I'm small, about love I know all, we little
ones can love and can woo. *(She repeats the same refrain several times.)*

Don Aarón. (Shows up a while later) Good evening.

Petronila. A very good one to you. *(Surprised by* DON AARÓN'S
presence, she stops singing)

Don Aarón. Go ahead, sing. I like *criollo* songs. Sing!

Petronila. And why should I sing if I don't want to!

Don Aarón. You don't want to? Too bad. You don't have to.
(Pause)

Petronila. The boss is out.

Don Aarón. You have a boss? What an ugly word! Boss, boss. It's
the same as slave! Men don't have bosses.

Petronila. But I'm not a man, you know.

Don Aarón. But you are people. And I meant people.

Petronila. I don't understand you. People who live at someone

else's place. How can they not have a boss then! I live at someone's place, you know.

Don Aarón. (*Looking at her mischievously*) It's true, you don't
understand. But you don't have to understand, you're a beautiful
criolla, and that's enough!

Petronila. Hey, watch it! An old tiger looking for tender flesh.
Don't think you're dealing with the *china* Tomasa, or with Fran-
cisca the *bichoca,*[11] or with Mary who has the four houses.

Don Aarón. What a presumptuous girl you are! I haven't said anything to you, and I don't have anything to say to you.

Petronila. I don't want you to say anything to me.

Don Aarón. All right, all right (*brief pause*). Tell the owner of the
house that I'll come back right away. I need to speak to him.
(*Leaves through the middle door.* PETRONILA *resumes her work
and begins to sing again. A few moments later* TOMASA *shows
up through the gate. She enters the yard, obviously looking for
someone.*)

Tomasa. (*Upon seeing* PETRONILA) Tell me, Petronila, have you
seen Don Aarón around here?

Petronila. He just left this minute.

Tomasa. Do you know where he went?

Petronila. Hey listen! Do you think I sleep around with Don Aarón
like some others do?

Tomasa. You're certainly testy, Petronila. Why should I think that
you sleep with Don Aarón! There must be something wrong with
you though, if he hasn't laid eyes on you yet.

Petronila. I've never been that brazen!

Tomasa. Just look at her, playing the saint! As if people didn't
know her. You've done right by yourself. He says the same thing
to all the women. A real charmer. As soon as he spots a *chinita,*
his eyes begin to cloud and he even forgets he has a memory.

Petronila. You shouldn't worry because of me.

Tomasa. It's obvious. You shouldn't be afraid. He can't help himself. He's just a show off.

Petronila. A show off? With less than that babies have been made.
(*Sarcastically*) Tomasa knows all about that, no?

Tomasa. Watch your tongue. You may lose your job yet.

Petronila. Thanks for the advice. I'll watch it because I don't have
anyone who's going to take care of me.

Tomasa. You don't have someone now, and you won't have anyone
later either, because you like them all and because you move
your tongue as much as you move your body. And I'm leaving.
I wouldn't want to disturb you. Maybe there are men hanging

around the house. (*As she leaves* DON AARÓN *enters through the gate.*) I was asking for you, Don Aarón.

Don Aarón. Did you ask Don Seba to bring the cart?

Tomasa. Not yet. I wanted to ask you if we're bringing flour. (PETRONILA *prepares to enter the house.*) Don't run away, Petronila. Don't run away. Let's see if it's true what they say about his charm.

Petronila. If that's the case, I'm staying. (*She turns back.*) Go ahead. Do you think I'm afraid of him?

Tomasa. (*To* DON AARÓN) She says you're chasing after her, and that you propositioned her just now.

Don Aarón. I'm not going after her. I'm not chasing her. But I like her, sure I like her. She's pretty, that Petronila. But she's wild. She kicks too much. Whatever I say, she kicks! I think she doesn't like me.

Tomasa. (*Furious*) Then is it true, Don Aarón?

Petronila. There you have it! You see? This'll show you. Petronila doesn't shoot off her mouth for nothing.

Tomasa. (*To* DON AARÓN) This very night I'm leaving your farm, Don Aarón. This is how you repay a woman's sacrifices! (*Hysterically, she begins to cry. Suddenly*) You're right. You're a lecherous old man. You and she are the same. A nice team to be pulling a cart together! Dirty old man! Bad Christian! (*New burst of crying*) I'm leaving your farm this very night! I'm leaving with the boy. (*Leaves angrily through the gate*)

Don Aarón. (*With satisfaction*) She's jealous, look how jealous she is. You're silly and you talk too much. (*Leaves through the gate.* PETRONILA *exits through the middle back door after remaining alone on the stage for a few seconds.* KOHEN *and* GOROVICH *return through the same door.*)

Gorovich. (*After both sit down*) What does the sheriff want? Could he have decided to proceed against Leibovich? If that's the case, we're on time, because we haven't sent the petition yet.

Kohen. Who knows what the chief wants. Let's see. Let's see. (*Suddenly becoming very angry*) It gets me so mad that that man should be so crazy. (*Pause*) Don't you know what's going on?

Gorovich. What? Has he done something else?

Kohen. Let me tell you. You know Leibovich's son?

Gorovich. Of course I know him. I baptized him for the second time. They call him Gath & Chaves[12] because he's such a show off. In the past, whenever he came home on vacation, he would be wearing something flashy to call attention to himself. One year he wore a hat with a wide brim! Some wide brim! Another time, he wore a tie, a really gaudy tie. He had the obsession of saying that everything came from Gath & Chaves. That's why I gave him that nickname. It fits him like a glove, believe me. *(Short pause)* What were you going to tell me about that stupid kid?

Kohen. What do you think? Without anyone's permission he wants to marry Cecilia.

Gorovich. This time the Leiboviches really got the better of you. And what does she say?

Kohen. It looks like they're serious. I'm not sure. The other day I was standing here and suddenly I look up and I see the boy coming over. He says hello and I don't say anything, waiting for him to speak to me. Don't you think that was right?

Gorovich. Very well done.

Kohen. He was quiet, very quiet and he was hitting his spats with a whip, like a policeman. After a while, when we were both quite bored, he tells me, "I came to talk to you, Señor Kohen." "Go ahead, talk," I answered him. Then he said, "I love Cecilia and she loves me." I looked at him as if he was crazy. "And she loves you?" I asked him. "Yes," he answered. "Well. And what do you want?" "Your . . ." How did he put it? He said one word. . . .

Gorovich. Authorization?

Kohen. No . . . What's the word?

Gorovich. Consent.

Kohen. That's it! "I came to ask for your consent so that we can marry. I came to ask for her hand."

Gorovich. He's a bold one, that Gath & Chaves.

Kohen. Then I got good and angry. "I don't give my permission. I didn't bring up Cecilia for you. Your father is my worst enemy and you're just like him. Even worse, you're a bigger anti-Semite than him."

Gorovich. Very well said. And what did he answer?

Kohen. I said even worse things to him. I said to him, "Your father is a man who looks for *chinas* from the shacks." *(He pronounces these last words emphatically and with great eloquence. As soon as he finishes his last sentence,* DON AARÓN *appears from the back of the stage.)*

Don Aarón. *(Seeing* GOROVICH*)* I have no luck. I always come across Doctor Gorovich. That's just no good. *(To* KOHEN*)* He can't stand me and I can't stand him.

(Gorovich gets up furiously, heading for the back door.)

Don Aarón. It's my pleasure. Right through here, Doctor.

Kohen. Stay, Doctor Gorovich.

Gorovich. No thanks, Mr. Kohen. I have a delicate stomach, you know. *(Leaves)*

Don Aarón. Maybe, maybe. *(Pause)* I need to talk to you.

Kohen. Right away, right away. *(He leaves as if to catch up with* GOROVICH, *and returns at once.)* Sit down. *(They both sit down.)*

Don Aarón. My son Goyito. . . .

Kohen. If that's what you want to talk about, forget it. We have nothing to talk about.

Don Aarón. That's what you think. I have something to say. I don't care if you don't listen to me. Goyito is in love with Cecilia and wants to marry her. Believe me, I don't think that's any great honor. It's no pleasure for me that a son of mine, whom I love more than anything else in the world, marries the daughter of a merchant I despise.

Kohen. How dare you insult me in my own house!

Don Aarón. I'm not insulting you. I'm saying the truth. I hate business and I hate businessmen too. I can't stand them, but that has nothing to do with anything. I cannot force my son not to love your daughter. I'm not such a fool. If he loves her, I have to keep silent, that's all. You have to do the same. But you don't. You have no right to deny them permission to get married. Parents should be careful before saying "No." When my Goyito told me he was in love with Cecilia, I told him, "Cecilia is a girl who one day goes this way and the next day goes that way. As the *tapes* say, she dances too freely with her body. Second, she likes fancy dresses too much. She's not for you." But he answered me, "I'm in love with her, Papá." "All right, go ahead, marry her then." It's useless to say no. Then they do as they please.

Kohen. Mr. Leibovich, you can teach your own children, not me. I know what I'm doing. I don't want my Cecilia to marry a son of yours. And that's it. *(The strident whistle of a train is heard as if from a very short distance away.)* You are my worst enemy. You are a man who wants the ruination of business and of all businessmen. I cannot allow my daughter to marry a son of yours. And I'm happy my Cecilia is a good girl and listens to me. When I say no, it's no. And I have nothing else to say.

Don Aarón. This has nothing to do with other matters. Foolish men believe you can say "No" to feelings and that feelings will get scared. Not only do you believe that, but you also believe another foolish thing. You believe that men who are not happy with money, like you, are evil, perverse. You're very wrong.

These are men who cannot stand injustice. You don't know what kind of a man I am.

Sheriff. *(Who appears from second door)* A very good afternoon to you, Señor Kohen. How are you, Don Aarón?

Don Aarón. You're just the man I have to speak to.

Sheriff. Whenever you want, Don Aarón.

Don Aarón. Can I speak here? *(As if it were a secret)* I don't have any more ideas. All I want now is a lot of money. Now I'm talking just like Señor Efraín, Señor Roter, Doctor Gorovich, and Señor Kohen. It's not necessary to get rid of money. What I need is even more money. What do you think about that, Sheriff?

Sheriff. Wonderful, Don Aarón! It had to be that way.

Kohen. Now you're a businessman too?

Don Aarón. I'm not talking to you. I'm talking to the sheriff *(Indignant)* I am not a businessman. *(To the* SHERIFF *)* I wanted to ask you a question.

Sheriff. With pleasure, Don Aarón.

Don Aarón. So, now I'm not a dangerous man any more. . . .

Sheriff. Of course not. Why should you be dangerous?

Don Aarón. Men who have a lot of money aren't dangerous?

Sheriff. Of course not! The questions you ask! Take all the money you can. Nobody will bother you.

Don Aarón. Sorry, Sheriff. I was mistaken.

Petronila. *(Appears breathless at the second door)* Boss! Boss! Cecilia ran away to Buenos Aires.

Kohen. *(Shocked)* What did you say?

Tomasa. *(Through the gate)* Don Aarón! Don Aarón! Goyito left for Buenos Aires with Cecilia.

Petronila. *(To* KOHEN*)* Yes, Boss. She just ran away on the train with Don Aarón's son.

Don Aarón. *(Joyfully)* With Goyito! Beautiful, beautiful. That I like. I'm so pleased!

Kohen. This man is a criminal. *Vey is mir!*[13] What can I do! How shameful!

Don Aarón. *(Rubbing his hands together)* I'm happy. My son is a man. He does what he has to do. *(Remains pensive)* You don't have to do anything. Nothing at all. Nothing's going to happen to your daughter. You're a lucky man. Your daughter is in good hands. Goyito is a good man who is not after money. He's like me. He ran away with Cecilia because he truly loves her with all his heart. He's not after your money, like some others. *(Unconsciously he approaches* KOHEN *and cordially pats him on the back, to everybody's surprise.)* Don't worry. You can rest easy. Cecilia's better off than all of us.

Gorovich. Señor Kohen, your daughter has run away on the train with that scoundrel Goyo Leibovich. *(*GOROVICH *excitedly rushes backstage.)*

Don Aarón. We already know, Mr. Busybody. Go look for other news in town. . . .

The End

NOTES

1. *Tape:* or guaraní Indian, colloquial term for a native from the interior provinces of the Argentine north.

2. *Criolla* (feminine): born in the New World.

3. *Mate:* from Quechua Indian, a beverage made from local tea leaves, mixed with hot water, infused through a metal pipe, and served in a gourd—the national drink of Argentina and Uruguay.

4. *Gringo:* (fem. gringa): a foreigner of European origin.

5. *Colono* (fem. colona): Eastern European immigrant settlers of the Argentine countryside in the twentieth century.

6. *Gurisa* (feminine): from the Guaraní Indian, colloquial term for a native from the interior provinces of the Argentine north.

7. *Sulky:* Horse-drawn carriage.

8. *Alpargatas:* espadrilles, sandals made of hemp.

9. *Chino* (fem. china): native Indian man.

10. *Aladios:* ethically unsound. Found in José Hernández's 19th–century epic poem, *Martín Fierro.*

11. *Bichoca:* Argentine colloquialism, cripple, generally referring to an animal.

12. *Gath & Chaves:* major department store in Buenos Aires until the 1950s.

13. *Vey is mir:* (Yiddish) My god!

Alberto Novión: *Petroff's Junkshop*

ALBERTO AURELIANO NOVIÓN (1881–1937)

We have chosen to include Alberto Novión, a non-Jewish writer, in this anthology because his play, *Petroff's Junkshop* (1934), presents a sharp contrast to those written by Jewish authors. Novión was born in France in 1881 and was brought to Argentina as a child. Samuel Eichelbaum asserted that the extraordinary and uninterrupted success that Novión enjoyed during his thirty-year career "could be explained by the freshness with which he recreated the humble settings he described so well" (Orgambide, 468).

Most of Novión's production, however, over one hundred plays, often written to satisfy the demands of particular actors, was comical and superficial, owing to the rising commercialization of the theatre at that time. Novión's strength, like his contemporaries, Florencio Sánchez, the brothers Discépolo, and Alberto Vacarezza, lies in his talent for revealing the reality around him, particularly the evils of poverty that he observed in the *conventillos* or tenement houses. Like Florencio Sánchez in *La gringa* (The foreigner) (1904), Novión explores the lives of the *gauchos* who were being displaced by industrialization and the advance of twentieth-century civilization. He also describes the sufferings of the *colonos*—the immigrants who came to settle the land. Novión's plays can be appreciated, if not for their literary value, at least as vivid documents of an era, brought to the stage with the skill and ear for dialogue that characterized his theatre.

The *sainete* included here, *Petroff's Junkshop,* is a humorous short play that caricatures the Jew in a light-hearted manner. Novión's intention was to entertain an audience that was mostly immigrant. He follows the same pattern as other writers of the genre known as the *género chico criollo,* popular in the 1920s, when the rising middle class needed to produce a commercial theatre for its consumption. After the 1930 coup d'etat in Argentina, however, this type of theatre began to be replaced by radio and cinema.

Petroff's Junkshop includes stock characters such as the old,

55

miserly, prejudiced Jewish father, his lovely Argentine daughter who speaks grammatically correct Spanish with no trace of a Russian accent, and the gentile Argentine boyfriend with whom the daughter elopes. It also touches on a fascinating, yet sordid subject in Argentine letters: the White Slave Trade, the importation of Jewish women from Poland into Argentina, and in particular the role of the Jew as *caften,* or slave trafficker. The most renowned play on the subject of Jewish prostitution, *Ibergus* (Regeneration) by Leib Malach, gained notoriety in the Jewish press of Buenos Aires when first staged in 1930, but did not have further repercussions since it was written in Yiddish.[1] The next full-length drama in Spanish to explore this theme was Samuel Eichelbaum's *Nadie la conoció nunca* (No one ever knew her) (1923).

NOTE

1. Leib Malach's *Ibergus* was translated into Spanish by Nora Glickman and Rosalía Rosembuj (Buenos Aires: Pardés, 1984). For a critical study on the subject, see Nora Glickman's "The Jewish White Slave Trade in Latin American Writings," *American Jewish Archives* 34, no. 2 (Nov. 1982): 178–89.

Petroff's Junkshop

List of Characters
Sofía
Catalina
Fedorowa
Petroff
Isaac
Alejandro
Nicolás
Torcuato
Pancho
Rafael
Antonio
Domingo

A Comic Sketch in One Act and Twenty–Three Scenes

Premièred in the Teatro Nacional of Buenos Aires, April 1920

A junkshop. Clothing, saddles, lassos, books, etc. Shelves from right to left, each with a door that faces the backroom. A counter in front of each door. Center stage, a showcase that faces the street. A door in the center. It is night. The set is illuminated by a light hanging in the middle of the store. Actors enter from right and left.

Scene I

ALEJANDRO *is seated at the counter and* FEDOROWA *exits stage right with two plates wrapped in a napkin.*
Fedorowa. See you later, Alejandro! I'm bringing food to my husband Isaac.
Alejandro. Enjoy yourself, Doña Fedorowa.
Fedorowa. (At the entrance door) Oh, how well you're looking today! *(Exits)*
Alejandro. (Remains sitting at the counter, mending a pair of pants. He sings.)
Ay, Aurora, you've abandoned me,
I who loved you so much . . .

(Pancho appears.)
    And in your black treachery
    you've forsaken me . . .
    Ay, Aurora, I'm still in love with you!
(Calling out without moving) Rabinovich! Rabinovich! Someone!

Scene II

ALEJANDRO, PANCHO, *and* PETROFF *enter stage left.*
Petroff. What do you want?
Pancho. Good evening.
Petroff. Good evening.
Pancho. Can you buy rings here?
Petroff. Anything money can buy you can get here.
Pancho. How much can you give me for this diamond ring?
Petroff. Let's see it! *(He examines it.)* How much do you want for
    this piece of crap?
Pancho. Well . . . Whatever you think.
Petroff. Tell me what you'll sell it for.
Pancho. Well, give me thirty pesos.
Petroff. Thirty pesos? Thirty kicks in the head I'll give you. What
    do you take me for, a fool? Do you think I find my money in
    the street?
Pancho. So, how much will you give me?
Petroff. I'll give you . . . I'll give you . . . three pesos.
Pancho. How much?
Petroff. Three pesos.
Pancho. (He gives him a punch.) What good are three pesos to
    me? What, do I look like I'm starving to death? Three pesos!
    I'll throw it on the street before that!
Petroff. So throw it on the street!
Pancho. Give me fifteen!
Petroff. Not one more than three . . . if you want it, take it; if not,
    we never spoke . . .
Pancho. And what am I supposed to with three pesos?
Petroff. You buy yourself an automobile . . .
Pancho. Get out of my way! Cheap Jew! Gimme back the ring!
    (He grabs it angrily.) Aren't you ashamed to offer three pesos
    for a diamond ring, that when you go like this . . . it looks like
    it's shining? Out of my sight, go away! . . . Cheap Jew!
Petroff. You're the cheap one!
Pancho. Three pesos! I feel like grabbing your beard and pulling
    it off.

Petroff. Lemme see you do that! Grab my beard! Go ahead! Pull
it off, you creep! If you want three pesos, Okay, if not, you better
get out right now.

Rafael. (From the door) Che, hurry up, the cops are coming. . . .
How much did he offer you?

Pancho. Three pesos.

Rafael. Tell him to go take a bath. *(Exits)*

Pancho. Go take a bath, go on! When I want three pesos, all I
have to do is stamp my foot, and there they are.

Petroff. So go stamp your foot on the floor.

Pancho. On your head I'm gonna stamp, you murderer! *(On his
way out)* You bum!

Petroff. You're the bum! You steal everything and then you want
to sell it to the poor *ruso*[1] so that they put him in jail.

Pancho. In jail? *(From the door)* They should hang you, that's
what they should do! *(Exits)*

Petroff. They should only hang your sister! *(Mumbling to himself)*
Compadrito![2] Good for nothing!

Alejandro. How brave those Argentines are when they get angry!

Scene III

PETROFF, ALEJANDRO *and* NICOLÁS, *from the street.*

Nicolás. Can I come in?

Petroff. C'mon in, Nicolás . . . I was waiting for you. How come
you took so long?

Nicolás. I had a lot of work at the Registry sending goods to the
country. So? Did you talk to Sofía? Is it okay with her to marry
me, to be my wife?

Petroff. And even if it's not okay with her, what do I care? I say
she'll marry you, and she'll marry you . . . whether she wants
to or not!

Nicolás. Bravo Rabinovich! If you get Sofía to marry me, I'll give
you another junkshop on Junín street and I'll also give you a
diamond ring to wear on the biggest finger you have!

Petroff. Dear Nicolás! *(Embracing him)* You're the greatest man
I've ever met in Buenos Aires. I'm beginning to love you as if
you were my dear old mother . . . Even if the whole house falls
down you'll marry Sofía! I'm going to call her right now and
you'll see she's prettier than a silver basin that's just been pol-
ished! *(Calling to the left)* Sofía! Sofía! My beloved daughter!
Do you wanna come into the store? I'm gonna show you so-

methin' real cheap and nice! Fix your tie, Nicolás, the day is dawning . . .

Scene IV

The above and SOFÍA, *from left.*

Sofía. Were you calling me?

Petroff. Come, look who's here . . . Nicolás! The boss of the Registry of Corrientes and Junín.[3] He's got a lot of money and wants to marry you.

Sofía. Me?

Petroff. Do you know what he just told me? That he's going to give you an automobile with a horn and everything! Look how beautiful! You're gonna spend your life blowing the horn.

Nicolás. I'm in love with you.

Petroff. Look how nice. He told me that when you have a little *ruso* he's going to be the one carrying the bottle so that the baby can drink. What do you say to that?

Nicolás. I'm going to give you a diamond bracelet with a watch on top so that you can see the time in the morning, in the afternoon, at nighttime, whenever you feel like it.

Sofía. And why so many gifts?

Nicolás. Señorita Sofía, I'm madly in love with you even though you can't tell.

Petroff. Nicolás is a very serious man. He falls in love from the inside, but outside he acts like a fool.

Nicolás. What's your answer?

Sofía. Caramba! I don't know what to say just like that. Let me think about it a little.

Petroff. Don't be silly. What's there to think about now? She wants to play hard to get. This is a business that's good for you and me, and that's that. You're going to marry Nicolás because I tell you to, because I feel like it. So there.

Sofía. You're the boss in the store and in the business, but when it comes to feelings, I'm the only boss. Do you understand? Look, I'm an adult.

Petroff. Che, che, che . . . Don't get off the trolley without ringing the bell because the sidewalk may be wet, even if it hasn't rained. Don't come to me with feelings when you know that in a junkshop they don't pay anything for that stuff. You marry Nicolás because I want you to, because I've given my word. And here you do as I say, and if you don't like it, there's the door, and once you leave you're not coming back.

Sofía. Don't worry . . . You won't have to tell me twice. I'm sick
of living in this house. I'll never be happier than the day I can
get far away from all these rags.

Petroff. So just go with Nicolás.

Sofía. And where do you expect me to go with this scarecrow?

Nicolás. What are you saying?

Petroff. What did you say? What does that mean, scarecrow? What
the . . . it sounds like a dirty word to me . . . Get out of here
right now!

Nicolás. Leave her alone, Petroff!

Petroff. I said, get out of here!

Sofía. I don't feel like it!

Petroff. So you're not leaving?

Sofía. Don't you hear that I'm saying no?

Petroff. So . . . stay there . . . what a mule she's turned out to
be, Nicolás!

Scene V

The above and ANTONIO. *He walks from the back of the store
to the counter on the left.*

Antonio. A package of *43s*.

Petroff. No *43s* left.

Antonio. Give me a package of *Barriletes* then.

Petroff. No *Barriletes* left either.

Antonio. So what brand do you have?

Petroff. The one that has nothing to do with you! So now you're
going to make me carry the brand you like?

Antonio. What do you have a tobacco shop for, then?

Petroff. To make you waste your time. Get out right now, if you
don't want me to call the cops . . . If you want cigarettes, pick
up the butts from the street.

Antonio. Your mother's a bigger butt-picker, you Russian thief!

Petroff. Scarecrow! (ANTONIO *exits. To* SOFÍA) So, my dear, what
do you have to say? Are you marrying Nicolás, or not?

Nicolás. Leave her alone, Petroff. I'll come tomorrow for the
answer.

Sofía. Don't bother, Don Nicolás. It's not worth your coming tomorrow. My heart's already taken. I've given my word.

Petroff. What do you mean, you've given your word? Let's see
the contract.

Sofía. My fiancé has the papers.

Petroff. And how much did he give you for the deal?

Sofía. He offered his life in exchange for my word, just like I would give my life if he asked for it.

Nicolás. And how much is your life worth?

Sofía. Ask my fiancé.

Petroff. And who is your fiancé? Alejandro? Or some Argentine *compadrito*?

Sofía. You'll meet him when he asks for my hand.

Petroff. What's he gonna ask for?

Sofía. My hand.

Petroff. What he'll get is my foot. What do you say to all of this, Nicolás?

Nicolás. That I want her more than ever. That woman will be mine whether she likes it or not. Do you give me your word that you're not against this? I'll buy her from you. How much is she worth?

Sofía. How horrible! I'll die first. *(Exits stage left)*

Nicolás. How much is she worth?

Petroff. Well, whatever you think, as long as it has more than four zeros.

Nicolás. Five thousand pesos?

Petroff Stretch yourself.

Nicolás. Six thousand?

Petroff. A little more.

Nicolás. Seven thousand?

Petroff. Add another half.

Nicolás. Seven thousand five hundred?

Petroff. I'd like it to be a round number.

Nicolás. Eight thousand?

Petroff. I don't quibble about money. You give me ten thousand pesos and we don't talk anymore.

Nicolás. It's a deal.

Petroff. Do you want us to sign an agreement? Let's go to my private office.

Nicolás. Let's go. *(Before leaving,* NICOLÁS *raises his hand towards the same door through which* SOFÍA *left, and pronounces some ceremonious sentences in Russian.* PETROFF *does the same. Then they both exit.)*

Scene VI

ALEJANDRO *and* CATALINA. *She enters from left.*

Catalina. *Che,* Alejandro, what happened to Sofía?

Alejandro. She had a fight with her father.

Catalina. Why did they fight?

Alejandro. Because her father wants to force Sofía to marry Nicolás Patogroff against her will!

Catalina. Sofía's so lucky. . . . Everybody wants to marry her, but nobody ever says nothing to me. . . . It makes me mad!

Alejandro. And what do you want them to say to you?

Catalina. What they'd say to any pretty girl like me . . . love words . . . "Hi sweetie pie," "You're so good looking," "What a dish."

Alejandro. And what do you think, that people don't have anything else to do but talk nonsense? Now look at me when I stand at the door of the junkshop to watch the girls go by. When they see me, they say to each other, "Just look what a miserable face that guy at the door has." And that guy at the door is me.

Catalina. But you don't have such a miserable face. A little, maybe a little, but not so much. *(Coquettish) Che,* Alejandro. Do you know something? I'm ashamed to say it . . .

Alejandro. If it's a dirty word, save it for your parents.

Catalina. No, it's not dirty. Just the opposite. It's a nice word, very nice, but it's so difficult to take the first step.

Alejandro. It can't be that hard, when you spend your whole life walking.

Catalina. If you felt the same way . . . if you were faithful to me . . .

Alejandro. Sorry, sister, I'm not that hungry.

Catalina. And yet I don't know what power your eyes have, that day by day I'm falling more in love with you.

Alejandro. You're confusing me, Señorita Catalina. Do you think I'm such a lowlife to marry you?

Catalina. What do you mean, lowlife?

Alejandro. Get out, get out of here. I was never close enough to you for you to talk to me this way.

Catalina. What are you saying? What would you like better than to marry me, you shitty little Russian? Since when were you so lucky?

Alejandro. Don't tickle me under my arm because I get sentimental. Have you ever looked at yourself in a mirror?

Catalina. Yes, I have. And I'm much prettier than you.

Alejandro. Have you ever seen me in a new suit?

Catalina. Yes, I've seen you, and you looked like a whipped dog on a chase.

Alejandro. Then why are you flirting with me, acting like you wanna marry me?

Catalina. Because women are like that. We see a man, we fall in love, and that's it. We want to get married. I saw you, I fell in

love, and I want to get married. And you have to marry me. If
you don't, I'll have you thrown out on the street.

Alejandro. Better they throw me out on the street and a trolley
runs me over, before I do something so horrible!

Catalina. Honestly, you're a miserable character!

Alejandro. And you're pretty pushy.

Catalina. A husband like you is just what I need.

Alejandro. Knock on some other door, not this one.

Scene VII

The above and TORCUATO, *from the door.*

Torcuato. Psst! Psst! Catalina!

Catalina. Torcuato!

Torcuato. Don't call me Torcuato! It gets me mad! Call me Tito!

Catalina. Tito!

Torcuato. Domingo's there, and he wants to talk to Sofía . . . Did
the old man leave?

Catalina. Come here, come on in! Don't you need cigars?

Torcuato. Save me two *toscanos*⁴ for later. What should I tell Domingo, to come or to wait at the corner?

Catalina. Angel lips!

Torcuato. Cut the lies . . . *Che,* does the smack I gave you yesterday still hurt?

Catalina. You left me with one side of my face still burning.

Torcuato. I'll come back later to fix the other side. What shall I
tell Domingo?

Catalina. Tell him that the old man is inside talking business with
some guy. That if he wants to come in, he should pretend he
wants to buy cigarettes.

Torcuato. All right. I'll tell him. Bye.

Catalina. *Che,* Tito, I'm reading a book of the prettiest poems.
I'm folding down the page of all the ones that I like . . . to lend
it to you later.

Torcuato. Don't be stupid. Just put five pesos on all the poems you
like. See you later. *(Exits)*

Catalina. Okay. See you later. *(To* ALEJANDRO*)* Now that's a boyfriend. He even hits me and everything. Not like you, who
doesn't know how to do anything.

Alejandro. Ha, ha, so I don't know how to do anything? It's clear
you never heard me whistle fast.

Catalina. Creep! *(Exits left)*

Alejandro. More than you know.

Scene VIII

ALEJANDRO. SOFÍA *enters stage left.* DOMINGO *appears from the back.* CATALINA *reappears later.*

Domingo. Sofía! *(Goes to the counter)*

Sofía. (Behind the counter) Domingo! I have so much to tell you. This can't go on . . . Alejandro, would you go to the store and buy me a spool of black thread, number 40?

Alejandro. Sure. *(He gets up, puts his hat and jacket on, takes the ten cents that* SOFÍA *took out of the register and exits, whistling quickly to show off for* CATALINA. CATALINA *had left while* ALEJANDRO *was putting on his jacket.)*

Scene IX

CATALINA, SOFÍA, DOMINGO, TORCUATO.

Catalina. And Tito?

Domingo. What Tito?

Catalina. Torcuato.

Domingo. He's outside. *(He goes to the door and shortly after* TORCUATO *appears. To* SOFÍA*)* What's the matter? Why such a serious face?

Sofía. They want me to marry a man I don't love. My father's already said yes and he's forcing me to go through with it. Right now they're inside arranging the conditions and setting the price on my marriage, as if I was just another piece of junk from the store.

Domingo. That can't be!

Sofía. We can't lose any time, Domingo. You have to save me . . .

Domingo. And I will save you, no matter what it takes!

Sofía. What are you going to do?

Domingo. Right now I can't think of anything. But I'll come up with something. You just get your things together. No—don't get anything together. Tonight, before they close the shop, you'll come with me.

Sofía. Where?

Domingo. I don't know . . . somewhere . . . will you do it? *(Pause)* Do you doubt my love and my word?

Sofía. Oh, Domingo! Yes! I'll follow you wherever . . . and the sooner the better. I'm sick of this life, of living far from you, of everything. Take me wherever you want!

Domingo. Thank you, Sofía, thank you! You'll never regret it!

Catalina. (From behind the counter on right) Why don't you like to be called Torcuato?

Torcuato. Because it's a silly name. Like some kind of dandy. And I don't go for dandies. Just give me a *chambergo,* a *faja*[5] and five pesos a day. Then I'm the happiest man in the world. Hand me a *toscano.*

Catalina. They're on the other counter.

Torcuato. Don't forget to give them to me later. But don't be so damn stupid to hide them in your stockings. They get ruined. What's that, way up on top?

Catalina. That? Some silver forks and knives. Papá got them for fifteen pesos.

Torcuato. Pass them over here. I'm going to take them to the junk shop across the street to see how much they'll pay for them. *(He hides them underneath his jacket.)*

Domingo. Then we're set. Once they're all in bed, I'll whistle from outside, you'll open the door, I'll come in, we'll grab your things and we'll go.

Sofía. Okay.

Domingo. (Taking her hand) See you later.

Sofía. My father!

Scene X

The above, PETROFF *and* NICOLÁS.

Domingo. Do you have a package of *43s*?

Sofía. Papá, do we have *43s*?

Petroff. We don't have 30 or 84 or anything. It looks to me like that one is Sofía's Argentine boyfriend . . . Nicolás, get in front of that door and don't let him leave . . . So, a package of *43s,* eh? . . . What're you doing here?

Domingo. Buying cigarettes . . .

Petroff. Buying cigarettes? You're coming to flirt with my girl, to take her away from me. But Sofía is not going to marry you! Sofía belongs to Nicolás.

Nicolás. She's my woman.

Domingo. You're lying, you rat! Sofía will never belong to a dog like you!

Nicolás. A dog, you said? Say that again! Maybe you want me to cut up your face, *compadrito!* If you step foot in this house again, you'll remember me for the rest of your life. *(He takes out his gun.)* That's the woman I love. And the man who wants to have her better be a match for me. So now you know. Ha, ha, ha! Just look at your boyfriend now, trembling like a leaf. Ha! And these are the famous *compadritos.* Ha!

Petroff. Make him get on his knees and apologize!

Torcuato. (*He pounces on* NICOLÁS *like a wolf and takes his gun.*) Hands up! Get out of here Domingo, or they'll put us in jail. Just let them catch me! Hands up! This will be my eighth murder. Get away, Domingo!

Catalina. Don't, Torcuato!

Torcuato. I said don't call me Torcuato!

Domingo. Ha, ha, the tables are turned!

Torcuato. Yes, these are the famous *compadritos*! On your knees!

Domingo. Ha! Let's go Tito! Leave them. Don't get yourself in trouble for these cowards.

Torcuato. (*He drops the silverware.*) Hands up!

Petroff. My silverware!

Torcuato. (*He picks it up.*) Let's go.

Domingo. Let's go.

Torcuato. And now, *arrivederci,* gentlemen! *Se non ti vedo più, felice morte!*[6] (*He exits with* DOMINGO.)

Scene XI

The above without DOMINGO *and* TORCUATO.

Catalina. What a guy my Torcuato is!

Petroff. What do you have to say, Nicolás?

Nicolás. Argentines, what *compadres*![7](*An argument is heard from within.* ISAAC *and* FEDOROWA *appear, yelling at each other in Russian.* PETROFF *and* NICOLÁS *join in the argument in Russian. They give the impression that they are discussing something of great importance.* ISAAC *carries a showcase full of cigarettes on his shoulders.*)

Scene XII

SOFÍA, CATALINA, FEDOROWA, ISAAC, PETROFF, NICOLÁS *and* ALEJANDRO.

Isaac. (*Once they have calmed down*) Yes, sir. This is the way I found that brazen woman giving away cigarettes to a cop and making love to him. Cheating woman! We just came from the police. I told them everything and they said that if they catch them talking, they're going to arrest them and put them in the same cell. (ALEJANDRO *exits stage right.*)

Fedorowa. I'm innocent, Isaac!

Isaac. "I'm innocent?" I'm going to grab your neck and wring it!

Fedorowa. And didn't you say you were a *Maximalista*?[8]

Isaac. I'm a *Maximalista* to outsiders. In business I'm a Conservative. Get inside! I don't wanna see your face! Get lost! You're a greedy woman who's never satisfied with what you have, always asking for more!

Fedorowa. You're going to kill me!

Isaac. You're the one who's going to kill me, giving away cigarettes all over.

Fedorowa. (*As she leaves from stage right*) I'm so miserable! (*Exits*)

Isaac. You sure are.

Petroff. Let's go to the dining room, Nicolás. We have to have a talk.

Nicolás. Let's go . . . (*As they reach the counter on left*) You first.

Petroff. After you. (*Exits with* NICOLÁS)

Scene XIII

SOFÍA *and* ISAAC.

Sofía. Isaac, I'd like to have a serious talk with you.

Isaac. What's the matter?

Sofía. Papá wants to force me to marry Nicolás and I want . . .

Isaac. I agree with you. I'm so mad at Nicolás that I could grab his hat and shove it down his throat. Once he lent me 200 pesos and then he had the nerve to collect them.

Sofía. I love another man, Isaac.

Isaac. I figured that.

Sofía. And there was almost a tragedy just now. Papá doesn't even want to talk to him. He makes me so upset, I could die.

Isaac. And you wanna talk to your boyfriend? That's very easy.

Sofía. Where? How? He won't let him set foot in the store and he watches me day and night.

Isaac. You can talk to him here in the shop. When everyone's asleep I'll let him in and you two can talk until dawn. What do you think?

Sofía. Great! You're so good, Isaac! That's just what's going to happen. Domingo is coming tonight at eleven and he'll whistle from outside for you to open the door.

Isaac. That's settled then.

Sofía. I owe you my happiness, Isaac. (*Exits left*)

Scene XIV

The above and ALEJANDRO, *with a sack of clothing.*

Alejandro. (Enters stage right) Adiós! I'm just in tears! Because Señorita Catalina is teasing me and I came here to work and not to waste time.

Isaac. And why don't you like Catalina?

Alejandro. Because she wants to marry me, and to make love with other men.

Isaac. And what do you care?

Alejandro. What do you mean, what do I care?

Isaac. Enough nonsense already! You come live with us. Leave that *(referring to the sack of clothing)* and close the shutters. It's time to leave the shop.

Alejandro. I'm staying only because you're asking me to stay. Otherwise I wouldn't. *(He puts down the sack and closes the shutters.* ISAAC *takes out an accounting book, and counts the money. After* ALEJANDRO *has closed the shutters, he returns with a cot and puts it in front of the counter, on the right. Then he uses an empty box as a night table, and puts a bottle with a candle on top of it.)*

Scene XV

The above, PETROFF, *and* NICOLÁS. *They enter from left.*

Nicolás. So, we agree?

Petroff. We agree.

Nicolás. I'll be here at midnight with an automobile. When I honk three times you open the door, and I'll come in. You make Sofía go to bed in the store, in Alejandro's bed. Then I'll cover her nose with chloroform, she'll pass out and we'll take her to the automobile. And then . . . happiness, my dear Petroff! Happiness for everyone!

Petroff. It seems perfect to me. Leave it all to me.

Isaac. (Behind the counter) I gave five, he takes two, I have four left. I gave seven, I got eight . . . one's missing.

Petroff. Very good. See you later.

Nicolás. So it's settled. At midnight.

Petroff. Three honks.

Nicolás. Exactly. *Adiós,* Isaac.

Isaac. Adiós, Nicolás. If I sell four packs of cigarettes and they steal one from me, I don't make a thing.

Scene XVI

PETROFF, ISAAC, ALEJANDRO.

Petroff. (Returns, after closing the back door) I have something to tell you, Isaac.

Isaac. What's the matter, Petroff? (ALEJANDRO *starts to get undressed.)*

Petroff. I was told that at night people enter the store and take stuff. You've got to watch Alejandro.

Isaac. I understand.

Petroff. I've decided that tonight Sofía will sleep in the shop, so that by tomorrow we'll know who's coming in and robbing everything. What do you think?

Isaac. Sofía's gonna sleep in the shop? It's a good idea.

Petroff. Alejandro! *(He has just pulled his pants down.)* Don't go to bed. Tonight you're not going to sleep here. Go sleep next to the coal cellar. I hear robbers are coming, you understand?

Alejandro. How terrible! I'm not staying here! *(Exits left and* SOFÍA *appears.)*

Scene XVII

PETROFF, ISAAC *and* SOFÍA.

Petroff. Sofía, my dear, Isaac and I have decided that you're gonna sleep here tonight, because it seems that Alejandro lets a friend in at night and gives him merchandise. You stay here to watch. Are you afraid?

Isaac. Of course she's not afraid!

Sofía. What a rat that Alejandro is! Don't worry! I won't open the door for anyone!

Petroff. Do you sleep very soundly?

Sofía. Like a log.

Petroff. Very well. Don't open the door for anyone. You sleep there.

Isaac. Good. I'm going to sleep. Until tomorrow. *(Exits right)*

Sofía. See you tomorrow, Isaac.

Petroff. Sleep well.

Scene XVIII

SOFÍA *and* PETROFF.

Petroff. (He gets a ladder before putting out the light. The room is dark. He lights a candle.) Good, dear Sofía. See you tomorrow. Forgive me if I was a little rough . . . It's my character, you know? Don't pay any attention to Nicolás. He's not a bad man.

Sofía. See you tomorrow. *(She turns the light off.)*

Petroff. *(Exiting left)* Poor thing! The last thing she expects is that tomorrow she won't be in this junkshop anymore . . .

Scene XIX

SOFÍA *and* ISAAC. *In the darkness.*

Isaac. *(Returning)* Sofía . . . Sofía! Are you there?
Sofía. Yes.
Isaac. Where are you? I don't see you.
Sofía. Here.
Isaac. Haven't they called from outside?
Sofía. Not yet. What time do you think it is?
Isaac. It's probably around ten thirty.
Sofía. We still have half an hour left.
Isaac. Should we see who's more ticklish?
Sofía. You think it's time to play games now?
Isaac. Shhh . . . Quiet! People are coming.
Sofía. From where?
Isaac. From there! *(He points to the back of the store, on the right.)* Hide! *(*SOFÍA *hides behind a closet.* ISAAC *jumps in the cot and covers himself.* FEDOROWA *appears with a ridiculous nightgown and a kerchief on her head and a lantern in her hand. The room is lit up.)*
Fedorowa. *(She goes towards the cot.)* Alejandro! Alejandro! My sweetheart! Who loves you? Who pulls your ear like I do?
Isaac. *(Mumbling)* Pig! Shameless hussy!
Fedorowa. Who are you?
Isaac. Your husband, Isaac.
Fedorowa. Don't shout at me! I'm sleepwalking!
Isaac. Shhh! Quiet! Go inside and I'll deal with you later.
Fedorowa. *(Making believe she is a sleepwalker)* Who loves you? Who pulls your ear like I do? Don't you see I'm dreaming and I don't know what I'm saying? *(Exits stage right)*

Scene XX

ISAAC *and* SOFÍA. *Later,* ALEJANDRO *and* DOMINGO.

Sofía. *(Laughing)*
Isaac. Did you see that?
Sofía. Poor Doña Fedorowa!
Isaac. Poor Doña Fedorowa? Poor me! That woman is such a cheat!
Sofía. Shhh! Quiet! I thought I heard something.

Isaac. It wasn't me!

Sofía. Shhh! (ALEJANDRO *appears from left dragging himself across the floor with a huge rifle.*)

Isaac. There he is!

Sofía. Who?

Isaac. I thought I heard three knocks. (*They pay attention. A whistle and three knocks are heard from within.*)

Sofía. It's him! Open up!

Isaac. Slowly! (*He opens the door very cautiously.* DOMINGO *appears.*)

Sofía. Come in! I'll explain everything to you! (ISAAC *closes the door.*)

Alejandro. (*Standing up behind the counter, pointing the rifle*) Halt! Who's there?

Isaac. Alejandro! It's me, Isaac. Put your gun down!

Domingo. This is an ambush!

Alejandro. What's going on?

Domingo. Quiet! We're lost!

Sofía. Don't worry! Old Isaac is on our side and wants to protect us.

Domingo. Thank you.

Isaac. (*Lights a match*) You better not say one word about it, or I'll cut your throat with a knife.

Alejandro. Here comes Petroff.

Isaac. Petroff? You better hide, fast! All of you over here. Alejandro! Get in bed, fast! Right now! (DOMINGO *and* SOFÍA *under the counter.* ISAAC *goes to the right,* ALEJANDRO *gets into the cot.*)

Scene XXI

PETROFF, *with a lantern in his hand.* ALEJANDRO, SOFÍA *and* DOMINGO.

Petroff. I think there are cats on the roof. (*In front of* ALEJANDRO) Poor thing, she's snoring like an angel . . . (*Three honks are heard.*) There he is! Nicolás! Dear Sofía, goodbye forever. May happiness always be with you. (*Three honks are heard again.*) He's in such a hurry . . . She's coming! (*He opens the door.*)

Scene XXII

The above and NICOLÁS.

Nicolás. So?

Petroff. She's sleeping like a little bird.

Nicolás. Here's the perfumed chloroform. Soak the sponge in it and put it under her nose.

Petroff. (*Taking it from him*) My poor darling child!

Nicolás. If you put it underneath the sheets, you'll make ten thousand pesos.

Petroff. May all this be for your happiness. (*He puts the sponge under the sheets, under* ALEJANDRO's *nose.*)

Nicolás. Is it done?

Petroff. Yes.

Alejandro. It smells like perfume.

Nicolás. Now, to the automobile! (*As the two of them lift the body, they realize their mistake.*)

Petroff. This is heavy!

Alejandro. What are you doing to me?

Nicolás. Alejandro!

Petroff. Where's Sofía? Son of a bitch! She got away! Sofía! Sofía! Turn on the light!

Alejandro. What were you doing to me?

Petroff. (*Sees* DOMINGO) Aha! What is this? Thieves in the house?

Nicolás. Leave it to me! Now you're in my hands! Now there's no one to defend you!

Petroff. (*Seeing* SOFÍA) Goddamnit! Sofía's here? What the hell are you doing here with that *compadrito*? Alejandro, call the police.

Sofía. No, don't call them. Forgive me, Petroff . . . forgive me!

Domingo. Don't get on your knees. Don't kneel in front of these miserable characters who wanted to buy and sell you like merchandise from the junkshop. Let them call the police, they'll know how to put them in jail for being *caftens*![9]

Nicolás. What did you say?

Domingo. Just what you heard.

Nicolás. Say that again, you louse! I'm going to slit your throat, just like a dog!

Petroff. Don't murder him Nicolás, you'll mess up the floor. Sofía! Get in!

Domingo. Sofía! Don't move from my side!

Nicolás. Leave that woman!

Domingo. Don't move!

Nicolás. Let her go! Help me, Petroff!

Petroff. Let my daughter go!

Domingo. (Taking out a knife) I'll kill the first one who takes a step!

Nicolás. (Taking out a gun) If you don't leave that woman, I'll put a bullet in your head.

Scene XXIII

The above and ISAAC.

Isaac. What's going on? What's all this? What's that one doing with the toothpick in his hand, and you, with your gun?

Petroff. Isaac, that's the thief who's been coming at night to rob my store. *(The two speak in Russian.)*

Isaac. And Nicolás, what are you doing in the store so late?

Sofía. He made a deal with Papá to steal me. They have the automobile outside.

Isaac. Goddamn! Goddamn! Goddamn!

Nicolás. That bum wants to steal my woman from me! Sofía is mine!

Isaac. Who do you belong to?

Sofía. To Domingo!

Isaac. So why are you lying?

Nicolás. What? You're going to object? Sofía will be mine, no matter what! And I'm taking her right now! Let's go, Petroff!

Isaac. Just one minute!

Nicolás. Out of my way!

Isaac. (Takes out two large pistols from his jacket) If you take one step, you lousy bum, I'm going to fill your face with more holes than a sponge. Sofía's not going with you. She's going with the other guy, because I say so, and because I feel like it. And if you don't like it, I'll unload these two pistols in your face. Throw that gun on the floor! Throw it! *(To* DOMINGO *and* SOFÍA*)* And you can get going because the automobile is waiting outside. Hurry up! *(*SOFÍA *and* DOMINGO *run out.)*

Petroff. What are you doing, Isaac?

Nicolás. Cretin!

Isaac. Don't move! If I really get mad, I'll make you pay for it! *(Three honks are heard from inside.)* They're gone!

Petroff. And with an Argentine *compadrito*! It's your fault that my daughter ran away with an Argentine *compadrito*!

Isaac. Don't feel so bad, Petroff. They love each other and it's

better that she went off with a *compadrito* than with a *caften,*
like this miserable character who has four wives. Get out of here!
Petroff. Get out of here!
Nicolás. What?
Petroff. I'm telling you to get out!
Nicolás. You too? Give me back my money!
Petroff. What money?
Nicolás. The money I lent you!
Isaac. You want the money? Petroff, grab the rifle.
Petroff. Get out of here!
Isaac. Out! Out. Out! Out, dog! *(As* NICOLÁS *leaves, yelling in Russian,* ISAAC *and* PETROFF *yell back at him, also in Russian, progressively raising their voices.)*

Curtain

NOTES

1. *Ruso:* The word *ruso* (Russian) is interchangeable with *Jew, sheeny,* or *Yid* in popular Argentine speech.
2. *Compadrito:* an arrogant, Argentine street character.
3. *Corrientes* and *Junín:* two central streets in Buenos Aires.
4. *Toscanos:* cigars.
5. Articles of clothing worn by a gaucho: *chambergo,* a slouched hat; *faja,* a cloth belt that twists around the waist.
6. If I never see you again, have a happy death!
7. *Compadre:* colloquial term of endearment, friend or buddy.
8. *Maximalista:* a radical left wing party, advocate of the Russian Revolution.
9. *Caftens:* In this context, *caftens* refers to Jewish men accused of bringing women from Poland to Argentina, to turn them into prostitutes. This phenomenon, known as the "White Slave Traffic," occurred at the turn of the century and was eradicated by the 1930s. See N. Glickman's study "The Jewish White Slave Trade in Latin American Writings," *American-Jewish Archives* 39, no. 2 (Nov. 1982): 178–189.

César Tiempo: *The Tithe*

CÉSAR TIEMPO (PSEUDONYM FOR ISRAEL ZEITLIN, 1906–1975)

César Tiempo is well-known both as a poet and as playwright. His first book is in the form of a poetic diary. Written in 1927, *Versos de una . . . (Verses of a . . .)* is an apocryphal creation, signed by a presumed Jewish prostitute of Russian origin, Clara Beter. Tiempo was forced to write this poem anonymously. The work of this immigrant, in Leonardo Senkman's opinion, can be seen as a metaphor for the failure of the Jewish immigrant in Argentina, a land that promised prosperity but brought about humiliation instead.[1]

Tiempo's plays, written primarily for a gentile public who had little knowledge of the real Jew, were attempts to present Jewish culture for them. Still, many of his characters, like the matchmaker or the *schnorer,* who were probably familiar to his Jewish audiences, provided additional interest because of their speech patterns, which included many humorous and colorful Yiddish expressions or derivations such as: *krekhtsen* (to complain); *Vey is mir!* (Woe is me!); and biblical allusions from the *Song of Solomon,* comparing a character to a flower in Sharon, for example. Like Samuel Eichelbaum's *Aarón the Jew,* Tiempo's plays relate to the experiences of integration that Jews underwent during the first decades of immigration, both as poor city dwellers and as pioneers in the Jewish colonies of Entre Ríos.

La alfarada (The Tithe, 1938), Tiempo's one-act play included in this anthology, has an interesting history. It was written during the so-called *década infame* of the 1930s marked by the rise of nationalism and xenophobia in Argentina and of Nazism in Europe. This coincides with the period of considerable effort on the part of the Jewish community to integrate into Argentine society. This period also marks the contrast between the liberal policies expounded by many political democratic leaders and the crushing of these ideas with repressive coup d'etats and the suppression of individual liberties.

César Tiempo

Tiempo reacted to the anti-Semitic campaign promoted by creole nationalists and to the writings of Martínez Zuviría by writing two different types of responses, both in 1935. Zuviría, under the pen name of Hugo Wast, had written the novels *Kahal* and *Oro,* in which he fictionalized the plots of the infamous *Protocols of the Elders of Zion* and epitomized them in the Jews of Buenos Aires. In response, Tiempo wrote an article for the newspaper *Mundo Israelita* entitled "La campaña antisemita y el director de la Biblioteca Nacional," which referred directly to the public office that Hugo Wast held at the time.

Tiempo's second response, *The Tithe,* was presented as an autonomous piece by the Teatro Independiente Company of Buenos Aires in 1935. It follows the three-act dramatic farce about Blacks, Jews, and theatre people, entitled *El teatro soy yo* (I am the theatre), which opened in November of 1933. Tiempo's thesis play cycle culminates with the play "Creole Bread," which offers the author's definitive solution to the question of Jewish integration in a Catholic country. This four-act play, which in 1937 received the highly acclaimed Premio Nacional de Teatro, has been regarded by the critics as a lengthy *sainete* with a thesis, because it was written in defense of the fusion of the races and in rejection of the closed ghetto existence of the Jews. "Creole Bread" proposes integration and assimilation to the new land and customs, achieved through the force of love—love for the land and respect for honest work. As Leonardo Senkman points out, this is the principal reason for the success of the play, since it was defended both by Jewish and non-Jewish critics, by liberals and by conservatives.[2]

Although the publication date of the one-act play *The Tithe* chronologically precedes that of "Creole Bread," it can be regarded as the second epilogue to the play. The author considers it "a gravely comic comedy . . . in four acts and two outcomes." But given the success of the optimistic second version, the first, grim version, was never performed again. It is this first version that is included in this anthology.

All three plays deal with racial and religious conflicts caused by the love of a man and a woman of different backgrounds and religions. Curiously, while Tiempo puts emphasis on the issue of brotherhood between Myriam Sambatión, a Jew, and Gaspar Liberión, a black man, in "I Am the Theatre," the worst discrimination is experienced by the black man. Myriam does not side with him until she herself is discriminated against and fears for her own demise. Tiempo confronts both writers, each carrying the weight of generations of suffering and injustice—the Jew through pogroms, the Black through lynchings. "I Am the Theatre" is important in that it anticipates the interracial conflict of the mixed couple. It is significant that only when it is too late—at the moment of Gaspar's death by suicide—Myriam confesses her love to him.[3]

In writing *The Tithe,* Tiempo uses a Pirandellian device that permits him to discuss his other dramatic writings from within the theatre and to develop some of his stylistic trends. Here, Myriam Sambatión, protagonist of the Tiempo play "I Am the Theatre," presents herself as the Jewish author of a play entitled *El cinturón de lino* (The linen belt). Like one of Unamuno's characters, Myriam is "a creature of the author" who turns against César Tiempo and also claims to be the "legitimate" creator of his main character, Solomón Lefonekho. The title of the play, *The Tithe,* which Myriam Sambatión defines as an "epilogue" to her previous play— "The Linen Belt"—refers to the tax that the Moors and Jews of Spain had to pay in Christian territory. It is the "onerous and painful" tribute that modern Jews pay as the price for living in the Diaspora. This imposed tax, she further explains, is "the pound of flesh that Shylock once demanded, and now is demanded from him, with interest." (p. 83)

The Solomón Lefonekho that the spectator meets at the beginning of *The Tithe,* far from being a just, Solomonic judge, is a destroyed man. He has lost his nobility and his dignity. He is now sordid, degraded, even cruel. Whereas before he drew on the Bible for inspiration for his pronouncements as a justice of the peace, now, like Hamlet, he dismisses it as "all words." (p. 87) Myriam Sambatión refers to Solomon's experience as his "crucible." Although he is rich, he is unhappy, and in addition he drinks. The action of *The Tithe* takes place two years after Solomón's daughter eloped with a non-Jew, with whom she spent one week before returning home. Mañe, Solomón's wife, is portrayed as a caricature of the martyred Jewish mother ("This is going to kill me," p. 93) who sides with her children, although she condones her husband's behavior.

In "Creole Bread," in response to Lía's elopement, her aggrieved, prejudiced father had said *Kaddish* for her, the Jewish prayer for the dead. His humiliation is so strong that he resigns as judge in Buenos Aires and moves to the country to start a new life. But Jehovah appears and pleads with him to be more understanding of his daughter and promises him that one day she will return to her family. Soon Lía does return, and her lover asks Solomón to accept the sincere love that he has for her. The conflict ends happily as Solomón seems reconciled with the new reality: It seems that the country sky makes us all good. And love makes us all equal. At this juncture, in recompense for his services, the townspeople ask Solomón to become their superintendent.

While in "Creole Bread" Solomón is a caricature of the good Jew, in *The Tithe* we see his unforgiving, evil side. It becomes Solomón's obsession to keep the dowry that he obtained by pure chance when he won a lottery ticket, in order to find his "adulterous" daughter a "proper" husband. No one in his family can touch any of the money because it "burns and scorches like a hot coal." (p. 94) "It is cursed money . . . God told me: a good dowry washes away any stain, and the bigger the stain, the bigger the dowry." (p. 89) Solomón becomes so materialistic that he loses his better judgment. He rejects his son's typically Jewish vocations of artist and musician in favor of more practical careers. To further turn Solomón into a demon, Tiempo has him hit his younger son, because the boy generously lends some of his money to his friends. In desperation with himself and his condition, Solomón threatens to set fire to his own household.

At the point of madness, Tiempo shifts the scene from a naturalist-realistic setting, to a surreal plane. Here, in an oneiric scene, four Solomón-like figures appear. This dream sequence is accompanied by a background of Jewish melodies played on the violin by Rubén, Solomón's son. The ghostlike figures remind Solomón of his happy past and urge him to "listen to your heart" and forgive his daughter. Transported back to happy times, Solomón is proud of his children. He is proud of being a *gaucho* who drinks *mate* and contemplates the terrible possibility that his daughter might one day fall in love with a *goy*. Solomón is awakened from his dream by Kukle the matchmaker, who offers him a middle-aged engineer groom for his daughter. From this experience, Solomón realized that when he had nothing "I was much happier than now," even if he had to contend with "bad debts, running here and there, giving free advice at the court, creating miracles, defending my own people." (p. 102)

Yet in spite of all his efforts, Lía elopes for the second time with her same lover, leaving her father dumbfounded: "I did everything for her. Everything. To everyone else I seemed cheap, greedy, moneygrubbing; but I wanted to save my last penny so that she would be happy after what she did. I wanted to be a worthy father, but evil has a younger throat than mine and it screams, '*The Tithe* is hard.'" (p. 104) Only at the very end, after Lía's elopement, does Solomón show some willingness to change. Again Tiempo links this episode to another in his earlier play "I Am the Theatre." Here he has Solomón reluctantly purchase the art of a deceased Jewish painter, Minjowsky, in order to help the community erect a monument in the artist's name. His personal tragedy turns him into a lonely man, desperate in his misery to do some good for others, now that his own life is in shambles.

NOTES

1. Leonardo Senkman, *La identidad judía en la literatura argentina* (Buenos Aires: Ediciones Pardés, 1983), 171.

2. Alberto Kleiner, in *La temática judía en el teatro argentino* (Buenos Aires: Libreros y Editores del Polígona Sur, 1983), 46, mentions the musical adaptation of *Pan Criollo,* entitled *Pan trenzado* (Jewish Bread or *Challah*) presented in 1972.

3. A large number of Argentine plays dealing with the issue of interracial and interreligious love end in tragedy. It seems to be the playwrights' way of handling a very difficult social problem. Some of the solutions and the metaphors used by Argentine writers to describe these hopeless relationships are analyzed in "The Jewish Image in Argentine and Brazilian Literature," Nora Glickman's Ph.D. diss., Columbia University, 1978.

The Tithe

List of Characters
Solomón Lefonekho
Solomón I, II, III, IV
Myriam Sambatión
Rubén
Mañe
Lía
Kukle
Bamberg
Doctor Tuckman
Naum
Maid
Janitor
Seamstress *(silent)*
Samson

Prologue

MYRIAM SAMBATIÓN, *dressed in red, rushes out in front of the closed curtains and faces the public.*
Myriam. Ladies and gentlemen, your attention, please. Before the curtain rises, allow me to share with you some inevitable, urgent words that are boiling inside me like water in a samovar. By an indiscretion of the prompter, the play that is about to be performed came to my attention. The drama of Don Solomón Lefonekho, or rather of Don Jeremiah Jobman, is none other than the comical drama of the protagonist of my play "The Linen Belt." This is a true case of literary symbiosis. César Tiempo, the author of "I Am the Theatre," of which I am the protagonist, incorporated me into his character, Gaspar Liberión, because he's afraid of his own shadow. The act that will unfold before you is mine and mine alone, and the fact that I am a creature of the author, does not diminish the magnitude of his crime. The style, feeling, rhythm and dramatic substance of *Alfarda* belong exclusively to me. There is not even a glimpse of the poet who supposedly is the author of the *Book for the Sabbath Rest,* not in its music, not in its language. If he had drawn that sketch, overflowing with the festive or morose humor of the Jews, in my

opinion he would surely have given up his artistic convictions. He would have questioned what Cansinos Asséns calls "the virtue of subtlety." I ask the critics here present to allow me this single quote. Perhaps you are the same ones who during the opening of the play in which I was the protagonist, mercilessly pointed out my obsession, as if the innocent pleasure of quoting was forbidden to a girl like myself . . .

The poet may have wished for "a crass and strong piece, full of intention, of layers, of connections, serious and weighty and amusing too, like the work of a carpenter"; or for a popular piece, ample and grave, where an army of artists collaborate with their wooden tools and their iron utensils to fill the piece with content. Disenchanted with the sterile and precious work, he would have broken his most subtle loom, his loom of clouds and dreams, and he would have sat on the benches of the artisans who patiently create the simple work of modest mien that justifies itself in its offspring: usefulness and solidity. He would have renounced the sterile graces, opting for the grave and heavy fruits with the conviction that solitary art, even the most fully realized, is worthless when compared with public and social art. Social art increases its number of interpreters and fills its vessels with emotion in the great heart of the masses.

What is the worth of a man's art—he would have asked himself—in the face of that other art created by the masses in ultimate and definitive communion with the artist, on the luminous stage, when dreams made in solitude become alive, like life itself? But César Tiempo cannot yet celebrate the jubilation of a strong and complete work. I am the real author, and he should regard this offering as a precocious grandfather would.

The drama, or rather the epilogue of the comic drama of this Jew of ours, belongs to me. Tiempo has substituted the parable of the linen belt, decayed by the waters of the Euphrates, a sign of the vanity of all that is hidden—with the more concrete expression, more terse in its symbolism, of *alfarda. Alfarda* was the name of the tax that the Moors and Jews of Spain had to pay in Christian territory. The Jew in the modern world continues paying that tax with more painful currency. The pound of flesh that Shylock once demanded, is now demanded from him, with interest. Pounds of flesh and spirit are the price of the Diaspora.

Wherever Jews find shelter, they offer the best of their lives and their knowledge. They are constantly creating, and the history of civilization attests to that. Nevertheless, their tithe, their *al-*

farda, is more onerous and painful than that of any other people
on this earth. They are generous, but their surroundings make
them petty. They are dreamers, but their surroundings make
them materialists. They must renounce their poetic tradition, the
melodious light of the candelabra, the sweet pause of the Sabbath, the spiritual direction of their children, and in the material
sense, the beard, the prayer shawl and the glass of tea. They
offer everything and they give more of themselves than anyone.
Their words have become deeds, and their spirit glows under
the heavens. But the *alfarda* becomes more bitter and heavy
every day. Don Solomón Lefonekho was an architect of his own
destiny, and here in the play he appears in the twilight of his
life, transfigured into a sordid and cruel man, a contradiction of
his own spirit. Life has carved him ruthlessly, it has destroyed
his heart, it has shattered his dreams. The crucible has burnt
him and what was once a vigorous pillar, has now become a heap
of crumbled stones. The crucible is the *alfarda,* and the *alfarda*
is the . . . (*The* JANITOR *of the theatre appears.*)

Janitor. Miss, please . . . (*He points to his watch.*) It's . . . (*He
says the exact time.*) The play has to begin. The management
allowed you to get this off your chest because they were saving
on the orchestra. But now it's getting late and . . .

Myriam. But I . . .

Janitor. Nothing doing. Don't force me to make another scene.
The respectable public has not come to hear you, or to see this.
So . . .

Myriam. All right, I'm going, I'm going. But I want you to know
that you're not letting me talk. I'm sure that this is another of
César Tiempo's schemes. He'll pay for this. He'll pay for this.
(*She leaves the stage, still complaining.*)

(*The curtain rises immediately and the play begins.*)

(*Waiting room that is also used as* SOLOMÓN'S *study. Bright chandelier and covered chairs, on top of the unusual desk inlaid with
ivory, a small terracotta statue. Hanging from one of the walls,
a seascape. Next to it, a calendar conspicuously displayed. A
row of cash registers somewhere in the room. Doors on the left,
right, and rear. The stage is empty when the curtain goes up.
Only* DON SOLOMÓN'S *voice is heard. He is pretending to complain as he argues with someone in the background.*)

Solomón. One peso seventy is fine, my friend.

Voice. Believe me, Señor. I can't do it for less than two pesos. The
wires alone cost me that much.

Solomón. One seventy and there's no more to be said. Just bring the ladder and get to work, you hear? You know there's always something for an electrician to do around here. If it's not an iron, it's a switch, or like now, when my son got it into his head to do some experiments . . .

Voice. I'm very sorry, Señor. But believe me, I can't.

Solomón. All right then, we'll look for someone else. You people get greedier every day. How about one eighty?

Voice. No, Señor, I'd never sell myself for ten cents.

Solomón. And I'd never buy you for two pesos. Good bye. *(To the* MAID*)* Show him out. (SOLOMÓN *goes into the living room, wringing his hands.)*

Voice. (From a distance) Don't bother.

Solomón. No, it's no bother. Who knows, you might take something from the hallway. People are getting more and more dishonest every day. *(Walks to the desk)*

Maid. (Entering) Señor, a man wants to see you.

Solomón. Who is it?

Maid. He says you know him.

Solomón. Yes, but what's his name?

Maid. He says you know him, but maybe you don't remember his name.

Solomón. What does he want?

Maid. To speak to you.

Solomón. How is he dressed?

Maid. Oh, he looks a mess.

Solomón. Tell him I'm not in.

Maid. I've already told him that you are.

Solomón. You get stupider every day. Do you have a boyfriend?

Maid. Señor.

Solomón. Answer me!

Maid. Sí, Señor. And you should see how good he is . . .

Solomón. He's the one you give my suits to?

Maid. My fiancé drives a bus . . .

Solomón. That's why he goes by so fast, so I can't recognize my own suits! Let that man in, and tell him I'll see him for two minutes. I'm very busy. *(He folds himself up like a question mark, and waits for the untimely visit.)* Ay, ay, ay!

Maid. (Enters, followed by NAUM*)* He can only see you for two minutes. Do you understand? *(Exits)*

Naum. (Approaching fearfully) Good afternoon, Señor.

Solomón. You told the maid that I know you?

Naum. Excuse me, Señor. I thought you would remember.

Solomón. Who are you? I've never seen you before. If you start off by lying, you'll have to leave right now.

Naum. Forgive me, Don Solomón. You know how poverty can confuse people. How can you remember me when it was almost two years ago? A year and a half, at least. However, I could never forget you. We talk about you at home, like a member of the family. More than that, like a greatly beloved man.

Solomón. How much do you want?

Naum. You think I'm lying to you, Señor? Don't you remember you were the judge who decided a case in my favor? I was a machine operator, and the boss didn't want to pay me what was coming to me. He swore he didn't owe me anything, and you made him swear on the cross. It was amazing how you did it.

Solomón. (Unimpressed) Ah, yes, yes . . . I think I remember. But I have nothing to do with that anymore. I don't even want them to remember me over there. Don Solomón Lefonekho is someone else now, and he has a higher mission to fulfill. There's nothing I can do for you.

Naum. Your Honor, I mean Señor Lefonekho, believe me when I tell you that I thought about this a great deal before coming to see you. This is very painful. I've been looking for work all over the place, and I can't find anything. My wife is still sick in the hospital, and when she comes out tomorrow, we won't have anywhere to go. They're evicting us tomorrow.

Solomón. And why are you coming to me, of all people? I don't know any of the judges who are there now.

Naum. The court has given me all the extensions possible. I . . . I'm sorry . . . I don't mean to offend you but . . . they told me that you lend money and . . . as you can see, I have nothing, but I swear on the lives of my wife and my children, that I will work at any job, be your slave, until I return what you lend me. Only enough to pay my rent. Only for that. (DON SOLOMÓN *turns white with anger and can barely respond.*)

Solomón. Who told you that? Who? *(He shakes him.)* It's not enough that they have dragged my name through the streets? Now they want to brand me a money-lender? They want to destroy me, that's what they want!

Naum. They told me so. I didn't want to believe it, but when you're in need . . . you know . . . people think you're so rich . . .

Solomón. Sure, people would like me to throw everything to the dogs. *(As he speaks, the front doorbell rings.* DON SOLOMÓN *pays attention to it for an instant and then continues.)* They've made me rich, and I enjoy their money. I'm just a beggar, a miserable, disgraced father who should crawl for the rest of his life . . . everyone is saying that, isn't he?

Naum. No, Don Solomón, calm yourself. I wouldn't have allowed anyone to say that. I believed the story about the money because poverty blinds us. But I wasn't very convinced. That's why I hesitated . . .

Solomón. Miserable, miserable creatures!

Naum. You're right. I can still hear your words to the jury: "He who shuts himself off to the cries of the poor, will one day cry out and not be heard." And you used to tell me . . .

Solomón. Don't remind me of the Bible. It's all just words. How much do you owe?

Naum. Three months, fifty four pesos.

Solomón. For each month?

Naum. No, for the three months.

Solomón. Oh! (*He takes a checkbook out of a locked drawer and prepared to fill it out.*) What day is today?

Naum. (*Confused*) Well . . . if . . .

Solomón. I know, I know . . . (*Before he hands over the check, he reads and rereads it repeatedly, dries the ink from the blotter, then puts the checkbook away and carefully locks the drawer.*) Here, you can cash it today. Exactly fifty four pesos. Not one cent more. (*He walks him to the door.*) You've caught me at a bad moment. Look, you go this way, then you turn on Azcuénaga until you get to Santa Fé. The bank is there. Just go in and they'll pay you.

Naum. Thank you, Don Solomón. Believe me, I'm going to pay you back. But if you would have added an extra five pesos, only that much to buy a little something for the children . . . Don't take this wrong, okay?

Solomón. Just get out. You can't be generous with anyone. The more you give, the more they ask for.

Naum. It has nothing to do with that, Señor. Please understand.

Solomón. Get out, just get out or I'll take the check back and you won't get a thing. Do you think money is a gift from heaven?

Naum. Sometimes I do.

Solomón. All right then, when you go out now, stand in the middle of the street with your mouth open to see if it drops like manna. You ingrate! (*He rings a bell.*) Take him to the door. (NAUM *exits.* DON SOLOMÓN, *who during the previous scene had been following what was going on in the next room, sneaks up to the door, and enters suddenly. Voices are heard and soon* DON SOLOMÓN, MAÑE, LÍA, *and the* SEAMSTRESS *come out.*)

Mañe. But Solomón . . .

Solomón. Out! Get out of here! *(He crumples up a piece of fabric and throws it down. The* SEAMSTRESS *picks it up.)* She doesn't need any more dresses. So, you think we're still going to dress her up like a queen.

Seamstress. Then you . . .

Solomón. Then I order you to leave and never set foot in this house again. The young lady doesn't need rags, or dresses, or anything. She should walk around in a sack.

Lía. Papá!

Mañe. But this is a disgrace! Just be quiet. Don't pay any attention to him, Señorita.

Solomón. What do you mean, don't pay any attention to me? *(He grabs the* SEAMSTRESS *violently by the arm and drags her to the door.)* Get out of here, we don't need you anymore. *(The* SEAMSTRESS *exits, followed by* MAÑE. LÍA *remains frozen.* DON SOLOMÓN *runs to a liquor cabinet, takes out a goblet, fills it with wine, and drinks it as he shakes his head.* MAÑE *comes in, and surprises him.)*

Mañe. Do you think what you did was right? We'll be the laughing stock everywhere. That seamstress sews in the best homes in Palermo and she's going to everybody. *(Suddenly becoming aware of his drinking)* What are you doing? Drinking again? *(She tries to take the bottle away from him.)* Give it to me!

Solomón. *(Slapping her hand)* Leave this alone! It's the only decent thing in the house. And it's just like it came into the world, without clothes and without lies. *(He puts the bottle away.)*

Mañe. Solomon, each day I know you less. You're like another man. Do you think it's nice what you've done?

Solomón. Ask her if she thinks what she did to us is nice.

Lía. Papá, again?

Mañe. But it's been two years already. How can you remember that? You should have a little more consideration for the girl.

Solomón. And did she have any consideration for me? Dresses, dresses. Are you preparing her for a dance, eh? So you'll go to the dance with a pretty face . . . The distinguished daughter of a rich Lefonekho, blind and dumb. He gives her dresses, jewelry, money, as if nothing happened. Big deal, she lived for a week, and what's a week, with a lazy good-for-nothing, a *sheigetz*.[1]

Lía. Oh! *(Tries to leave)*

Mañe. But that's over now. Lía, wait! And you, most of all, should remember this. Are we going to spend our entire lives tied to that ugly memory? Do you think that's a good idea? Tell me. Before, you were half crazy when she didn't come home. And now that we have her with us, you seem completely crazy. How much longer can the poor thing go on suffering?

Solomón. No, don't bother the señorita. The señorita is an angel, of course. While she's here she'll have to learn to respect her father. Later on, when she gets married—if she can get married at all—her husband will give her all the luxury she wants. That's why the father-in-law has to hoard and slave. But until he arrives, I will not spend a penny on you. I can't touch the money from your dowry. It's sacred! Sacred!

Mañe. But she's not asking you for anything. They were a few dresses I was ordering . . . The girl has to be presentable. She can't go anywhere. She can't have any friends in.

Solomón. She doesn't have to go anywhere, she doesn't need to have any friends in. She has nothing to do with them, nothing to say, nothing to tell. Here she has luxury, comfort. What else does she need? Her future husband, if he ever shows up, is going to come through that door. Together we'll all meet him right here. Then you—if he wants to take you—will go with him. You'll have a name that will cover everything over. Even what didn't happen. Don't worry, we're not going to marry you off to just anyone. That's why we have this lovely house and we live in this beautiful neighborhood, and Señor Lefonekho, the Jew Lefonekho, has so much money, so much money. But not a cent can be touched. It's all for the dowry.

Mañe. But Solomón, bear in mind that we won't give her everything.

Solomón. Everything! Everything! It's a great shame. We don't need a thing. We will secure the good name of our daughter, and we'll go back to being poor like before. I don't want to keep a cent of that cursed money. God told me: A good dowry washes away any stain, and the bigger the stain, the bigger the dowry.

Samson. (*Runs in carrying some texts and notebooks under his arm*) So what's the matter here? (*To* LÍA) Why are you crying? Did the old man beat you up?

Solomón. Just go inside.

Samson. Papá, look at my report card. I got an "A" in history and an "A" in drawing. How about that? Rubén is a great musician and I'll be a great artist.

Solomón. We'll talk about that later. Corn is valuable not because it looks up at the sky, but because it gives bread. Do you think you're going to become rich by drawing?

Samson. And why should I become rich? I'm going to draw for the love of art. That's why you have the money.

Solomón. Who told you that?

Samson. No one had to tell me. At school everybody asks me for money to buy sandwiches during the break, and I lend it to them. What's wrong with that?

Mañe. Go on, put the books down and I'll make you a hot chocolate.

Solomón. With whose money?

Samson. Mamá gives me something every day.

Mañe. But Solomón, I can't just give him what he needs for the train. The boy needs to have some change.

Solomón. Yes, to give it away to the thieves at school.

Samson. Papá, they're my friends. What's wrong with that? It's better that I do them a favor now with some change, then spend all the money in bars when I'm older.

Solomón. What? What are you saying? Who taught you that?

Samson. My friends tell me that when I don't want to lend them any money. "Why worry about pennies? When your father dies, you'll inherit a fortune. And you'll see what a good time you'll have." What do I know? (DON SOLOMÓN *strikes him in the face and he bursts out crying.*)

Solomón. And that's what they teach you in school? Thieves! Ignoramuses! You're waiting for me to die so you can spend my money. Come over here so I can hit you again. Get over here!

Mañe. Leave him alone, stop hitting the boy . . . That's all we need. Come on, get out of here. You're getting worse and worse.

Solomón. Shut up! (*She tries to answer.*) Shut up. Don't answer me. Just don't answer me. We're all idiots. I can't live in this house any longer. One day I'll set fire to the whole house and we'll dance with our tongues hanging out. My God. My God! (*Exits left, delirious*) With our tongues hanging out . . .

Samson. (*Stops sobbing*) How did I know I wasn't supposed to say that?

Mañe. All right. That's enough. Go and wash your face. Papá is very nervous. Go ahead.

Samson. And all I wanted was to ask him for some money to see Lupe Vélez.[2] (*Or any other popular actress of the moment*)

Mañe. If you tell him that's what the money is for, he'll kill you. He really will.

Samson. I have such lousy luck. (*Exits crying*)

Lía. Mamá, I think the best thing for me would be to move in with Grandma. It would be a relief for both of us.

Mañe. With Grandma? And how will you make the trip to Domínguez?

Lía. Alone, what's wrong with that? No one is going to eat me up.

Mañe. And you think your father is going to let you go?

Lía. I know he won't, but we don't have to tell him.

Mañe. And who will pay for the trip?

Lía. You will.

Mañe. Me? How? Where am I going to get the money? You know he doesn't give me a penny. You want me to ask for it now? It's hopeless. He's going to think it's for the seamstress. Besides, I don't want you to make that trip. It doesn't make me happy at all. Your father is going to die of grief. And me? Don't think it makes me happy to have you so far away. You're my only companion. I almost went crazy that last time.

Lía. Don't remind me. But you can see that my life in this house is impossible. Or rather Papá makes it impossible. Everything is criticism. Everything is an excuse to insult me and exaggerate the madness of what happened then.

Mañe. You're right, Lía. Papá has changed since you came back. Before he was so simple, so good. Do you remember how he used to make us laugh? I look at him and it makes me very sad. We're not young any more. We could enjoy the few years that are left to us. First Rubén will get married, then you.

Lía. Not me, Mamá. Who'd want to marry me?

Mañe. That's your father's obsession. He wants to find you a husband, and he'll do it. He'll find you one.

Lía. Yes, but it can never be. Imagine, Mamá, a man who would take a girl who has done what I did, because they offer him money. That's a sorry thing. It would be undignified even for me, and I'm a nobody.

Mañe. Don't say that, dear. You're a good girl because you understand. All right, you did that terrible thing, but that's in the past. Papá is not so dumb as to tell the whole story to every man who wants to marry you.

Lía. No! No! I can't stand it! I would die of shame if I got married and there was even one guest who remembered what happened. Besides, I could never look my husband in the eye and not feel guilty. Never.

Mañe. Lía, darling!

Lía. That's why it's better if I just go away. We'll all be better off. There in the country, far away, I'll try to start a new life. Sometimes I think you should have let Papá kill me the night I returned. It would have been the best thing. *(Weeping)*

Mañe. My child, don't talk like that. We all love you here. Your father isn't well. He just isn't. *(RUBÉN enters from rear.)* Ah, Rubén is here . . .

Rubén. Hello, everyone, what's going on?

Mañe. Nothing, problems with Lía.

Rubén. I bet you had a fight with Papá.

Mañe. Yes, he threw out the seamstress.

Rubén. But he's impossible! He gets worse every day.

Lía. Look, Rubén, I think I should go to Domínguez. It's the best thing for me. I've explained it all to Mamá.

Rubén. (To the MOTHER) So what do you say?

Mañe. It makes me so frightened. If you went with her . . .

Rubén. I can't. I have classes. Besides . . .

Mañe. And she needs some money. It's useless to ask Papá.

Rubén. I don't have any. I just began to teach this course. Who knows when we'll get paid. And as for Papá, I can't count on him. But why don't you ask him?

Mañe. He won't give it to me. He'll think it's for the seamstress and he'll be furious.

Rubén. And what if we tell him what it's for?

Mañe. He'll put us against the wall and shoot us. Are you crazy?

Rubén. It won't be so bad. I'll talk to him.

Lía. I don't want you to. He'll start up again. It makes me sick to hear him. It just poisons my blood.

Mañe. Lía, it's your father you're talking about.

Lía. He doesn't treat me like a father.

Mañe. And do you think you acted like a good daughter?

Lía. Mamá, you too? *(About to cry.* SAMSON'S *voice, from inside)*

Samson. Mamá, the milk is spilling.

Mañe. And the maid? What is that girl doing? Damn it. Come with me, Lía. I think we're all going to end up in a madhouse. *(They begin to walk out arm in arm.)*

Rubén. Listen, Lía, I think I just saw someone you know at the other corner.

Lía. Someone I know?

Rubén. Yes, you know who. That ex-secretary.

Mañe. What do you mean? That man is around here?

Lía. It can't be.

Rubén. I saw him clearly. I passed by him twice because I thought that I was wrong. He wanted to say hello to me, but I didn't respond. I don't know why I didn't shake his hand. I suppose that you . . .

Lía. What do you suppose?

Rubén. Haven't you written to him?

Mañe. But Rubén, how can you believe that?

Lía. What's on your mind?

Rubén. But you can't tell me that you're not getting letters from him.

Lía. Me?

Rubén. I've seen at least two. I know his handwriting well. Look, I've even seen letters of his asking Papá to rehire him when there was all that trouble at the court.

Mañe. Is that true?

Lía. Yes Mamá, he writes to me. And what am I supposed to do?

Rubén. Don't open the letters. Return them. Do you know what would happen if Papá found out?

Lía. That's why it's better if I go to Grandma's house as soon as possible. Here . . .

Rubén. Please be careful.

Lía. You too? Is there anyone who trusts me in this house?

Rubén. Yeah, those who don't know you.

Mañe. Rubén, what are you saying? Come on Lía, let's go. All of this is going to kill me. (RUBÉN *shrugs his shoulders and the women exit.* RUBÉN *exits from stage left and reappears following* DON SOLOMÓN, *who is carrying some papers that he puts on his desk.*)

Solomón. (*Making broad gestures of disagreement*) No, no, no! Don't talk to me about that.

Rubén. But Papá!

Solomón. I told you no. I don't want to know anything, and that's that.

Rubén. I'll have to ask for a bank loan. Do you like that idea?

Solomón. Who's going to sign for you?

Rubén. You're also going to deny me that?

Solomón. Yes, Señor. And don't talk to me in that tone of voice, because I don't owe you a thing. On the other hand, everything you are—without even working a single day in your life—you owe me.

Rubén. I'm always aware of that, Papá. You don't have to remind me of it. Now I'm asking you for another little favor. It would be a great opportunity for me to go to Brussels with my teacher. He could really help me perfect my studies, and then there would be great concerts in Paris, London, Rome, Moscow. Don't you see, Papá? Lefonekho's name would be all over Europe.

Solomón. It's not a bad idea. The only thing is, you've got the whip but you don't have the horse. And you want me to be the horse, the one who puts up the money for the trip.

Rubén. I swear I'll pay it back, and even more.

Solomón. More *krekhtsen*[3] is that what you mean? More complaints. I know what a crybaby you are. I also had my dreams, but I never let the bread burn in my stove. With one eye I looked at the sky and with the other at life. We were terribly poor but you never lacked for anything because your father was not the kind to fall asleep while making plans. He knew how to carry them out. There are men who are human rifles, their muzzle points skywards. They only have to whistle and the prey falls at their feet. But you have to know how to aim, my boy.

Rubén. Yes, but now you're rich and . . .

Solomón. It's all appearance, like the waters in the sea, deep down it's all mud. None of us can touch that money, because it burns and scorches like a hot coal. It's Lía's and she has to take it with her.

Rubén. But you deny her everything! She can't even have a lousy peso for a dress.

Solomón. So, you think I should give her everything so she can live in luxury, as a reward for her fine conduct? She'll have the money as her dowry, and it will be a triumph for her. But until she finds a man who wants to marry her, she'll have to suffer what we've all suffered for her sake.

Rubén. And you intend to give away every penny to the man who takes her? What if he turns out to be a worm who marries her only for her money, a cheat, a good-for-nothing?

Solomón. And why would any other kind of man want to marry a girl who's been dishonored?

Rubén. But Papá, what you're doing is terrible. All that is over, and now . . .

Solomón. What do you mean "is over"? The shame in a decent home like ours has left its traces, not like those of a bird in the air, nor like the traces of an adulterous woman who just eats and wipes her mouth and says "I have not sinned. I have not sinned." It was her crime and it won't be mine. I want to make a woman out of her, a woman who can hold her head up high with a good name and . . .

Rubén. Next to a creep who marries her for her money and makes her life impossible.

Solomón. We'll find that out later.

Rubén. When it's too late.

Solomón. The important thing is for her to get married.

Rubén. You talk about it as if Lía's marriage would free you from a punishment. You're chained to her dowry more than to your feelings as a father.

Solomón. Don't try and tell me about my duties.

Rubén. I said feelings, not duties. Lía is not a wooden doll you can give away to anyone who asks for it.

Solomón. Still, she ran away with the first one who came along.

Rubén. She loved him.

Solomón. Before you said that she was crazy, a slut, and now you're defending her disgrace.

Rubén. That's over now, and I suffered through it as much as you did, as much as she. But she's my sister and I'm not going to let you punish her more than she deserves.

Solomón. What are you saying? That you're not going to let your father . . . Do you realize what you're saying?

Rubén. Yes, Papá. I'm not going to let you do something crazy. It hurts me to see you act so stupidly at your age.

Solomón. Get out of here before I smash your head! *(He raises his fist and* MAÑE, LÍA *and* SAMSON *run in response to the shouting.)* I'll make a man out of you. I go crazy because of you, and all of you attack your father. Nice children . . .

Rubén. Papá, but not this! I won't allow it. . . *(Prevents him from hitting him by holding his arm. All this takes place rapidly.)*

Mañe. But Solomón, are you crazy? Look what you're doing. *(*LÍA *and* SAMSON *watch in shock.)*

Solomón. Get out of here, all of you! I don't want to see you anymore. I can't stand the sight of you. I don't have a family anymore. My family is dead! My whole family is dead! Get out! Get out!

Lía. Papá!

Solomón. Don't call me Papá. Everybody out! I don't know you. I don't need to know you. *(Everyone backs out the door.)* Wife, children, everybody. I don't need you anymore. *(After mumbling or praying in a soft voice, he reaches for the bottle and feverishly gulps down two or three glasses. Then he goes to his desk, transformed, but possessed by an implacable bitterness. He sits down holding his face in his hands and begins to sob faintly. After a while four* SOLOMÓN *figures enter on tiptoe. They are a vivid image of* SOLOMÓN. SOLOMÓN I *and* II *enter through the rear door.* SOLOMÓN III *and* IV *through the right door. They circle around him slowly as in a dream. The voices repeatedly grow louder until, in a single voice they burst into a scream and become quiet again, as in a rondo. If possible, the four* SOLOMÓNS *should be the same size, wear the same clothing and have the same voice as* LEFONEKHO.)

Solomón I. What are you doing, Solomón?

Solomón II. What did you do?

Solomón III. What are you doing?

Solomón IV. What are you going to do?

Solomón I. No, no. God could never have commanded that.

Solomón II. You haven't seen God.

Solomón III. Unfortunate are those who see His face.

Solomón IV. To see Him is to die.

Solomón I. God sends rivers to arid lands, and not hatred and madness into the soul of man.

Solomón II. Woe to those who fight against their Maker. They will be as ground to dust.

Solomón IV. Woe to your petty, yet great madness, Solomón.

The Four Together. Woe unto you!

Solomón I. How happy you were when you were poor!

Solomón II. How blessed your house!

Solomón III. And how they praised your genius at the court.

Solomón IV. You loved good people and they loved you in return.

Solomón I. Solomón, just remember!

Solomón II. Listen to your heart.

Solomón III. You were simple, like a handful of sand.

Solomón IV. And like a handful of sand you want to slip through God's hands.

Solomón II. Throw away the gold. The gold and the hatred.

Solomón III. Don't you love your wife?

Solomón I. Don't you love your children?

Solomón II. Do you remember Rubén's concerts?

Solomón III. And little Samson's mischief?

Solomón IV. And Lía's beauty, and her diplomas, and the *mates* that she served you when you returned home?

Solomón I. She is good. She is surely good.

Solomón II. You should forgive her. (SOLOMÓN *gets upset.*)

Solomón III. She loves you.

Solomón IV. She respects you.

Solomón I. Oh, that was madness.

Solomón III. You would rather see your house destroyed than forgive.

Solomón IV. Would you rather see your house destroyed, than forgive?

(The light has dimmed gradually and now there is total darkness. There is a spotlight on one corner of the stage where a counter

and part of a window can be seen. With his back to the public, DON SOLOMÓN LEFONEKHO *is fishing money bills with his rod. He looks rejuvenated. His memory has transported him to happier years, when he wasn't upset by his daughter's behavior and he was as happy as a conservative vote in a Buenos Aires election. From within, one can hear the clear tones of a melody interpreted by* RUBÉN *on his violin. The recording used can be by Heifetz or Mischa Elman and it can serve as background music for this dream sequence. Enter* MAÑE)

Mañe. You're all alone?

Solomón. Your father taught me. Do you remember? It's better to be in hell, alone, and tormented, than in paradise, next to an idiot. *(He laughs.)*

Mañe. If you mean me, thank you very much. Are you angry with me?

Solomón. It was a joke, Señora. How can I be angry with you, when you prepare such delicious lentil soup? Besides, if this is hell, then I must be the devil . . .

Mañe. You're already a redhead . . .

Solomón. But I'm missing the tail . . . *(They laugh.)*

Mañe. (Referring to the music) How do you like it?

Solomón. He plays like an angel. If Joshua had known our Rubén he wouldn't have had to go round Jericho seven times and make all his people shout for the walls to come down. He would have played and the wall would have tumbled down by itself.

Mañe. Oh, you do exaggerate!

Solomón. Truly, we have to be grateful for life. A daughter like Lía, a son like Rubén who draws tears from stones when he plays, and a little devil like Samson. That's why sometimes I'm so pleased, I could give away all my money so that the poor people would have as many dreams and would be as happy as we are.

Mañe. You give away everything and you don't even know who you're giving it to. Because you're so good, people take advantage of you.

Solomón. And hasn't life given us everything? You go out into the street and right in front of you is a piece of land stretched out, and at each corner you hear a crazy melody and see stars tossed into the wind. You look at the sky and the fine drizzle from the sun falls on your eyes and makes you want to cry and to applaud God, who gives you everything and only asks us to go to the synagogue and greet Him with our hats on. *(*LÍA *enters with a* mate *that she offers to* DON SOLOMÓN.*)*

Lía. A *mate,* Papá.

Solomón. Thank you, dear. You already know that your father is a *gaucho*[4] and he can't think without a *mate.* You're getting prettier each day. When you get married, who is going to make me *mate* the way you do, and adorn this house like the flowers of Sharon[5] in the spring?

Lía. Papá!

Mañe. Solomón, what are you saying?

Solomón. Let me talk. Who knows if one day this pretty girl will fall in love with a *sheigetz.* *(He laughs as he pats* LÍA'S *head.)*

Mañe. Why with a *sheigetz*? Aren't there enough nice Jewish boys? Should she have to look at someone who's not one of us, a *goy*?[6] My God, that's all we need!

Lía. But Mamá, who's thinking about that?

Solomón. If you want to scare your mother to death, talk to her about this. *(Laughing)* Ay, Mañe, Mañe, if you were a *gaucho* like I am, you wouldn't be so scared. If some better looking Italian had made love to you, wouldn't you have married him?

Mañe. What are you talking about? Crazy, you're crazy! There's no cure for you. *(They all laugh. The set darkens, the four* SOLO-MÓNS *reappear.)*

Solomón I. Solomón!

Solomón II. Solomón!

Solomón III. At your age, you need the warmth of your people more than ever.

Solomón IV. More than ever.

Solomón I. Your window is no longer open to the world.

Solomón II. It isn't open to the world any longer.

Solomón III. You look out, and all you see are dark clouds.

Solomón IV. Only dark clouds.

Solomón I. The storm approaches and you're far from everyone.

Solomón II. Far from everyone.

Solomón III. Solomón, come down to earth with your simple soul.

Solomón IV. With the simple soul you've always had.

Solomóns II, III & IV. *(They all retreat and when they reach the door they ask)* Will you do it, Solomón?

Solomón II. What about it, Solomón?

Solomón III. Solomón.

Solomón IV. Solomón. *(All exit simultaneously.* KUKLE *enters behind the* SOLOMÓNS, *as they disappear into the background.* LE-FONEKHO *raises his tired head.)*

Kukle. Don Solomón! Don Solomón! Good news. Good news. Look how I wasn't afraid of risking my life to bring you the news. I came by bus. By bus. Do you realize? *(He pats him on the back.)*

Solomón. What are you saying? What's happening? I don't understand a word. Were you talking to me just now? Who are you?

Kukle. Kukle, your old friend, if you grant me the honor of counting me among your friends. But what does that matter? Don't you recognize me? Go on, Don Solomón, you must be tired. You look sleepy. It must be work, business . . . thinking and eating too much is always bad for you. All right then, if you wish, I'll come back another time.

Solomón. (Somewhat recovered) No, no. Since you already bothered to come, talk. What do you have to tell me?

Kukle. About the "engeniere", the "engeniere" . . .

Solomón. What do you mean?

Kukle. About the engineer who came to see your daughter the other night. He likes her, he really does. He likes the house, he talked a lot about you . . . What didn't he talk about? I tell you, he's in love with the whole family.

Solomón. Yes, but what did he say about my girl?

Kukle. Very nice things, very nice. He's an engineer. He doesn't beat around the bush. He looked at her once, and that was enough. What else? Oh yes. He was very happy with the idea of having his own factory. He says he'll make greater progress in industry than Argentina did during the last five year plan. Phew! The man knows a lot. What doesn't an engineer know? Everything! Everything! Well then, we can get ready for the engagement party.

Solomón. Yes, but first we have to see what Lía has to say. I want to ask the girl.

Kukle. What does your daughter have to do with this matter? He's the one who has to decide. And he agrees with everything, that you give him a factory, that you give him the hundred and fifty thousand . . . Or are you going back on your word about the money? You know that it all stays in the family, the same as if you had it in a safety box.

Solomón. If Lía accepts, he'll have that and much more. Everything will be for them.

Kukle. And what about me?

Solomón. There'll be something for you too, there certainly will. I don't want to be left with a single penny. I don't want to know anything about the money. But the engineer's not so young, you know, and . . .

Kukle. What do you call "not so young"? Do you want a fifteen-year-old boy? He's a real man. He's all right at forty–five. A man who's just beginning.

Solomón. He's almost twenty-five years older than the girl. He may be a good man. I know his family. I like them. He's a serious man, but . . . Tell me, does he know about Lía?

Kukle. I didn't tell him. If he knows it, it's not through me.

Solomón. But he does know it . . .

Kukle. Why should we suppose that he knows it? Let's say he doesn't know it.

Solomón. All right. Tonight I'm going to talk it over with the girl. Calmly. I hope she wants it. It would be very fortunate for everyone.

Kukle. I should say so.

Solomón. But not against her will.

Kukle. Of course he won't take her with chains. She can talk. One can talk to her. One can reason with her, one can persuade her. He's an "enginiere." He's respectable.

Solomón. Don't talk to me about that . . .

Kukle. But, Señor Lefonekho. It's just an opinion. The last thing I wanted was to offend you . . . Just tell me.

Solomón. I didn't like what you said about the last name.

Maid. *(Enters with a calling card)* Señor, may I come in?

Solomón. What's the matter?

Maid. There are two gentlemen who wish to talk to you. *(She hands him the card.)*

Solomón. *(Puts on his glasses and reads it)* Doctor Tuckman. Doctor Tuckman, a lawyer. I don't know what he's here for. I don't owe a penny to anyone. And who's the other one?

Maid. Oh, he's very nice, very nice.

Solomón. I didn't ask for your personal impression. I'm not interested. What I asked was who is he?

Maid. I don't know, Señor. He comes with the other one.

Solomón. Let's see. Have them come in. *(The* MAID *moves backstage.)* Are they well dressed?

Maid. Ay, Señor, don't ask me about clothes. *(Exits)*

Kukle. Well, I'm leaving. You know, you have business. You don't need anybody here to listen in. But look, if it's someone here to see your daughter, remember that my candidate is first. Okay? You have to do things right. What's first is first. There are plenty of lawyers, but an engineer is something special.

Solomón. I'm telling you . . . don't worry.

Kukle. Fine, with your permission . . . I'll . . .

Solomón. No, stay here, my friend. Stay. In case they're coming here to ask for something, if there's another person around, it won't be so easy. Do you understand?

Kukle. If you think so.

Solomón. Stay, stay awhile.

The MAID *enters with* DOCTOR TUCKMAN *and* MR. BAMBERG. *It's dark outside.*

Doctor. (To KUKLE) Good afternoon, Señor Lefonekho, or rather good evening. I'm sorry, I couldn't see you in the darkness. Pleased to meet you. This is Mr. Bamberg, director of the magazine *Tzar Haumah.*[7]

Bamberg. Very pleased to meet you.

Solomón. A friend. *(They greet* KUKLE.)

Maid. (From the door) Shall I serve coffee, Señor?

Solomón. I'll let you know. Besides, the gentlemen are probably in a hurry. *(*MAID *exits)* Of course, so much to do.

Doctor. We've interrupted the many engagements we had for the express purpose of coming here. Did you know Minkowsky, the painter?

Bamberg. He was that great artist who lived in Buenos Aires some years ago. He was a deaf mute and had shows in the best museums in Europe. Julio Payró published a very enthusiastic article about his work in *The Nation. (To* KUKLE) Did you ever see any of his paintings?

Kukle. Maybe, maybe . . .

Doctor. And so, Señor Lefonekho, in the Liniers cemetery there is not a single monument to that great artist who died among us. It would be an honor for the community to mark his presence here, his posthumous presence, and if I may say so, it's also our duty.

Bamberg. Besides, it's necessary to rescue his paintings, his wonderful paintings that will be lost forever in mercenary hands.

Doctor. Some of his valuable pictures are in the hands of close relatives, and we are authorized to sell them at a truly exceptional price with the double purpose of raising funds for the monument and helping out his family, who is going through hard times.

Solomón. I had heard something about it, but I don't understand how I can help you. I'm no art critic.

Doctor. I was coming to this. A group of professionals and intellectuals from the community have decided to form a committee to visit our fellow Jews who are known for their generosity, and invite them to buy some of the paintings.

Bamberg. As a matter of fact, it's almost an obligation.

Solomón. Perhaps it is. I don't doubt it. But what I don't understand is what have I got to do with this? Who do you think I am?

Doctor. You don't expect us to believe that you can't afford five hundred pesos or a thousand, at the most two thousand pesos for a beautiful painting.

Solomón. What you're asking for is totally outrageous. Look at this little statue. *(He caresses it theatrically.)* Don't you think it's lovely? Well, my wife bought it at a sale for ten pesos.

Kukle. And that's just what it's worth, just what it's worth.

Solomón. Well, this happens to be a bargain. Let's change the subject. And that beautiful picture *(pointing to the seascape)* . . . Come closer. It even looks natural. If you touch it with your hand, you'll feel the wetness of the water. It's something truly natural. Isn't it? And the color? I imagine you've travelled, don't you think that the sea is exactly that color at certain hours? In the morning, golden honey, a bottomless vessel. At six thirty or seven in the afternoon, a red currant drink. And later, the blue that tints the water darker and darker.

Kukle. I remember when I came from Europe, I kept eating garlic so I wouldn't get nauseous.

Doctor. You'll forgive me, Señor Lefonekho, but this painting is really in poor taste.

Solomón. I don't know if it's in very good taste or in very bad taste. Since I'm a lawyer, I don't dare give an opinion on art. But this is just what I was getting to. Don't look a gift horse in the mouth. This painting, which at least is eye catching, was given to me by a painter who one day won a prize in my agency. He gave it to me and even at that, I didn't want to take it because I didn't know what to do with it.

Bamberg. Ah, do you own a lottery agency?

Solomón. I once did, and let me tell you that I was much happier than now, with bad debts, running here and there, giving free advice at the court, creating miracles, defending my own people. I was happier than I am now with everything I possess. *(He immediately corrects himself.)* With everything they say I possess. And they are lies, all lies!

Doctor. But Señor Lefonekho, I see that among your many virtues, modesty stands out, and I'm pleased to point that out to you. I agree, you might not be as rich as Rothschild, but you cannot deny that you are in a position to acquire a picture for a meager thousand pesos, a picture that in a few years collectors will fight over for ten or twenty thousand pesos.

Solomón. That's all right. All right. Whatever you say. But it would be criminal on my part to make you waste your time. How many pictures do you have for sale?

Bamberg. About thirty.

Solomón. Let's say two thousand pesos for each one, just to round it out. That would be sixty thousand pesos. Right?

Doctor. More or less.

Solomón. Exactly. According to your figures, in a few years they would be worth between six hundred thousand to a million pesos.

Doctor. Exactly. And even more in the United States.

Solomón. And you're coming to involve me in this scheme, to make me steal the money of the family of a painter like Minkowsky? How dare you think that about me? Who do you take me for? Please, gentlemen.

Kukle. It's as clear as water.

Doctor. (Laughing politely) You're a formidable logician, Señor Lefonekho. But I can assure you that this is no laughing matter. The widow and the brother of the artist are living in poverty. At the cemetery, an inscription on a poor tombstone is the only monument to his glorious name. We have to remedy both of these unfortunate situations, and that's why we are here. A painting for you, a painting for someone else, and that way, among us, we'll solve this matter without resorting to the humiliation of charitable collections through the newspapers.

Solomón. I assure you that I can't help you. Frankly it's impossible for me to give you a penny. I knew the painter very well. I even like his work. My son took me to see an exhibition of his that suddenly brought me back to my hometown, to my old memories. You know my son is the musician Lefonekho.

Bamberg. Yes, we know him very well, Rubén Lefonekho. He shows great promise. I believe he's about to leave for Europe, isn't he?

Solomón. So they say. And there you have it, there it is. And don't you think I would like to send him to study there? But I can't, I just can't.

Doctor. Forgive me, Señor. But I'm connected with various banks and I understand that in one of them alone you have more than two hundred thousand pesos.

Solomón. (Startled) It's in my name, but it's not mine. It isn't mine. I swear to you, it's not mine.

Bamberg. We believe you, Señor, we do. But remember that you too have a son who is an artist, and God forbid, one day he may need other people to beg for him or for his family . . .

Solomón. Is that a threat?

Bamberg. How can it be a threat? I said, "God forbid."

Solomón. Yes, "God forbid." I would like to be able to explain this to you. I don't want you to leave with a wrong impression of me, but I can't, I just can't!

Doctor. It's hard for us to believe you, but what can we do? *(They exit slowly.)*

Solomón. I can't, I simply can't!

Kukle. Word of honor! (MAÑE *and* SAMSON *enter breathlessly.*)

Mañe. Solomón, *oy,* Solomón! *Vey is mir!*[8] *Oy,* Solomón!

Solomón. What's the matter, woman? Quickly! What's the matter? Is it the girl?

Mañe. Yes, what a disgrace! What a disgrace!

Solomón. But what happened? Talk woman, talk!

Mañe. Lía, Lía ran away again with the same guy! Rubén saw her!

Solomón. What are you saying? Are you sure?

Mañe. Yes, yes, they saw her. Rubén followed them. I hope she doesn't do anything crazy.

Solomón. It can't be. I can't believe it. Watch what you're saying. There are strangers here.

Doctor. You'll forgive us. We . . . (MAÑE *weeps silently.*)

Solomón. (He has inadvertently put his hand on KUKLE'S *shoulder and speaks to himself.)* She refused to understand me. She didn't want to understand me. I did everything for her. Everything. To everyone else I seemed cheap, greedy, money-grubbing, but I wanted to save my last penny so that she would be happy after what she did. I wanted to be a worthy father, but evil has a younger throat than mine, and it screams, "The *alfarda*[9] is hard." What else do they want from me? What else, my God?

Doctor. Señor, calm yourself.

Mañe. Solomón, please, don't . . . *(She doesn't dare continue.)*

Solomón. What else? What else? *(He is mad with anguish.)*

Kukle. Señor Lefonekho.

Doctor. Well, we . . . *(He doesn't know what to say.)* I hope everything works out. I hope you'll forgive our coming.

Solomón. What else? What else? Do you understand now why I couldn't help you? How blind, how blind I've been!

Doctor. We're leaving. We hope . . . *(They walk towards the door. When they're almost gone* LEFONEKHO *calls them back in a thin voice.)*

Solomón. Don't go! Don't go! I'll buy all the pictures. I'll buy them all!

Curtain

NOTES

1. *Sheigetz* (Yiddish): gentile young man, can have a negative connotation for a non-Jew.
2. *Lupe Vélez:* popular performer of the time.
3. *Krekhtsen* (Yiddish): complaints.
4. *Gaucho:* a native of the Pampas of Argentina.
5. *Sharon:* from the *Song of Solomon,* "I am the rose of Sharon and the lily of the valley."
6. *Goy* (Yiddish, from Hebrew): gentile, literally "of another nation."
7. *Tzar Haumah* (Hebrew): the sorrow of the people.
8. *Vey is mir!* (Yiddish): Oh, my God!
9. *Alfarda:* tribute or tax.

Germán Rozenmacher:
Simón Brumelstein,
Knight of the Indies

GERMÁN ROZENMACHER (1936–1971)

When Rozenmacher published his first collection of short stories entitled *Cabecita Negra* in 1962, he quickly became one of the most acclaimed narrators of his generation. This was followed by *Los ojos del tigre* (Eyes of the tiger) (1968) and other stories. Rozenmacher's first play, *Réquiem para el viernes en la noche* (Requiem for a Friday night) (1964) represents the conflict among the generations of a traditional Jewish family living in Buenos Aires. *El avión negro* (The black plane) (1970) written by the group of playwrights Roberto Cossa, Carlos Somigliana, Ricardo Talesnik, and Germán Rozenmacher, brought about thematic and technical innovations in the Argentine theatre. The last production of Rozenmacher's tragically short career was an adaptation of *El Lazarillo de Tormes,* produced for the first time in 1971. In addition to his playwriting, Rozenmacher was a drama critic and a journalist.

Simón, caballero de Indias, was the original title of the play written in 1970 that later became *Simón Brumelstein, el caballero de Indias* and was first produced in Buenos Aires under the direction of Luis Brandoni. Rozenmacher's own personality, taciturn and anguished, as well as his own life situation—the son of a cantor, married to a non-Jewish woman over the objections of his family— are conveyed through his protagonist. Ricardo Halac remembers that during the first reading of *Simón Brumelstein, Knight of the Indies* for his fellow playwrights, Rozenmacher was very tense. When he finally entered "the world of dreams, fever and delirium," he began to sing Jewish melodies and to sway. "We felt he was transporting us to another dimension of larger significance."[1] Simón, therefore, cannot be regarded merely as a cynic who tries to avoid his responsibilities, but rather as a conflicted man undergoing a profound crisis.

106

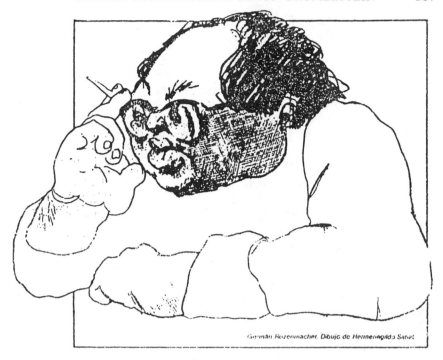

Germán Rozenmacher, Dibujo de Hermenegildo Sabat

Germán Rozenmacher

Simón can be seen as the symbol of the Wandering Jew. He is
the eternal misfit, the dreamer who seeks to escape from life when
pressures become unbearable and who resorts to outrageous fantasies when he can no longer face his drab existence. Like Pirandello's *Enrico IV,* Simón's moods shift constantly between illusion
and reality. Memories of the past come to plague him when he
decides to break away from the mediocrity of his life. David, the
protagonist of "Requiem for a Friday Night," represents a younger
Simón emerging from adolescence and experiencing the pain
caused by his father's religious dogmatism and moral rigidity.
Emotionally paralyzed, he can no longer stand his conventional
wife, his annoying children, and the petty demands of lower middle-
class life. Simón flees from the outside world and hides in a rented
room that becomes his world: Chantania. There he commends himself to the Talmud, to Spinoza, and to the Cross. He takes shelter
in the love of Guadalupe, the landlord's wife. The room becomes
his bastion where he can be a Quijotesque hero fighting his personal and political demons. In moments of despair, he poignantly

asks God to "throw [him] a lifeline" ("Tírame un cable, Adonai").
(p. 135)

Simón is besieged not only by the ghost of his grandmother, but
also by those who ostensibly come to "save" him: the Priest-Rabbi,
the psychiatrist, his wife, his cousin. He is profoundly ambivalent
about being a Jew and rejects the stereotypes represented by his
family. At the same time he longs to strengthen the connection
with his ancestry. In admiration of his imaginary *marrano* ancestors who sought land in unconquered territories and succeeded in
their endeavors, Simón adopts the persona of the Knight of the
Indies, a Spanish conqueror, a direct descendent of the intrepid
discoverers of America, romantic and chimeric, powerful and tena-
cious in pursuit of their ideals.

Rozenmacher's character, like the other protagonists in the plays
included in this anthology, is tormented by his spiritual dilemmas.
He is the most heretic, the most heroic, the craziest, the most
schizophrenic antihero in this gallery of misfits. Simón succeeds
in alienating himself not only from his Jewish world represented
by his wife, children, business, and community, but also from the
Christian world, the people of the street, the church, and the
Catholic religion. Even more tragically, he disengages himself from
the woman he loves and who loves him.

Plagued by the ghosts of his father who never forgave him for
abandoning his religion, Simón reverts back to the simpler faith of
his grandmother's generation. From her he learned the traditional
Jewish songs and that God's presence is in each act of love and
freedom. But as Simón fantasizes about the possibility of sharing
his faith in one God with all human beings, he embraces Christianity and sees God in the figure of Jesus.

Like other characters in Rozenmacher's stories, Simón finds a
place where he can realize his fantasies: like the lonely man in
"Tristezas en una pieza de hotel" (Sadness in a hotel room), who
finally exchanges words of comfort with a strange woman in a
shabby hotel room; or like the failed artist of "El gato dorado"
(The golden cat) who plays a Jewish melody to a solitary cat in a
run-down bar. Yet it happens that the cat is a golden cat and that
the music he plays is the one he had been searching for all his life.[2]

If in the end Simón escapes into madness, it is because he realizes that there is no El Dorado, no Chantania, and that the promised land lies within himself. Alone in his imaginary kingdom,
Simón may feel nostalgic for his *marrano* ancestors who took pos-
session of the Indies, yet he fears the threat of inquisitorial voices,
past and present, who accuse him of belonging nowhere and tell

him, "You will never cease to be a stranger." (p. 140) An exile from all lands, Simón is a stranger to Judaism, to Christianity, and even to the gentile woman he loves. For Simón it is impossible to belong to any community. When he finally abandons everyone, he does so to follow his own internal voice, incomprehensible as it may be to anyone else. He becomes the Jewish heretic searching for his own way: the Knight of the Indies.

NOTES

1. Ricardo Halac, "Recuerdo de Germán" (Program Notes to *Simón, Caballero de Indias,* Teatro Tabaris, Buenos Aires, July 1982).
2. Germán Rozenmacher, "The Golden Cat," trans. Nora Glickman, *Latin American Literary Review* 9, no. 19 (Fall–Winter 1981): 79–85.

Simón Brumelstein, Knight of the Indies

List of Characters
Simón Brumelstein, a jeweler from Calle Libertad
Guadalupe, his lover
Pingitori, landlord
Wife of Simón
Katz, rich jeweler, Simón's cousin
Priest
Rabbi
Psychiatrist
The three above characters are played by the same actor.
Bobe, Simón's grandmother
Simón, Simón's child (extra)
The Bull (extra)
Two Nurses (extras)
Pair of Dancers
Errand Boy, worker (extra)
Father

A play in two acts

Act I

Two walls of a room: one on the side and one in the back. There is no third side wall; it is lost in the shadows that cover half the stage. Those shadows reveal the dreams, fever, and delirium that only SIMÓN BRUMELSTEIN *and his accomplices witness. As in old apartment houses, the room has high walls; it is papered with large flowers; bare electric cables creep up the walls towards the ceiling. A chandelier, at one time ostentatious, hangs from the ceiling on that half of the stage where the room is visible. There is a table that is used as a desk and also serves as an eating place, foot rest, book shelf, a place for leaving cookies, cards, clothing samples. There is also a green rug with a small lamp and a jewelry box. A clock hangs on the wall. There is an enormous medieval map, possibly torn off some Shell station calendar; it is a vulgar, fantastic map of the Americas, featuring sea dragons. The word "Chantania" is written on top in arabesques. There is a manual Singer machine and a dummy, with a woman's dress on it, perhaps an unfinished robe. A cross hangs prominently on the wall. There*

*is a marble top dresser, which, like the chandelier, seems a remnant
of better times. A three-paneled mirror hangs over the dresser. On
the marble top there is a large glass box lined with blue velvet.
Inside the box, there are jewels and clocks on display, like in the
windows of jewelry stores. One in particular, small and rococo, is
an exquisite music box. Also lying on the dresser—a very fine piece
of French-style furniture—is a pair of watches. There is a sofa on
the side wall under the cross. At present it is unmade. The small
window over the sofa opens to an air shaft. Voices, sighs, complaints, fragmented conversations can be heard coming through
that window, along with the infernal, resounding noises of children
playing in the courtyard of the tenement. The voices of women
talking to each other from window to window or from door-to-door
can be heard. A red velvet curtain covers the narrow, medieval
window. There is a door at the rear wall, near the black shadowed
area from which the dreams will appear.*

It is very hot. This is apparent in SIMÓN BRUMELSTEIN, *a drawn,
emaciated man in his forties, with fiery, dreamy eyes, as beautiful
as flames that slowly burn themselves out; he is seated on a Vien-
nese chair, wearing an old-fashioned, sleeveless undershirt, pajama pants, and bedroom slippers; he is resting his feet on the
table; he is dishevelled; his beard is overgrown; his eyes stare aim-
lessly around the room. Thunder can be heard in the distance. The
curtain is drawn.* GUADALUPE *is seated at the sewing machine,
which she pedals as she sews a tailored suit. There are remnants
of cloth scattered on the floor.* GUADALUPE *is about thirty-three;
she is attractive; she wears pants with a defiance typical of certain*
barrio *women. More thunder. On the table is a kettle over a hot
plate and a* mate. SIMÓN *fills the* mate. *He takes a sip from it and
looks at her.*

Simón. *(Softly)* It looks like rain . . .

Guadalupe. *(Goes on working)* Yes.

Simón. Did you see?

Guadalupe. *(Stops working and looks at him as she pins her
   hair)* What?

Simón. The room. It's turned grey . . . .

Guadalupe. *(Looks at him)* It's true . . . all grey . . . *(She stands
   up, moves closer to him and strokes his head; then his hands
   meet hers in his hair.)*

Simón. How nice, don't you think?

Guadalupe. *(She looks at him with passionate eyes.)* To make love
   in this dim light, in this weather, in this heat . . .

Simón. To make love in the rain that's about to fall. *(As he says*

*this, he grabs her and she falls on her knees before him ador-
ingly. She rests her head on* SIMÓN's *lap, then caresses his body
while he lifts her up. They kiss and embrace, fondling each other
with the same voluptuous, ferocious freedom of animals in heat.
She pulls him up from the chair, puts her hand under his clothes
and strokes his chest hungrily and shamelessly as* SIMÓN *guides
her towards the bed. They sit there, sensually kissing each other.*
GUADALUPE *takes a puff of the cigarette she has been holding
in her mouth, then passes the smoke to* SIMÓN, *who has been
waiting for it with his mouth open. He exhales. They are very
happy; their bodies too are happy to discover each other. She
looks at him, her mouth half open with desire, with joy, with the
truth they feel when they are together. She moves away from
him.)*

Simón. (Seated on the bed) Don't give me that crazy look.

Guadalupe. What look? *(She locks the door and leans on it, as if
imprisoning him. She stares at him, hungrily, playfully.)*

Simón. That look, like just now . . . *(The light is grey and the
faraway thunder can be heard. Children make noise in the corridors. The couple draws closer to each other, embraces and bites
each other with enormous, beautiful, authentic longing and pleasure, like kids, like grown-ups. She pushes him onto the bed,
takes off his undershirt while he removes her blouse. In the
dream space a huge sail appears, revealing a Malta cross stirred
by the wind. There are tools, harness rigging and tackle on a
ship. High up in the mast stands a sentry wearing a helmet,
dressed like one of* Solís's[1] *soldiers.)*

Simón. (Below her) Can you feel it?

Guadalupe. (Kissing him) Mmmm?

Simón. The wind.

Guadalupe. (Stroking his head) What wind?

Simón. The one that moves the sails of the galleon. . .

Guadalupe. (She smiles and leans towards him.) Is it there?

Simón. Shall we sail on?

Guadalupe. (Climbing on top of him) Shall we?

Simón. (Laughing) You're always ready.

Guadalupe. (Hungry and smiling) Always . . . *(Pause)* The fact is
I have so much stored up hunger . . .

Simón. Me too . . . after all, the world could end at any moment.
*(He draws his hand towards the zipper of her pants and slowly
pulls them down. A persistent bell rings from outside. Both stop
short as if petrified. The image of the galleon disappears.* GUA-

DALUPE *sits tensely on the bed.* SIMÓN *grabs his undershirt and puts it on.)*

Guadalupe. (Nervously) Who can it be?

Simón. Señor Pingitori . . .

Guadalupe. No, it's very early. *(She fixes her pants and once again puts on her usual hardened expression.)* I don't understand . . .

Simón. The client with the tailored suit . . .

Guadalupe. No, Simón, it's not her turn for a fitting today.

(Another emphatic doorbell. GUADALUPE *sighs and walks towards the door.)*

Simón. Well then, go. . . (GUADALUPE *leaves.* SIMÓN *takes a cigarette and lights it; he is very disturbed and feels somewhat guilty. In the area of the stage where the dreams are enacted, suddenly, in chiaroscuro, the image of his father, crucified, appears. He looks very tall, his arms are tied to the cross, and from there he looks at* SIMÓN *without speaking. He should be lit from below, to emphasize his head and his hands on the cross. Shaken by the vision, nervous and frightened)* Are you there again? *(Pause)* So speak . . . say something . . . *(Pause).* Of course, you're not there . . . *(Furious)* Don't worry, that woman is clean . . . she may be a *shiksah*[2] O.K., but she's clean. That's enough for me . . . *(Exasperated)* Does she have syphilis, is that what you want to know? Not as far as I know . . . and if worse comes to worst, Papá, what can I tell you . . . I prefer to take penicillin. *(Pause; he walks around anxiously.)* But that's not the only reason you're there. So speak then! Do you want me to believe you're there? You want to make me nervous, right? *(He approaches the image on the edge of the room in the dream area. In a tense, anguished voice)* What do you want to say to me?

Guadalupe. (From outside) No, sir, you can't come in. *(The image disappears.)*

Katz. (Out of breath) Come on. Come on. Where is he?

Guadalupe. (Her voice getting nearer) How dare you push your way into my house? Listen to me, that man lives here, but he's my tenant. You need my permission to come in here . . .

Katz. (His voice getting closer) I'll wait for him. *(Still panting)*

Guadalupe. (Her voice even closer) Wait out there, in the dining room. No! . . . What do you think you're doing? (KATZ, SIMÓN's *cousin, bursts in through the door. He is a balding, red-haired man in his fifties. He pants like an elephant. Behind him,* GUADALUPE.)

Simón. (Looks at him as if he were looking at a ghost) You?

Guadalupe. But who is this man, Señor Brumelstein? *(Pause)*

Simón. I'm sorry, Señora, but I didn't call him. *(*KATZ *looks around the room, breathing heavily, then, with surprise, he looks coldly and bitterly first at* SIMÓN, *then at* GUADALUPE.*)*

Katz. My name is Katz. I'm his cousin . . . Katz, famous jewelers. *(With certain arrogance to the lady)* You must have heard the name. *(Looks around the room)*

Guadalupe. And so what . . . Yes, I've heard the name. And that gives you the right to barge into my own house?

Katz. *(Looking around for a place to sit)* So this is your office . . .

Guadalupe. Don't you understand what I'm saying? I'm no pushover.

Simón. Excuse him, Señora Lupe . . . this one's a lost cause. *(Breathing heavily and uneasily,* KATZ *sits on the disheveled bed, disgusted and practically choking.)*

Katz. So this is your office . . .

Simón. How did you wind up here?

Katz. A whole year looking for you. *(He pants and covers his face with his hands.)* And this is your office. *(He gasps and lowers his head, trying to listen to his heart.)* I climbed up five flights. *(Accusingly)*

Simón. The elevator's not working. It hardly ever works.

Katz. That's why you moved in here . . . nice place, eh? Some nice place for a jeweler . . . No one can find you here.

Simón. So how did you find me then? *(*GUADALUPE *and* SIMÓN *look at each other.)*

Katz. *(Between gasps)* And that fried fish smell all over the halls . . . and those kids, running and shouting . . . and the women gossiping from door to door . . . and you're trying to tell me that this is where you decided to put your jewelry store?

Simón. Who gave you my address?

Katz. Downstairs, isn't there a sign? "Simón Brumelstein, jeweler . . . Fifth Floor, C . . ."

Simón. There's no sign downstairs.

Katz. *(Shrugs his shoulders and becomes calmer)* So I just thought there was. I passed by and I came in. *(To* GUADALUPE*)* Does the gentleman pay rent?

Simón. That's my business, Katz.

Katz. Ay, Simón, you were always the black sheep of the family, you were, but those three sons of yours that you left when you ran away . . . Who feeds them? I do. Isn't that your business? *(*SIMÓN *is enraged by* KATZ's *reproach; he moves closer to him* *as if to hit him, but instead he grabs his head and gives him a violent, disgusting kiss on the mouth.)*

Katz. What are you doing? (GUADALUPE *gestures to* KATZ *that* SIMÓN *has gone crazy.)*

Simón. Is this what your life is about? To come to me with all your blame? And what about you? How many more years are you going to be around, Jonas Katz? *(Comes closer to him, threateningly)* Listen, have you ever been fucked in the ass? Have you ever tried it? It's great . . . You never let them, you never dared? It's great, you should really try it.

Katz. (SIMÓN *has grabbed him by the wrists.)* Let go of me. Let go.

Guadalupe. Do you see? Don't make him nervous. Get out . . .

Katz. Let me go. *(Tries to free himself but he can't)*

Simón. *(Exasperated)* So, you don't like men. Okay. You like women. *(To* GUADALUPE *letting* KATZ *go)* Not them either . . . jewelry he likes, watches . . .

Katz. Don't act crazy with me, you hear.

Simón. You're the crazy one . . . raising your voice at me. Do you know where you are? In my country *(pointing at the map)* Chantania . . . you're in my country. What right did you have to come in here, eh? Who gave you permission? Do you have a visa?

Katz. Three kids I told you . . .

Simón. So what if I ran away from them? I sent them all to hell . . . so what . . . (KATZ *looks at him scornfully; he looks round the room and towards the rococo clock.)*

Katz. This clock is mine. (GUADALUPE *moves in front of* KATZ *and almost snatches it away from him.)*

Guadalupe. Well . . . I don't know . . .

Katz. *(To* SIMÓN) The family garbage, that's what you are. Not a doctor, not a jeweler, no title, no money, nothing . . . the only thing you bring are headaches . . . That's the only thing you're good for.

Simón. *(Laughing)* Come on. The only thing I'm good for? And what about the ranch?

Katz. What ranch?

Simón. And the gold mine . . . down here.

Katz. Come on, come on, sonny . . . we're talking about three mouths . . . stop that shit. It's enough that you killed your father with a heart attack. I have to take care of your family too? *(Looks at the other clocks, rushes to the showcase and opens it.* GUADALUPE *moves in front of him.)*

Katz. Eh! Just junk, useless stuff. A gold mine I'll give you.

Simón. (*Laughing*) Señora Lupe, go ahead, give this poor creep the fancy clock he wants.

Guadalupe. No, it's yours.

Simón. Give it to him, what I have in the mine is more than enough to rub in his face . . . a title . . .

Katz. Yes, what about it? Everyone in the family has a title, even I, I have something. What do you have?

Simón. (*Laughing*) A galleon. Do you have a galleon?

Katz. What galleon, where galleon?

Simón. From my ancestors, the first Brumelsteins who arrived from Spain, the conquerors who founded this country. Knights of the Indies, like me . . . they arrived in a galleon like all the aristocrats, and since the Indians were after them, they moved their galleons to firm land, and they turned them into fortresses . . . very few galleons survived. I, for instance, have one, that's the stamp of nobility, cousin Katz.

Katz. Stop that nonsense. You've always been a good talker, but in the moment of truth . . .

Simón. I'm also a gentleman. No, wait a minute . . . (SEÑOR PINGITORI *comes in.*) Just like Señor Pingitori . . . he's one too, with that last name, don't be fooled. (PINGITORI *is exaggeratedly well-dressed, wearing a blue suit, white shirt, vest, and tie.*)

Pingitori. Ah, excuse me . . . you have guests. Is the food ready, dear?

Simón. Come in, I'll introduce you . . . the owner of the house, who put that cross on the wall so that I'd never forget that I'm a Jew, just a temporary tenant . . . My cousin, Señor Katz, a real gentleman. Who wouldn't want to be a gentleman in Chantania, eh?

Pingitori. Oh, is that so? (*Cold, distant, with the aristocratic air of bank clerks and civil servants, somewhat uncomfortable because of the situation, he makes a move to leave.*)

Guadalupe. (*Questioningly to* PINGITORI) How did this man get here?

Pingitori. I haven't the slightest idea.

Katz. What's going on here? It was you who called me . . .

Guadalupe. So you went out looking for him.

Katz. It took him months to find me, but he did.

Simón. (*To* PINGITORI) So, my friend, you want me to leave this place.

Pingitori. (*Somewhat confused*) Well, I . . .

Katz. What's the problem here . . . You don't like this tenant, he doesn't pay his rent, okay then, you've got the right to evict him. Don't landlords have any rights?

Simón. (Laughing) And why didn't you call the police? Do you want to know why? Because I'm very rich. Here in Chantania, I'm the one who calls the shots.

Pingitori. (Nervously, he walks to the windows and closes it.) Lower your voice, please. (GUADALUPE, *breathing between clenched teeth, opens the window defiantly.)*

Guadalupe. You're crazy closing the window, it's so hot!

Simón. He has class. *(To* KATZ*)* Señor Pingitori here may work at the post office, he may earn 23,000 pesos, but he has class. It shows, right? That's obvious.

Pingitori. Look, I think that everything's been said here already.

Guadalupe. Bring me a beer, with some cheese . . . we'll have a picnic.

Simón. I don't want to. I don't want anything.

Pingitori. (Frozen, to KATZ*)* Do you see? He hardly eats.

Guadalupe. So why do you want to get rid of him? What I would do, if it were up to me . . . but why does he bother you so much?

Pingitori. My plan isn't to evict him, but the whole thing bothers me. *(To* KATZ*)* Just look at him, he's shrunken. He just drinks *mate,* do you see? (SIMÓN *is seen drinking* mate.*) Mate* all the time. He never eats.

Katz. Can a person live like that?

Simón. So you found me, you creep. *(Sips from his* mate)

Guadalupe. (To PINGITORI*)* But I don't understand. This gentleman is a jeweler, you can see that. What are you complaining about? Why didn't you tell me before that you wanted him to leave? You could consult me, you know. I'm your wife.

Katz. And the rent? Doesn't that worry you?

Guadalupe. (To PINGITORI*)* We have to talk about these things, the two of us, or else, what am I here for?

Katz. But he pays you? With what, if he doesn't even do anything?

Simón. Oh, don't you know, with the gold mine I have down here . . .

Katz. (Furious) Gold mine, gold shmine! Charlatan, conman, liar. Pure blah-blah-blah, that's what you are, just blah-blah-blah. *(To* PINGITORI*)* You know, he was such a revolutionary. We all thought he had left, what do you know, to throw bombs, to work at a factory, but no, he was here . . . and without paying any rent.

Guadalupe. What do you mean without paying? *(To* PINGITORI*)* Look, he sold you watches in installments, and he sold jewelry to the whole neighborhood. The only thing you have to do is to go from apartment to apartment and collect the payments.

Pingitori. *(Exasperated)* And what do you want from me, that on top of everything I should put a sack on my back and go collect from all that riff-raff?

Simón. No, please, Madam, how are you going to let him get involved with the neighbors?

Pingitori. Look, Don Simón, when you first came here, I won't deny it, you dazzled me . . .

Simón. Of course. You were expecting an easy deal, eh? Smuggling, jewelers, right? You even told me the rent was going to go up every six months. You thought you would get rich at my expense.

Pingitori. *(To* KATZ*)* Not true . . . first he told me that this was going to be his office, nothing else, and now it turns out that he moved in here. He sleeps, he eats here.

Guadalupe. Don't be such an asshole.

Pingitori. Guadalupe, please . . .

Guadalupe. Don't call me Guadalupe.

Pingitori. Then mind your language, watch your words. *(Walks to the window and closes it)* The whole neighborhood doesn't have to find out . . .

Simón. What class, eh?

Pingitori. I already told Señor Katz that we're a family, that this is a decent, normal, moral home. It might be an office too, but . . . you'd never guess what this man does here!

Guadalupe. What does he do? I spend the whole day here sewing and . . . as far as I know . . . what do you mean you'd never guess what Señor Simon does here . . . what do you think he does?

Pingitori. *(Evasively, to* KATZ*)* You'll see.

Simón. This man is a real gentleman. How can he collect rent from the riff-raff around here? Please . . .

Pingitori. That, at any rate, is what you have to do, Simón. You have to work, my friend, for this country to move forward, although there are so many undesirable types . . . *(He looks at* KATZ *for agreement.)*

Guadalupe. Your Italian father would have collected from them quickly enough.

Pingitori. *(Closing the window)* Guadalupe . . .

Guadalupe. Stop it already *(threateningly)*. Don't call me Guadalupe . . . That name is horrible and you know I hate it.

Pingitori. But this man spends the whole day lying around here on his back reading, reading and looking at the ceiling.

Guadalupe. If you don't like it, you know what you can do. *(Her declaration makes him feel ashamed and he leaves.)*

Pingitori. Excuse me.

Katz. Those books, eh? What about those books? One day the police will give you a fine old time, Señor.

Guadalupe. (To KATZ*)* Get out of here.

Simón. (To GUADALUPE*)* Please, leave . . .

Guadalupe. (Surprised, looking at him) You want *me* to leave?

Simón. Please.

Guadalupe. (Looking at him for a moment) All right. *(She leaves.)*

Katz. (Looking at SIMÓN *as he drinks* mate*)* This is the way you ended up, great *khokhem*³, big wise guy . . . nice diet, eh? Cold *mate,* cold water . . . and I'm stuck with the debts from your jewelry store. *(Comes closer to him)* . . . and you wanted love, happiness, who knows what other nonsense . . . the revolution . . . and you ended up like a criminal inside this hole. This may be enough for you, but your family, your wife, your children, it's not their fault. You're a *luftmensch.*⁴ You're in the air, you live from the air, and that can't be! There's a two-by-four jewelry shop on Calle Libertad that's waiting for you. You don't like that idea? Too bad. You just better face it, *che.*⁵ Of course, here you live like a king . . .

Simón. Tell me, are you a good Jew?

Katz. What? Go on, you're putting me on . . . what does that have to do with it? *(Glances over the books on the table)* When the police come . . . *(He randomly picks up a book and opens it with disgust. When he sees what the book is, his surprise grows and he no longer understands anything.)* Spinoza . . . what is this doing here? *(Grabs another book)* The *Talmud*⁶ . . . what . . . what is all this? *(He hides his surprise.)* Well . . . it's obvious you have nothing else to do.

Simón. When I was a kid I used to read it . . . at religious school . . . Do you remember? Where Papá used to send me to become a rabbi.

Katz. So this is what became of you. *(Surprised)* But what rabbis are you talking about? I'm under the impression that brood is doing some job on you, really taking care of you! And you talk to me about the Talmud now? Have you really gone mad? But . . . but . . . look, you're just an assimilated Jew, you broke with everything, you didn't even finish school . . . nothing . . . a heart attack for Papá, that's all you were. You destroyed everything.

Simón. Yes, I was thinking about all of that, like *Elisha Ben Abuia.*[7]

Katz. Like who?

Simón. *Hu kafar binetiot*[8] . . . that's what the *Haggadah*[9] said. Do you remember? No, how are you going to remember if you're such a thickskull?

Katz. So . . . you're an assimilated Jew and now you're talking to me in Hebrew? Look, let's end this once and for all. *(Approaches the rococo clock that* PINGITORI *had left on top of the mantlepiece)* This is mine. I'm cashing in on something for all that you owe me. *(Takes a piece of paper from his pocket)* I finally found you, and here it is.

Simón. *(Looks at it without taking it)* What's this?

Katz. It's a contract. *(Avidly)* Sell me the jewelry store . . . this way it's not going anywhere. I can turn it into something big, *che,* and I'll give you some money so that your wife and children don't go hungry.

Simón. What do you believe in, cousin?

Katz. What? Look here, I didn't come here to discuss theology.

Simón. Do you believe in God?

Katz. Look, you're an atheist. What's going on here, what kind of joke is this? You broke with everything that's Jewish and now you speak to me in Hebrew . . . but of course, one gets old and goes back home, right?

Simón. You understand shit. I asked you something, and yet . . .

Katz. *(Confused)* Why are you looking for problems? You're looking for something that's not there. There are Jews, there are Christians, but who cares about that anymore? God must be there, in Heaven, but here I'm the one who has to pay bills, and you talk nonsense to me, to pass the time. But you won't get me off the subject.

Simón. Don't you understand, you numbskull? I've thought about it a lot this past year. The Jewish God, taken to its logical conclusion, breaks with the tribe, with the letter, with the words of the law and ceases to be a Jew . . . now he belongs to everyone, like Jesus, do you see? Can you grasp it? *(Drinks another* mate*)*

Katz. Jesus . . . what a mess you have in your skull.

Simón. Not really, it's very simple. I'm more of a Jew than you are . . . Spinoza is more of a Jew than many Jews. You know why? Like Elishah Ben Abuia who rode a horse on the Sabbath as he conversed with Rabbi Akiba. Is there anything more Jewish than heresy, than Christ? When one fulfills the rules he stops being a Jew and becomes a human being, a total man. It may look like he's no longer a Jew, but he's more Jewish than ever

. . . like Elisha Ben Abuia who rode a horse on Saturday and it wasn't allowed, but he did it for that very reason . . . *(Pause)* You don't understand shit! Go to hell!

Katz. (Interested) Che, then why don't you go to Israel? Sell me the jewelry and go.

Simón. Why don't *you* go? You want me to tell you why . . . because if you leave, who's going to tell others to leave?

Katz. I went there already, several times.

Simón. Like to the *Salada*[10] . . . they don't need people like you over there.

Katz. Ah, but now you agree with Israel?

Simón. No, what does that have to do with me?

Katz. (Persuasively) I mean it, I have a friend through the ORT[11] who can get you a free ticket there . . . why not? Why don't you give it a try?

Simón. (Laughing) Haven't I told you already that I have a country? Chantania is my country.

Katz. How many went, just like you?

Simón. (Smiling) And that's just the way they came back. What do you think Israel is? An old age home?

Katz. No, no, you'll go there and see if you like it. When you were a kid didn't you use to go to the *Moshavah*[12] to camp, to prepare for *kibbutz*[13] life? Do you remember when you used to go camping in Luján for two weeks? Go, you'll work the land. You're just the type who might like that strange kind of life.

Simón. Dear cousin, if Hitler had known you, just you, what a ball he'd have had in the crematorium . . . the world would have been spared the murder of six million Jews.

Katz. Why?

Simón. By cremating you he'd have had more than enough.

Katz. You're an anti-Semite to boot.

Simón. No, I have respect, but for those who leave, not for you.

Katz. All right, *che*, enough nonsense *(counts on his fingers)*, your car payments, I'm paying them. *(Continues counting with his other fingers)*

Simón. Leave me alone! Don't you see I'm into something else? I'm busy!

Katz. (Counts two more items) The apartment, you dumped everything on your wife. And I have to pay for your apartment. *(Offers him the contract)* Sell it to me, and we won't talk about it anymore . . . . Or buy my jewelry shop on Calle Florida, with the gold from that mine of yours. *(Furious,* SIMÓN *takes out a long*

sword of Toledo steel from behind the dresser and jumps on
KATZ, *who jumps back astonished.)*
Simón. Señor!
Guadalupe. Here's your suit from the cleaners.
Simón. Lock the door. (GUADALUPE *locks it.* SIMÓN *puts down
the Toledo sword, grabs the contract and tears it in half. Then he
prods* KATZ's *stomach with the sword.* KATZ, *who had remained
silent, draws back.)* You want me to show you what I have?
(Grabs GUADALUPE *and kisses her on the mouth)* First, . . . and
what do you have? An old pig who gave you children. Second
. . . (GUADALUPE *lays out the suit.)* The best seamstress in town
. . . *(It's a black doublet with golden braid trimming and match-
ing breeches. As she dresses him, he removes his pajama trousers and with a triumphant smile he makes a trumpet like sound
with his mouth, as he hums a medieval tune. She hands him the
doublet which he puts over his shorts. Then he sits on the bed,
and she helps him on with a pair of cheap soft leather boots
that go up to his groin. He then puts on the collar, Philip II
style. He walks to the dresser and puts on a false beard. He then
walks to the curtain, he tears it off and puts it on as a cape. He
looks like a coarse innkeeper and also like a ghostly Velázquez
knight. She removes the cheap jewelry from the little display
window and puts it on* SIMÓN's *fingers while he puts on his
gloves.)* I shit on the tiles of all the professionals in the family. I
shit on your jewelry shop. You've conquered America, haven't
you? No, cousin, you're mistaken, I did. I discovered a treasure
under the earth and I have it here, hidden. What Solís, Pizarro,
and Cortés couldn't find, I found, I, Knight of the Indies, Simón
Brumelstein. And I have an enormous ranch . . . miles and miles
. . . you can spend days on horseback. If you could ride like I
can, you never leave it. So what do I care about your contract?
Shove it up your ass. *(Now accompanying himself with his
palms, he dances an ancient* jota[14], *slow like a* pavanne, *a* jota
*of an Indies knight. He sings it with lustful eyes and using his
hands more than any other part of his body, almost clownishly
and yet with enormous dignity. Someone bangs at the door.* GUA-
DALUPE *opens it.)*
Pingitori. (Coming in) Ah, we've begun already. Is he in costume?
Do you see how he plays?
Katz. (Dumbfounded) But you never told me anything about this.
Pingitori. He's pretending, he's faking.
Katz. What? He's pretending? *(Very anguished and afraid)* No,
no . . . *(He moves backwards, towards the door.)*

Guadalupe. And it's not the only one. I've sewn more for him. Would you like to see them on?

Katz. (Desperate) No, no, no! My God! . . . a *meshugener!*[15] *(Runs away)*

Pingitori. (Looking) Are you going . . . to work a while longer? *(*GUADALUPE *looks at him.* PINGITORI *lowers his eyes and leaves.* SIMÓN, *overcome by tremendous excitement, falls flat on the bed, laughing. Pause.* GUADALUPE *goes to the sewing machine.)*

Guadalupe. This will teach them that they shouldn't disturb us. *(Pause. As if talking to herself)* Let them, just let them think you're crazy . . . we have the right to be left alone, don't we? *(*SIMÓN *takes off his false beard and his collar and unbuttons his jacket.)*

Simón. Do you realize? Israel, that's where he wants to send me. *(Nervous smile)* I told him that my country is Chantania. *(Suddenly depressed)* But . . . *(Approaches the mirror)*

Guadalupe. Our country . . . the country of both of us, here inside, alone, happy.

Simón. (Looking at himself in the mirror with certain uneasiness) I don't understand . . . *(as if he were seeing himself for the first time)* How did I come to his? I assimilated, and he wants to send me to Israel . . . but I don't want to be a Jew. I want to be a man, that's all.

Guadalupe. (Looks at him, draws closer to him and hugs him) I love you, Simón, I love to play with you . . .

Simón. (Pulls away from her) Leave me alone, it's hot here.

Guadalupe. It's not hot in the galleon.

Simón. What galleon? Stop fooling around. *(She hugs him.)* Is that the only thing you've got on your mind? *(Makes the obscene gesture for fucking)* And he's right, three kids. I've got three, and I left them, just like that . . . I left them.

Guadalupe. (Sweetly) For me . . . you're the secret king of the world, you're my master . . . and you've discovered an enormous treasure that . . .

Simón. (Paces nervously) Ah . . . don't just repeat mechanically every piece of shit I say. *(*GUADALUPE *hangs on him like an abandoned child and leans her head on his shoulder. Slowly he, or rather his skin, softly touches hers, recognizing it.)*

Guadalupe. Why shouldn't we have our own world? When the outside world is like shit. *(Weak knocking at the door)*

Pingitori. (His voice) Lupe . . . *(Pause. Both of them kiss. In a pitiful voice)* Dinner is ready . . .

Guadalupe. Yes? *(She bites his lips with a vengence.)*

Pingitori. (His voice) Lupe . . . the crackers you like.

Guadalupe. (Defiant) Then come in . . .

Simón. (Separating himself from her) No, you're crazy.

Guadalupe. Then let him go away from here, let him leave this house. I can't stand him. What is he? A man? No. A companion? Not even that. What good is he? He's a husband, an eternal husband, but I don't love him anymore. *(In the dream area the* PRIEST *appears.)*

Priest. (Smiling) So Old Shloime Brumelstein had a galleon, did he? Well, I'm telling you that the ship he arrived in was the "Flandria" . . . *(*SIMÓN *turns his back on him and embraces* GUADALUPE. *She moves away from him and looks at him. Someone knocks at the door.)*

Guadalupe. You look wonderful. Isn't it a little tight under the arm? *(Speaking softly in his ear)* There's a plot . . . *(More knocking at the door)*

Pingitori. (His voice is heard, shaky, but pretending to sound natural.) Lupe . . .

Simón. What plot?

Guadalupe. His, against us . . . we have to get rid of him. Get him out of here. *(In the dream area* PINGITORI *appears, kneeling now, and the* PRIEST *hits his naked back with a whip.* SIMÓN *walks around trying to put his ideas in order.)*

Simón. (To GUADALUPE*)* But listen to me . . . if he . . . he called my cousin. *(Transition)* All right then! Let's get this out in the open once and for all! We can't spend our whole life locked in here.

Guadalupe. Why not? But without him. Just the two of us. He's one too many.

Priest. For being a cuckold. *(A lash on* PINGITORI's *naked back)*

Simón. I really screwed him, didn't I? I tricked him, he welcomed me into his house . . .

Guadalupe. And what would you like? For me to stay with him? To humiliate you? To humiliate me? *(A bell rings outside.)*

Priest. For being a cuckold. *(Another lash)* And this corrupting Jew to the torture chamber . . . *(The* PRIEST *makes a Nazi salute looking at* SIMÓN.*)*

Simón. (To the PRIEST*)* But what are you doing? Do you think I believe in that, in ghosts? Look, in this country no one persecutes anyone. No, I won't play your game.

Guadalupe. What's going on now? What do you see?

Priest. (To SIMÓN*)* And how does one punish the fornicator, the lustful, the one who jumps into bed with the women he shouldn't? You live for pleasure, right? In a strange country which isn't yours and which you'll never be a real part of . . . you Jew . . . (*The image disappears. The knocking on the door stops.* SIMÓN *walks restlessly around the room. The door opens and* SIMÓN's WIFE *comes in. She is rather fat and ugly, seems lonely, spent, and carries a suitcase. She looks around the room, annoyed and humiliated by her behavior, and almost immediately walks toward the sofa with tired, pathetic ease. She opens the suitcase.*)

Wife. How are you?

Guadalupe. (*Looks at her and at* SIMÓN) And this?

Simón. (*Looking with embarrassment at the woman who entered*) This is . . . my wife . . .

Guadalupe. Ah! Everyone is dropping in today. (GUADALUPE *to* SIMÓN) And what does she want? (*Moves closer to the* WIFE) You come in here too as if it were your house.

Wife. (*Without looking at her*) A man opened the door (*pretends to act naturally*), you know?

Guadalupe. Uh, huh, very well. (*To* SIMÓN) I don't know her, you never introduced us. (*To the* WIFE) I'm your husband's wife . . . the real one, as soon as you give him the divorce.

Wife. (*Lighting a cigarette and smiling*) What divorce? He never said anything to me. (*To* SIMÓN, *affectionately*) How are you, Simón?

Simón. (*Looks at her, recognizing her*) I'm okay. (GUADALUPE *perceives a strange, dense, painful and old feeling growing between these two people, that makes her a little uneasy.*)

Wife. At least you could have called. Why didn't you? (*Pause*) I only have a little time. Luisito has the measles, and I called the doctor. He could come any moment . . . (*Pause*) Where are your things? (*Opens the dresser*) You look thin . . . aren't you taking vitamins anymore?

Guadalupe. But, don't you understand? He doesn't love you anymore, Señora, he has nothing to do with you. (WIFE *looks at her with a tired, weary smile, measuring her up*)

Wife. You're pretty, more than I am, sure, sure . . . but you don't understand. Between Simón and me, there are many things . . . Right, Simón? (GUADALUPE *and* WIFE *look at him.* SIMÓN *brews* mate *and turns his back on them, as he sits in a chair. Sounds are heard from a flute. In the dream area, a* YOUNG MAN *appears, sitting on his haunches.*)

Guadalupe. Do you think that I'm holding him back? (*The music is very sweet. So is the boy. He is sixteen. Gradually,* SIMÓN *feels his presence and moves towards the dream realm. The music is "Kinder yorn" (Childhood years). It is soft and melancholy. The* YOUNG BOY *has long hair, and he holds a wooden flute.)*

Simón. And how is Simón?

Wife. He missed you a lot when you left. He used to wake up crying at night, shouting "Papá, Papá." Then one day he left and I never heard from him again.

Simón. (With tearful eyes) Did he take his flute with him?

Wife. And his long hair. You let him grow it that way.

Simón. (With pride and sadness) That boy is like me . . . *(To* GUADALUPE*)* You know he's the same sign as me. He's an Aries, like me, like my father.

Wife. He has your eyes, Simón, . . . and also your sweetness. And he's also crazy, like you . . .

Simón. You know? Sometimes I dream about him.

Wife. And I don't? *(*GUADALUPE *looks at them and slowly sits down on the bed.)*

Simón. (Very softly, addressing the image he sees) I wanted to look after you, my little boy, I wanted to protect you so that nothing would ever happen to you . . .

Wife. Yes, it's obvious.

Simón. Do you know what I dream about? That one day I'm in a car . . . because I'm going to have a car, you know?

Wife. We already have one . . . and I don't know how I'm going to pay for it.

Simón. I mean another car, another one . . . with my gold mine. And I'm going on the highway, and suddenly, on the side of the road, there's Simón, alone, with his hair blowing in the wind, sitting, absorbed in his thoughts, playing the flute. Simón . . . my own flesh and blood, my oldest boy . . . the thing I love most in the world . . . and then the car comes closer to him and when I pass him, I love him so that it hurts, and that's why I accelerate so that he doesn't see me . . . because he's looking for me, you know, and I don't want to hurt him. And the car is lost in the distance . . . and he's still there, behind, alone, following his road, and I never see him again. *(The vision and music fade away. The* WIFE *pulls out a horrible yellow tie from the suitcase, the kind of tie a poor Jewish jeweler from Calle Libertad would wear.)*

Wife. Look what I brought you, Simón. *(Tries it on him)* The one you like.

Simón. What?

Wife. This is a tie for a jeweler . . . What are you doing there, all dressed up? This is not a carnival . . . What are you doing with your life? You always dressed properly. Do you think these are clothes for a jeweler?

Simón. (*Wraps himself in his cape and says in a haughty tone*) What?

Wife. (*Tired*) Let's go. Anita is coming back from school, the doctor is coming to check Luisito. Let's go . . . don't make me waste my time.

Simón. Ah, does that still exist?

Wife. What?

Simón. In the contingent world . . . Does that nonsense still go on? (*He walks as if he were a lord.*) What's the matter now? Why are you bothering me, don't you see I'm busy? I have problems, leave me alone!

Wife. In the . . . (*She doesn't remember the word at first, but then she does*) contingent world, your youngest son has the measles.

Guadalupe. Wasn't it the mumps?

Simón. I always say, if you let him out without a sweater . . . here it gets cold just like that. You know what the weather's like around here.

Wife. The weather outside . . . (*with disgust*) because inside there's an odor.

Guadalupe. Of what?

Wife. Of being closed in . . . it stinks.

Simón. (*Haughtily*) Bah . . . those are just details.

Wife. That's the way it is. For me life's a pile of details, one next to the other. I have to pay the doctor, for instance . . .

Simón. (*Shrugs his shoulders*) Let him come to see me.

Wife. What for?

Simón. I have florins, doubloons, maravedis[16] . . . anything you like, a pile of maravedis that the first Brumelstein brought when he left Spain.

Wife. *Shimeleh!*[17] What Spain, what are you talking about?

Simón. (*Goes to the display cabinet and opens it*) There they are— sapphires from the mine . . . they're priceless. Take something. (WIFE *looks at him with scorn, sadness, desperation, passivity, strength, patience.*) Well? Take one, you idiot. (*To* GUADALUPE) Look who I married. The daughter of the vendor from the market. Chicken seller, her mother used to sell chickens. A Brumelstein married to a chicken seller's daughter. Did you ever hear of such a thing?

Wife. Simón, our little shop . . . it's not working out. I can't do it all alone, Simón.

Simón. That's why I'm giving you a sapphire.

Wife. Junk, just worthless junk, and the watchmaker who worked next to the display window, that boy . . . I had to fire him. I couldn't pay him.

Simón. What? You hired somebody without letting me know?

Wife. (*Getting more exasperated*) And who did you expect to repair the watches when you left?

Simón. Nonsense. No one consulted me.

Wife. And where were you? The jewelry shop is going to the dogs, your cousin wants to swallow me up. He wants to buy it from me . . .

Simón. I know, I know already.

Wife. Sure you know. And what good does it do me? I have to take care of the kids, the jewelry shop, the house, everything . . . Anita, Luis, the other one who left, your cousin, and your relations and mine. Everything is falling apart and I can't take it all by myself, Simón . . . and the debts, and the car, and the house, and the cracked glass. Did you know the display window is broken? Details, details, details.

Simón. (*Suffocated*) Get out of here.

Guadalupe. This is the way you want to get him to go with you? Poor strategy, believe me, very poor strategy. (*Leaves almost triumphantly*) I leave him to you . . . do what you can with him.

Wife. Besides (*pause*) . . . besides, I miss you Simón.

Simón. Come on, don't cry, you hear? You want me to go back to you, right? You humiliated yourself, you came all the way down here, to take me back . . . but I like her.

Wife. I don't care what you do outside the house.

Simón. Don't you? That's what I don't like. Do you understand why I left, why I ran away? I went with many women . . . and you knew it, but it was outside the house. And what happened, Elena? Why did it all end? I loved you, we were Romeo and Juliet . . . but look, look at yourself, those wrinkles, look at that double chin. You're fat and flabby and ugly . . . I want young people around me, firm flesh, that's what I like. What do you think? That making love is work? No . . . (*He lifts up her skirt.*) Look at those varicose veins. Is this what has become of the girl I married? This used to be my Juliet. (*Smiles imperiously*) Get out of here . . . my God . . . I don't love you anymore. It's terrible, but that's the way it is. (*While he lifts up her skirt, the* WIFE *is crying, deeply upset. Her voice is choked.*)

Wife. You're so bad.

Simón. Good, bad. I spent my whole life saying that. Be good.

What can you do? We're only here for an instant. How many
more years am I going to live? Look, I'm already forty, my dear.
(His voice becomes sweeter.) And what kind of life have I had?
What did I do? I'm going downhill.

Wife. What happened to our love, Simón?

Simón. How do I know how it died? Do you remember my little
business with your girlfriend Esther?

Wife. That was a long time ago. I forgave you.

Simón. But I didn't forgive myself, no, that was dirty. How could
I do it, when I loved you. I did that shit with her . . . I was
searching for purity. I loved you and she came along and I got
hot . . . I was a son of a bitch, just like now.

Wife. It can happen, Simón, it can . . . but I don't mind. What
matters is what lasts—me, you, and the children.

Simón. What do you mean, what lasts. Bullshit. And what about
purity?

Wife. What purity, Simón? I'm telling you that I can't handle it all
by myself at the jewelry shop. And I can't understand what you
want . . . purity, not purity . . . it has to end!

Simón. And one fine day Romeo and Juliet have varicose veins,
he has a prostate, he can't keep his eyes off other women . . .
no, not that same old way, not just a habit, no. *(His* WIFE *clings
to him in desperation.)* No, no . . . *(He pushes her away.)* I'm
with her, you hear, leave me alone. *(Shoving her toward the door)*
Leave me alone, just go away. *(Throws her out as he shouts)*
Leave me alone! *(Closes the door)*

Wife. (From outside) Open up.

Guadalupe. (From outside) He doesn't want to.

Wife. (From outside) Open . . . Simón. *(The knocks on the door
and the argument between the two women become a chorus of
barks and howls where the words uttered by the quarreling fe-
males are indistinguishable from an infernal clatter.* SIMÓN *covers his ears. In the dream area now the* PRIEST *appears. In the
style of a Talmudic scholar he has long curled sideburns, a
beard, and wears a skullcap on his head.)*

Priest-Rabbi. So this is your life, eh? A nice mess your life is.
What do you expect? With your head you want one thing, with
your body you want something else. What are you? A shithead.
Just a lot of pieces of shit fighting one another and not knowing
where to go. To the coffin, that's where, to the coffin.

Simón. Go wash your armpits, you filth, with your robe, with your
peyes.[18] *(He points to the long sidelocks.)* Go wash your armpits,
then we'll talk. *(Outside, a scream like a howl can be heard.*

Suddenly the stage becomes completely dark, except for SIMÓN's *face. A sudden change in light brings about absolute silence where* SIMÓN *is. A very sweet voice is heard, and the light spreads over the dream zone. It points to a Jewish cemetery, just a heap of stones. Perhaps twelve tombstones, randomly placed, some vertically, some slanted, others horizontally. In imitation of the Prague cemetery they are ancient, faded gothic and baroque stones. Weeds and branches grow all around them, as in an abandoned garden. The stones bear huge Hebrew inscriptions, some with carved fishes or scissors, according to the professions of their owners. Behind the tombstones, the* PRIEST-RABBI *is crouched, spying. The voice of a woman can be heard singing a Yiddish lullaby very softly as the curtain rises, and the* BOBE[19] *appears. She is wearing a small kerchief tied under her chin, like a Russian peasant, and she is singing a litany from a far off place. "There are green leaves on the branches of the trees, and the wind pulls them off. Sleep, my love. But it is warm inside; here the wind will not come in, because my arms are here to stop its fury." When he hears this song,* SIMÓN *feels very moved. Its sweetness is disarming, and he approaches the cemetery.)*
Bobe. *(*BOBE *walks toward him.)* I knew you would come. *(The* PRIEST *moves back and forth between them, stroking his beard like a rabbi. He smiles diabolically and cruelly.)* You must help me, Bobe. *(*BOBE *strokes his head.)*
Priest. (With a Jewish accent) Why should we?
Simón. Go away!
Priest. Pay me . . . You want me to pray for them. *(He fixes his purple skullcap on his head, like a Jewish* yarmulka.[20]*)* You want me to leave? Then pay me!
Simón. I can't stand it here anymore, Bobe.
Bobe. Why don't you come with us?
Simón. (In his anguish, he does not hear.) Who's going to help me? *(Sudden and short barrage of cries from the women,* "You bitch!" *and* "Get out of here!"*)* I feel like I have a mountain on top of me. How did it all happen? How did I wind up like this?
Bobe. To Yehúpets[21] . . .
Simón. What?
Bobe. Come to Yehúpets with us.
Simón. I can't, Bobe. I'm not from there.
Bobe. We're all young here, we're all so happy. What are you doing there, in America, in that world? *(Pause)* In Yehúpets, we only have one cow . . .
Simón. But what does that have to do with me?

Bobe. Here everyone is in his world. Everyone is in his glory. I plant alfalfa, wheat . . . and on Saturdays we ride the cow through the woods, and five *verstas*[22] away *pánio*[23] Dostoyevsky lives.

Simón. (*Smiling*) There you go again, Bobe, with your lies. You carry on with your stories there too? You're still babbling on over there? (*Gently*) And what do you want me to bring him? My custom jewelry? And what am I going to tell him, and who am I next to Dostoyevsky . . . A jeweler from Calle Libertad! Impossible! (*Anxious*) But where's the way, Bobe?

Bobe. Come along.

Simón. Where is it, Bobe?

Bobe. Here. (*Points to the graveyard, and walks towards* SIMÓN, *to take him along*)

Simón. Stop . . . I don't have time. I can't now, I have a lot to do over here.

Priest. You've got to fornicate, right? (*He hums in an ecclesiastic and apocalyptic style.*) Copulare cum bestias et ánimas . . .[24]

Bobe. Simón . . . I'm so happy.

Simón. What are you happy about, Bobe?

Bobe. I'm happy whenever you see me . . . (*She feels his forehead with her hand.*) I want you to know we look after you . . . I see you, and I love you, and I always take care of you, Simón.

Simón. And what am I supposed to do with your protection?

Bobe. (*Ceremoniously*) Do you know what I brought for you? Look what I'm going to give you. (*She opens a small purse.*) A *ruble*,[25] a whole ruble for you. The only one I have, for my little boy. Do you know how much you can get with this?

Simón. (*Laughing*) No, Bobe. What can I do with that? It's no good around here . . .

Bobe. (*Gesturing with her hand*) You'll use it, you'll use it.

Father's voice. Mamá, Mamá. (*Pause*)

Simón. He's here, too?

Priest. (PRIEST *strokes his peyes and fixes his yarmulka.*) Does it bother you? (FATHER *appears from among the stones with* SIMÓN *as a child next to him.*)

Father. Where's my white shirt, Mamá?

Simón. How young he looks, how happy . . . (FATHER *wears tzitzis,*[26] *a kind of bib used by Orthodox Jews, over his heavy undershirt. He's wearing a yarmulka and his face is covered with shaving cream. He has a shaving brush in one hand and a jar with his razor in the other. He wears suspenders and golden rimmed glasses.*)

Father. Let's go Mamá, it's getting dark. It's time to go to temple.

Simón. Sure. What do you care about the rest of the world?

Father. (Answers BOBE *as if she had spoken)* Yes, what do I care about that? *(Smiling)* Tomorrow is the Sabbath.

Simón. Papá. Señor Pingitori is suffering because of me. Listen to how they're fighting out there. I have to do something. I can't stay in here forever.

Father. (To BOBE*)* What's the big deal? Tomorrow is the Sabbath. That doesn't change, that always stays the same. It's eternal. For 3,000 years, tomorrow will always be the Sabbath. It's the only truth. Who cares what's happening outside? Eh . . . *(to* SIMÓN, *the child)* Listen to me, Simón. You have to go out into their world, to tell them things, to make a living, so you can eat. And for what? To go back home later to live the only reality that's pure and certain. And what's that? *(He strokes the* CHILD'S *head, and in the same rabbinical manner as he would chant the Passover Hagaddah, he chants softly, marking the rhythm with his index finger.)* Kings, governments, countries may change, but God is eternal . . . *(Stops singing)* And we too . . . we're His children, chosen by Him, God's blood, God's children . . . And how Simón? *(He kneels in front of him and chants.)* There's something that always remains the same. *(Speaking)* And what's that? *(Chanting resolutely)* On Saturday . . . *(Speaking)* whether they persecute us or protect us, what does it matter? We always live through one day that never changes and never dies. It's always the same . . . *(Chanting)* And how do we know this? *(Speaking)* Because there are always problems, there is always pain, the flesh rots, desire tears you apart, details fill your head and ruin your health, you struggle and scheme to put food on the table, but on Saturday, my son, you always feel young, you are always a king, always clean. *(Chanting)* That stays the same . . . *(Speaking)* We have stopped time, my son . . . and for three thousand years we've been drinking glasses of tea at home after lunch. *(Chanting)* Cities change, and so do years, countries, and even persecutions. *(Speaking)* But we go on and the glass of tea always remains the same. *(Stands up and begins to shave off his beard)*

Simón. Papá. It's all a big mess. I don't know.

Father. And you just realized that now? Now that you've broken off with me, now that you've ruined my health. A jewelry store is nothing to you, right?

Simón. It's not that, Papá.

Father. You have assimilated, you're like them. So fine. Whoever

doesn't respect the Sabbath, whoever kills his father with a heart
attack, will never get in here.

Simón. Listen to me, Papá. That Katz is cheating me. He's a hypocrite. But he respects the Sabbath, right? So anyway, Papá, does
that fix things up? Look at all the pain out there.

Father. Garbage. The whole world of yours is garbage.

Simón. Yes, but I have to live here.

Father. To Israel, that's where you have to go. To Israel, to start
a factory . . . to start a big jewelry store there.

Simón. But I don't want to be a Jew, Papá. I want to be a man.
And what you gave me is no good to me. So what do I do? How
can I manage?

Father. (*Laughing*) But you can't assimilate, because I am eternity.

Simón. Just crazy talk, you and your eternity. A breeze can destroy it. I have to do something, Papá. I have to make a move.
I have to go out into the world. Look what's happening there.
Don't you hear the screams? It's hell. The kingdom of this world
is hell, and you're no help to me, Papá. The only thing you do
is curse me. (*A tearful* GUADALUPE *comes running in.*)

Guadalupe. I threw her out. I threw her out. I threw her out by
her hair. Simón, we have to do something. We can't go on like
this. (*The stage becomes dark. The only lights, coming from the
dark zone, are on* SIMÓN *and the* PRIEST-RABBI. *The face of the
latter reflects a punishing smile.*)

Priest. El mole, El mole, El mole, El mole, El mole, El mole.[27]
(*Chanting*) Pray for your dead. Do not forget the death that you
have inside.

Simón. You'll have to make me.

Guadalupe. Sweetheart, beloved. (SIMÓN *grabs her and kisses her
with great passion, anxiety and vulnerability.*)

Simón. Oh my love, my love.

Priest. Pray for this soul.

Simón. (*To* GUADALUPE) You know? One day I saw my father's
soul leaving an apartment with a woman who wasn't my mother.

Priest. So you're starting up with the dead?

Guadalupe. Stop it already with your father. I'm here.

Priest. Yes, but where's the spirit?

Simón. (*Sarcastically to* GUADALUPE) The spirit wants to know
where he is. (GUADALUPE *takes* SIMÓN'*s hands and presses them
against her body. As his hands run over her body, she whispers.*)

Guadalupe. Here, right here. (*The* PRIEST *circles the two of them
like one of the mythological Furies and shakes* SIMÓN, *who is
the only one who sees and hears him. Now the* PRIEST-RABBI

*shouts with the plaintive, shrill and tearful chanting of those
who entone the prayers for the dead before the tombs in the
Jewish cemeteries. All of this with a tone of exasperated cruelty
and punishing sarcasm against* SIMÓN)

Priest. What was the name of this soul, this dead man that you
killed? Reb Shloime Brumelstein, son of Yosl, son of Yankl, son
of another, and another and another even earlier, of clean blood
and conscience. May God keep them all in his luminous paradise.
(*Chanting*) Ay, ay, ay, ay, ay, ay, ay, ay, where you'll never go.
Ahcha-hcha-hchay-chah cha, iab-iab-iab-iab-iab-iab-iab-iab
(*Swaying as he crosses himself.*) Leb-leb-leb-leb-leb-leb. (SIMÓN
lets go of GUADALUPE. *He runs to get the sword and chases
after the* PRIEST.)

Simón. Get out, get out!

Guadalupe. Who is it?

Simón. The Inquisitor.

Guadalupe. What does he want?

Simón. (*Running after the* PRIEST) Wash your armpits, wash your
armpits. (GUADALUPE *takes the cross and without seeing where
the* PRIEST *is, since he's always in a different place, holds it up
at random.*)

Guadalupe. Vade retro. Vade retro. Vade retro.[28]

Priest. (*In a natural voice*) That will be two hundred pesos. (*He
snatches the ruble from* SIMÓN's *hand and disappears into the
dream zone.* SIMÓN *remains still; he is trembling now and sits
down on the bed.* GUADALUPE *leaves the cross leaning against
the desk on the floor and goes to* SIMÓN's *side, where she sits
down.*)

Guadalupe. Simón . . . (SIMÓN *is quiet, in his own world.*)
Shouldn't we leave this place?

Simón. (*His eyes closed and his mind somewhere else*) Yes, yes.
But I'd like to know just one thing. (*Seated on the edge of the
bed, his hands clasped between his legs, he begins to sway like
a rabbi.*) You . . .

Guadalupe. What?

Simón. Not you. You, who took me out of Egypt! Aren't you on
the side of the oppressed? And who are the children of Israel?
Everyone is a child of Israel.

Guadalupe. Right, that's what Jesus said. (*A weeping* SIMÓN *with
his eyes closed, sways back and forth, stifling a scream, with his
hands clenched between his legs.*)

Simón. And why don't you help me to get ahead? (*Pausing*) Don't
you see what a mess I am? (*He pauses and falls on his knees,*

with his hands clasped in front of the cross.) Adonoy, Adonoy.[29]
Throw me a life-line. *(Swaying back and forth like a rabbi.* GUA-
DALUPE, *very moved at seeing him like that, kneels at his side.
He prays with closed eyes. A muffled bell is heard.)*
Guadalupe. He has to help us to get out of here, to begin again.
(Pause. The door opens. Pingitori comes in and sees everything.)
Pingitori. (Scandalized, he whispers.) They don't respect anything
anymore, right? As a Catholic . . .
Guadalupe. Hypocrite! (PINGITORI *looks at her threateningly and
a vicious glint lights up his eyes.)*
Pingitori. Yes, yes. *(Behind* PINGITORI *is the* PRIEST *in street
clothes. He sticks his head in and looks around with great care.*
SIMÓN *opens his eyes. He sees him and becomes afraid. He
stops. The* PRIEST *doesn't appear to be the least impressed by
what he sees.)*
Priest. Is the gas working here?
Guadalupe. (Sees him, then stops) Yes. *(Pause)* Why?
Priest. There was a gas leak. They told me it was here.
Guadalupe. There's no leak here.
Simón. (To GUADALUPE*)* Who's there?
Guadalupe. It's no one, sweetheart.
Simón. (Turning his back to the man) I'm not in for anybody.
Priest. It's really hot, isn't it? *(Pauses)* Okay. It's probably a mis-
take. *(He leaves.)*
Guadalupe. (To PINGITORI*)* Who was it?
Pingitori. Didn't you hear? He told you.
Simón. (With his back to him) From the gas company? And he
just comes in like that?
Guadalupe. And now? Who was that? What did he come for? *(She
throws herself at him.)* You want to keep me by force, right?
You hypocrite! *(She brushes him off.* PINGITORI *looks at her
somewhat upset but also unperturbed. With a pale and bitter
smile he frees himself from her.)*
Pingitori. A doctor from the asylum is here. He came to take a
look.
Guadalupe. (Frightened, in a very faint voice) What did he come
for?
Pingitori. To take a look. *(Pauses)* I called him.

Curtain

Act II

*(A heavy heat fills the room. There is a fan that works and hums,
but it does not cool. When the light goes on you can see that the*

room has been turned into a religious sanctuary: church candles, hearts of Jesus, crucifixes, the Virgin inside a crystal ball above the chest, small reproductions of saints in the mirrors. GUADALUPE *observes everything, seated on the bed.* SIMÓN, *with a T-shirt and pajamas is by her side, fanning himself with an old magazine. He looks towards the inside of the room.)*

Simón. Do you think it will work?

Guadalupe. With all this . . .

Simón. Do you think they'll dare come in? The neighbors won't let them . . . isn't it true that they won't let them take me?

Guadalupe. As far as the neighbors . . . they're dying of laughter behind your back. Don't you hear? *(Coughs, mumbling outside the window, nocturnal sounds of people who are sleeping but also of people who can't sleep and whisper in low voices, or eavesdrop.)* No one's sleeping.

Simón. (Fans himself) And with this heat . . .

Guadalupe. That's why they gave me all these saints. What do you think, that they're Catholics? They're hypocrites. Some believers! They're just hypocrites, like Pingitori!

Simón. Like Katz . . .

Guadalupe. They're the ones who nailed Christ. And everyday they nail him again. They nail each other. Simón, come on, let's go.

Simón. (He sits at the table and drinks a cold mate.*)* You brought all this? *(He grabs the jewelry box. Looking at the saints)* They can make miracles? *(He turns on the table lamp.)*

Guadalupe. Of course. But you have to help them, Simón. And should we just wait here until that guy comes? *(She stands up as she puts her shoes on.)* The people from the mental hospital are not big believers. (SIMÓN *turns the lights toward the red cushion that is on the table. It is like a small velvet tapestry. He gets up and goes to the showcase where he removes the jewelry that is inside and brings it to the table. He empties it all on the cushion next to the contents of the jewelry box. With the help of the magnifying glass that jewelers use, he looks at his possessions: rings, gold bands, necklaces, pearls, pins, bracelets, beads.)*

Simón. None of this is worth anything. All junk, costume jewelry.

Guadalupe. No, Simón. They'll be good for something.

Simón. If this is everything that I'm going to leave when I go, what good is it all? Outside or inside, it's the same . . .

Guadalupe. Simón, oh Simón. We have to leave. For me it's not the same. *(She pauses.)* I'm going to make a phone call.

Simón. Who are you calling?

Guadalupe. I'll be right back. *(She opens the door.* PINGITORI *quickly moves away.)* You're always there, spying.

Pingitori. (Peering at the door) You don't have to work so hard, love. Go on, lie down a while.

Guadalupe. With him? *(She pauses.)* So this is the game we're playing now? Should I go to the big bed with him? Or do you believe that I'm really working inside? This is where I live, where I'm happy, where I find pleasure. You hear me? Where I find pleasure, yes. Didn't you know it? I've always shown that to you. Before, I never said anything to you because of him, because Simón didn't want me to, but now . . . It's all clear now, isn't it?

Pingitori. Don't raise your voice. You're tired. Nothing wrong. Go on, lie down a while.

Guadalupe. (Fed up) Eh . . . *(She violently slams the apartment door as she leaves.* SIMÓN *slowly puts the jewelry back into the box. He stops, approaches the cross that is standing on a pedestal next to the table and kneels, his eyes wide open and tired.)*

Simón. If I could only believe, Señor. If you could help me get out of here, start again. It's not that I don't believe. It's just that *(somewhat anguished),* can't you give me a sign? You know what it is? My head's a mess, it's all mixed up. And I have no strength to fight. *(He looks at the cross with his arms fallen at his sides. First a halo appears, and the* BOBE *appears surrounded by the halo.)*

Bobe. What are you doing still up?

Simón. I can't sleep tonight.

Bobe. Is it hot there?

Simón. (Makes a sound indicating how hot it is) Pff . . .

Bobe. Did you eat? You want me to make you a little tea? *(*SIMÓN *shakes his head. She looks around the room.)* What is all of this? *(She looks at the cross with a smile.)* If I were alive, I would say you're a hooligan, a *sheigetz,*[30] *a grober young,*[31] a heretic. I don't know what else I'd say. But now . . . *(She smiles and strokes his brow.)* I will always be at your side, wherever you are. *(She takes out a package, a green velvet purse.)* Take this. You'll need this too.

Simón. (Looks at it) What is it?

Bobe. Put it on. It will keep you. This or that. *(She points at the cross.)* Someone has to help you. *(*SIMÓN *opens the purse and takes out a pair of philacteries. The* GRANDMOTHER *takes one and puts it on his forehead. It is a black wooden cube with a papyrus fragment inside that has the not-to-be pronounced* *name of God on it: "Shadai." A black leather string, like a hair band, holds up the cube and two black leather straps fall on the sides, one on each shoulder. The* GRANDMOTHER *puts the other philactery on her left arm and twists it around until it reaches her thumb. Then she takes out the prayer shawl—the* tallis[32]— *and puts it on.)* They were my grandfather's. I don't know. Maybe you can use them . . .

Simón. Deep down I've never prayed. Papá taught me. I used to say words in the *shul,*[33] but to really pray in the temple, I just couldn't. My words never reached heaven. They couldn't fly, and now *(he looks at the crucifix),* all together? *(He smiles with ironic sweetness.)* Some short circuit is going to go off up there!

Bobe. Use them. If they can't do you any good, they can't do you any harm either. That one *(pointing at the cross)* also used them. Did you eat? Because I can make you some bread and butter. *(She butters an imaginary slice of bread on the palm of her hand and offers it to* SIMÓN, *who rejects it.)*

Simón. They're going to come and get me . . . and I need strength.

Bobe. I know, so eat. *(*SIMÓN *takes the imaginary slice of bread and swallows it as if it were a host.)*

Simón. I don't want to go crazy, Bobe. I have to get out of here. *(The* GRANDMOTHER *sits down in a chair and beckons him with her hand.* SIMÓN *kneels in front of her and puts his head on her lap. An undefined anguish racks* SIMÓN's *body. He huddles there and fidgets restlessly.)*

Bobe. (She strokes him with utter serenity.) Nothing comes out? And nevertheless *(she caresses his head with great tenderness),* you know how to pray. That prayer that I taught you before you go to bed. *(The* GRANDMOTHER, *as old as the world, rocks herself, with her peasant scarf tied under her chin, her childlike air, her roots, her small and absolute truth, fragile and indestructible, as she repeats mechanically, in an ordinary voice)* It's always the same; *Shma, Israel, adoishem, elokeinu, adoishem ekhod.* Hear oh Israel, the Lord our God, the Lord is One. And afterwards *(she caresses his head),* good night to Papá, good night to Mamá, to Bobe, to Zeyde.[34] *Un ale mayne gute fraynt vos heyisn mir tsum gutn veg . . .*

Simón. (Repeats in a soft voice) And to all my good friends who always lead me on the right path.

Bobe. Amen. *(She lifts up his head and kisses his cheek.)* Good, and now, a cup of soup?

Simón. It wasn't that, Bobe *(desperate).* It wasn't that. *(He grabs his head.)* It was some kind of a sentence like that, I don't know where it's said, or where it's used, or even where it's written. How did it go? I need it so much. You know it.

Bobe. I'm not an educated woman, Simón. I was born, lived, and passed through the world with no one looking at me twice. *(She pretends to prepare bread and butter with her hands while rocking herself, and suddenly, mechanically, repeats a tongue twister with simplicity.) Vehavto eloihekho komoiho, bekhol levovkho, bekhol nafshekho ubekhol meoidekho.[35] (SIMÓN is relieved and breathes more restfully, like after an orgasm, like after quenching a long thirst.)*

Simón. Ah . . . *(He purrs as if a freshness had invaded him.)* There it is. *(He straightens up and with his eyes closed and his hands together, repeats.)* And you will love your God, with all your heart, with all your soul, and with all your being. *(He remains that way, in ecstasy. His GRANDMOTHER caresses his head and then looks at him for a long time as if she were saying goodbye to him.)* And I feel it now with all my being . . . *(Silently, his GRANDMOTHER pauses and looks around the room as she leaves.)* If I could get it out of me, how would I pray, Bobe? And you know what? Just now I feel that I could, that maybe I could, with my whole heart, with all my being . . . that the words could fly. *(The GRANDMOTHER fades forever into the dream area. PINGITORI slowly opens the door and enters with two bottles of beer and two glasses. Simón opens his eyes.)* Thank you, Bobe . . . *(He looks at the chair and seeing it empty, he panics.)* Bobe, where are you? *(Still kneeling, he looks around the room.)* Why did you leave me?

Pingitori. You can't sleep either? In a while it's going to be worse. *(SIMÓN becomes furious when he sees him. He stops and takes off the philacteries. PINGITORI walks around the room and pauses in front of the map. He looks at it, smiles and proceeds to leave the bottles on the table.)* Chantania . . . so this is your country. This is where it is, in my house. You had to come and discover it right here? It couldn't be next door. It had to be here.

Simón. Yes, General Pingitori.

Pingitori. In a while my men are going to come, all dressed in white, and they're going to take you away Jew, in a straight jacket. And you're going to stop screwing around with me once and for all.

Simón. I'll stop screwing the gentlemen around . . . *(PINGITORI looks at him and approaches the chest, opens it and starts to take out costume after costume.)*

Pingitori. What golden hands she has, eh? And all for you. *(He becomes wild, self-assured, fanatic, vengeful.)* Little suits, costumes.

Simón. Does it bother you, General?

Pingitori. (Comes across a general's cap and puts it on) No, because I already moved the tanks to the street, *marrano.*[36]

Simón. (Ironically) Why *marrano? (A* PRIEST *appears from the dream area hiding his fists inside his sleeves.)* What a sad thing, General. You're not even a gentleman. I have a galleon. But you earn 23,000 pesos a month. And what do you defend? The religion of the rich? The world of the rich?

Priest. (Mockingly) Marrano.

Simón. (To the PRIEST*)* No, Father . . . *(With exasperated, painful sarcasm)* Your blessings, Father. *(He throws himself to his knees.)* I've converted. (PINGITORI, *with his military cap on, sits down at the table and enjoys watching* SIMÓN's *delirium as he drinks his beer. To the* PRIEST*)* From a New Christian to an Old Christian. *(He raises his empty hands.)* Here are the records that prove the purity of my blood. On the other hand, Father, your nose. I don't like anything about your nose.

Priest. Pagan. You will never cease to be a stranger. You will wind up in hell, in the darkness of the outside shadows.

Simón. (To PINGITORI*)* Why, General? This house is yours, yes, but it is mine too. This table *(he raises his empty hands)* I bought recently, a short while ago.

Pingitori. Some picnic they're going to have with you. Some legal records, when just a little while ago . . .

Simón. In the year of our Lord 1484 . . . *(He looks at the* PRIEST.*)* from an agent from the Holy Office. I paid for it with all my maravedis and with my estate, with my house. *(To the* GENERAL*)* And now, you want to throw me out again, you want to rob me of everything?

Priest. Here is the miracle that smells of sulphur. *(He walks around* SIMÓN.*)* This is a mystery of history.

Simón. (To PINGITORI*)* This conversation, you know we had it before. *(To the* PRIEST*)* With the two of you.

Pingitori. (Drinking) With what two . . . there's nobody here.

Simón. (To PINGITORI*)* 1200 years ago in Aragón. I was your friend and everything worked to perfection. *(He bows.)* I was your banker, Your Majesty. *(To the* PRIEST*)* And a thousand years ago I cured you from a grippe that almost killed you.

Pingitori. (Sullen and amused) A grippe, where was it?

Simón. In a Polish convent, in an abbey in Cluny. What do I know, I don't remember anymore. But 500 years ago *(he looks at the two of them)* I was rich, just like now, and you both wanted to devour me, just like now.

Priest. (To the audience) What do we see, brothers? I see here a camel condemned to cross the desert of temporal life, weighted down with precious stones, condemned forever to solitude and helplessness, forever corrupting everything it touches.

Pingitori. So, Chantania was yours, eh? But no . . . I plotted. I took the tanks to the street and I'm going to wind up with your mine and with everything of yours. *(The* PRIEST *disappears.)*

Simón. Do you think you even know the way? I'm never going to show it to you. I had to come myself, not Pizarro not Cortés, not Solís, me, Simón Brumelstein. I founded Chantania, in my father's galleon. He sailed from Cádiz one afternoon in 1400 and left his land behind him forever. *(*GUADALUPE *enters.)*

Guadalupe. (To SIMÓN*)* What? What's going on here? You're still at it? Come on, let's go.

Pingitori. Where are you going?

Guadalupe. What the hell does it matter to you?

Pingitori. Where did you go?

Guadalupe. (To SIMÓN*)* Let's go. We have to move. *(*GUADALUPE *leaves.)*

Pingitori. (Disconcerted) Where? *(To* SIMÓN*)* To Israel?

Simón. (Wounded) And why?

Pingitori. There are very good mental institutions there, all full of Jews. It's your land. Right? No? Don't tell me that you're for the Arabs. Don't you know you're crazy . . . *(*GUADALUPE *enters with a suitcase and throws it on the bed. She goes out again.* PINGITORI, *terrified by what is happening, pours a glass of beer and offers it to* SIMÓN, *who is deep in concentration as he walks in his slippers from here to there, all over the room.* SIMÓN *ignores him.* GUADALUPE *enters with some of her own clothes and throws them in the valise.)*

Simón. Throw out all that.

Guadalupe. What?

Simón. Everything that's on the table, in the showcase . . . that watch, throw everything out.

Guadalupe. Why?

Simón. It's all fake. *(He grabs the jewelry box.)* Throw it out.

Guadalupe. (Grabs it) No . . . it's lovely. We can sell it. *(She puts it in the suitcase.)*

Pingitori. Where are you going? You can't leave me like that.

Guadalupe. (Defiantly) I can't? Just see if I can't. *(She leaves.)*

Pingitori. She's my wife. You know that? I'm married, I have the papers. This is a decent family. What do you want from me? (GUADALUPE *enters with a blue suit.*) The blue suit, what are you doing? It's the only one I have.

Guadalupe. In one year you used all of his suits, and now he doesn't have any. You want him to go downstairs dressed up like a Knight from the Indies?

Pingitori. And what will I wear tomorrow? I have to go to the office. I wash my shirts, my shorts, everything.

Guadalupe. There isn't any other suit.

Pingitori. What do you mean, and the grey suit?

Guadalupe. It's all torn.

Pingitori. But for him it's all the same. The grey one is missing buttons.

Guadalupe. So, sew them on.

Pingitori. It's awful. It's double-breasted, old, ugly. My boss will kill me. They're going to throw me out. (GUADALUPE *leaves.* PINGITORI *walks around, desperate now, while* SIMÓN *is seated at the table, pensively drinking cold* mate. GUADALUPE *comes in with black shoes.*) The black shoes too?

Guadalupe. You have the brown ones . . .

Pingitori. But they're going to pinch him. Black, they have to be black. There's a house rule, I told you a thousand times. *(He grabs his head desperately.)* Oh, God, what a mess, Guadalupe.

Guadalupe. Go on, continue. You tell everyone just what they can't bear to hear. I told you a thousand times that I can't stand that name.

Pingitori. Just a minute, please, one minute. Let's put things in order here. You're my wife . . . This guy comes from the street, and you're going with him, just like that? What are you, some kind of whore? And my family, and your family, what are they going to say? Look, we're happy . . . we get along well.

Guadalupe. We get along well? Do you know how I met Simón?

Pingitori. Here . . .

Guadalupe. No, in the movies.

Pingitori. What do you mean, in the movies? You never go to the movies alone. You never went without me.

Guadalupe. Yes, yes, I did. *(Shouting)* Every afternoon, you idiot.

Pingitori. *(Closing the window)* Don't speak so loud, watch your language.

Guadalupe. You're always so correct. But he wasn't so correct. He was next to me and he reached out his hand and put it under my skirt.

Pingitori. That's disgusting, filthy.

Guadalupe. So yes, that's the way everything began. And you can see that it's just lovely now.

Pingitori. Look. I don't want to know. I don't care . . .

Guadalupe. Yes, you know all about it. For a year you've known all about it.

Pingitori. I'm not so sure. (GUADALUPE *leaves. To* SIMÓN) Why didn't you talk to me?

Simón. What?

Pingitori. You never paid any attention to me. And I would have liked to be your friend. Back then, what can I say . . . I played the violin when I was a child, and you never said anything to me.

Simón. What was I supposed to tell you?

Pingitori. Good morning, good afternoon, lovely weather.

Simón. Brother, may God forgive me, but what can I do? She doesn't love you.

Pingitori. But there are norms, rules, you just can't do everything you want to. There are decent families. Why did you have to pick my family, to disrupt my family? (GUADALUPE *enters with more clothing. To* GUADALUPE) Look, whether you want it or not, you're going to have children with me, and go to bed with me, because here there's no divorce. Understand? We were married by a priest and that's that. I'm a Catholic. I go to mass from time to time. Where are you going to go with this crazy man? Because he's absolutely crazy.

Guadalupe. And what are you doing with that cap on your head?

Pingitori. What cap?

Guadalupe. He and I used to have such a good time. We invented clothes, countries, trips. We were very happy here. What did you just tell me? Where is it written that I have to stay with you if I don't like it? (GUADALUPE *leaves.*)

Pingitori. (*To* SIMÓN) Jew. What did you come here for? To change the order of things? Why didn't your parents stay in Russia? They would have all died in the gas chambers. (*He walks towards him and speaks with exaggerated sweetness.*) Why didn't Hitler kill you, huh? What did you come to this country for? We're the ones who built up this country.

Simón. (*Putting on the blue suit and laughing*) We . . . the gentlemen, the aristocrats . . . if you call yourself one, Pingitori, my dear General . . . whose side are you on? Would you like to tell me what you defend? I bet you defend the *Anchorenas*.[37] Yes, of course, some gentleman you are. (*Versaillesque music is heard in the dream area and it is interrupted by* SIMÓN's *sarcastic laughter. The lights go on in the background. The big chandelier is lit up. The drapery gives the impression of a fine ballroom. The drapes are drawn on each side. There is a kind of throne in the center, upon which* EL TORO *is seated. He is a very fat, half nude actor, wearing a bull's mask and a helmet with a large pair of horns. It looks like the masks that Greek actors used to wear. He has a large ring through his lips, and a large obelisque or phallic symbol hangs between his legs. He presides over the dance, a delicate minuet. The lights in the room are off, except for the chandelier which gives a chiaroscuro glow to everything.* SIMÓN *moves into the dream area as he dresses. A couple dances, she is wearing a long gown, and he, a general, is covered with medals. Both hold their masks in their hands. They are dancing and at the same time they are aware of the* BULL *who growls, burps, farts, breathes heavily, yawns, and exhibits every kind of physiological manifestation. At his feet lies a rug made from grass, on top of which is a peasant boy. He is dressed like a* gaucho *and caters to the* BULL's *every whim. He serves him water, alfalfa, wipes and combs his tail.)* What a smell of manure. *(The dancers don't pay attention, but you can see that they are holding their breath.)* Most Excellent Señor Presidente of Chantania, General Pingitori. *(The* PRIEST *enters wearing the triangular golden mitre of a bishop; his shoulders are covered by a long red cape.)* Your most Illustrious Reverence. *(Bows to the* MONK*)* Just as every year. *(He addresses himself to* PINGITORI, *who is framed in a spotlight wearing his general's cap, drinking beer at the table and looking at* SIMÓN *with sullen hatred.)* Let us celebrate with jubilation, the greatest festivity of our homeland, the Versailles of the Cows. We all know to what degree those who founded this country were, like our president, descendants of Knights. Here in Chantania, what is the highest compliment you can pay to anyone? "So and so is a gentleman," "So and so is a gentleman." And it couldn't be any other way. We all know to what degree the roots of our country are linked with morality, the law and above all, with the Minotaur, whose descendant *(he points to the* BULL*)* this year as every year, occupies the place of honor.

Bull. Moo . . .

Simón. Let us kneel before our president, who descends from the best families of Chantania. All you have to do is observe his class, his style. He is a true gentleman. *(The minuet dancers look at him with scorn.)* It's the norm and just because this year the inaugural address will be made by Simón Brumelstein, doesn't change the fact that we must obey the rules. *(To* PINGI-

TORI) Don't you agree, sir? *(The dancers kneel. The* PRIEST, *with his bejeweled hands, remains silent, looking at* PINGITORI.*)*

Priest. Look what we have come to.

Simón. It was the Minotaur god himself *(the three assistants turn their backs on him)* who fertilized the first cows who populated our ranches. And thus we are great and prosperous. *(Always addressing himself to* PINGITORI) This year *(he moves towards the* BULL) observe what hooves, what hind quarters, what liveliness in the eyes, what perfect legs, what grace.

Bull. Moo . . .

Simón. (*To* PINGITORI*)* It is the stud that all our cows anxiously await. Because sometimes the males are a bit castrated, then the cows wait for these 800 kilos of fat and semen. *(Chanting monotonously)* May it be for the good of all.

The Assistants. (In unison) May it be for the good of all.

Simón. (Softly singing) May you have bountiful energy. Let us adore the bull.

Chorus. Adoremus pro nobis.[38]

Simón. May it be in good time. *(He approaches the* BULL *and feels between his legs for the obelisque that hangs there.)* And I, as a member of one of the oldest and most respected families of Chantania, know how to emulate the Minotaur *(approaching* PINGITORI*)*, something that your Excellency never knew, doesn't know, doesn't dare to know because he's so very ethical and therefore, he'll never find out. *(To* PINGITORI*)* Me, like the bull, with your wife . . .

Voices. General Pingitori, do something. What about the law, and good manners?

Simón. (Hearing PINGITORI*)* Let's blow this up with all of you inside. (GUADALUPE *enters.* SIMÓN *walks towards her, provoking* PINGITORI *and kisses her. First she goes to the suitcase.)*

Guadalupe. Come on.

Simón. (To PINGITORI*)* We're going down to the street. The two of us. And what of it? We have to burn Chantania up, start all over. (GUADALUPE *and* SIMÓN *kiss each other. The bell rings.* PINGITORI *gets up and goes to the door. Suddenly a third door, leading to the world of dreams, which was not visible to the spectator until now, closes heavily, creating an asphyxiating atmosphere.* GUADALUPE *and* SIMÓN *look at each other.* GUADALUPE *closes the suitcase and* SIMÓN *finishes putting his tie on.)*

Guadalupe. Let's go.

Simón. Yes, yes. (PINGITORI *enters followed by the* PRIEST, *now dressed as a doctor, looking indifferent.)*

Priest. How are you, Simón?

Guadalupe. (Pauses) Who are you?

Priest. Doctor Ríos, pleased to meet you.

Guadalupe. (Alarmed) The gas man.

Priest. What gas?

Guadalupe. You were here before. *(She grabs the suitcase. The* PRIEST *blocks the door.)*

Priest. Where are you going, Señor? *(Pauses)* At this time of night? Are you going out?

Simón. (Frightened) We were leaving.

Priest. You, like that?

Simón. Like what?

Priest. Nude. (GUADALUPE *looks at* SIMÓN *in the blue suit.)*

Guadalupe. What do you mean nude? Did my husband call you, Doctor?

Pingitori. The neighbors. It's not just me alone.

Guadalupe. Look, I don't love him anymore. I don't think a psychiatrist can fix this up.

Priest. And who said I'm a psychiatrist?

Simón. (Smiling timidly) I guess I'm supposed to be crazy.

Priest. Oh yes? Do you believe that?

Simón. I don't believe anything. He said you were going to come.

Priest. All right, Simón. *(He points to the door.)*

Simón. What for?

Guadalupe. To come with me.

Pingitori. And the sewing machine? Are you going to leave it?

Guadalupe. I'll be right back, dear.

Simón. (Begging) Don't leave me, princess, don't leave me.

Guadalupe. (Calming him like a baby) I'll be right back, my love.

Pingitori. (To the PRIEST*)* Princess. *(With a smile)*

Priest. Aha.

Simón. (Defiantly) I call her that sometimes, because I love her. I have so many different names for her. So what are you going to do? Punish me for that?

Priest. Who's talking about punishing? *(Suddenly)* You are.

Pingitori. If that were all.

Priest. (To PINGITORI*)* Please leave. *(At first* PINGITORI *looks at the* PRIEST *with surprise, but then, as if a sinister look of complicity had crossed between them, he agrees.)*

Pingitori. All right.

Simón. (Noticing the look) Don't take me, Doctor.

Priest. Who is going to take you? *(Torturing, sadistic, but very calm)* You're going to come all by yourself.

Simón. Where to?

Priest. Wherever you want. But leave. They are waiting for you there.

Simón. Why should I leave?

Priest. Weren't you going to leave together? (GUADALUPE *enters with a big rope and goes to the suitcase that since the beginning of the play has always been next to the sofa, untouched by anyone. It always gave the room the air of someone just passing through and always on the verge of going on a trip. Firmly to* SIMÓN) What can you do?

Simón. I can recite the *Song of Songs* for you.

Priest. That's no good.

Simón. I can dream while I'm awake.

Priest. (*Murmuring with a strange and sarcastic voice*) Where you're going, you won't be needing that.

Guadalupe. Why not?

Priest. Where were you heading for?

Guadalupe. To take the train. (*She grabs the suitcase, winds the rope around it and ties it.*)

Priest. What do you have there?

Simón. Junk. You can have it.

Priest. A train to where?

Guadalupe. Just leave us alone, please.

Simón. Yes. What do you want from us?

Priest. Ah. (*Sadistic smile*) So, I won't ask any more questions. (*Pausing and putting his hands in his pockets*) All right. (*He takes out a cigarette holder and puts in a cigarette while the other two look helplessly at him.*) I wanted to help you, but . . . (GUADALUPE *looks at* SIMÓN *and moves towards the door.* SIMÓN *follows her. Two male* NURSES *wearing white coats and hats block the door.* SIMÓN *and* GUADALUPE *stop.*)

Simón. (*To the* PRIEST) Help us.

Priest. (*Resumes the interrogation indifferently*) Where were you going?

Guadalupe. To Berezategui.

Priest. That's what I like. So you were running away from me? From us?

Simón. No, I swear I wasn't.

Priest. (*Playing with the cross that hangs from his neck*) You were going to begin again. You were running away, isn't that it?

Simón. (*Nervously pointing to the nurses*) Please, make them leave.

Priest. (*Ignoring him*) But you can't escape. (*To* GUADALUPE) Are

you out of your mind? You were going along with him . . . Both
of you just wanted to do whatever you felt like. Don't you know
he's doomed?

Simón. To what!

Priest. To have visions, to hear things. And it can't go on like this.
He's locked up here all day. Doesn't he ever work? You have to
work. If you don't work, then you're sick in the head.

Simón. Jesus.

Guadalupe. You're no doctor.

Priest. (Smiles perversely) And in this place full of saints, you're
a Jew. Do you think that these saints were going to stop me?
(Bursts out) They have no power over me!

Simón. My God. *(Closes his eyes, screaming)* How can I get out
of here?

Guadalupe. I want to die. I want to die.

Priest. Come to me. (GUADALUPE *crosses herself, looking at the*
PRIEST *as if she were in front of the devil.)*

Guadalupe. God damn you!

Simón. (Smiling nonchalantly) Let the worldly kingdom that you
have promised me come forth.

Priest. So, you wanted to begin again? To be free? To be a man?
(Ironically) You wanted to change, move. *(Emphatically)* Let's
go, Simón.

Simón. Where?

Priest. Where were you planning to go now?

Guadalupe. I'm not going to say one more word to you.

Priest. But I know. I know everything. To the house of a friend of
yours, Right, Señora? The one who makes pants. To take any
job, right? To get lost in the country. That's right, isn't it? *(The
room gets darker.)*

Simón. What's that? *(Through the door his* FATHER *and a* CHILD
enter.)

Guadalupe. What's the matter, Simón? *(Taking his hands)* Be
calm, my love. Don't give up. Don't be fooled by them. We're
together. *(Whispering)* We're going to escape from here. We'll
beat them, we'll beat them.

Simón. I don't want to see them.

Father. (To the CHILD) Let's go Simón.

Simón. (Shouting) Take away these ghosts, Lord, give me strength,
give me your sword of fire.

Father. (To the CHILD) Do you see, Simón? *(They walk to the center of the darkened room where the only spotlights are on* SIMÓN

and the rest of the characters. The lights follow them as they walk.) I'm going to teach you what we came into the world for.

Child. Is it all right here?

Father. Yes.

Child. (Kneeling) And where is the lamb, Papá?

Father. God will give us one. *(He ties the* CHILD*'s hands behind him. He does the same thing with the* CHILD*'s feet. Then he blindfolds the* CHILD*. It takes no time to do it. Then he takes a long and shiny knife out of his pocket.)* He knows what He is doing. Repeat with me. Lord . . .

Child. Lord . . .

Father. Here I am.

Child. Here I am.

Father. Once again, like so many times before, I am going to be yours.

Child. Once again, like so many times before, I am going to be yours. *(The* FATHER *pulls the* CHILD*'s head so far back that the neck remains free. Then he lowers the knife.)*

Clamorous voice. No, don't do it! *(The* FATHER *throws away the knife and takes the* CHILD *in his arms and squeezes him, sobbing.)*

Simón. (Shouts) Are you crazy? And if the angel hadn't stopped you? And if he had been a second late?

Father. (Calmly looking at SIMÓN, *the man)* Fornicator. *(Then he unties the* CHILD*'s feet and hands, picks up the knife and puts it away.)* There are millions for whom the angel never arrived. *(Blackout on the* FATHER, *and spotlight only on* SIMÓN.)*

Simón. And if there are millions that the angel always arrived late for, what is it to me? How long can we wait for your angels, Lord? I don't want any more ghosts. I'm sick of them.

Priest. (His own voice) You are condemned to fight them like Jacob fought the Angel.

Simón. Sometimes I believe that there is no angel up there. *(Defiantly)* Yes, sometimes I feel it here. *(He bangs his chest.)*

Priest. (His own voice) That's your own business. Besides, your story is very insignificant. No one is interested in it. You're crying for something that's not worth it. *(He laughs.)*

Simón. (Shouting) Don't I even have the right to ask for my own dream of greatness? Don't I even have the right to fulfill it?

Guadalupe. Let's go, Simón. Let's get out of this room. Let's go outside.

Simón. I abandoned the House of David. And for that they're going to punish me until I die? But no, I didn't abandon it. Like you,

Jesus, I want the spirit, not the letter. Not these Pharisees, not these hypocrites. (GUADALUPE *holds him tightly.*)

Priest. *(His own voice)* The ship is in your hands. Here no one is persecuting you. You are your own fury. Go down to the street, just go ahead. Who's not letting you? *(Laughing)* Me, yes, me, because I have come to take you.

Simón. Not to the mental hospital, not there, please. *(The light returns to its normal brightness.)*

Priest. Who's talking about that? No, I've come to take you back to your old house.

Simón. What do you mean to my old house?

Priest. There's a house, a woman, and some children waiting for you. There's a dirty jewelry shop on Calle Libertad. There was a little man in the window. What crazy obsessions got into his head? That little man was you . . . Go back to your place. *(He walks around* SIMÓN *as he talks to him.)* You can't break away. Everything in its proper place. And yours is there.

Guadalupe. Let's go.

Simón. Don't leave me . . .

Guadalupe. Let's go Simón. Let's go to the street together.

Simón. Yes, others did it. Other Jews could assimilate, they could become men. It happens every day and no one ever went crazy.

Priest. Others did, but not you.

Simón. But I can't return to Yehúpets.

Priest. What do you mean? I'm taking about Calle Libertad, dinners with your wife, a car, a house, payments, trinkets, costume jewelry, fifth class smuggling, that's your place.

Simón. No it's not. My father was a prince. Every man is a prince. What brought me here? A dream of princes.

Priest. Your father was the owner of that second-hand shop and he died for you, some hell of a prince he was! Not a doctor, not a professional, you didn't finish anything, that's how he made it in America, in that second-hand store, and that's your place, too. Come on, let's go.

Simón. No, no.

Guadalupe. Let's go now, Simón.

Priest. Oh, so you don't want to? You want to go to the mental institution then? Well? (GUADALUPE *clings to him and* SIMÓN *to her. He looks at her. Suddenly he moves away from her. He begins to get undressed.)*

Guadalupe. What are you doing, Simón? Get out, get out. Go on. (SIMÓN *takes off the jacket, the shirt, the tie, the pants and the shoes. While he does all of this, a deathlike bell tolls. With great dignity he opens the trunk. He takes out his Knight of the In-dies suit.)*

Simón. Let two chamberlains dress me.

Guadalupe. No, no, no.

Simón. (To the PRIEST*)* America, the city of the Caesars? It's down here, imbecile. I found it and no one else knows the way. And what are you waiting for to dress me? There's electric shock, beatings and 1001 nights of howling madmen waiting for me out there. *(The* PRIEST *signals the two* NURSES *who are going to dress him. One puts on the doublet, the other, the tights.)*

Guadalupe. (Begging) Let's go outside, Simón, the two of us against all of them.

Simón. What? Could this hell be any worse? And the hell outside, what's it like? What do you do there? How do you live without voices and without guilt? They're all crazy, all of them. *(The* NURSES *put on his boots that reach his calves. Then the false beard, then the sword.* GUADALUPE, *seated on the bed, moans.* PINGITORI *enters.* SIMÓN *goes to the* PRIEST *and he removes the cross from his neck.)* You are not worthy. *(He puts it on himself.)* From one Jew to another. *(He goes to* GUADALUPE.) Don't be sad. I wasn't meant for you, don't be sad. Christ is in my blood. He will enlighten you.

Priest. (Scornfully) Luftmentsh.

Simón. Luftmentsh, that's what Papá was, a man of the air, who lives and doesn't want to change and leave any trail behind. What did you leave? What am I leaving? No, excuse me. There's no comparison. I'm leaving this palace. *(With great dignity he goes to the wall, pulls down the Shell station map that displays Chantania, and rolls it up. The* NURSES, *still waiting, go to him.)*

Guadalupe. No, leave the Knight alone, leave him alone. His head aches. Don't bother him, don't touch him. *(*SIMÓN *goes to the suitcase, takes the chest and gives it to* GUADALUPE, *along with the map.)*

Simón. Take it, Lupe. It's for you, gold and sapphires.

Guadalupe. What are they going to do to you?

Simón. (Smiling) Cure me. Of what, though? I'm already in a state of grace. *(Caressing the cross)* What they'll never know is that I'm a true Knight of the Indies and that I'm going to outlive them all. My lands are immense. *(Delirious)* I have a ranch as big as an entire country. *(Stops and returns to reality)* Let's go, the men don't have that much time. *(He takes the cape and wraps himself in it.* SIMÓN *looks at the room, taking leave of it all. He doesn't dare look at* GUADALUPE. *He leaves.* GUADALUPE, *crushed, remains seated on the bed.* PINGITORI *looks at her. Finally* GUADALUPE *raises her eyes and looks at him.* GUADA-LUPE, *tearful, closes the suitcase and leaves without looking back.* PINGITORI, *seated heavily in a chair, makes a move as if to follow her, but then lowers his head. He is all alone. He raises his head and looks at the audience.)*

Curtain

NOTES

1. *Juan Díaz de Solís* (d. 1516): traditionally considered the discoverer of the Río de La Plata.
2. *Shiksah* (Yiddish): gentile woman.
3. *Khokhem* (Yiddish from Hebrew): intelligent man.
4. *Luftmentsh* (Yiddish): daydreamer.
5. *Che*: Argentine slang for buddy, or also "hey you."
6. *Talmud*: body of Jewish civil and ceremonial law and legends comprising the Mishnah and the Gemara.
7. *Elisha Ben Abuia*: Talmudic scholar.
8. *Hu kafar binetiot* (Hebrew): literally, renegade from his religion.
9. *Haggadah*: narration read during the Passover *seder* (celebratory meal), which includes historical and Talmudic references.
10. *Salada:* a lagoon with salt water located in La Pampa.
11. ORT: international organization for the promotion of skilled trades and agriculture among Jews.
12. *Moshavah*: an agricultural training camp for Jewish youth who planned to immigrate to Israel between the 1940s and 1960s.
13. *Kibbutz*: a communal farming settlement in Israel.
14. *Jota*: popular dance from Aragón, Spain.
15. *Meshugener* (Yiddish): crazy, mad.
16. *Florins, doubloons, maravedis:* ancient Spanish coins.
17. *Shimeleh* (Yiddish): diminutive for Simón.
18. *Peyes* (Yiddish): long sidelocks worn by some Orthodox Jews.
19. *Bobe* (Yiddish): grandmother.
20. *Yarmulka*: skullcap.
21. *Yehúpets*: small town in Russia.
22. *Verstas*: a Russian measurement of 1,067 meters.
23. *Pánio* (Russian): mister.
24. *Copulare cum bestias et ánimas* (Latin): to have intercourse with beasts and people.
25. *Ruble*: Russian currency.
26. *Tzitzis* (Hebrew): the fringes of entwined threads worn by Orthodox Jews at the corners of their outer garments and at the corners of the tallis.
27. *El mole* (Hebrew): "El mole rakhamim"; part of a Hebrew memorial prayer.
28. *Vade retro*: Latin expression used to ward off a person or thing.
29. *Adonoy* (Hebrew): Lord.
30. *Sheigetz* (Yiddish): gentile young man, can have a negative connotation for a non-Jew.

31. *A grober young* (Yiddish): an unrefined person.

32. *Tallis or Tallith* (Hebrew): a prayer shawl of wool or silk with fringes at the four corners worn around the shoulders by Orthodox Jewish men.

33. *Shul* (Yiddish): synagogue.

34. *Zeyde* (Yiddish): grandfather.

35. *Vehavto eloihekho komoiho, bekhol levovkho, bekhol nafshekho ubekhol meoidekho* (Hebrew): And you will love your God with all your heart, with all your soul, and with all your being. From the *Shema Yisroel,* the prayer affirming the monotheistic principles of Judaism, recited three times a day.

36. *Marrano*: Jew in Medieval Spain who simulates acceptance or accepts Christianity, especially to avoid persecution.

37. *Anchorenas*: the surname of a powerful landowning family in Argentina.

38. *Adoremus pro nobis* (Latin): Pray for us.

Jorge Goldenberg: *Krinsky*

JORGE GOLDENBERG (BUENOS AIRES, 1941)

Equally acclaimed in the fields of drama and cinema, Goldenberg has worked extensively as a director, scriptwriter, and producer, and has been awarded numerous prizes for his screen writing and his theatre. His film *Reportaje a un vagón* (Interviews on a railway car) received a prize in the first Festival of Latin American Documentary Cinema.

He co-adapted the film version of Alberto Gerchunoff's stories *Los gauchos judíos* (The Jewish gauchos). He also wrote the adaptation of several films: *No toquen a la nena* (Don't touch the girl), *Hoy-cine-hoy* (Cinema today), *Juan que reía* (Laughing John), *Sentimental* (from a novel by Geno Díaz), and *Plata dulce* (Fast money), which was awarded the Filmwriters' Association Prize. He has also worked on the scripts of *La película del rey* (The king's movie), *Miss Mary, Sostenido en la menor* (A sharp minor), and *Pasajeros de una pesadilla* (Passengers in a nightmare).

Goldenberg began his dramatic career with "Argentine Quebracho Company," written with Danilo Galasse. This play was followed by "Fifty-fifty" (from improvisations by actors Miguel Guerberof and Patricio Contreras); *Rajemos, marqués, rajemos* (Let's get out of here, Marquis); the highly successful *Relevo 1923* (Relay 1923), awarded the Casa de las Américas Prize in Cuba in 1975; "Un país muy verde" (A very green country), presented by the Young People's Ensemble of the Payró Theatre; *Knepp; Poniendo la casa en orden* (Putting the house in order); and *Cartas a Moreno* (Letters to Moreno), which grew out of improvizations developed during rehearsals of the Young People's Ensemble. His adaptations of the classics for the Argentine stage include Shakespeare's *Measure for Measure* and Ibsen's *The Pillars of Society*.

Krinsky was written in 1977 while Goldenberg was in exile and has received numerous awards: the Union Carbide Prize for Theatre in 1983; the María Guerrero Prize from Spain and the Argentores Prize from the Argentine Writers' Union, both in 1986. In

Jorge Goldenberg

"Krinsky" and "Luba" in a scene from *Krinsky* by Jorge Goldenberg

"Krinsky," "Luba," and Harpo Marx in a scene from *Krinsky*

1993, the play was successfully presented in several French cities, including Paris and Lyon.

The playwright's choice of a Russian Jew in the New World as a protagonist reflects his nostalgia for the fate of the old immigrant after a long life of struggle. Dreams of the past and the ghosts of the dead gradually take over Krinsky's life. We learn about Krinsky, the historical character who inspired Goldenberg, from the prologue to the play, entitled "The Other Krinsky." He was a librarian at a Jewish institute and a traveling photographer who also wrote poetry, both in Yiddish and in Spanish.

As one of the theatre reviews from Argentina states, "Krinsky is a survivor on the map of memory."[1] Once an inspired revolutionary, in his old age Krinsky feels humiliated for being sick and poor, living among people he considers strangers, in a country that remains forever foreign to him. Luba, his lifelong friend and one great love, is now his only provider of occasional scraps of food. She has an obsession about cleanliness; at one point she literally picks Krinsky up like an old rag and sweeps him out of her way. His daily visits to Luba's store are filled with his endless discourses on the past (which Luba summarily dismisses), his stories of fighting in the Russian Revolution alongside Isaac Babel, and their endless arguing, which actively involves the audience as each one invites the public to take sides.

Where Krinsky is pathetic and amusing, Luba is practical and critical of everything Krinsky is, and does. Strange visitors come to Luba's store, all parts of Krinsky's and Luba's shared past: a Cossack; Harpo Marx, a grotesque, mute embodiment of the burlesque tradition in Jewish Hollywood; the mother; the actor who calls forth rich associations with Jewish performers from Eastern Europe in Argentina's theatre; two thugs who personify anti-Semitic persecution both in the Old World and in the New, at a period when xenophobia and chauvinism in Argentina could be captured in the slogan "Haga patria, mate a un judío" (Be a patriot, kill a Jew); and finally, the gentile girl, an idealization of the love Krinsky could realize only in his dreams.

At the close of the play the images of Krinsky's past reemerge. His "supposed" death is reenacted by a chorus of figures and by fragments of his memories, representing the complexity and the contradictions of his life. An original and amusing touch occurs when Krinsky suddenly jumps out of his casket and decides that he does not want to die yet, even if it was "the perfect death."

The linguistic elements in the play are provided by language switching. Readers can find most of the Yiddish expressions used throughout in the author's appended translated footnotes. In watching the drama, however, the non-Yiddish speaking audience depends purely on the translations that the characters alternately make for each other, or in the expressions used to paraphrase and explain what has been said. They resort to Yiddish because it best expresses the particular feelings they wish to convey. The bilingual dialogue results in an overlap of the two languages. When Krinsky expresses himself in Yiddish he makes no effort to make himself understood by the audience, since he has always emphasized his alienation from a culture that he considers foreign to an immigrant like himself.

Krinsky is also a love story of a stubborn man who dwells in his bittersweet memories, always faithful in his love for Luba, although she married someone else. The powerfully lyrical ending of the play—when Luba finally admits to hearing what Krinsky has always heard, the echo of horses on the Russian steppes—allows memory to triumph over the sordid present, creating a touching and melancholy moment.

NOTES

1. Rómulo Berruti, "'Krinsky', un sobreviviente en el mapa de la memoria," *Clarín,* Buenos Aires, June 3, 1986, no page.

The Other Krinsky

That other Krinsky (whose first name was Adolf, according to Argentine documented sources) died in 1977. In San Martín they maintain that his body was found two days after his death, lying on his bed and dressed in his grimy overcoat. They add that between the lining and the cloth of his coat outdated one-peso notes were sewn. There is disagreement regarding the meaning of those worthless notes; some say that they were good for increasing the insulation of that deteriorated piece of clothing; others just as easily attribute it to some perverse and senseless form of greed.

It is also said that he was buried just the way he was found, since no one dared undress him, and that a meticulous diary of his life—written in elegant Yiddish calligraphy—had been consumed by rats and moths.

I witnessed none of these events or conjectures since I was living in Caracas at the time, but I remember having known that original Krinsky as a child, when I was about ten years old. In fact, I must have met him even earlier, since all the iconography intended to give everlasting life to my parents' early years (particularly my mother's), my own childhood, and that of my brothers, comes from the photographs taken by that man. But the truth is that my memory recreates him with some clarity in his position as librarian of the "Mendele Cultural Home of San Martín" (previously known as the "Jewish Cultural Center of San Martín"). This Krinsky was not satisfied fulfilling the routine administrative demands of his job. At the very least, he was a functionary with an opinion. He not only decided what titles should be added, but also, mainly for the benefit of those of us who were beginners in the uncertain pleasure of reading, he attempted to impose his judgment on matters of aesthetics.

Thanks to the pressure he exerted on me, I read Dickens, Ehrenburg, Alexandre Dumas, and Eugenio Tarle's *Napoleon*. He never succeeded in making me read the Jewish authors in the original Yiddish, perhaps because the voyage through that literature was imposed on me for twelve years at a secular Jewish school. This decreased my pleasure in such readings—a pleasure which I tried to regain with great difficulty many years later.

During those years, whenever Krinsky was mentioned, one thought of him as a bachelor before any other judgment about him was passed. In spite of the tacit respect that a "scholarly man" enjoys among Jews, he was not greatly loved. His unkempt appearance, the darkish color of his fingernails stained by the acid of his photographic work, his awkward gesticulations, his bold scorn for ignorance, and above all, his inscrutable life as a bachelor in the small room he rented from Don Julio, inspired more ridicule than curiosity. I must imagine that among men, that attitude resulted from the ambiguous scorn provoked by any man who reaches a certain age without having known a woman. Among children like myself it went no further than frank, though carefully hidden ridicule. As far as the way women treated him, I can only imagine they showed a more compassionate attitude, along with veiled, erotic overtones.

All fantasy aside (that would not correspond to that Krinsky), I can affirm that the man showed some dignity. When, for reasons of ideological purity, the institution attempted to impose an advisor to assist him in the purchase of books, Krinsky submitted his resignation as a proper gentleman would. It would be tempting to link this episode to the beginning of what in San Martín became known as his "period of decadence," but it would be just a skillful way of obviating the gaps in my own memory and, even worse, of not admitting the minuscule interest I had for him at that time.

What I can attest to with certainty is that much later I met that same Krinsky again at my parents' store. His aspect revealed—in the minutest detail—the same features of the unkemptness of twenty-five years earlier as well as the visible traces of a stroke.

That morning I carried on me a volume of Isaac Babel's *Odessa Tales,* which I had been reading on the bus. Almost without returning my greeting, that Krinsky insisted that I tell him information about the book I was reading. Awkwardly and quite condescendingly, as if Babel's name were known only to a sect of the initiated, I gave him the information he requested, ignoring his unfamiliarity with the book. His comment was clear and unequivocal: "Babel . . . Why of course, he used to ride two rows behind me in the Budyonny Red Calvary. . . ."

The truth or fiction of his affirmation cannot be proven, but it is possible that at that moment the gestation began of that other Krinsky who has attempted to inhabit the following pages with some authority.

Regarding the other Krinsky, as with this one, let me add that perhaps he truly deserved the disturbing blessing of requited love.

Buenos Aires, January 1984

Poems Written by Adolf Krinsky

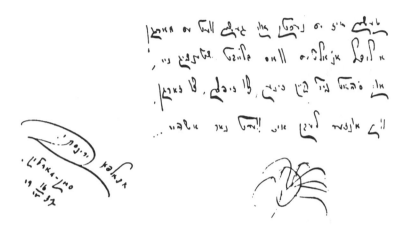

"Ocurrió ayer y ocurrirá mañana:
es una vieja canción, nueva por siempre,
y no tienen sentido gemido y congoja
si nuestra vida sólo vale un escupitajo."

It happened yesterday and it will happen tomorrow
It's an old song, yet always new
Crying and sorrow make no sense
If our life isn't worth the spittle.

A Lía:

18 Abriles? — La época bella,
Gratos recuerdos nos quedan de ella,
Recuerdos de sueños de mil fantasías
Las que cantan poetas en sus poesías...

Noches de luna, de amor, de ternura,
Tiempo de dicha — y también de locura.
En nuestra memoria, lo queda grabado,
Como algo sublime, como algo sagrado...

Y en el ocaso, al pasar de los años,
Que el tiempo nos roba, que nos hace daños
Buscamos consuelo en los recuerdos preciosos
Del lejano pasado, de los tiempos dichosos...

Adolfo Krimsky.

San Martín 19 V 41.

To Liah

Eighteen Aprils?—the beautiful time
Fond memories remain
Memories of a thousand dreams
That bards sing in their poems . . .

Moonlit nights of love and tenderness
Time of joy and of madness
Remain imprinted in our minds
Like something sublime, like something sacred . . .

And in the twilight,
With the passing of the years
While time robs us, wounds us.
We look for comfort in beautiful memories
Of the distant past, of joyful times . . .

San Martín, 10/19/41

Krinsky

Krinsky opened on May 30, 1986. It was a coproduction of the Teatro Payró and the Teatro Municipal General San Martín, Buenos Aires.

List of Characters
Krinsky
Luba
Cossack
Harpo Marx
Mother
Actor
Thug 1
Thug 2
Girl

One Act.

One Set.

Except when stated, all foreign phrases are in Yiddish.

A mesh curtain through which the inside of a store that sells cookies and canned goods can be seen. KRINSKY *appears from offstage. He is a short man in his seventies. He limps slightly, probably a result of hemiplegia. He looks dirty, but he hasn't "dirtied himself." His appearance is the product of a deliberate neglect of personal hygiene, like a patina that covers his body and his clothes, somewhat greasy and full of dull brilliance. He leans on a cane. He wears a cap with a visor, an oversized suit, a shapeless shirt that was once white, and a tie with a knot that was made to last forever. The heels of his shoes are shredded and he's missing shoelaces. His ripped socks reveal the dirty heels of their owner. He speaks fluently, although he pronounces the guttural "r" like the Jews of Eastern Europe. He drags around a huge old sack with difficulty. He stops on one side of the mesh curtain and speaks.*
Krinsky. *(To the audience)* She'll be here very soon. My name is
   Krinsky and I'm trying to be calm. *(Indeed* LUBA *does appear*

from the opposite side. She is a woman in her sixties. Her hair is almost totally white. She is somewhat heavy but energetic. She wears a purple skirt, and a blouse that emphasizes her hips, broadened in the course of time. She wears beige shoes with low heels, stockings, and woolen socks. She comes in carrying a shopping bag and humming a waltz.)

Luba. *(To the audience)* He's there for sure already . . . waiting . . . who knows how long . . . since he says he doesn't sleep anymore.

Krinsky. (To the audience) Now she's going to speak in Yiddish.

Luba. An *idyot, a ganstener idyot.*[1]

Krinsky. (To the audience, somewhat ashamed) I suppose no translation is necessary . . .

Luba. (To the audience) But why doesn't he come in once and for all? Why the same farce each and every time? If he's really going to come in . . . *vus makht er zikh interesant? Ver iz er, Graf Pototzki?*

Krinsky. (To the audience) She says why do I put on airs. Do I think I'm Count Pototzki? Me, Count Pototzki . . . That's how she treats me. But today I'm not going in . . . *(Somewhat ashamed)* . . . not yet anyhow . . .

Luba. (To the audience) Bobe mayses![2] He's going to go in and he's going to sit down on that little bench and he'll fill my head with stupid tales of Czar Nicholas's times, and he'll chase away my customers with that stinking smell of his.

Krinsky. (To the audience) You're going to agree with me that I can't allow such behavior. I have to . . . I'm going in now and I'll tell her, because this can't go on. *(He meekly enters the shop and walks towards the small bench that* LUBA *pointed out earlier.)* . . . Good morning . . .

Luba. (To the audience) I told you so. *(To* KRINSKY*)* Try to lift your legs because I'm going to mop the floor.

Krinsky. (Trying to lift his legs) How are things?

Luba. You already know how things are. I told you to lift your legs.

Krinsky. (Pointing to his left foot) This one . . . I can't do it . . . *(*LUBA *moves closer to him and with rough movements she pushes* KRINSKY'S *left foot through the cross-bar of the bench. To the audience)* She's doing this on purpose.

Luba. (To the audience) He likes it.

Krinsky. (To the audience) How can I like it when I can't feel anything in this foot?

Luba. (To the audience) He does feel something. *(*LUBA *returns to her job. After a painful pause,* KRINSKY *speaks in a low voice.)*

Krinsky. I don't want the paper today.

Luba. What?

Krinsky. I said I don't want the paper today.

Luba. *(Without interrupting her work)* There it is, underneath you.

Krinsky. I told you already, I don't want the paper today!

Luba. All right. *(She persists in her chore.* KRINSKY *tries to relax and to adopt a casual look, but it's useless. Finally, he picks up the paper.* LUBA *notices it. To the audience) Vus macht er zich narish?*

Krinsky. *(To the audience)* She says, what do I pretend to be, a fool? I don't pretend to be a fool. I'm trying to be calm. I . . .

Luba. You're a grown man now, you're half dead and you should have learned to behave yourself by now, and not to roam the streets *vee a betler!*[3]

Krinsky. Don't speak in Yiddish . . . they *(pointing to the audience)* don't understand . . .

Luba. They understand, they understand . . . and if they don't understand, it's better for you, you'll be less ashamed. *(To the audience)* Do you believe he's poor? Oh well. Poor he's not. He goes about like this because he likes it. He says he doesn't have time to bathe because he needs to think. But I bet he's got his pension and he must have hidden . . .

Krinsky. *(Interrupts her)* Luba, *vus darft ir dertseln?* . . . *Ikh beyt aykh zeyer* . . .[4]

Luba. *(To the audience)* Do you hear him? He speaks Yiddish. When he has to ask me not to tell you, he speaks in Yiddish.

Krinsky. (To the audience) And why not? Yiddish is a language, it's not just gibberish like some people go around saying. Yes sir! It's a full-fledged language, with its literature, its spelling rules, its declensions. It's something very interesting; it was born in the ghettos of Germany in the sixteenth century.

Luba. *(Interrupts abruptly)* Who cares? Just tell me! Why do you go on talking and talking? *(To the audience)* He thinks that because he was once a librarian and read many books the whole world has to know it . . .

Krinsky. I'm a photographer.

Luba. *(Corrects him spitefully)* You were a photographer.

Krinsky. I was many things . . .

Luba. Sure! Of course! *(To the audience)* Take out a pencil and write this down: he was a photographer, a Bolshevik soldier, a prisoner, an immigrant, a prisoner again, a librarian, a starving man. You can add it all up now. What's the score? What is he now? A useless old bachelor.

Krinsky. (*To the audience*) A woman like her shouldn't speak that way . . . it sounds so vulgar . . .

Luba. Vulgar, schmulgar! It's the truth!

Krinsky. It's not the truth!

Luba. All right. It's not the truth, but what is the truth? C'mon, tell us. We're all here, listening.

Krinsky. (*After a pause*) Please, I want to walk. Get me out of here.

Luba. The floor is still wet and your shoes are dirty.

Krinsky. (*To the audience*) . . . and now she'll take pity on me and offer me a cookie . . . but this time, this time she'll finally realize who she's dealing with, this time . . .

Luba. (*Handing him a cookie*) Take a cookie (KRINSKY *doesn't react.*) What's the matter? Are you deaf too?

Krinsky. (*To the audience, after taking the cookie and putting it in his mouth*) I'm a wretch . . .

Luba. Don't talk with your mouth full, you slob. I just cleaned the floor and you're dirtying it with crumbs. (LUBA *leaves.*)

Krinsky. (*To the audience*) Perhaps I haven't earned the right to ask you for anything. I was too inconsistent. But if you still can do it, believe this: today I'll be an eagle. An eagle! And she, she . . .

Luba. (*Returns with a bucket and a mop*) Talking again? (*To the audience*) What big deal has he been telling you about?

Krinsky. (*Ashamed and watching the public's reaction out of the corner of his eye*) . . . nothing, just nonsense . . .

Luba. And what else could you tell them?

Krinsky. I want to walk.

Luba. Wait until I finish cleaning up the mess you made. (*As she mops the floor,* LUBA *accidently bumps into* KRINSKY'S *sack.*)

Krinsky. Be careful! It's fragile.

Luba. What garbage are you carrying in there?

Krinsky. My camera.

Luba. *Oy!* I'm going to faint! Are you going back to work?

Krinsky. Why not?

(*Suddenly a* COSSACK *in Marshal Budyonny's Red Cavalry barges in. He is wearing a fur cap and an immense cape that reaches almost to his ankles. He wears two cartridge belts across his chest and an old Mauser. He is the living image of the Russian posters of the twenties. He looks somewhat disheveled. There are bloodstains and traces of gunpowder on his face. His attitude is exultant, happy and rather authoritarian. He appears, like the other characters, from some unexpected corner of the stage. In fact, all the characters remain on stage throughout the play, yet their presence is not noticed by the audience, except in the form of shadows or silhouettes, until they become part of the action.)*

Cossack. Where's the photographer?

Luba. (To KRINSKY*)* What kind of drunks are you bringing me now?

Cossack. (To LUBA*)* Who's the photographer, Grandma?

Luba. Grandma my ass!

Krinsky. I'm the photographer.

Cossack. You? (KRINSKY *replies with a half humble, half bashful gesture. The* COSSACK *gives him the once over and laughs. He comes closer to him and sniffs him.)* You stink.

Luba. Because he never takes a bath. And from what I can see, neither do you.

Cossack. We have no time, Grandma. We can't give the Whites a rest.

Luba. I'm not your grandma, hooligan!

Cossack. (He laughs at KRINSKY.*)* C'mon, old man. Take my picture. Fast!

Krinsky. (To LUBA*)* Please, help me down from the bench.

Luba. Let the drunkard take you down.

Cossack. C'mon already! *Iop tvu iu mat!*[5] (KRINSKY *tries to get down, but he can't manage to dislodge his left foot because he refuses to use his hands, and he falls with a crash. The* COSSACK *laughs.* LUBA *comes to* KRINSKY'S *aid.)*

Luba. (To the audience) Old "Ivan" is laughing . . . *(To* KRINSKY*)* Let me help you.

Krinsky. I can do it myself. Leave me alone.

Luba. I'll leave you alone. I'll leave you alone. You can also drop dead alone for all I care.

Krinsky. (Back on his feet after a great effort) Don't take offense, Luba . . .

Luba. Me? That's all I need, to take offense. Let me tell you, I have no time for that.

Cossack. What are you waiting for, old man?

Krinsky. (Opening his sack) I'm coming!

Cossack. (Impatiently and with rough movements he helps KRIN-SKY *take out his old camera and tripod from the bag.)* Ready. Let's go.

Krinsky. Spakoyna,[6] things have to be done right. *(Hands the* COS-SACK *a comb and a piece of rag. The* COSSACK *takes them and laughs as he tidies himself up, cleaning his face and combing a lock of hair peeking out from under his cap.)*

Cossack. I like you, old man. I see you know your job. Let's get started now.

Krinsky. (Puts his head under a black cloth. The COSSACK *poses as if he were in a poster.* KRINSKY *gives him directions on where to stand until he is satisfied that he's in the right place.)* Hold it.

Cossack. (He moves just as KRINSKY *is about to shoot.)* Wait a minute! Do you know how to write?

Krinsky. I know how to take photographs.

Cossack. Don't confuse me, old man. Do you know how to write or don't you?

Krinsky. Of course I do.

Cossack. Then write me a big sign that says "Soviet Power Is Here!" so that you can see it well in the photo. *(To* LUBA*)* Hurry up, Grandma, get me some paper and paint!

Luba. I'm not your grandma and I don't have those things.

Cossack. (In response he picks up a piece of red cloth and gives it to KRINSKY*.)* I could slit your throat for being so cheap.

Luba. You could also slit my throat just because you feel like it.

Cossack. (Laughing heartily) It's true! You have brains, Grandma, you do . . . *(To* KRINSKY, *forcefully)* Write this down in a nice handwriting! I can't read, but I can tell whether a handwriting is nice or not. *(*KRINSKY *does as he's told. He carefully writes down an inscription in Cyrillic letters. Suddenly, the* COSSACK *interrupts him, lifting him up by the arm until he is almost suspended in the air.)* Don't you dare write any garbage because if you do I'll strangle you! With these hands of mine I'll strangle you! *(To* LUBA*)* Don't be afraid, Grandma. You know what happened? On Kolia Rybakov's photograph they wrote, "I'm a son of a bitch." When they killed him in Zhitomir, I picked up all his things and I was about to send them to his family when the Commissar happened to pass by. And it wasn't just anybody. He read the sign and right away he ordered me to cut Rybakov's photo from the rest of the picture. What a pity; it was a beautiful photo. But you couldn't send it like that to his family. It would have been a disgrace for him and for the Red Army . . . *(To* KRINSKY*)* So you better watch out, old man!

Krinsky. (Without taking his eyes off his work) It wasn't in Zhitomir . . .

Cossack. What do you know?

Krinsky. It was in Lublin . . . I was there . . . *(The* COSSACK *is surprised. He walks over to* KRINSKY *and looks him in the face, lifting his head up by the chin.)*

Cossack. You were there? *(He studies him carefully. Then he lets go of him kindly and speaks to him almost tenderly.)* How old you've grown, comrade . . . How could it be?

Luba. (Interrupting) Why don't you just hurry up! *(To the audience)* Some nice show for the customers.

Krinsky. (Putting the finishing touches on the sign) It's ready.

Cossack. (Admiring the inscription) Molodietz! Molodietz!⁷ *(The* COSSACK *poses again, this time raising the sign.* KRINSKY *puts his head back under the black cloth of the camera.)*

Luba. (To the audience) Now tell me, really, with friends like this, how can he be different? And not that he's stupid, mind you, he's a whiz . . . but he has no practical sense. If he were a little more practical, he would have gone to an old age home already. Calm, well-looked after, very clean, waiting for death like you're supposed to.

Krinsky. (To the COSSACK*)* Ready?

Cossack. Ready.

Krinsky. On your mark . . .

Cossack. Hooray!

Krinsky. (Shoots the photo with the magnesium flash) It's done.

Cossack. If they don't kill me, I'll come for it tomorrow. *(Approaches* KRINSKY *again and kisses him on both cheeks)* Thank you, comrade. *(Kisses* LUBA *in the same way)* To your health, Grandma. Long life to you! *(Pointing at* KRINSKY*)* And pay him the respect he deserves, he's a very brave comrade. *(The* COSSACK *leaves in a hurry.* LUBA, *disgusted, wipes her cheeks. Right after that, she takes the sign that* KRINSKY *painted, crumples it and throws it in the garbage. Almost at the same moment the* COSSACK *reappears.)*

Cossack. (To KRINSKY*)* You're a Jew.

Krinsky. That's something you don't choose . . .

Cossack. (Smiling joyously) Don't worry! *(To* LUBA*)* And you neither, Grandma. It's all past! With Soviet power, you won't be Jews anymore! *(After declaring what he believes to be good news, the* COSSACK *leaves.)*

Luba. Ikh kak oyf die freyd!⁸

Krinsky. Please Luba, don't talk like that . . . *(To the audience)* . . . She said some vulgarity which I'm not going to translate because . . .

Luba. I said the truth! I shit on that happiness! *(Referring to the* COSSACK*)* He's an animal, a brute and an anti-Semite!

Krinsky. It isn't so . . . . it's . . . he had an idea . . .

Luba. A shitty idea!

Krinsky. Please, Luba . . . he died sixty years ago . . .

Luba. So much the better!

Krinsky. Don't say that *(To the audience)* I loved him . . . I always wanted to be like him.

Luba. (To the audience) Do you see? Do you see what I told you? Do you see who he uses as an ideal? What good were all the books he read? *(She returns to her obsessive cleaning. After a brief pause,* KRINSKY *recites in a monotone.)*

Krinsky. "With a confusion of happenings
　　　and a tangle of events
　　　little by little
　　　day turned into shadows.
　　　Two in the room,
　　　me
　　　and Lenin.
　　　A faded photograph . . ."

Luba. (Interrupts, laughing) You and Lenin no less? Lenin had nothing else to do but pay attention to you? *(To the audience)* Did you hear that? Lenin and him. *(To* KRINSKY*)* Do me a favor, eat another cookie and shut up.

Krinsky. I was reciting a poem by Mayakovsky.

Luba. May he rest in peace.

Krinsky. He committed suicide.

Luba. He probably had nothing better to do.

Krinsky. Why do you make fun of everything, Luba?

Luba. I'm not making fun of anyone. I'm busy. *(*LUBA *keeps on cleaning.* KRINSKY *watches her uneasily. From time to time he takes a furtive glance at the audience.)*

Krinsky. How's your husband?

Luba. Fine, thank you.

Krinsky. He's not coming in today?

Luba. No.

Krinsky. So you'll be by yourself.

Luba. (To the audience) A genius, didn't I tell you?

Krinsky. Sorry, I'm saying stupid things today.

Luba. How about yesterday?

Krinsky. Probably yesterday, too.

Luba. (To the audience) At least he's honest.

Krinsky. Today I came for a special reason.

Luba. To tell me you're going to take a bath.

Krinsky. To tell you something.

Luba. You said it already. You can leave now.

Krinsky. Something important.

Luba. You always think you say important things.

Krinsky. (*To the audience*) I could very well take offense and I would be more than justified.

Luba. (*Standing right in front of* KRINSKY, *surprising him*) So, okay, say it once and for all.

Krinsky. (*Terrified*) What?

Luba. Weren't you going to tell me something important?

Krinsky. Of course.

Luba. So, say it.

Krinsky. Very well, Luba . . .

Luba. Yes.

Krinsky. Luba . . .

Luba. (*To the audience*) You've got to give him some credit. He's learned my name by now.

Krinsky. (*To the audience*) It's not so easy . . . (*To* LUBA) it was almost fifty years ago . . .

Luba. (*Interrupting*) Fifty years ago I wasn't I and you weren't you.

Krinsky. Listen to me Luba . . .

Luba. I'm listening, I'm listening.

Krinsky. No, no . . . I don't want to force you . . . If you prefer . . .

Luba. Say it, say it once and for all. What are you waiting for? (*After a brief pause during which* KRINSKY *only manages to make awkward gestures,* HARPO MARX *bursts in with a clamor. He blows his horn and stands before* LUBA *with a very broad smile.*) Oy! Another one! What do you want? (HARPO *answers by blowing his horn and gesturing.*) What do you want?

Krinsky. . . . he doesn't talk . . .

Luba. If he wants a handout tell him to come when my husband is here. ("*Offended,*" HARPO *produces an endless string of sausages from the pockets of his huge raincoat and offers them to* LUBA. *She reacts in total surprise.*)

Krinsky. (*He explains to her.*) He doesn't want charity. He's Harpo . . . Harpo Marx . . .

Luba. Doesn't he have any other place to go? (*Meanwhile* HARPO *has brought his harp and passionately starts playing a fragment of Liszt's Hungarian Rhapsody No. 2. The first few bars are followed by a concentrated silence.* KRINSKY *anxiously watches* LUBA'S *reactions, as she gradually becomes more relaxed. It is obvious that the music moves her.*)

Krinsky. (*Unable to contain himself*) Did you hear it? Did you hear how beautifully he plays?

Luba. Shh . . .

Krinsky. You like it, right? (LUBA *doesn't answer.* KRINSKY *insists.*) It moves you . . . It is clear that it moves you . . .

Luba. (On the verge of tears) Please be quiet.

Krinsky. I'm quiet, I'm quiet . . . shhh . . . *(When the music ends,* LUBA *is clearly moved.* HARPO *looks at her with a smile of complete satisfaction. But suddenly, without transition, he guides her hand to his thigh, repeating the routine he uses in several of his films.* LUBA *detaches herself mechanically, without fully registering the sensuality implied in* HARPO'S *move, concentrated as she is on the suggestive voluptuousness of the music.* HARPO *persists in his behavior as* KRINSKY *looks on anxiously. This time, however,* LUBA *notices what* HARPO *is doing and, disgusted, violently shakes him off.)*

Luba. What are you doing? Have you gone crazy?

Krinsky. (To HARPO*)* She doesn't like it. She doesn't like it at all. *(*HARPO *looks at* KRINSKY *but insists on having his thigh fondled. To* HARPO, *shouting)* I told you no!

Luba. (Drily) Tell him to leave.

Krinsky. Can't he stay a little while longer?

Luba. No. *(Before* KRINSKY *manages to say anything,* HARPO *leaves, completely heartbroken, dragging his harp behind him. Only then does* LUBA *express her irritation.)* Disgusting wretch! *(To the audience, referring to* KRINSKY*)* And he doesn't really know him, he didn't know him . . . he never knew him!

Krinsky. . . . but he plays beautifully . . . you liked it . . .

Luba. Me? *(To the audience)* Did you hear him? *(To* KRINSKY*)* I don't like that trash.

Krinsky. (To the audience) You saw her. She was crying.

Luba. (To the audience) Me crying? Me? *(She touches her eyes with her fingers.)* Dry, you see? All dry! Me crying! Please . . . *(To* KRINSKY*)* Don't talk such nonsense, will you?

Krinsky. Forgive me . . . it seemed to me . . . you were moved by the music.

Luba. Of course I'm moved by music, but not by the music of that crazy man. *In der heym,* back in my village, when I was young . . . that was music. When *Kol-Nidre*[9] was sung in the *shul*[10] even the officers at the garrison, those anti-Semitic dogs, came to listen and with such respect! And when the garrison band played . . . that was music; you would even forget they were *goyim;*[11] . . . *(To the audience)* I know, I even know it before he tells me; you don't know what the word *goyim* means. All right, a *goy* is just one; *goyim* are many.

Krinsky. Many what?

Luba. Many *goyim;* many of the others ones . . . *(To the audience)*

And I swear to you that band played so well that you would forget who they were.

Krinsky. You never forget.

Luba. Over there I used to forget.

Krinsky. And how about here?

Luba. What do you mean here? Where are we?

Krinsky. Where are we?

Luba. You tell me.

Krinsky. You said "here."

Luba. All right. "Here" is another awful place. Are you satisfied now?

Krinsky. (After a pause) Tell me, Luba . . . before . . . you were moved, right?

Luba. You're starting with that again?

Krinsky. A little . . . just a little bit . . . but weren't you moved . . . admit it . . .

Luba. What's the matter with you today, Krinsky?

Krinsky. What's wrong with admitting that you were a little moved?

Luba. And what if I was?

Krinsky. S'vet mir zayn besser.[12]

Luba. (To the audience) Do you get it?

Krinsky. They don't get it because they don't understand Yiddish.

Luba. (To the audience) He says that he'd feel better if I admit that the music of that madman moved me. *Nu? Vi gefelt aykh?*[13] *(To* KRINSKY*)* All right. Suppose I agree, what's going to happen?

Krinsky. (Reassured) It already happened.

Luba. What happened?

Krinsky. It happened to me.

Luba. (To the audience) That one should reach an age to say such things . . . frankly, it isn't worth it. He talks for the sake of talking. Because he's alone all day, by himself, so he comes here and talks . . .

Krinsky. I'm not alone.

Luba. Don't tell me someone had the guts to go to your room.

Krinsky. I have my rats. I feed them from my hand.

Luba. (Disgusted) Don't be such a pig! *(To the audience)* That's the way bachelors always end up . . . *(To* KRINSKY, *amused)* Tell me, Krinsky, why didn't you ever get married?

Krinsky. You know.

Luba. How am I supposed to know? Did you ever tell me anything?

Krinsky. If you'd think about it, you'd know.

Luba. If I thought about it, I'd tell a couple of things you wouldn't like.

Krinsky. (Terrified) No, no . . . please . . .

Luba. (To the audience, laughing) What do you think about this big shot?

Krinsky. I didn't say I was brave.

Luba. The Cossack said . . .

Krinsky. That's another kind of bravery.

Luba. Tell me the truth, you never found a girlfriend?

Krinsky. (Almost provocative) Sure I did.

Luba. So?

Krinsky. So . . . better we should talk about something else.

Luba. (Amused) Do you know what my husband says? That you laid the prettiest girls on your bed . . . in photos . . . you laid them there to get dry . . . *(Laughing)*

Krinsky. Your husband is an idiot.

Luba. (To the audience) There! What do you think? A real rooster, no?

Krinsky. (Suddenly sorry) Luba . . .

Luba. (To the audience) What have you got to say about my guest?

Krinsky. Luba . . . I didn't.

Luba. (Savagely) You didn't what? Stop stuttering already.

Krinsky. I didn't mean to offend . . .

Luba. How about that? I must be a complete fool. My whole life I believed that "idiot" was an offensive word . . . It's only because I feel sorry for you, otherwise, you don't step foot in here with your filth and your foul smell!

Krinsky. Forgive me . . . *(He makes a clumsy, apologetic gesture which causes a bottle to fall down and break.)*

Luba. (Viciously making fun of him) "Forgive me . . . forgive me . . ." What else are you planning to break? *(She exits.)*

Krinsky. (To the audience) Is that all there is to me? You already heard what I was . . . what I could have been . . . I beg you, be patient with me . . . What agony, *Got mayner,*[14] what agony . . . *(He recites a fragment from the* Song of Songs *as if addressing* LUBA.*)*
"Open to me, my sister, my love,
my dove, my undefiled:
For my head is filled with dew,
and my locks with the drops of the night . . ."
(The MOTHER *appears. She is an old lady dressed in dark clothes, a kerchief on her head. She looks like a pious Eastern European Jew. Her movements are slow but precise. She recites*

her part of the Song of Songs *as she approaches* KRINSKY *and she strokes his hair.)*

Mother. "I have put off my coat.
How shall I put it on?
I have washed my feet;
how shall I defile them?"

Krinsky. (Smiling sadly) Ot bin ikh, alt un troyerik . . . [15]

Mother. Veyn mein kind, veyn . . . ruik . . . [16]

Krinsky. (Pointing to the audience) Zey kukn . . . [17]

Mother. Zolen zei kukn, vos hartes dir?[18]

Krinsky. (To the audience) My mother tells me to cry and not to worry what you may think . . . but I do worry, I always worry.

Luba. (Comes in and resolutely faces the MOTHER.) Can I help you, Señora?

Mother. (To KRINSKY*) Kikhlach.*[19]

Krinsky. (Nodding) Kikhlach.

Luba. I asked you what you want.

Mother. I don't speak your language.

Luba. You can see that I understand you anyway. What do you want?

Mother. Cookies.

Luba. Cookies?

Mother. Cookies . . . *(While* LUBA *offers her various sorts of cookies, the* MOTHER *questions her.)* . . . How old are you?

Luba. How about you?

Mother. I have run out of years.

Luba. So have I. Here are your cookies.

Mother. (Points to KRINSKY*)* Is the gentleman with you?

Luba. What do you mean "with me"?

Mother. I mean . . . is there anything between him and you . . . *(Luba laughs heartily.)*

Krinsky. (Furiously, rebukes the MOTHER*)* What are you saying? What are you saying?

Mother. (To LUBA*)* He seems to be a good man . . . an honest man . . . *(*LUBA *keeps on laughing.)*

Krinsky. (To the MOTHER*)* Shut up.

Luba. Which cookies do you want?

Krinsky. She doesn't want any cookies.

Luba. (Brutally, to KRINSKY*)* Then she should leave.

Krinsky. (To the MOTHER*)* Please, leave . . .

Mother. Are you throwing me out?

Luba. (Laughing, to the MOTHER*)* You heard it right. He's a strong-willed man.

Mother. Don't treat him like that . . . he's a delicate person . . . As a child he couldn't fall asleep at night if I didn't hold his hand . . . I had to sleep with gloves on because the winter was so cold . . . He's a delicate soul . . .

Krinsky. (Annoyed, to the MOTHER*)* I am not a delicate soul. And I don't need anyone to stick up for me.

Mother. All right then, so I'm leaving.

Luba. (Ferociously) And what about the cookies?

Mother. (Crying as she exits) He says I don't need cookies.

Krinsky. (Follows his MOTHER *as she exits)* Don't cry . . . don't cry please . . . *vein nisht, ikh beyt dikh* . . . [20] *(The* MOTHER *doesn't listen to him and exits. A desolate* KRINSKY *speaks to* LUBA*.)* That was my mama . . .

Luba. A customer is a customer. I don't ask anyone for their papers.

Krinsky. Do you know why she came?

Luba. To buy cookies.

Krinsky. No.

Luba. (Harshly) Then why?

Krinsky. (To the audience) I can't say it just like that, so fast.

Luba. I'm waiting for you to answer me . . .

Krinsky. I never sent her the ticket . . . she stayed behind and the Nazis killed her.

Luba. (Goes back to her cleaning and straightening) Sooner or later she would have died just the same. We all die . . .

Krinsky. Your whole family too . . .

Luba. (Annoyed, to the audience) Why does he have to talk about that?

Krinsky. (To the audience) Because . . .

Luba. (Violently, to KRINSKY*)* Because you're morbid, that's why.

Krinsky. No . . . I just remember, that's all.

Luba. And you think that I don't have any memories? Every day, every hour, every minute. So tell me, Lord of Filth, what do I do about that?

Krinsky. I . . .

Luba. (Implacable) Tell me what I'm supposed to do right now. Give me a good answer or get out of here. *(*KRINSKY*, who has once again climbed onto the bench, doesn't answer.)* So? What's the matter? Have you lost your tongue?

Krinsky. Get me down, I'm leaving.

Luba. You can get down by yourself.

Krinsky. No I can't.

Luba. Then crawl down. *(*KRINSKY *gets off the bench with diffi-*

culty and starts to leave. He walks a few yards. LUBA *softens.)* Where are you going? (KRINSKY *doesn't stop.* LUBA *addresses the audience.)* So where can he go? To feed the rats?

Krinsky. (To the audience) I want to leave for good.

Luba. (To KRINSKY*)* Come here. I need you to help me. *(To the audience)* I'm not really that bad . . . I can't stand to see him like that . . . *(To* KRINSKY*)* Come over here, Krinsky.

Krinsky. (Stops, addresses the audience) I'm not coming.

Luba. Come on, you help me and then you can go. (KRINSKY *looks at the audience as if to apologize beforehand for his imminent change of heart.)* What are you waiting for?

Krinsky. For you to say please.

Luba. Otherwise you won't do it?

Krinsky. No.

Luba. All right then, *zol zayn,*[21] please.

Krinsky. (To the audience) But afterwards I'll be going.

Luba. Of course. *(To the audience)* He's like a puppy, poor thing.

Krinsky. (Addresses the audience, as he walks back) I'm just a mess.

Luba. (Energetically, she climbs a stepladder next to a shelf.) Start handing me those boxes. (KRINSKY *complies. He does everything slowly, trying not to make any mistakes. Amused, to the audience)* Nu?[22] What do you think of my assistant?

Krinsky. (Offended) Look, you asked me to . . .

Luba. You're right!

Krinsky. (Pointing to the audience) Tell them that you asked me.

Luba. (To the audience) I did ask him. So now they know it, I even said "please." *(To* KRINSKY*)* Are you satisfied?

Krinsky. (More humiliated than satisfied, keeps on working. After a moment he can't stand the silence.) What if I tell you a joke?

Luba. If you like . . .

Krinsky. No, no, if *you* want me to.

Luba. All right. Tell it.

Krinsky. (To the audience) She wants me to. You're witnesses . . . *(To* LUBA, *enthusiastically)* Okay, a Jew unexpectedly meets another Jew he knows in Nepal . . .

Luba. Where?

Krinsky. In Nepal.

Luba. What's that?

Krinsky. A country.

Luba. Where is it?

Krinsky. (Impatient to continue) What does it matter where it is?

Luba. I don't know, whatever you say. *(To the audience)* He wants to tell a joke but he talks crazy and he can't stand it if anyone asks him a question.

Krinsky. (To the audience) She's the one who wanted me to tell it!

Luba. So tell it already.

Krinsky. Two Jews meet in Nepal. One asks the other, "What are you doing here, so far away . . . ?" And the other one says, "Far from where?" (KRINSKY *waits for* LUBA *to laugh, but she never does.*)

Luba. So you think that's a joke?

Krinsky. It's a joke.

Luba. It's pathetic, it's not a joke. *(Unexpectedly, an* ACTOR *from the old Jewish vaudeville theatre bursts in. His appearance reflects a poorly concealed decadence. He could be an actor-master-of-ceremonies from the last cabarets of the Warsaw Ghetto. He still retains a certain sparkle in his gestures, a certain professional elegance in his movements, inevitably spoiled by clumsiness and forgetfulness. Nevertheless his showman's smile is indelible.)*

Actor. You're mistaken, Señora! It is a joke, and a very good one. It's almost a classic.

Luba. Look here, don't butt in!

Actor. Right now I'm going to tell you another one. Once there was . . .

Luba. (Interrupts him) I don't want to hear anything!

Actor. (To KRINSKY*)* What's the matter with this woman? *(To* LUBA*)* Let me sing something for you then . . . *(At a sign from the* ACTOR, *a familiar cabaret theme is heard.)*

Luba. (Screaming) Oh, no! *(The music stops.)*

Actor. What will it cost you? A potato? A carrot? I'm telling you, in the Warsaw ghetto I charged much more, even in the worst of times . . . Oh, what a time that was!

Luba. I don't want to hear anything.

Actor. There's something wrong with you.

Luba. Get out of here. You're dead.

Actor. Did I say I was alive?

Luba. I don't talk to dead people.

Actor. Are you afraid of me?

Luba. You don't exist.

Actor. Precisely! There's nothing to be afraid of, Señora . . . Let me tell you something . . . for nothing.

Luba. (To the audience) Why don't they leave me alone?

Actor. You don't want to talk about your family. You don't want

anyone to tell you jokes. There's something wrong with you
Señora. You better do something about it.

Luba. I'm just fine!

Actor. Then why are you screaming?

Luba. (*Controlling herself*) I'm not screaming.

Actor. That's what I like, Señora. (*Suddenly a curtain is heard
going up. The* ACTOR *arranges* LUBA'S *hair, skillfully paints her
lips, straightens her clothing, moves her towards the stage and
presents her to the public.*)

Actor. Damen und Herren![23] Wielmonznye panye![24] Khosheve[25]
guests! Please welcome, for her one and only performance . . .
(*Trumpets sound*) . . . Madame Luba! (*At the* ACTOR'*s signal,
the music begins and* LUBA *starts to sing with a certain shyness
that wears off as she continues.*)

Luba. (*Sings*) *Kinderlakh kumt nor aher do tzu mir*
Ikh vel aykh a mayse dertseyln:
Es hobn tsvey brider gazlonim gevoynt
in fintsern vald in di heyln . . .
(*As she finishes the first verse, the instrumental music is heard,
and* KRINSKY *translates the lyrics for the audience. He is moved
and proud of* LUBA'*s performance.*)

Krinsky. It's an old children's song that goes more or less like this:
Children, come close to me.
I'll tell you a story.
Once upon a time there were two brothers
who were thieves,
and who lived in a cave in a dark forest . . .

Luba. *Eyner fun zey iz a yunger geven,*
der tsveyter an alter a blinder.
Der alter flegt zitsn un hitn di heyl,
der yunger flegt geyn khapn kinder . . .

Krinsky. (*Translating*)
One of them was young.
The other was old and blind.
The old one stayed home to guard the cave.
The young one went out to kidnap children.

Luba. *Eyn mol in a fintsterer nakht . . .* (*The music keeps playing
but* LUBA *stops singing. She seems distracted. The* ACTOR, *distraught by the pause, makes a sign for the last bar to be repeated. Then* LUBA *repeats the verse.*) *Eyn mol in a fintsterer
nakht . . .* (*The music continues, but* LUBA *stops.* KRINSKY, *in
desperation, talks to the audience.*)

Krinsky. I'm going to take advantage of this momentary lapse to translate that verse . . . It says that once, on a dark night . . . *(He gestures to* LUBA *but she walks off the stage. The music stops.)*

Actor. A shud! A shud!²⁶ It was going on so well.

Luba. Please get out.

Krinsky. Not yet.

Actor. I have to tell a joke. I need . . .

Luba. But then you'll go.

Actor. Afterwards you'll ask for more. In the ghetto they never let me leave the stage . . .

Luba. Hurry up.

Actor. (Pulls himself together and enthusiastically begins to tell his joke) It's like this. An Armenian, tired of being outsmarted by a Jew, tells him this riddle. It's very funny. He says to him . . . Listen to this . . . he says . . . *(The* ACTOR *becomes sad and can't continue.)* It's not really very funny, you know?

Krinsky. But if it's very good, tell it!

Actor. No.

Krinsky. (Furious) Tell it, damn you!

Actor. Forgive me. I can't. She's right. I'm definitely dead and I don't matter at all . . . *(The* ACTOR *starts to leave.* KRINSKY *holds onto him trying to keep him from leaving, but the* ACTOR *gives him a shove and* KRINSKY *falls on the floor.)* I'm sorry, *brooder,*²⁷ I'm sorry . . . *(He exits.* KRINSKY *is still lying on the floor.* LUBA *comes over to help him get up, but* KRINSKY, *unexpectedly violent, doesn't let her.)*

Krinsky. Don't help me! *(More gently)* I want to stay like this . . . *(*LUBA *sighs and gestures to the audience, indicating the enormous amount of patience that* KRINSKY *demands. She returns to her cleaning as she looks from time to time at* KRINSKY. *After a pause* KRINSKY *addresses the audience from his position on the floor. He points to the sky.)* When I was young I used to make a deal with Him: ten years of my life in exchange for fifteen minutes, five hundred years later . . . A stupid thing, I should have known that there's no one to talk to . . . Believe me, there's no one to talk to.

Luba. What are you going to do now, Krinsky?

Krinsky. I'll stay here.

Luba. (To the audience) Just as long as he doesn't get it into his head to drop dead . . . *(To* KRINSKY*)* Do what you want, but don't go and die on me here.

Krinsky. Why not?

Luba. Because you just don't do that in a store. *(To the audience)*

You have to talk to him like a child. (KRINSKY *doesn't move. To the audience*) He's moving; he's alive. *(To* KRINSKY*)* All right. That's enough now. You got what you wanted. Now get out. (KRINSKY *doesn't move.)* You're in the way. This is a business, people come here. Everything has to be clean here. *(She tries to push him out of her way with the broom but she can't. Finally, she has no choice but to drag him by his clothes, trying to get over the disgust she feels from such close contact with him. With a great deal of effort she drags him to a corner. She is very annoyed as she speaks.)* Ugh! A *shmutsike khaye!*[28] *(She looks at her hands with disgust and exits.)*

Krinsky. (To the audience) Do you know what she called me? Filthy beast . . . a filthy beast. (KRINSKY *gets up with difficulty and shaking his head, exits. Almost immediately she returns, drying her hands.)*

Luba. Listen Krinsky . . . *(She looks around, then at the audience.)* Don't tell me he left . . . *(She looks all around the store.)* Krinsky! Krinsky! *(To the audience, somehow surprised)* He actually left! *(She resumes her work although with somewhat less energy.)* That's really something, isn't it? . . . People can get used to anything . . . Well, I did everything I could for him. And not just now, always, since I first knew him. Before, it was another story. He was nice . . . but that's not really the right word. He was . . . original! That's it, original . . . *(An anxious* KRINSKY *appears from a corner listening to* LUBA'S *words and begging the audience, through signs, not to let on that he's there.)* One thing, though: ugly, he was always ugly. A bogeyman . . . but that didn't matter. You would laugh with him. What didn't I do to get him a girlfriend? I arranged get-togethers and parties. But he was very proud. He made fun of everything. He thought he was superior . . . Once he asked a girlfriend of mine, poor thing, if she believed in free love. She, *nebekh,*[29] the only thing she wanted was to get married. The truth is that it didn't matter much to her with whom, *abi*[30] a marriage. You know, an older girl, a very good girl . . . She was ashamed already . . . poor parents . . . When Krinsky said free love she asked him what he meant and the scoundrel told her. Later he came to tell me that my girlfriend fainted. And the two of us had a good laugh. The truth is he said it like a joke, to scare her, because he didn't really believe in those things. He was always a decent sort . . . (KRINSKY *interrupts, complaining.)*

Krinsky. (To the audience) It's not true. I did believe in those things!

Luba. I thought you were gone.

Krinsky. I was leaving.

Luba. And what stopped you?

Krinsky. The lies that you're telling them about me. *(To the audience)* I believed and still believe in free love.

Luba. Oh yeah? And what does that mean? Explain it to me.

Krinsky. (Warming up) All right. Let's take you for example.

Luba. (To the audience) How stupid of me. Why did I have to ask him?

Krinsky. You already have your man, no? (LUBA *shakes her head in resignation.)* Very well. Let's suppose that at the same time you have something with me.

Luba. (Overly precise) What do you mean, "something"?

Krinsky. You know . . . something . . .

Luba. I don't know a thing. You're the one who says you know.

Krinsky. (To the audience) I'm getting there. *(To* LUBA*)* All right. You want something . . . and so do I.

Luba. I don't know what you mean.

Krinsky. That you have to do it and no one should feel guilty about it. *(To the audience)* There, I said it. I said it to her! *(To* LUBA*)* So, what's your answer?

Luba. To what?

Krinsky. To what I just proposed.

Luba. My answer is that your head doesn't know what your mouth is saying, that you talk to hear yourself talk, that the books you've read unfortunately got all mixed up in your brain, that the best thing would be for you to go to an asylum, to take a bath and not to come here anymore with crazy stories, because I want some peace. Just get out of here once and for all!

Krinsky. (To the audience, while he exits with some shreds of dignity) Now I'm really going. *(But when he is about to walk out the door a pair of* THUGS *stop him. They are wearing long raincoats, wide-brimmed hats and generally conjure up the stereotyped image of Gestapo agents.* THUG 1 *grabs* KRINSKY *by the neck while* THUG 2 *keeps guard in front of the door.)*

Thug 1. This time you won't escape, you creep! (THUG 1 *drags* KRINSKY *to the bench and pushes him down brutally.* LUBA *is about to react but* THUG 2 *takes out a pistol and threatens her.)*

Thug 2. Take it easy or I'll kill you, old lady.

Luba. I'm going to call the police.

Thug 1. (Laughs heartily) Just try it!

Luba. Farsholtene fashistn![31]

Thug 1. (To KRINSKY, *while he sizes him up)* So, you're the famous

Krinsky, the big-mouth little Russian. *(He struts around.* KRIN-SKY *remains calm and dignified.)* You're just a piece of shit. But I have to admit that you do have some talent . . . We've spent years looking for you, but you'd disappear and then you'd turn up where no one expected you.

Krinsky. It's not that I'm so talented . . . It's just that you guys are stupid.

Thug 2. Calm down, little Russian. Don't get too chatty.

Thug 1. All right, let's get to work. We've got a lot to talk about.

Luba. He doesn't have anything to say to you!

Thug 1. You're going to talk too. *(He pulls some Yiddish newspapers out of his coat and waves them in* KRINSKY'S *face.)* What does it say here?

Krinsky. Just what you read.

Thug 1. No one can understand these filthy scribbles. What does it say?

Krinsky. Di kapitalistishe ordenung guet fatal tsu ir untergang.

Thug 1. (Patiently) And what does that mean?

Luba. He wrote it a long time ago!

Krinsky. No, I wrote it today!

Thug 1. What does it mean?

Krinsky. (Defiantly) The capitalist order is marching fatally towards its downfall. *(*THUG I *is surprised. He feels strangely uneasy. He asks in an almost intimate tone)*

Thug 1. How did you come up with that?

Krinsky. It's a scientific fact.

Thug 1. Are you sure?

Krinsky. Quite sure.

Thug 1. And when is it going to happen?

Krinsky. Soon.

Thug 1. (Exasperated) When?

Krinsky. (Very proud) Soon.

Thug 1. And what's going to happen to me then?

Krinsky. You're going to die.

Thug 1. And if I let you go?

Krinsky. You're going to die anyway.

Thug 1. But if I let you go! I can say I never found you . . .

Krinsky. It doesn't depend on me . . . It's a matter of history.

Thug 1. What do you mean, history?

Thug 2. Just pull the trigger and don't waste your breath.

Krinsky. History records everything.

Thug 1. Lies! The only one who remembers everything is God!

Krinsky. Suppose that's true, how are you any better off because of it? *(Out of control,* THUG I *smacks* KRINSKY *in the face.)*

Luba. Don't hit him! Do you hear me?

Thug 2. (Covering LUBA'S *mouth with the gun)* Quiet, my love, quiet.

Thug 1. (Waving the newspapers in KRINSKY'S *face)* Who wrote this?

Krinsky. I did, you already know that.

Thug 1. Who else?

Krinsky. No one else.

Thug 1. (Grabbing him by the hair) Who else is involved in this?

Krinsky. (Impassively) No one else.

Thug 1. You're lying.

Krinsky. Right.

Thug 1. (Pulling his hair even harder) Where is this printed?

Krinsky. I'm not going to tell you.

Thug 1. Don't be so sure . . . *(He points to* LUBA.) Who's she?

Luba. I'm Luba.

Thug 1. (To LUBA) I didn't ask you. *(To* KRINSKY) Who's she?

Krinsky. She doesn't have anything to do with this.

Thug 1. I asked you who she is!

Krinsky. I don't know.

Thug 1. (Putting the barrel of his pistol against KRINSKY'S *head)* Talk or I'll finish you off. You know I could easily do it. I'll count to three. One . . . Two . . . *(*LUBA *unexpectedly gives* THUG 2 *a hard shove, leaving him dazed as she shouts to* KRINSKY.)

Luba. Now! *(With an unsuspected skill,* KRINSKY *strikes* THUG I'S *arm, forcing him to drop his pistol.* LUBA *picks it up while* THUG I *throws himself on* KRINSKY. LUBA *fires and* THUG I *falls dead.* THUG 2 *rushes for his gun but* LUBA *shoots first, killing him too. After a tense moment,* KRINSKY *gets off the bench with difficulty and goes over to the bodies. He listens for their heartbeats.)*

Krinsky. They're dead.

Luba. (Comes over to him) Help me with the bodies. We've got to get rid of them, no? *(*KRINSKY *helps* LUBA *to drag the bodies further inside the shop.)*

Krinsky. Thanks, Luba . . . You just risked your life for me . . .

Luba. Shut up and get to work.

Krinsky. We'll have to get out of here.

Luba. We'll see.

Krinsky. We'll have to change identities . . You'll put on a wig and dark glasses and I'll take care of fixing up the passports.

Luba. Just stop talking and help me. *(They leave the "bodies" inside the shop.)*

Krinsky. Let's get out of here. They can come any minute. We have to cross the border before dawn . . .

Luba. That's enough, Krinsky.

Krinsky. But we're in danger. Let's see. Let me figure it out . . . They do a patrol every two hours . . . in two hours . . .

Luba. Stop, Krinsky.

Krinsky. (Desperately) We can't stay here!

Luba. It's all right. Didn't you hear me?

Krinsky. Yes . . .

Luba. And don't do this to me again. Do you hear me?

Krinsky. Are you sorry?

Luba. That doesn't matter. But don't do it again. *(She picks up the newspapers that were left scattered all over. To the audience)* At least they're good for wrapping boxes.

Krinsky. Luba, give me the pistol.

Luba. For what?

Krinsky. I'm leaving. *(To the audience)* I have to get out of here . . . I don't want to, but if I'm caught everything will be in danger. *(To* LUBA*)* Don't worry Luba . . . If they get me I'll say that I killed them.

Luba. Thank you very much. I didn't expect anything less from a gentleman like you.

Krinsky. Maybe we'll meet again. But if not, if something happens to me, I want you to know that I always . . . *(To the audience, excusing himself)* I don't have any time, they might come at any moment. (KRINSKY *exits. Almost immediately a* GIRL *appears. She is around twenty years old. She is dressed elegantly in stylish European sports clothes from the 1930s. Everything in her bearing reveals the innocent arrogance of a young woman who knows she is loved. It is natural arrogance, in no way irritating or provocative. She is simply happy with herself.)*

Girl. Good morning, Señora.

Luba. Good morning.

Girl. Could you please call Mr. Krinsky?

Luba. He's not in. He doesn't live here.

Girl. But he'll be back. He hasn't gone away forever, has he?

Luba. I don't know.

Girl. It would be horrible.

Luba. (Alarmed) Why?

Girl. I have to see him.

Luba. What for?

Girl. You won't make fun of me?

Luba. Why should I make fun of you?

Girl. Because I assume a lot.

Luba. I'm listening.

Girl. (Shyly) I don't know how I had the nerve to come. Look at me. I'm trembling.

Luba. Why?

Girl. Can I be frank with you?

Luba. Try me.

Girl. I think I'm in love with him.

Luba. (Upset) You're lying. (KRINSKY *returns, hurriedly.*)

Krinsky. No *(to the audience),* you heard her. *(To the* GIRL*)* Say it again!

Girl. (Bewitched) Mr. Krinsky. Dear Mr. Krinsky.

Krinsky. (To LUBA*)* "Dear Mr. Krinsky," did you hear that? "Dear Mr. Krinsky."

Luba. (To the audience) He shouldn't have done this to me.

Girl. (To KRINSKY*)* Can I give you a kiss? *(*KRINSKY, *very moved, accepts with a humble nod. The* GIRL *kisses him first with modesty and then passionately.)* You don't know how long I've waited for this moment. *(She falls into* KRINSKY'S *arms again.* LUBA *quickly pulls her away with a shove.)*

Krinsky. Why? Why?

Luba. Because it's a lie. And because you shouldn't do this to me. *(The* GIRL *cries silently.* KRINSKY *tries to console her. To the audience)* She was beautiful, wasn't she? A flower . . . Maybe I shouldn't be the one to say it. *(Suddenly she checks herself.)* What an idiot! What am I telling you these things for if you won't believe me anyway? How could you believe me? Better just forget it. *(She goes back to cleaning.)*

Krinsky. No! *(He drags the* GIRL *toward the stage and tries to show her off in front of the audience. The* GIRL *complies, but she can't help looking back at* LUBA *with growing interest. To the audience)* Look at her, please!

Luba. (To the audience) Forget it, just forget it . . . What do you want to remember for?

Krinsky. (To the audience) Don't listen to her. *(To the* GIRL, *almost violently, making her face him)* Don't listen to her! I want you to kiss me again. *(The* GIRL *does it, but mechanically. Her attention is on* LUBA.*)* Not like that! Like before!

Luba. (To the audience) She won't be able to.

Krinsky. (To LUBA*)* Yes, she will! *(To the* GIRL*)* She doesn't know anything. She doesn't really know you. You'll have to begin all over again.

Luba. Don't waste your time, Krinsky . . . *(The* GIRL *speaks to* LUBA *without leaving* KRINSKY'S *side.* KRINSKY *desperately moves her arms to make her embrace him with passion as if the* GIRL *were a puppet.)*

Girl. Did you ever get married?

Krinsky. What does that matter? It doesn't mean a thing! Marriage is a bourgeois institution!

Girl. (Gently to KRINSKY*)* Wait a moment, Krinsky.

Krinsky. I can't wait.

Luba. (To the GIRL*)* If I tell you it was for love, will you believe me?

Girl. Yes. I wouldn't have done it for any other reason.

Luba. You were very proud then.

Girl. Yes.

Luba. That was what he liked.

Krinsky. (Clumsily embracing the GIRL*)* Me! You have to talk about me!

Girl. (To LUBA*)* What happened afterwards?

Luba. Afterwards? I don't know. It was all too fast.

Girl. What was he like? How was he?

Luba. He was beautiful.

Girl. I remember . . .

Krinsky. (He protests, full of anguish.) It's not true! That's an arbitrary affirmation. Beauty isn't an absolute. In Africa . . .

Luba. Light eyes, thick moustache . . . He would stand there in silence and look at you . . .

Girl. Yes . . . Yes . . .

Krinsky. (To the GIRL*)* We used to ride at night. We used to ride with fury and perfection.

Girl. (To LUBA*)* When is he coming back?

Krinsky. Never! You have to listen to me. I used to ride a sorrel mare with a star on her forehead.

Girl. (To LUBA*)* Would he recognize me?

Luba. Sometimes, each time a little less.

Krinsky. An arrow flying over the steppes!

Girl. I love him.

Krinsky. (To the GIRL, *more and more desperately)* Listen to me, please. The cavalry marshal said to me: "Comrade photographer . . ."

Girl. (To LUBA*)* I love him, isn't that so?

Luba. I think so . . . I think it's inevitable. (LUBA *and the* GIRL *embrace.)*

Krinsky. (Almost defeated) "You over there, comrade photographer, you're the best rider in the whole Red Cavalry. . . ." (KRINSKY *slowly exits humming a cavalry tune. Suddenly, the* GIRL *goes towards* KRINSKY *before he can leave. She takes his hands.)*

Girl. What should I do, Krinsky? It's not right that I introduce myself to you and say, "I'm in love with you . . ." A decent girl wouldn't do that . . . He'd have to say it to me. Isn't that so?

Krinsky. When you came in you said you were in love with me.

Girl. You know it wasn't true.

Krinsky. You said it. Everyone heard it.

Girl. I'm asking you, please . . . Tell me what to do . . . You're a sensitive man.

Krinsky. I'm not sensitive! I'm mean! I'm jealous! I'm cruel and violent! *(The* GIRL *laughs.)* I'm capable of killing!

Girl. (To LUBA*)* Mr. Krinsky is charming . . .

Krinsky. (Shouting) No! *(Unexpectedly, he removes the pistol from his pocket that* LUBA *used to kill the thugs. He points it at the* GIRL*.)* And now? What do you have to say to me now? *(There is a moment of great tension.)* It's over! It's all over. *(Wearing a fierce expression,* KRINSKY *fires . . . But only a trickle of water comes out of the pistol.* KRINSKY *becomes deeply depressed. The* GIRL *notices it.)*

Girl. Believe me, I'm sorry . . . I'm sorry . . .

Krinsky. I'm an eagle.

Girl. Of course, of course you are. *(She kisses him on the cheek.)* Goodbye . . . *(She exits.* KRINSKY *watches the* GIRL *leave. Then he speaks to the audience.)*

Krinsky. What more can I do? Tell me, without faith what can an old man do? *(From the semidarkness, as if in response to the question, the* ACTOR *hisses at* KRINSKY. KRINSKY *tries to determine where the sound is coming from.)*

Actor. Psst! *Kum aher . . .* [32] *(The* ACTOR *emerges from the shadows, and* KRINSKY *approaches him.)* In my opinion, the best thing you can do now is get yourself a good death. *(The* COSSACK *unexpectedly interrupts.)*

Cossack. Konyechno![33] The comedian is right! A good death, with a good scream that you can hear forever. That's it!

Actor. There's no reason to exaggerate, an ordinary death will do also.

Cossack. Don't pay any attention to him. He talks that way because he went to the slaughterhouse like a sheep. He didn't even know who he was anymore. Do you know how I died? That was really some death! I bled to death riding my horse . . . Dead, that's how they took me off the saddle. *(The* MOTHER *appears unexpectedly.)*

Mother. He's not up to riding, the poor thing, he never was up to it . . .

Krinsky. (To the MOTHER*)* Did you hear what they're saying?

Mother. Yes.

Krinsky. Nu? What should I do?

Mother. I'm an ignorant woman . . . Whatever you decide will be all right with me.

Krinsky. And with Papa?

Mother. (Smiling ironically) Papa never knew about these things . . . The only time he didn't talk about work was when he told me he was dying, and then he died, and he didn't say another thing . . .

Krinsky. (To HARPO, *who looks at him, frightened, from a corner next to his harp)* What do you say? *(*HARPO *only manages to make a feeble sound with his bugle.)*

Cossack. Come on photographer! What's the problem? We're going to give you a funeral like you've never seen before.

Actor. Listen to me, it's the best way.

Krinsky. (To LUBA*)* And what about you? . . . Don't you have anything to say?

Luba. (Pointing to the GIRL*)* Better you should ask her. It's a good idea. *(The* GIRL *spontaneously offers her opinion.)*

Girl. I will kiss your dead body and cry until I faint. Afterwards, I'll dress up in mourning.

Krinsky. But it will be a lie . . .

Girl. And who's going to find out?

Krinsky. Me.

Girl. You're going to be dead, silly.

Actor. Of course!

Cossack. A big parade, with the coffin suspended on the soldiers' shoulders, all the cavalry as an escort, and a speech that will make the enemy shit in their pants with fear.

Krinsky. All right. I accept. How do we do it?

Mother. Mit eydlkayt,[34] in bed, clean. I'm going to cry, and slowly, slowly . . .

Actor. Not that way, woman! That's no death for a Krinsky. *(He points to the* THUGS.*)* What do we have these two for? It's nothing for them. We'll do a good staging and that's it. Let's see, get ready. *(He starts placing the characters in the "drama" ac-*

cording to his own instructions. To KRINSKY) You go over here, and you face them as you cover the retreat of your comrades who left through this door. You have your gun?

Krinsky. Only water comes out of my gun . . .

Actor. It doesn't matter! They're going to shoot first. And you, before you take your last breath, cover the door with your body.

Cossack. (Scornfully) What? What kind of retreat can he cover if he dies first? It's obvious you don't know anything about war.

Actor. And you don't know anything about metaphors!

Cossack. (To KRINSKY) Don't pay any attention to him! Listen to me, take this carbine. *(He hands him his carbine.)* You stand there in front of the door and shoot the two of them. One dies at once, and you can shoot the other while the first is agonizing. Then you can die because you're sure your comrades are safe. *(To the* ACTOR) That's covering a retreat like you're supposed to!

Luba. Why don't all of you let him decide for himself? After all, he's the one who's going to die, isn't he?

Krinsky. I . . . I want to have a wound here. *(He points to his chest.)* Then I want her to come over *(referring to the* GIRL) to hold me in her arms and close my eyes.

Luba. If she can stand the smell.

Actor. Señora! A little respect.

Luba. All right. Forgive me. *(To the* GIRL) Do you want to do it?

Girl. Yes.

Mother. It doesn't seem proper to me . . .

Krinsky. It's only once, Mama, *loz mikh.*[35]

Mother. S'iz nisht eydl.[36] She has a husband . . .

Krinsky. Not yet. *(The* COSSACK *decides to speed up the process.)*

Cossack. Anu davai![37] I don't really agree with this kind of death, but at least you have good taste, comrade. *(He laughs.)* The Jewess is worth it. (HARPO *starts to play a sad melody on the harp while the* ACTOR *sets the stage. He paints the wound on* KRINSKY'S *chest and places the* GIRL *so that she holds* KRINSKY. *He gets excited seeing his own handiwork.)*

Actor. It's a Pietá! A Pietá with a light, romantic touch!

Cossack. Hurry up, you good for nothing! He's bleeding to death! *(The* ACTOR *places the weeping* MOTHER *at one side; he places the* COSSACK *with his arms crossed on his carbine and his chin resting on his arms, and himself standing in front of the stage bowing expressively. The setting he has created is balanced, although somewhat conventionally "pretty."* LUBA *observes it all as she continues cleaning, apparently not paying any attention. Suddenly the* ACTOR *notices that both* THUGS *are there.)*

Actor. What are you doing here? This isn't a place for you. Get out! I said get out!

Thug 1. (As he exits) We'll be back, we always come back. *(Once the* THUGS *leave the* ACTOR *takes his place again. After a pause during which only* HARPO'S *sad arpeggios are heard, the* GIRL *closes* KRINSKY'S *eyes, kisses him and speaks through her tears.)*

Girl. He's dead. *(Everyone, except for* LUBA, *respectfully approaches the body.)*

Mother. He's beautiful. Isn't he? *(The* COSSACK *begins to curse in Russian as he weeps convulsively.)*

Cossack. My comrade photographer! My comrade from Zhitomir! White Russian scum! They're going to pay for this! *(The* ACTOR *dries his eyes causing his makeup to run. He makes a sign to* HARPO, *who is crying from his ears, and the two of them bring over the coffin. Carefully, with everyone helping, they place* KRINSKY'S *body inside. When they are all about to raise the coffin the* MOTHER *approaches* LUBA.)*

Mother. Why don't you come too? He would have liked it.

Luba. What has become of him now?

Mother. That's what I mean . . . You're not compromising yourself in any way. *(*LUBA *and the* GIRL *exchange a quick glance to decide what to do. Then* LUBA *approaches the coffin and takes one of the handle rings. All together they raise it to their shoulders and walk towards the stage while the second movement of Beethoven's Third Symphony is heard. When they are almost at the stage they stop. The* ACTOR *separates himself from the group, takes a step forward, takes a wrinkled piece of paper out of his inside pocket, puts on a pair of glasses with just one temple and reads.)*

Actor. Ladies, gentlemen, comrades, *khaveirim,*[38] *liebe fraint.*[39] A puff of air. A gentle breeze. A *vintele.*[40] Perhaps only this has been felt on the surface of the planet. Perhaps not even that. Nevertheless, this was Krinsky. He wanted to be a man, isn't that enough? *Nisht genug?*[41] Must I list his accomplishments so that you can consider him your equal and admit that you've lost something great by his death? Will the testimony be necessary of those who admired him, of those he admired, and who only knew that they loved him after it was too late, to get a little heartfelt sorrow from you? I don't ask that his name be inscribed in your memory of *eybik.*[42] Eternity, after all, is no more than a word of consolation . . . And that is all I'm asking, a good word in the heart, *spassiba,*[43] *a groysn dank.*[44] *(The* COSSACK *aims his carbine at the sky and fires.)*

Cossack. *Slava,*[45] Krinsky! *(He fires again.)* Eternal glory to comrade Krinsky! *(A crowd is heard repeating the last sentence.* LUBA *is deeply moved. But suddenly* KRINSKY *sits up in the coffin.)*

Krinsky. In spite of all this, I can't go this way . . . *(The surprise is absolute. They all lower the coffin and watch* KRINSKY *as he gets out of it with great difficulty.)* I thank you very much, but . . .

Luba. You've ruined everything. It was so beautiful, so moving . . .

Krinsky. Forgive me. I thought it was for the best, honestly . . . *(The people who were gathered, exit, carrying the coffin with them.* LUBA *starts cleaning again. To the audience)* I would have died, believe me. I would have if I could have been certain that my death would provoke some great cataclysm, so that all of humanity would present itself before me in an act of contrition and grief. But as I already told you, I'm an old man without faith . . .

Luba. *(To the audience. She makes a scornful gesture.)* Folgt mikh,[46] just forget it. *(*LUBA *returns to her cleaning.* KRINSKY *watches her.)*

Krinsky. But still . . . something . . .

Luba. Don't be an *akshn,* Krinsky. *(To the audience)* I'm telling him not to be so stubborn. Don't give me "but still . . ." Here's another cookie . . . *(*LUBA *goes back to her work.* KRINSKY *humbly takes the cookie and eats it distractedly. Suddenly he lifts his head as if he were listening to some sound.)* What's the matter?

Krinsky. Shhh . . . *(There is a pause.* LUBA *tries unsuccessfully to hear the sound that* KRINSKY *hears.)* Don't you hear it?

Luba. No. *(The game changes.* LUBA *begins to talk about herself in the third person, as if the actress were telling the story. Almost immediately* KRINSKY *does the same. To the audience)* But Luba lied. For the sake of Krinsky's memory, I beg you to try to believe that she lied, that in reality, she clearly heard the neighing of the sorrel mare on the steppes . . . *(*KRINSKY *speaks as he sheds his ragged clothing and takes off his makeup to reveal a young and svelte man.)*

Krinsky. *(To the audience)* And it was then that Krinsky, the legendary Krinsky, did away with his miserable shell, laughed wisely, and approached her in silence . . .

Luba. *(To the audience)* And loved the woman.

Krinsky. And the woman loved him as no one had ever loved before.

Luba. Only then was he ready to leave. He mounted his horse with a leap, and with a victorious cry galloped off.

Krinsky. The hooves of his sorrel mare still resound over the steppes.

Luba. Listen . . . listen . . .

(After a brief pause, final blackout)

Caracas, Jan. 1977
Buenos Aires, Aug. 1980
Buenos Aires, Jan. 1983

NOTES

1. An idiot, a complete idiot.
2. Old wives' tales, literally, grandmother's tales, although the expression originally referred to Buovo's stories.
3. Like a beggar.
4. Why do you have to tell them? Please, I beg you . . .
5. Son of a bitch (Russian).
6. Calm down (Russian).
7. Bravo, well done (Russian).
8. I shit on that happiness!
9. Prayers for the Day of Atonement.
10. Synagogue.
11. Gentiles, non-Jews.
12. I would feel better.
13. So, what do you think of that?
14. My God.
15. Here I am, old and sad.
16. Cry, my son, cry . . . be still
17. They're looking.
18. Let them look. What do you care?
19. Cookies.
20. Don't cry, I beg you.
21. So let it be.
22. Well, so?
23. Ladies and Gentlemen (German).
24. Distinguished public (Polish).
25. Distinguished guests.
26. A pity, a pity!
27. Little brother
28. Filthy beast.
29. Poor thing.
30. As long as it was.
31. Rotten fascists!
32. Come here!
33. Of course! (Russian)

34. With nobility.
35. Let me.
36. It's not decent.
37. Come on! Let's get going! (Russian)
38. Friends.
39. Dear friends.
40. A little breeze.
41. Isn't that enough?
42. Forever.
43. Thank you (Russian).
44. Thank you very much.
45. Eternal glory (Russian).
46. Listen to me.

Ricardo Halac: *A Thousand Years, One Day*

The Edict of Expulsion, March 31, 1492

In our principalities there are numerous bad Christians, who Judaize the Marranos and they deviate from our holy Catholic religion, which is manifested to a great extent through the contact of Jews with Christians. Wishing to correct this evil, we ordered at the *cortes* that gathered in Toledo in 1480, the isolation of the Jews in all the cities and the allocation of special areas into which they might reside. We also initiated in our principalities an Inquisition that has existed for the past twelve years, and which has condemned many guilty ones. According to the report of the inquisitors, there has come to light the great harm to the Christians due to their contact with Jews, who strive to mislead them to their accursed faith. The Jews endeavor to mislead them [the Marranos] and their children, they give them Jewish books for prayer, they tell them which fast days to observe, they bring them 'matzot' for Passover, and point out to them which food to eat, and which to abstain from—in general, they urge the observance of the Mosaic faith. All this leads to the degradation of our holy Catholic faith. We therefore came to the conclusion that one effective means against all these evil deeds would be to halt altogether the contact of Jews and Christians by banishing the Jews from our principalities; but at first, we were contented with ordering them out from the cities of Andalusia, where they perpetrate the greatest harm. But neither this, nor the righteous judgment of Jews, who have abused our holy faith so much, served to halt these transgressions. . . .

Therefore, we have decided to order all Jewish men and women to leave our kingdom, with the understanding that they will never return. And with this, we order all Jews—men and women of all ages—who live in our principalities, that no later than the end of July of this year they should depart from our royal principalities and senorias with their sons and daughters, with households and servants that are Jewish—and that they should not dare to come back here, neither to reside, to pass through, nor for any other reason. If they shall fail to comply with this order, and if they are to be found in our principalities, they shall be condemned to death, and their assets confiscated without any trial. We command that from the end of July, no citizen in our kingdom is to dare to keep openly or secretly a Jewish man or Jewish woman under threat of forfeiting his entire property, which is to be turned over to our treasury. However, in order that the Jews should be able to dispose of their enterprises in the course of this interval, we take them under our royal protection, and assure them inviolability of person and property, so that until the end of July they may reside here in peace, buy, exchange, donate their belongings and estates according to their wish. We also permit them to take along their belongings by sea or by land, in addition to gold, silver, money, coins, and other things, which are otherwise prohibited by law of our principalities to transport.

Simon Dubnov, *History of the Jews From the Later Middle Ages to the Renaissance.* 6 vols. (New York: Thomas Yoseloff, 1969) 3:334–35.

RICARDO HALAC (BUENOS AIRES, 1935)

Halac's theatre evolves over two decades that coincide with a period of transformation in Argentine drama. His first period has been described as one of a "reflexive realism" marked by introspection in plays like *Soledad para cuatro* (Solitude for four) (1971), *Estela de madrugada* (Morning stella) (1965), and *Fin de diciembre* (End of December) (1965). His later period, of a more "critical realism," draws him closer to the traditional, classical Argentine theatre of the 1920s influenced by Florencio Sánchez and Roberto Payró. The "grotesque," characterized by exaggeration, dominates Halac's later work. *El destete* (The weaning) (1978) is a mordant critique of children's upbringing. *Ruidos de rotas cadenas* (Clamor of broken chains) (1983) deals with the economic crisis of the lower classes of Argentina. *Lejana tierra prometida* (Far away promised land) (1981), a more avant garde play, is influenced by Roberto Arlt. Halac's theatre shows the disconformity, inertia and frustration of young middle-class people drowned in a world of incomprehension.

Mil años, un día (A Thousand Years, One Day) was originally entitled "The Kabbalah and the Cross." Halac began to write this play in 1986. After having been rewritten several times, the definitive version was performed for the first time at the Teatro San Martín in Buenos Aires in 1993, at which time it was published by Ediciones Corregidor. The play, set in fifteenth-century Spain during the Inquisition, fictionalizes the intimate relationship between Queen Isabel and her personal physician, Isaac Levy, a Jew envied and despised by other members of the court. Halac uses this situation not so much to recreate a historical moment, but to establish some important parallels between the condition of the Spanish Jews and that of any other ethnic minority under oppression and harassment.

Halac presents the transition period of the Spanish state ruled by Queen Isabel la Católica, triumphant after the Moorish wars. Under her reign she expects Spain to move from a sense of euphoria to one of sobriety, as her authoritarian state of "the sword and the cross" are used interchangeably to reinforce each other. *A Thousand Years, One Day* emphasizes the opposition of the Catholic church to tolerance and spiritual progress. The harmony shared by three different religions under Arab rule for seven centuries is replaced in 1492 with the expulsion of Jews and Mohammedans from Spain.

The text repeatedly suggests that the cruel methods used for the

Ricardo Halac

"Queen Isabel" and "Isaac Levy" in a scene from *A Thousand Years, One Day* by Ricardo Halac

expulsion of the Jews will have repercussions throughout history. Implicit here is Halac's association of what took place then, with future historical events, in particular with the atrocities perpetrated during the Holocaust. In addition, Halac strongly hints at the close link between the expulsion and the first voyage of Christopher Columbus, whose mysterious life seems to reflect the agitated and precarious condition of the *conversos* (converted Jews) of Spain.

The Kabbalah is presented as a mystical philosophy, attractive to Jews because they believed it would provide them with essential keys to understanding human behavior and divine mysteries. Many of them resolutely believed that God would intervene at the last minute and revoke the Edict of Expulsion. They also put their faith in the Kabbalah because they hoped that the popular superstitions, traditions, and mythological motifs contained in it would help them transcend the misfortunes of their material world. But the Kabba-

EL EDICTO

El 31 de marzo de 1492 Isabel y Fernando firmaron en el Palacio de la Alhambra de Granada el "Edicto general sobre la expulsión de los judíos en Castilla y Aragón". Dice así:

"En nuestros reinos hay pocos judainizantes, malos cristianos que se apartan de Nuestra santa iglesia católica, hecho que tiene su origen ante todo en la relación existente entre los judíos y los cristianos. . . Según el informe que nos ha sido presentado por los Inquisidores no existe ninguna duda de que la relación entre cristianos y judíos que intentan inducirnos a abrazar a su condenada religión, origina uno de los peores males. . Todo ello tiene como consecuencia inevitable la corrupción y degradación de Nuestra santa Religión Católica. . . Por todo ello hemos tomado la decisión de expulsar de las fronteras de Nuestro reino a todos los judíos de ambos sexos.

"Así que por este decreto disponemos que todos los judíos que viven dentro de los límites de Nuestra soberanía, sin distinción de sexo ni edad, abandonen Nuestra propiedad y señorías reales dentro de un plazo que terminará a final de julio, con sus hijos e hijas y con sus servidores judíos y que no se atrevan a pisar más este país, ni en el tránsito para ir a establecerse a otro sitio ni bajo ningún otro pretexto. Si no tuvieran en cuenta esta órden y fueran descubiertos en Nuestro territorio serán castigados con la muerte y con la confiscación de todos sus bienes sin juicio previo. En consecuencia, recomendamos que a partir de final de julio en nuestro reino nadie se atreva a ofrecer cobija, abiertamente o en secreto, a un judío o una judía, bajo pena de confiscación de todos sus bienes a beneficio del Tesoro Real. Les permitimos salir de Nuestro reino por vía marítima o terrestre llevando consigo los bienes de su propiedad a excepción de oro, plata, dinero en moneda y otros efectos que están incluidos entre los de exportación prohibida".

The original Edict of Expulsion. English translation appears on p. 196.

lah proved to be ineffective as a practical vehicle for salvation for the Jews when they faced real danger.

In *A Thousand Years, One Day* three generations of a Jewish family are brought to life. A central character is Sara, who combines the traditional, self-sacrificing Jewish mother figure with that of the modern, assertive female. Ezra, the religious grandfather, is the voice of wisdom, of fear, and of warning of worse times to come. ("We are not loved here." "This is not our country." p. 246) His grandson, Yehuda, confronts the fatalism of his elders and does not forgive the errors of the past. He is the young rebel who will not run away, but rather will join others in resisting and fighting back. Isaac Levy, the father, on the one hand, is attracted to the glamour of court life and, on the other, is tied to his Jewish roots. Isaac is the prototype of what will become the Renaissance man: a scholar, a scientist, and a lover of life. In the eyes of traditional Jews, he is too secular, an assimilationist. Yet he shares with them a love for their country, Spain. Thus he resists the idea of departure and exile until the very end.

Halac presents a tableau of Spanish society and its relationship with the Jews about to be expelled from their homeland. In this tale of betrayal, Isaac's supposed friends take advantage of the situation to advance themselves: Rodrigo, the constable, wants Isaac's daughter and is eager to put the wheel of torture into use against the heretics; Devoto, an original character in Latin American theatre, the *converso,* is after Isaac's position at court. He instigates Isaac to read kabbalistic books in order to confuse him and to provoke the Queen's fear of his possible demonic powers. The poor Christians, represented by the peasants, are aggressive toward the Jews, whom they blame for their misfortunes. Nevertheless, they are powerless to detain the Inquisitorial process that will eventually turn against them as well.

There are several recurrent metaphors that add richness and significance to the play. The Jews, ready to leave the country at a moment's notice, are always seen carrying bags containing their material belongings. These bags are symbols of their state of impermanence. The symbol of the wheel suggests two possible interpretations: the wheel of time, irreversible and ominous, moving forward towards the moment when the Edict of Expulsion will be implemented, and those Jews who still remain unconverted in Spain will be sentenced to death; the wheel of torture, a symbol of the New Order that Spain represents under the Inquisition.

The bells that herald the expulsion of the Jews on August 2, 1492, at midnight, awake rejoicing in the Christians, but mourning in the Jews. In contrast, the *shofar*—the ram's horn—is blown during the Jewish holidays to reach the Messiah and plead with him to save humankind. The *shofar,* along with other ritualistic objects—the *tallith* and the candelabra—imbue the play with a religious atmosphere. The kabbalistic rituals—throwing letters into the air, performing physical motions and prayers at the Jewish cemetery, and pronouncing secret words—are meant to attract God's attention to the suffering of the Jews and remind the audience that these Jewish motifs are set against the background of the Inquisition.

The Christian symbols—the bells, the sword, the cross, the crown, the feathers, the flags—are all reminders that Spain is about to pronounce itself as a united trinity of crown, people, and religion, as prescribed by the Holy Tribunal of the Inquisition. The dramatic, devious presence of Torquemada, garbed in black, epitomizes that concept.

A Thousand Years, One Day is about the failure of the individual to alter the course of history. It is about turning to the supernatural—Kabbalah, mysticism, and rituals—when rational solutions, political strategies, and economic coercion fail to make an impact on the oppressors. Isaac Levy learns that man stands alone, that one has to decide one's own fate and cannot manipulate destiny. In this sense, it is a twentieth-century existentialist play that stresses the precariousness of the human condition, where fate can be determined by chance, a single word, or the stroke of a pen.

The strength of *A Thousand Years, One Day* lies in Halac's ability to establish a natural connection between the specific instance of the Jewish exodus of 1492 and the conditions of exile that has become a recurrent theme in Jewish history, one universally shared by other groups who have suffered mass displacement. Written only a decade after the military dictatorship in Argentina, the play can also be read as a metaphor of repression and precariousness under that totalitarian regime.

NOTE

1. Osvaldo Pelletieri, "Ricardo Halac y sus veintinco años de realismo," *Latin American Theatre Review* (Spring 1987): 85–89.

A Thousand Years, One Day

First performance, San Martín Muncipal Theatre, Buenos Aires, June 14, 1993.

List of Characters
Isaac Levy, the Queen's doctor
Isabel, the Queen
Sara, Isaac's wife
Ezra, Isaac's father
Yehuda, Isaac's son
Raquel, Isaac's daughter
Devoto de la Cruz, a convert
Sancho, the mayor
Rodrigo, the constable
Juan, the priest
The Kabbalah teacher
The disciple
Raquel as a child
Yehuda as a child
Male peasant 1
Male peasant 2
Female peasant 1
Female peasant 2
Torquemada
Jewish leader 1
Jewish leader 2
Jewish leader 3
Court official
Ladies, Pages, Spies, Soldiers, Peasants, Clergy, and Jewish people.

Scene 1. *The Cemetery.*

Jewish cemetery of a small village in Spain, July 31, 1492. The Edict of Expulsion of the Jews decreed by the Catholic monarchs, is about to expire. There is fire in the sky or on the ground. A group of Jews, their heads and shoulders covered with talliths *(ritual shawls), sway back and forth, as is their custom when they pray. They sing in a grave, plaintive voice. There are also families with children, watching from a distance, with heavy bundles containing all their belongings.*

Isaac. Lord . . . Lord . . . *(At a given moment,* ISAAC, *the protagonist, cannot go on praying. His prayer shawl falls and he can barely stand up. His mind wanders.* RAQUEL, *his daughter, seeing him in that condition, puts the shawl around his shoulders and takes his arm.)*

Raquel. (Forcing him to repeat with her) "Fathers and forefathers . . ."

Isaac. Fathers and forefathers.

Raquel. "Fathers and forefathers whom we have buried here . . ."

Isaac. Fathers and forefathers whom we have buried here . . . *(*ISAAC *hears a very sweet voice, which is actually a* shofar, *or a ceremonial ram's horn, that conjures up memories from his past. His wife* SARA *lowers her shawl and looks at him, concerned.)*

Raquel. "We haven't come to say goodbye because we don't want to go . . ." *(*ISAAC *covers his face with his hands and weeps.* RAQUEL *repeats her words, waiting for him to follow her.)* "We haven't come to say goodbye because we don't want to go . . ." *(*SARA *goes towards him and lifts his arms.)*

Sara. You brought all these poor people here to the cemetery. You told them you were going to speak with God, and that He was going to save us.

Raquel. Courage, Papá! *(Distraught,* ISAAC *begins a prayer.)*

Isaac. "Fathers and forefathers . . . souls that weep because we must leave . . ."

Raquel. Your arms! Don't lower your arms!

Isaac. Sara, where am I?

Sara. Isaac, the Edict runs out in an hour! There's not much time left! If they find us . . .

Isaac. (Overcome) Fathers and forefathers buried here . . . Nobody knows us better than you! Because you brought us to this world . . . You cradled us until we grew . . . in this land that we don't want to leave today . . . *(He takes a few steps.)* Please! Enter our bodies, speak through our voices . . .

Raquel. Like that, Papá, like that!

Isaac. And ask God to let us remain here! *(The prayers become louder. The worshippers feel the souls of the dead in their bodies.)* God, let us stay in Spain! Stop the Edict! Forgive us . . . *(He gathers his strength and lifts his head.)* Come what may! *(Frightened, some families step back.* SARA *and* RAQUEL *move towards them.)*

Raquel. Let's not separate now!

Sara. A miracle . . . a miracle is going to happen! *(All alone,* ISAAC *falters.)*

Isaac. God, don't punish us anymore . . . (RAQUEL *and* SARA *join the worshippers. Suddenly* ISAAC *begins to hear other voices singing in Spanish that blend with those of the worshipers.)* What is this . . . *(Laughs, distracted)* Forgive me, your Majesty. I left without saying goodbye. *(He attempts a bow. The Spanish song becomes louder.)* Well, if it isn't Juan, Sancho, Rodrigo and Devoto, drinking wine and without me! Do you think that's right? You're having a good time . . . *(He approaches them slowly, leaving the area of the cemetery and entering a new space. In his mind, time moves backward, while behind him the praying figures lower their hands, doubling over, as their prayers go unanswered.)*

Scene 2. *The Farewell at the Tavern.*

A tavern, a table set with food. ISAAC'S *friends have organized a farewell party before he leaves Spain.* SANCHO *the mayor,* RODRIGO *the constable,* JUAN *the priest, and* DEVOTO *the convert, along with other neighbors—the town notables—are all present. They are singing and laughing.* SANCHO *dances as if he had castanets in his hands. A woman comes and goes bringing wine.*

Sancho. What are you taking, Isaac?

        What are you leaving, Isaac?

        Today you're here,

        Tomorrow there,

        Isaac, oh Isaac,

        You won't forget us . . .

(Resolutely, ISAAC *goes to the table.)*

Rodrigo. Isaac, our guest of honor!

Sancho. Jesus, Mary and Joseph . . . I haven't stopped drinking since we arrived!

Rodrigo. The blood of Christ.

Juan. You took a long time.

Devoto. This is where you should have been! It's your farewell party! *(Sudden silence.* JUAN *stops and embraces him.)*

Juan. Our . . . our beloved friend . . . *(*ISAAC *is silent. He tries to maintain his composure.)*

Sancho. You won't forget us!

Isaac. Can one ever forget one's friends?

Rodrigo. What, there's no more? Father Juan drank all the wine!

Juan. Not so. My nose is red because of my cold . . . *(Silence. He looks at* ISAAC.*)* Your family?

Rodrigo. Ready for a trip with no return. Isn't that so?

Isaac. Yes, and it's hard to decide what to take and what to leave. *(He feels dizzy and sits down.)* Can I have some wine?

Devoto. If there's something that we have plenty of here, it's wine! *(He gives him a jug.)*

Juan. Wine and friendship . . .

Sancho. How you'll miss the wines of Spain, damn it! *(He bites his lips. Silence.)*

Juan. The things we lived through as children! Who can take those childhood memories away from you!

Sancho. And the memories of life at the palace? Because this country doctor, gentlemen, made it to the court! *(They all applaud. Laughter.* RODRIGO *drinks more.* ISAAC *hears something, surprised.)*

Isaac. Do I hear bells?

Rodrigo. They're announcing the departure of the Jews. It's a big event for the people. *(On guard)* Why, do they bother you?

Isaac. They sound like victory . . . *(He finds it hard to hear them. In his memory time goes wild; suddenly he hears a Jewish song and he sees* SARA *singing. Lights on the space that is his house)*

Sara. Packing and unpacking . . . as always. *(Sighing, she sits down on a pile of pillows, legs crossed, Arab style, and unties a package.)* What should I do? Take more warm clothing? Where we're going, will it be hot or cold? I'll have to make a home all over again. Only God knows what's going to happen to us! *(Dreaming)* I'd love to see what snow is like. *(*ISAAC *is in a trance as he listens to her.* SANCHO *pats his shoulder.)*

Sancho. Isaac, the Edict says that at twelve midnight on the thirty first, time is up. Any Jew who is found after that . . .

Devoto. You should pay attention to what it says.

Sancho. (Looking at him) Just like somebody else I know.

Devoto. Why? I converted. I'm not Jewish anymore. I'm like the rest of you. *(*SANCHO *laughs slyly.)*

Juan. Let's hear your farewell speech, Isaac.

Rodrigo. Yes. We want to hear you . . . *(Silence)*

Isaac. I can't tell you anything.

Sancho. (Standing behind him, he cranks him up, as if he were a puppet, while imitating him.) I thank you for this lovely party that the town's most important people organized for me . . . the mayor, that is me, Father Juan . . . *(*ISAAC *pushes him away.* SANCHO *falls on top of* RODRIGO. *He points at him.)* Ah, we're also celebrating Rodrigo's promotion to Chief Constable . . . *(He slaps his back noisily. Applause)*

Juan. (To ISAAC, *taking him aside)* If your father feels bad because of your leaving, let him come to see me.

Rodrigo. Devoto, do you realize that if you had not converted, you would also have to leave now, like Isaac?

Sancho. (Pretending to have castanets, he sings.)
Devoto is here,
Devoto will not leave . . .
Ay, what a cross my friends,
We have to put up with him . . .
Abraham . . . Abraham . . .
Take off your mask . . .

Rodrigo. Abraham!

Juan. That was your name before you converted.

Rodrigo. Does the name Abraham bring back memories?

Devoto. No. (RODRIGO *looks at him questioningly.)* I mean yes.

Sancho. But they're the same person!

Devoto. When I was a child, my name was Abraham. My father called me Abraham! "Abraham, don't hide . . . Abraham, don't cry over everything!" . . . The Edict brings back memories. But it's only because Isaac is going away. *(A sudden shiver runs through him.)* Please don't denounce me.

Rodrigo. Raquel, your dear daughter . . . is she leaving with you? *(Suddenly* RAQUEL, ISAAC'S *daughter, appears in the space that is their house, where there is now a lit candelabra.)*

Raquel. Mamá! Mamá!

Sara. I'm here Raquel! (RAQUEL *falls on her knees next to* SARA, *dropping the books that she was carrying.)* My treasure . . . I can't carry another thing . . . I can't.

Raquel. But they're Papá's books. It says here in the Bible that Joshua won a battle by holding his arms up high. When he got tired, the people helped him.

Sara. Let's forget about those stories for now . . .

Raquel. Papá used to tell me those stories when I was a little girl, to put me to sleep. (RAQUEL *hides her face in her mother's lap, as her mother strokes her hair.)*

Sara. Yes, my dear. When we are far away we'll have to remember those stories to gather strength from them. *(While she rocks her, she sings.* SANCHO'S *loud voice brings* ISAAC *back to reality.)*

Sancho. Constable!

Rodrigo. Chief Constable . . .

Sancho. If you had become a Jew, now you could leave with Raquel. *(Laughs scornfully, while the area of the house fades out. For a moment* RODRIGO *becomes the center of attention. He stops, quickly pulls out a short sword, and examines its sharpness.)*

Rodrigo. In the New Order that now rules Spain, there is no place for those jokes.

Sancho. All right. It's not that important.

Rodrigo. If you weren't my friend, you would have to respond for that insult. *(*JUAN *quickly steps between them.)*

Juan. We're here to celebrate! A friend is about to leave us, a great doctor . . .

Devoto. I'm a great doctor too.

Juan. Yes, luckily we have Devoto!

Sancho. Please don't expel the converted doctors too! If you do, who's going to take care of my wife, who always has some ache?

Devoto. Let Isaac speak!

All. Let Isaac speak! *(Silence. Suddenly* ISAAC *raises his head and looks at them.)*

Isaac. Childhood friends . . . *(A glimmer of rebellion can be seen in his eyes.)* I'm not leaving. *(They all look at each other, baffled.)*

Rodrigo. This I never imagined.

Juan. What are you saying, Isaac?

Isaac. I was born in this land, just like all of you. It's my home too. Didn't we go to the harvest celebrations together? Didn't we discover women, wine and song together? *(Silence. Each one is immersed in his thoughts.)* Then Juan became a priest and we used to walk at night, talking about God, I, as a scientist, he as a religious man. *(His voice breaks. They are overwhelmed with anguish.)* Sancho, I was at your wedding!

Sancho. Yes, but I wasn't at yours.

Isaac. I helped deliver your first child with these hands. Rodrigo, wasn't I at your bedside . . .

Rodrigo. When . . .

Isaac. When you struggled between life and death from a wound you received in a fight!

Rodrigo. You left before I recovered.

Isaac. It's true. But I also left my family. They called me from the court, and I went. I was always very ambitious. *(Silence. He turns to them.)* But I never forgot my people . . . *(A shofar is heard.* ISAAC'S *face takes on a strange light.)* My roots are here! And since it is not fair that we should have to leave, a miracle is going to happen! Time will move backwards to the moment when our expulsion was decided! They'll put the Edict in front of the Queen, and instead of signing it, she will tear it up. These are God's surprises! The Great Juggler. *(Silence)*

Rodrigo. (He adjusts his belt.) The Edict is very clear, Isaac. When time runs out, whoever hides a Jew . . .

Isaac. Rodrigo, time will move backwards.

Devoto. Would we be giving you a farewell party if you weren't leaving?

Isaac. The Kabbalah led me to understand. Thanks to your help, Devoto.

Devoto. (Looking around him, worried) My help?

Isaac. Didn't you send me to the teacher who taught me everything?

Devoto. You got everything wrong! The Kabbalah is meant to help you escape from the sorrows of life! It's not a manual to ask God for solutions! *(Takes him by the hand to where he can't be heard)* Did you thank me in front of everyone to ruin me? If you don't leave, you'll die . . .

Isaac. (Smiling strangely) No. I have one more ritual to perform.

Devoto. A ritual? What ritual? *(Pulling his hair out)* You're going to drive me crazy.

Isaac. A ritual that I learned from the master.

Devoto. (Turning to the others) Listen! Now Isaac believes in black magic!

Sancho. (Drunk) How I envy you, Isaac! You're going to travel. You're going to visit new countries.

Juan. Wherever you make your home . . . continue to be the great person you've always been. (ISAAC *hears more bells. It anguishes him not to know where they're coming from.)*

Isaac. Stop those bells! *(He touches his body; he pinches himself.)* Am I dreaming? Teacher! I have to give them a sign! *(They look at him in amazement as another section of the stage lights up. It is the holy place where the* teacher *of the Kabbalah appears, wrapped in a cape.)*

Devoto. Take a good look at him! Palace doctor, famous professor, erudite in many subjects . . . today he wants time to move backwards! *(Suddenly* SANCHO *breaks into song. The drunkest ones get up and start tapping like flamenco dancers.)*

Sancho. Isaaac . . . Oh, Isaaaaac . . .

The Rest. Don't forget us.

Sancho. You will forget us . . . Yes, you will forget us.

The Rest. What are you taking, Isaac?

What are you leaving, Isaac?

Today you are here.

Tomorrow there.
Isaac, oh, Isaac,
You won't forget us . . .

Isaac. And what does this mean? Are you throwing me out?

Sancho. Yes! And now your friends will carry you to the gates of Spain . . . *(They all lift him up and carry him on a throne made from their hands.)*

Isaac. Leave me alone. I don't want to go . . .

Rodrigo. And we'll throw you out . . . ! *(They stay there, laughing, while* ISAAC *falls. He falls and falls . . .)*

Scene 3. *The Kabbalah Teacher.*

Isaac. Where am I? *(Surrounded by wilderness, the* TEACHER *sways back and forth, following ritual movements.)*

Teacher. What does it matter where? Perhaps you should ask yourself why your steps led you here. *(Silence.* ISAAC *sits up. Looks at him)*

Isaac. I am looking for a teacher.

Teacher. That's a good sign. You've begun to listen to your heart. But I don't know where your teacher is.

Isaac. On the contrary, I believe that I have found him.

Teacher. He who has lived in darkness for a long time, cannot see.

Isaac. Teacher . . . *(Holding his head)* For the love of science I have read a great deal.

Teacher. Knowledge honors God . . .

Isaac. I relieved the pain of those who suffered. I enlightened the ignorant . . . But evil is forever advancing. And I don't know how to stop it. Why?

Teacher. It is not in our power to explain it. Evil is part of God's creation. But He has also given us an antidote: the possibility of deciphering the Book. *(He lifts his hand, revealing the Bible.)*

Isaac. Men kill each other . . . yet we're all the same. We're made of the same stuff! The same head, the same body, the same heart . . . *(He breaks down.)* Teacher, the knowledge that accompanied me all my life is of no use to me anymore. Does the Kabbalah help you to see God?

Teacher. One has to love God without attempting to see Him.

Isaac. Why, if one could see him, would one stop loving him? *(The* TEACHER *brings his face towards him, with an inscrutable expression. He raises the* shofar *and plays it. A* DISCIPLE *appears nearby.* ISAAC *becomes upset.)* Teacher, did you hear how they stopped a killing in Toledo? They called a teacher like you! He discovered in a synagogue that there was one incorrectly written word in the Bible. That error obstructed God's light! They corrected it and evil vanished . . . I'm not lying! It is written in Toledo! *(He looks at him, visibly upset, full of doubts. The* TEACHER *shakes his head.)*

Teacher. One mustn't cling to those stories. Despair clouds the mind. *(The* TEACHER *plays the* shofar *for a long time.* ISAAC *looks at the sky in wonder.)*

Isaac. We must find the error! The mechanism of the Universe is stuck somewhere. The wheel of time turns and turns, but it is always in the same place. Since is doesn't move, it oozes hatred, evil . . .

Teacher. This place, don't you find it blissful?

Isaac. Should I calm down? *(He laughs and starts raving.)* How do I do that?

Teacher. *(He helps him to lie down and take off his clothing.)* Recapture a moment in your life when you were happy.

Isaac. In my life happiness and sorrow are entangled like day and night.

Teacher. God reads our minds, but he looks into our hearts first. *(He guides him in a relaxation exercise.)*

Isaac. Teacher, will you be my guide? How will I ever repay you? *(At a sign from the* TEACHER *the* DISCIPLE *begins to sing. He sings to put* ISAAC *to sleep, but* ISAAC *resists.)* Teacher, we must do something before it's too late.

Teacher. Now just look for a moment of your own light . . .

Isaac. *(Closing his eyes)* The happiest moment?

Teacher. And go to sleep with it . . . *(The soft sounds of the* shofar *are heard. Its long wail blends with a lullaby that the* DISCIPLE *sings, while the* TEACHER *exits.* ISAAC *laughs in his sleep.)*

Scene 4. *At the Palace of the Queen.*

The setting changes. Now a woman is singing a delicate courtly song. The chirping of birds is heard along with the sound of a fresh water fountain. We are in a patio of the royal palace. ISAAC *is sleeping, bare-chested. He is awakened by a noise.* QUEEN ISABEL *appears with her entourage.*

Isabel. Doctor . . . I'm looking for you all over, and here you are . . .

Isaac. *(Stands up and bows)* Your Majesty!

Isabel. How long have you been hiding in this terrace?

Isaac. *(Happy to see her)* I was reading . . . and I fell asleep.

Isabel. Now I understand why you're still fresh at dawn, telling witty stories, while my courtiers are all falling from sleep! Why are you hiding that book?

Isaac. It's one of those books that . . . *(He smiles, leaning towards her.)* I have to keep learning so that you won't lose interest in me.

Isabel. The book! *(She extends her arm, leaving him with no alternative but to hand it to her.)* Hmm. It has Hebrew letters. *(She gestures to the entourage to leave.)* But, what a surprise, it's written in Spanish . . . *The Book of Splendor.* What is this? I'm extremely curious and I want an answer right away. *(She looks at him.* ISAAC *clears his throat.)*

Isaac. Your Majesty . . .

Isabel. Isabel.

Isaac. Isabel . . .

Isabel. Your Majesty. *(They both laugh.* ISAAC *sighs, enjoying the sun.)*

Isaac. Once upon a time, a young man went to see the great scholar Eliezar. "Is it true what you say," he asked him, "that God gave us the chapters of the Bible in the wrong order?" "Yes," the rabbi responded, "because whoever knew the correct order could bring the dead back to life." *(Silence. The* QUEEN *takes a few steps.)*

Isabel. How interesting! And you want to perform miracles like that one?

Isaac. No! I'm a physician. A scholar. *(He points to the book.)* But the kabbalists, it's they who interpret dreams, they exorcize demons . . .

Isabel. To defeat the demons, we Christians not only believe in God but we also trust our swords.

Isaac. I know! *(Laughing)* Your Majesty, may I? *(He takes the book back and leafs through it.)* The only miracle I want is to stop the passage of time. My time . . . *(She listens to him attentively as he recites.)*
"Oh God, so many ages and generations
have passed through this land.
And I was nothing in any of them."

Isabel. Very beautiful . . . Who wrote that?

Isaac. It's from a Spanish poet I admire, a Jew . . . *(bows as he smiles)* and a general, too: Schmuel Ha-Naguid.

Isabel. *(Sighing)* I would so love to lie down, close my eyes and enjoy the fresh air like you. But I can't! *(Pauses, looking around)* This is the prettiest terrace in the palace.

Isaac. Why?

Isabel. Because this is where you hide.*(He looks at her and smiles gratefully. He seems like another man: strong, sure of himself. She reaches for a cluster of grapes from a basket. A noise is heard; it is someone who is spying on them, and who leaves.* ISABEL *walks around. In the distance a woman's singing is heard again.)* What a headache! I don't know if it was last night's conversation, or the wine we drank . . .

Isaac. Isabel, wine goes to your head.

Isabel. Why don't I realize that and why do I drink so much? Isaac, what marvelous stories you told me yesterday. I'd like to remember them all. *(She looks at him as she fills his hand with grapes. He eats them without reacting.)* How come you know so much?

Isaac. Why didn't I ever stop asking myself about our past? I don't know. Who knows . . . maybe that's why I studied a bit of everything. Later, when I became a doctor, I discovered that health is a balance between mind and body.

Isabel. How strange Jews are!

Isaac. Oh, yes? You think so? *(Silence. He laughs.)* I wish we weren't so strange. What does our history mean? It can't be explained. When something happens to us, we never know if it's a reward or a punishment . . . *(He feels a pain.)*

Isabel. Talk to me more . . .

Isaac. About what?

Isabel. About everything. *(She eats. She shrugs her shoulders.)* Talk to me about the Kabbalah.

Isaac. I can't. *(Shaking his head)* It's only for the initiated.

Isabel. I am Queen. No one can know more than I do. *(She laughs, extending her hand.)* Isaac . . .

Isaac. *(Puts his hand on hers.)* Your skin . . . it seems calm now, but it's like a dormant sun.

Isabel. Yes, my hands are hot . . .

Isaac. What you just said is true. *(He walks away.)* You are the Queen. You have God on one side and King Fernando on the other. He is strong and able with weapons as well as men. He commands and they obey him.

Isabel. Isaac, with him it's different. It's a long story. Together we are a symbol that stands for a united Spain.

Isaac. I feel cold. *(He takes a few steps. He laughs.)* Very cold! *(Two people appear, look at them and leave.* ISABEL *throws him his jacket, smiling.)*

Isabel. Cover yourself in my presence, vassal, or I'll have you locked up in a dark dungeon!

Isaac. Don't laugh at me if you love me! As a child I used to dream that people were following me. I run and run . . . but they were always behind me. *(He looks around him and cries out.)* You see? They're spying on us! *(She laughs heartily. Then she leans her head on her hand.)*

Isabel. I love your stories, Isaac. They say so much. I love your humor too, so mordant . . . With you I am in mortal sin. But I don't care! I've earned heaven with my conquests. Now I want to laugh, or spend my time listening to my personal physician . . . *(mockingly)* who, since I neglected him a bit, has begun to read some strange books. *(She sits down on the ground.)* Come over, sit by my side. *(He clears his throat, uneasy. He approaches her with caution. Two figures, covered from head to toe, pass by, frightening him. The doves flap their wings.)*

Isaac. An inner voice keeps telling me, "You must leave, Isaac . . ." Why don't I listen to it?

Isabel. Come here, Isaac. It's an order. *(He sits down silently. They look at each other.)* I want another grape. No, in my mouth. Another one! *(She laughs at his nervousness.)* They're preparing a celebration for tomorrow.

Isaac. *(Eating)* In honor of whom?

Isabel. Me! Who else? And therefore . . . *(She asks for another grape, which he puts in her mouth.)* in honor of my doctor, who will accompany me.

Isaac. *(Bowing)* I love to see how they flatter my Queen.

Isabel. I'll introduce you to one of my protégées, the Duchess Inés, who's dying to meet you.

Isaac. Is she suffering from something? Do I have to examine her?

Isabel. No! I forbid you to do that. Am I clear?

Isaac. Can I look at her, at least?

Isabel. Only from afar.

Isaac. Can I tell her my stories?

Isabel. No! I know how that ends!

Isaac. Isabel . . . Isabel . . .

Isabel. *(Sighing. She scratches herself frantically, then playfully.)* Ay, doctor Levy, see how I look because of you . . . *(She shows him her arm and her chest which he examines carefully.)*

Isaac. Your skin is remarkable.

Isabel. Cure me. Don't make me suffer!

Isaac. *(Playing along with her)* Please, let me see your other arm.

Isabel. Look at it carefully.

Isaac. Oh, another eruption.

Isabel. Say "My poor little Queen . . ." *(He laughs.)* Say it, you miser! Who are you saving your sweetest words for? *(She feels an itch and begins scratching again.)* This is driving me mad! *(Whimpering)* Do something for me!

Isaac. Like what?

Isabel. Recite one hundred Our Fathers. Right now!

Isaac. Isabel . . .

Isabel. Your Majesty.

Isaac. What does your confessor have to say about this?

Isabel. That it's a punishment I deserve for flirting with the devil. *(He pretends to be the devil to frighten her; she screams, crosses herself, and gets up.)* Jesus, Mary and Joseph! *(They look into each other's eyes and burst out laughing. Suddenly her expression hardens.)* I have to go! *(Her entourage returns.* ISAAC *becomes nervous.)*

Isaac. This is going to end, Isabel!

Isabel. Nothing ends in Spain if I don't end it.

Isaac. (Imitates the gesture she used earlier to describe the sores spreading through her body.) Your armies advance, expelling the Moors . . . each victory drives you further away from me.

Isabel. But what about these meetings?

Isaac. These meetings? They are games we invent to avoid seeing reality. I am a Jew. Everybody says that when the Moors are defeated . . .

Isabel. (Interrupting him) Sharing walks, meals, and readings can be done without offending God.

Isaac. When the Moors are defeated there will be a new order, where there will be no place for me. Not for me, not for those like me . . . *(Silence)*

Isabel. Don't bring up that subject again. Not with me, not with anyone else. That's an order.

Isaac. Yes, Your Majesty. *(With an exaggerated bow)* Or is it Your Holy Majesty? Or Most Eminent Isabel la Católica? In the future I don't believe that I can be your personal physician. Did you look for someone who . . . ?

Isabel. Isaac! *(She instinctively reaches for the large crucifix on her chest. Her voice becomes more tender.)* Last night God appeared to me in a dream. He gave me a sacred sword and signaled me to use it. *(She pauses.)* And look, this morning I was informed that our armies continue to advance. Isaac, our history is a runaway horse that no one can stop. They don't call me Isabel la Católica for no reason! *(Bells are heard.* ISABEL *notices that he is disturbed.)* What's the matter, Isaac?

Isaac. *(He becomes stiff as he listens to the bells.)* Don't laugh at me, but lately the bells . . .

Isabel. *(Straightening his hair)* Dear one. Nothing makes me laugh if it frightens you . . .

Isaac. They are calling for a hunt . . . *(Frightened by his own images)*

Isabel. Nothing is going to happen, Isaac.

Isaac. They are calling for a hunt . . .

Isabel. My fragile man . . . it's just your imagination . . . they're only bells. *(She caresses him. Isaac's face becomes distended.)* Let's see, what do you hear now? (ISAAC's *children appear cautiously from behind, calling him. They are young; she is eleven, he is thirteen.* ISAAC *shudders.)*

Isaac. It's the voice of my Yehuda . . .

Raquel. Papá!

Isaac. My Yehuda and my Raquel! *(Instinctively he reaches for his jacket, but it's too late. He bumps into* SARA, *looking grave as she follows their children. She is young and attractive, dazzled and excited.)*

Raquel and Yehuda. Papá! Papá!

Isaac. *(He hugs both of them tenderly.)* Yehuda! . . . I don't know, but you look bigger to me! And my Raquel, you look beautiful with your long hair! Isabel . . .

Isabel. What?

Isaac. How did you know I wanted to see them?

Isabel. We know each other very well, Isaac. (ISAAC *notices* SARA's *furtive glance. She is followed by guards. The royal entourage takes its place next to the* QUEEN.)

Isaac. She is the Queen! *(The children look at her, exhilarated, while he helps* ISABEL *put on her cape.)* Your Majesty!

Isabel. This visit is only for a short while. Hurry, Isaac. I need you. *(Tension in the air. No one moves.* SARA *goes to* ISAAC.)

Sara. How are you, Isaac?

Isaac. How are you, Sara? You look very beautiful.

Sara. It's the joy of seeing you and of feeling that the children are happy.

Isabel. *(Smiling)* I would love to know your village, Isaac.

Isaac. Did you hear that, Sara? *(To the children)* What do you say? Shall we invite her?

Isabel. I would also like to know your home.

Isaac. It's a modest house in a modest village.

Isabel. You fill it with your light. Isaac is a wonderful person, Sara.

Sara. That's why I chose him as my husband. *(She curtsies deeply. Pause.* ISABEL *smiles.)*

Isabel. You're happy, Sara . . .

Sara. How should a woman feel when her family is together again?

Isabel. Doctor Levy is very important in the court.

Sara. And in the village too. Everywhere he goes people love him and respect him. But it's important that he be happy too.

Isabel. You have a beautiful family, Isaac! *(At her command, they bring a basket.* ISABEL *takes presents out of it.)* Raquel! This necklace is for you to wear when you're a young woman. Never forget that a Queen gave it to you. Yehuda! In this mirror engraved in gold you will discover how much you look like your father.

Sara. And he also looks like his grandfather. And they say that he looks like me when he smiles . . . But I'm only concerned that he be honest and intelligent when he grows up.

Isaac. Your Majesty, can I invite Sara to the celebration tomorrow?

Isabel. Of course!

Isaac. I would love you to hear her sing. (SARA *lowers her head.)*

Sara. I only sing in my house for my people.

Raquel. Can I wear the necklace now?

Yehuda. Your Majesty, can I take the mirror?

Isabel. All right, say goodbye to your father now! Hurry, I need you, Doctor. *(She exits, followed by her entourage. At her signal the guards also follow.* ISAAC *remains alone with his family.)*

Isaac. Well, tell me! Are you all happy to be here? *(He laughs as he claps his hands.)* This is a palace . . .

Raquel. A real palace?

Isaac. Of course! *(Laughing, he throws a wineskin at* YEHUDA.*)* Have you ever tasted wine?

Raquel. He only drinks milk.

Isaac. (Shrugging his shoulders) At court all the children drink wine.

Sara. We're from the country, not from the court.

Isaac. Sara, you look beautiful . . . *(He wants to touch her. She becomes tense and closes her eyes.)* Come over here. *(He sits the children on his lap.)* I missed you so much.

Raquel. Papá, I brought you this little house as a gift. I made it with my own hands.

Yehuda. Papá, can I have more wine?

Isaac. As much as you want!

Sara. Isaac, don't let him have any more. He's only a little boy.

Isaac. He's on his way to becoming a man.

Raquel. (Showing her work) This is my father, and this is me, Raquel.

Isaac. And this is our house in our village. *(He presses them against him.)* How happy I am with all of you! How would you like to live here?

Sara. Isaac, don't take them away from me! *(Suddenly* ISAAC *sees that there are people watching him from above. In a defiant gesture, he sits on the throne that is nearby. The children point this out to* SARA, *who grabs her chest.)*

Isaac. You know, there's a celebration at the castle, tomorrow. *(The children laugh excitedly.* YEHUDA *picks up the mirror, looks at himself and sticks out his tongue. He lifts the wineskin and drinks from it.)* Did you see it well when you first came? This is a real castle surrounded by water, with turrets and archers who watch from the towers. Unless they lower the drawbridge, no one can enter!

Raquel. Can we visit it, Papa?

Sara. That's enough, Yehuda! Isaac, he's getting drunk!

Isaac. Then he's learning something. *(He laughs and hugs him.)*

Yehuda. And are they going to let us enter the castle?

Isaac. Of course! And there will be dukes, marquises accompanied by clowns, musicians and acrobats. *(SARA wants to leave but he takes her by the hand.)* Sara, we'll go together.

Sara. Do they invite Jews?

Isaac. I'll tell the Queen to lend you one of her dresses.

Sara. So that I look like a courtesan . . . ? You used to like me the way I was. *(YEHUDA laughs.)*

Raquel. Mama, I want to go there.

Isaac. If you sang, you would make a good impression at the party.

Sara. When you left, you took away the moments that made me want to sing. Now the house is filled with silence.

Isaac. (Attempting to draw her close to him) I also feel your absence. That's why you're here . . .

Sara. Oh yes? I saw what your work is like when I came in . . . And they told me that at court your stories are heard till all hours of the night.

Isaac. You're very capricious, Sara . . .

Sara. Did you hear what the Queen said, children? She said, "Say goodbye to your father, quickly. Hurry, Doctor. I need you." *(The children laugh. She prepares them to leave.)*

Isaac. Well, what have you decided? Are you coming to live here or not?

Sara. Isaac, I prefer to be queen in my own home.

Isaac. If I had stayed at home, Sara, I never would have become anything!

Sara. And I saw for myself how you live here . . . you have certainly triumphed. The Queen treats you like a favorite.

Isaac. No. She saw that I was sad and she sent for all of you. She gave me a surprise.

Sara. What a shame that I can't do the same when I miss you.

Isaac. Sara, living here has its advantages . . . Yehuda can go to the university. (YEHUDA *laughs. He can hardly stand up.*)

Sara. That's how he's going to study?

Isaac. I am an important man now! I have power. (*He tries to kiss her, but she turns her back to him.*) I see that it's going to be difficult to live together. You'd be saying no to me all the time. And I like to live this way, Sara. It gives me pleasure to enter the reception rooms with the Queen, to see how everyone bows before her, and then they gather around to listen to me . . . I can also practice my profession and get acquainted with whomever I want.

Sara. As if you were a nobleman . . . I look at you and I don't know you!

Isaac. Stop it, Sara! (*Silence*)

Sara. Why did they bring me here, so that you could humiliate me?

Isaac. (*Looking them over*) Why are you dressed like this? If what I send you is not enough, tell me so! The way you look, I don't know how they let you in the palace . . .

Sara. Now we embarrass you!

Isaac. Sometimes it really annoys me to listen to you.

Sara. I behave this way, Isaac, because I feel you're in danger . . . and even though I don't know how, I would like to protect you. Your father . . .

Isaac. What, has something happened to him?

Sara. Oh, the poor old man! (*Gathering her children to leave*) We shouldn't see each other again, Isaac. (ISAAC *stops her, upset.*)

Isaac. I asked you about my father!

Sara. He is . . . very sad. Goodbye! (*She exits quickly taking* YE-HUDA *and* RAQUEL *with her.*)

Isaac. Wait! You forgot the necklace and the mirror . . . Wait! (*But darkness swallows them up. While* ISAAC *closes his eyes, the area becomes filled with spies.*)

Scene 5. *With the Teacher.*

The sound of the shofar *is heard. The holy place where the* TEACHER *is gloomily blowing on the* shofar *is lit up.* ISAAC *awakens and stands up.*

Isaac. Teacher, I recaptured a glimpse of past bliss close to the Queen, with the birds and the water fountain . . . But it slipped through my fingers! What good is it to remember happiness in the midst of pain? I feel a threat in the air.

Teacher. Isaac . . .

Isaac. Yes . . .

Teacher. Raise your eyes. What do you see in the sky?

Isaac. Stars, shining stars. *(The wind whistles. The space is filled with stars.)*

Teacher. I'm going to give you a surprise . . . Those stars are searching for each other. Their greatest wish is to be together. Ah, if they could only become one . . .

Isaac. Of course. *(He becomes anxious.)* Because together they would give off a great light . . .

Teacher. Yes.

Isaac. Immense! That would end all our misfortunes!

Teacher. Because they would light the path of the Lord to us.

Isaac. Yes. *(He pauses and is overwhelmed with anguish.)* But they are alone in the sky. Teacher . . . why are they scattered?

Teacher. Isaac . . . *(A sad smile crosses his face.)* Whoever can explain it, can also explain why man is like a wolf to his fellowmen. *(He raises the* shofar *and blows it.* ISAAC *confronts him.)*

Isaac. Wait! From here only those small isolated lights are seen, but it is there below where men are evil.

Teacher. *(Observing him in silence)* That's why you climbed the mountain, to find answers.

Isaac. But I want to bring the answers there, where the pain is. *(The* TEACHER *doesn't answer.* ISAAC *becomes rebellious.)* Why should one look for them here, where one speaks and listens only to his own echo? *(Silence)* What is God without man, who is down below? Justice, beauty, love, mercy, sacrifice, nothing exists if man does not exist!

Teacher. Man does not exist if he doesn't know God.

Isaac. And God is nothing without man! *(Silence. The* TEACHER *turns his back on him, pensively.)* Teacher, man's suffering is the measure of all things.

Teacher. Isaac, the doubts that consume you, the burden that weighs on your heart, prevent your soul from taking flight.

Isaac. I don't know if I want to give up this burden! It is the weight of those I know and those who suffer. Now I carry their fear, their rage, their despair, their madness . . .

Teacher. Isaac, why don't you allow each person to look for their own path to reach God when they need it? Didn't you wait until you lost your way before you came to me?

Isaac. (Closing his eyes) Yes . . .

Teacher. (Smiling at him) Never forget that I can lead you in your path because you climbed the mountain to ask for my help.

Isaac. (Yielding, surrendering himself) Yes . . . help me, please . . .

Teacher. So, to begin, Isaac, I have to tell you that if you want to enter the world of the occult you have to leave everyday life behind you. *(He raises the* shofar.*)* If you don't, divine splendor will never touch you. *(He blows the* shofar *for a long while.* ISAAC *raises his head and looks at the sky. He is filled with doubts.)*

Scene 6. *At the Entrance to the Town Hall.*

(The shofar *continues to be heard. In the village, next to the entrance to the Town Hall,* RODRIGO *listens nervously to that unfamiliar sound. At his feet, strange metal instruments. He busies himself with them as* DEVOTO *passes by and looks at them with surprise.)*

Devoto. Rodrigo!

Rodrigo. Devoto . . .

Devoto. What an interesting instrument.

Rodrigo. The hammer.

Devoto. What?

Rodrigo. Hand me the hammer.

Devoto. Your hammer . . . Señor Constable . . . *(All of a sudden he climbs onto a beam of the instrument and swings on it.)* It reminds me of the scaffolding for the fairs where we used to play as children.

Rodrigo. Nails!

Devoto. (Looking at him from above) What?

Rodrigo. Hand me the nails! *(*DEVOTO *jumps down and gives them to him.* RODRIGO *keeps on working.)*

Devoto. When did this arrive?

Rodrigo. I received it today.

Devoto. What's it for?

Rodrigo. Does a doctor like Devoto de la Cruz have to ask, or does he just know? *(Suddenly* DEVOTO *grows pale.)*

Devoto. These . . .

Rodrigo. Yes!

Devoto. are instruments . . .

Rodrigo. Yes! Yes!

Devoto. of the Holy Inquisition.

Rodrigo. You guessed! Give me those chains. (DEVOTO *whimpers.)* They say that when someone is inside one of these instruments . . . *(He skillfully maneuvers* DEVOTO *into it; when he wants to escape,* RODRIGO *pulls him back with the chain.)* they quickly come to their senses and talk.

Devoto. Ay, I'm stuck.

Rodrigo. They just keep on talking.

Devoto. Rodrigo . . .

Rodrigo. Yes, they blurt out everything they know!

Devoto. This is hurting my neck. I'm going to choke . . .

Rodrigo. (Proudly) This instrument is a product of the New Order. How do you like the New Order, Devoto?

Devoto. I just love the New Order!

Rodrigo. (Encouraging him to repeat after him) Long live the New Order.

Devoto. Long live the New Order! *(He coughs, almost suffocating. With pathetic eyes he begs* RODRIGO *to let him out.)* Rodrigo, it hurts me here . . .

Rodrigo. Just by seeing them, people will understand the New Order. And if the exhibit doesn't convince them, the Holy Office will put them to use.

Devoto. Why are you doing this to me? Aren't I your friend? I always loved you, I lent you money . . .

Rodrigo. Devoto, I heard that sound again.

Devoto. What sound? *(As* ISAAC *returns home carrying his bag, he sees* DEVOTO *and* RODRIGO. *He slows down and spies on them.)*

Rodrigo. We both know what I'm talking about! *(He tightens some screws. Inside,* DEVOTO *starts kicking.)*

Devoto. Ah . . . you heard a *shofar.*

Rodrigo. A what?

Devoto. A *shofar! (He imitates the sound with his lips.)* The horn that the Jews blow in the synagogue. It has three sounds . . . one long, tooooo . . . one short, tooo, and one in between, too-oo-oo . . .

Rodrigo. Why do they play the *shofar* . . . the Jews?

Devoto. The *shofar* recreates the sorrows of the heart.

Rodrigo. The sorrows of the heart? Ha, ha! Then it's for lovers . . .

Devoto. No, no! (RODRIGO *turns the screws again.* DEVOTO *whimpers.*) They say that one day it will announce the coming of the Messiah.

Rodrigo. The what?

Devoto. The redeemer of humanity. (RODRIGO *unexpectedly grabs him by the jacket and shakes him.*)

Rodrigo. Devoto, I don't want to hear any nonsense from you! I want to know who is playing it! I want names!

Devoto. My neck . . .

Rodrigo. (*He walks away, nervously.*) I'm listening to you.

Devoto. For the last few nights some Jews have been meeting in the synagogues to practice their rituals.

Rodrigo. Black magic, eh?

Devoto. They are mystical rituals, related to black magic, where they invoke God . . .

Rodrigo. God? What God?

Devoto. Their God . . . not ours . . .

Rodrigo. Devoto, there is only one God! Ours! We're Christians, aren't we?

Devoto. We're Christians, yes, we're Christians . . . but Rodrigo, that's the way they address God. It's as if we would speak to Him without priests.

Rodrigo. That's a sin! They can burn you for being a heretic! And what do they expect to get from that?

Devoto. They expect God to tell them when their suffering will be over. (RODRIGO *remains pensive for a moment.*)

Rodrigo. And does God answer them?

Devoto. No. God says nothing! He doesn't answer anything! (*He begins to bang.*) I want to get out! Rodrigo, I want to get out!

Rodrigo. No one is going to blow the *shofar* anymore in this town.

Devoto. Please! (*Silence.* RODRIGO *opens the instrument.* ISAAC *leaves in disgust.*)

Rodrigo. Let's continue this talk somewhere else.

Devoto. Rodrigo . . . I can breathe again! (*He hugs him and laughs.*)

Rodrigo. You were afraid . . . eh?

Devoto. I was! My foot fell asleep. (*He limps.*) Ha, ha! Better asleep than sawed off!

Rodrigo. (*Fixing the machine and arranging the instruments of torture*) And now, to the tavern!

Devoto. I need a drink! "Devoto, Rodrigo is ordering you to have

some wine!" *(He laughs.)* Ay, how good it is to drink wine when
I'm forced to . . . *(They leave arm in arm, humming.)*

Scene 7. *Sara's House.*

The lights come up on the part of the stage where SARA'S *house
is. She sings as she cleans some pots.* YEHUDA, *an adolescent
now, feeds his grandfather, who is very old.* ISAAC *enters.*

Isaac. Raquel! Yehuda! (SARA *clutches her chest. Her intuition
told her that he was going to come.* ISAAC *drops his bag on the
floor and opens his arms.)* I'm home again! *(He looks at them
with affection.)* How are you, Sara?

Sara. (Lowering her eyes) Fine.

Ezra. Help your grandfather stand up, Yehuda.

Isaac. Can I help too? *(He helps, then he looks at him.)* Papá . . .

Ezra. Isaac! *(He embraces him.)* You've come back to us! *(To*
YEHUDA, *hesitating)* Did you know that he was coming today?

Yehuda. No, he wasn't coming today.

Isaac. (Touching him) Why is your beard so dirty? Isn't anyone
taking care of you here? *(He wants to touch* YEHUDA, *but* YE-
HUDA *pulls away. He points at him angrily.)* You and I have
to talk.

Ezra. You came, Isaac . . . (YEHUDA *sits the* GRANDFATHER *down,
and continues to feed him.* ISAAC *is aware of his hostility but
says nothing.)*

Isaac. Listen! I've travelled all the way from Granada without
stopping. Do you know what's going on? *(Silence)* News travels
fast. I thought that you would find out before I arrived. Granada
has fallen! The last of the Moors were defeated. Boabdil, the
sultan I had the honor of meeting, a cultured man and a patron
of the arts, surrendered. From now on, all of Spain is Christian.

Ezra. (Addressing his grandson) What is he saying?

Yehuda. Eat, Grandfather, eat!

Ezra. Granada has fallen and there's trouble. I knew that there
was going to be trouble!

Isaac. Happily, the Monarchs acted quickly and guaranteed that
as of today, Moors, Jews and Christians will be able to live
together, in peace.

Yehuda. I would like to know just how they guaranteed it . . .

Isaac. (Surprised at his comment) In writing, foolish boy! They
signed documents. How else would they guarantee it? Doesn't
this boy understand anything? You'll have to be more alert if
you're ever going to attend the university!

Ezra. There's trouble . . .

Sara. Yehuda, don't feed him without tying something around his neck so that he doesn't get himself dirty.

Yehuda. *(Cleaning him up)* What's the matter, Grandfather, that you're so nervous?

Ezra. Isaac gets angry and shouts. I knew something wrong would happen . . .

Isaac. I met with the leaders of the Jewish community, Papá. They're not stupid! They went over the documents that the Monarchs signed, word for word! Then they called me to ask me what I thought. They value my opinion.

Yehuda. Because they know he lives at court and that he's close to the Queen.

Sara. Enough, Yehuda! *(To* ISAAC*)* What did you tell them?

Isaac. That both Isabel and Fernando can be trusted.

Sara. *(Silence)* What does that mean? That there won't be any more persecutions? That the killing of the "heretics" will end? That they won't build any more stakes to burn people?

Isaac. Sara, *(sighs, distraught)* sometimes there are sinister people around the Monarchs who acquire power, no one knows how. They grow like mushrooms! They are the ones who nowadays side with the Inquisition. What do they want? To get rid of all of us who are different. They whisper in the Monarchs' ears that it's easier to control a country where everyone is like everyone else. *(Silence. A smile spreads over his face.)* But I told them what the Monarchs signed. This is a country made up of different communities, who have lived here for a very long time, with their language and customs. They are proud of their traditions. No one can destroy their roots. It's impossible! *(*SARA *continues with her household chores. A bell is heard.* ISAAC *becomes upset.)* That bell! *(Hiding his feelings)* Yehuda, I remember when you were little and I used to take you to the plaza. Then we would go to the country and run through the fields.

Yehuda. How many times did you take me?

Sara. Isaac, everything has changed! They forbid us to do so many things we used to do! We Jews not only have to live together, but now we can't go further than the marketplace . . .

Isaac. What?

Ezra. My brother went to Granada to denounce all this! Your uncle, Moisés . . . What happened, didn't he get there?

Yehuda. Grandfather, keep eating. *(Silence)*

Isaac. But in life not everything is sorrow. Sara, Yehuda, look what I brought . . . Sara, Granada is a Persian market! *(He goes through his bag.)* You can find cloth from Egypt, necklaces from Smyrna, dresses from Salonica . . . *(Silence)* Why isn't Raquel here?

Sara. She went to see her fiancé Halil.

Isaac. It's forbidden to go further than the marketplace and you let her go alone to another town?

Sara. She didn't go alone! *(Silence)*

Isaac. I brought gifts for everyone. Let's see how this dress looks on you . . .

Sara. (She takes it and smiles.) What's the matter with it? The Queen doesn't wear it anymore?

Isaac. You want to start fighting? *(He pulls her to him, forcing her to look at him.)* I chose it with you in mind.

Sara. I like . . . the color . . . *(She moves away, touched.* EZRA *stands up, tottering.)*

Yehuda. Is there something wrong, Grandfather?

Ezra. (He pushes him aside, brusquely.) We can't go any further than the marketplace! And if my brother is not back yet . . . something must have happened to him!

Isaac. Listen! *(He claps his hands.)* I have plans! *(*EZRA *looks at him, breathing heavily.)* I know, I know. Each time I come home I say the same thing . . . but this time it's different! I want you all to come and live with me!

Ezra. We're from the country, not the court.

Isaac. Yes, but here they have you all imprisoned!

Yehuda. Didn't you see the instruments of torture? How strange, they're on display in front of the Town Hall. Then the Holy Office will arrive, and then the interrogations will begin. It's always the same. And no document signed by the Monarchs is going to stop them.

Isaac. These things go on in other places too! And they'll continue . . . for a while. That's why I want you to come and live with me, so that in the meantime you can study.

Yehuda. Didn't you say that I'm stupid?

Isaac. I began to teach at the university to show my sympathy with the New Order.

Yehuda. The same Order that burns anyone who doesn't agree with it?

Isaac. Profound changes are taking place here and we have to prepare ourselves to understand them! *(His tone is somewhat apprehensive.* EZRA *becomes excited.)*

Ezra. Yes, Isaac, perhaps Yehuda can follow in your footsteps at the court. But who can assure his success today?

Isaac. Papá, it was because of discussions like these that I had to leave this house!

Yehuda. Wasn't it because Mamá bored you?

Ezra. Isaac, *(holding his head)* you've lost your roots.

Isaac. We're starting with that again.

Ezra. And now you'll do the same thing with your own son . . .

Isaac. And he shouldn't study? Should he stay here, so he won't stray from our traditions? Yes, I know, Papá, that you're sorry for having made me study, for my having come so far . . .

Ezra. What good is it? *(Breathing with difficulty.* YEHUDA *holds him up.)* Why are they sending you those books?

Isaac. (Surprised) What books?

Yehuda. The ones that arrived from the court. *(*ISAAC *runs over to the books and begins to leaf through them, feverishly. An overhead light reveals* DEVOTO, *who is walking through a corridor of the castle.)*

Devoto. I sent you the *Sepher Yetzira* and the *Sepher Hazohar al Ha-Torah,* the *Shoshan Edut* and the *Sepher Ha-Rimon,* also known as the *Book of the Pomegranate Tree.*

Ezra. Who sends you books about the Kabbalah?

Isaac. You're still questioning the books I receive? No one has the right to censor what I read, Papá!

Ezra. I know who it is, that renegade Abraham . . .

Isaac. Now he goes by the name of Devoto de la Cruz, and he's a great doctor!

Ezra. That "devotee of the cross" does it because he wants you to convert, like he did.

Devoto. You have to read those books very carefully. Even the most pious person can lose his mind in their pages.

Isaac. I'm studying the Kabbalah, which isn't the same thing!

Ezra. Our law forbids the Kabbalah!

Isaac. Our law doesn't forbid anything! How could it forbid learning? Your concept of the law was always very narrow. It questions the Kabbalah, which isn't the same thing.

Devoto. Some Jews believe that by mastering that knowledge they can alter fate.

Yehuda. Your visits always upset us.

Isaac. (To his son) No!

Yehuda. Yes!

Isaac. In Spain, Papá, everyone is free to . . .

Yehuda. Free, you said? Who is free in Spain?

Devoto. The books I sent you are all different. Each kabbalist has his own method. (ISAAC *holds his head, confused.* EZRA *walks unsteadily.*)

Ezra. I should never have allowed you to mix with the village boys.

Isaac. "I should never have allowed you to mix with the village boys!" Why, did they contaminate me? How is one supposed to live isolated from the world? They learn from us just as we learn from them!

Devoto. Oh, and please, don't confuse a *shofar* with a bell, lowering your arms with raising them, or fasting with praying, because all the Kabbalah teachers agree on one thing: fate hangs on one small detail . . . (*He exits, laughing. The lights from the palace go down.* SARA *enters wearing her new dress. She stops and looks at them.*)

Sara. I heard shouting. Now I realize how many men there are in my home, and each one thinks differently. Even Yehuda . . .

Isaac. I wasn't wrong when I chose this color. It brightens you, Sara. (*He goes to her and hugs her. Silence.*)

Sara. How long are you staying?

Isaac. I don't know, I don't know when I'm going back. I came following an impulse. I needed to be with you. But you didn't like it. (*He caresses her.*) What am I supposed to do? Send a messenger?

Sara. (*Takes a hand-mirror and looks at herself*) They sent a messenger for us that time. Raquel was very little, Yehuda drank wine and we found you with her . . .

Isaac. (*Takes her hand and kisses it*) You look fresh and young like a bride!

Sara. (*Upset*) I have nothing for you to eat.

Isaac. Sara . . . We have to learn to live in the New Order. You are my family . . . Let's not be divided any longer! (RAQUEL *arrives, as if in a trance.* SARA *cries out.*)

Raquel. Ay, Mamá! They left . . .

Sara. Raquel, what's the matter with you?

Ezra. Papá is here.

Raquel. I want to die . . .

Sara. (*To* YEHUDA) Bring water, quickly! (YEHUDA *exits quickly.* ISAAC *steps back, deep in his dreams. Slowly light comes up on the mountain. The* shofar *is heard.*)

Raquel. Leave me alone . . . just leave me alone . . .

Sara. Isaac, where are you?

Isaac. (*Kneels down and takes his daughter in his arms*) Here I am, Raquel . . .

Sara. Raquel, what happened?

Raquel. My fiancé Halil . . .

Sara. What? *(She moves toward* RAQUEL *to listen to her, as* RA- QUEL *sways convulsively, laughing and weeping.)*

Raquel. Five families, they left in a single day! The peasant woman told me to stop searching because there was no one left in the village. They were the last to leave! They left, Mamá . . .

Sara. It can't be. How could your fiancé just abandon you?

Ezra. Let's be calm. Raquel, Papá brought presents.

Yehuda. *(Defiantly, to his father)* Now do you see? They're going to make our lives impossible!

Sara. *(Shaking her head)* This situation is hopeless . . . *(In the holy place on stage, the* TEACHER *stands up and performs ritual movements.)*

Isaac. *(On his knees, with* RAQUEL *in his arms. He raises his eyes.)* God, how should I interpret this? Is this happening because you are not part of me?

Sara. Isaac, this is when we need you with us! Why were they so scared? Why did they escape without telling us? Where is your daughter's fiancé?

Yehuda. "Everything will turn out fine." That's what he's going to tell you, just like always.

Sara. Find him! Both of you! Search in the next village. Maybe they haven't left Spain yet. *(Crying)* We should have left with them. We should have left too.

Yehuda. We don't matter to him. His mind is there. And if it hadn't been the Queen, he would have fallen in love with someone else . . .

Ezra. Look for my brother too! Isaac, don't forget your uncle!

Sara. Go! You have to find them!

Raquel. Papá! *(She embraces him, as the suffering image of the* TEACHER *disappears.)*

Scene 8. *Farewell in the Palace of the Queen.*

Artillery salute. A patriotic Spanish march can be heard, sung by a crowd. Lights go up in the corridors and in a hall of the palace where high level officials of the Crown begin to gather. ISAAC *walks among them, calling attention to himself, alone and disturbed. They greet him and bow with irony, spying on him and gossiping.* ISAAC *looks around, perplexed, and leans against a pillar. The bells toll frantically. The* QUEEN *enters from the opposite side of the stage followed by her entourage. She walks resolutely to the hall where the people are gathered.* ISAAC *steps in front of her.*

Isaac. Your Majesty!

Isabel. I don't want to be bothered now.

Isaac. It's me, Isaac. *(She stops and looks at him. His appearance frightens her.)*

Isabel. When we were discussing the situation of the Jews, we invited you to participate. But you got up and left!

Isaac. There were so many people, I thought that it wouldn't be noticed.

Isabel. No one has ever done anything like that to me! In front of Fernando, the cardinal, our loyal noblemen, heroes of the Reconquest . . . I'm sorry, but we cannot converse at this moment, Doctor.

Isaac. If you intend to sign the Edict, this is a farewell, not a conversation.

Isabel. It's a shame, Isaac, that you didn't participate in the discussion. It was so hot in that room . . . I asked for another meeting because I don't see clearly what decision I should make.

Isaac. What you decide will allow me to live or condemn me to die. *(Silence.* ISABEL *frowns. She watches her followers who have removed themselves a respectful distance away.)*

Isabel. You're always exaggerating . . . *(She draws near him, overcome by intense sensual feelings.)* For me, the Edict is one thing, and you are another.

Isaac. The Edict is one thing, my family is another, Spain is another . . .

Isabel. And the two of us . . . one! Together, we've always felt a strange communion, somehow like a mystical bond. *(She smiles at him, fanning herself.)* Isn't that so, Isaac? *(She goes towards him and touches him, ignoring her entourage that moves even further away.* ISAAC *looks at her intently. Indeed, they are bound by a strange intimacy.* ISAAC *takes her hand and caresses it.)*

Isaac. If you sign an edict that expels us from this country, what kind of communion can there be between us? *(More dignitaries gather in the hall. The whispering grows.* ISABEL *becomes impatient.)*

Isabel. Find out why they're making so much noise. Is everyone there? *(She turns to* ISAAC *while someone walks towards the hall.)* My dear one, you're so pained. What's the matter? There are papers I sign that don't concern you! *(*DEVOTO *appears surreptitiously and spies on them from behind a pillar.* ISAAC *grabs him by the jacket and drags him in front of them.)*

Isaac. Allow me, my much esteemed Queen, to introduce to you the very eminent doctor . . .

Devoto. (Bowing exaggeratedly) Devoto de la Santa Cruz.

Isaac. He's an excellent physician. (DEVOTO *kneels on the ground and lowers his eyes.)*

Isabel. I have an excellent physician.

Isaac. I might not be here. (ISABEL *moves away, taking* ISAAC *with her.)*

Isabel. Isaac, I will never allow anyone else to examine me . . .

Isaac. Your Majesty, never say never in the New Order. (ISABEL *sighs, touched.)*

Isabel. What can I do to reassure you? Let's bring Yehuda and Raquel to live here.

Isaac. More names are missing.

Isabel. Sara too. Do you see how I remember?

Isaac. More names are missing.

Isabel. Ezra, your father.

Isaac. Still more names are missing! Now my family is everyone. Even the naive ones from Granada who believed in you! (ISABEL *paces from one corner to the other. The whispering of the functionaries becomes unbearable.)*

Isabel. There are moments when I hate to be Queen. *(She notices* DEVOTO *who is following her everywhere.)* Come! *(Laughing, she drags him, following a sudden whim.)* I want you to kiss Isaac's hand, as if he were the King!

Isaac. I don't feel like it today.

Isabel. (To DEVOTO*)* Come on, show me what you can do. You must be very efficient if you want to be at my side! *(In a leap,* DEVOTO *prostrates himself at* ISAAC'S *feet and covers his hand with kisses. He continues to stare at her intensely.)*

Devoto. King Isaac, at your feet. Whatever you wish, Your Highness!

Isaac. If I were king I would order all the inquisitors who believe in the benefits of the stake, to throw themselves into the flames so that they could scientifically explain the purifying effect of the fire.

Devoto. (Following him everywhere on his knees, murmuring) Yes, Your Excellency! Just as you wish . . . *(Taking notes)* All the inquisitors . . . should throw themselves . . . into the fire!

Isaac. I would also order the wheel of time to return to the moment when the Queen signed the Edict . . .

Isabel. What's done, Isaac, cannot be undone.

Isaac. Then I abdicate and leave.

Devoto. Your Majesty, don't do that, please . . .

Isaac. (To DEVOTO*)* Enough! (DEVOTO *does a cartwheel in the*

*air and stands up, happy. Spies disappear and then reappear
somewhere else.* ISABEL *fans herself nervously.)*

Isabel. They're demanding that I take harsher measures, the noblemen, the Inquisition . . .

Isaac. I was happy here . . . for a thousand years. I never knew I
was just passing through.

Isabel. I defend you in spite of what they say about us.

Isaac. I never dreamed that my feelings toward you would ever
be returned. *(His voice breaks.)* That's why they were so beautiful. *(Bells begin to toll frantically.* ISABEL *sees how* ISAAC *becomes anguished. She takes his hand.* DEVOTO *places himself
where he can listen.)*

Isabel. Isaac, I'm going to command them to close the last patio
for us, later on. We can take refuge there when it's all over . . .

Isaac. After you've signed . . . ?

Isabel. *(Gesturing for him to sit next to her)* Do you like my new
perfume? *(The Queen's throne is brought into the hall. Everyone
makes way to grant her her place of honor. The voices become
louder. The messenger returns and signals her with his eyes that
everyone is awaiting her arrival.* ISABEL *becomes exasperated.)*
Can it be possible that I'm not going to have even one moment
to think calmly?

Isaac. Isabel, what if God appeared to you in your dreams and
ordered you to stop the expulsion?

Isabel. My confessor is the only one who reads my dreams.

Isaac. And what would happen if tomorrow the Inquisition burned
me at the stake?

Isabel. *(Smiling)* Would you be that cruel, to leave me all alone?

Isaac. Then . . . there's nothing we can do together anymore . . .
(He is about to leave, when she stops him.)

Isabel. Isaac! *(She extends her hand.)* I want my ring. *(*ISAAC *looks
at her in surprise.)* Yes, the royal ring, with the emblem of Cas-
tille that you stole from me.

Isaac. That I stole from you?

Isabel. All right, that I gave you. The same thing happened with
an embroidered handkerchief that you asked me for. *(She smiles
suggestively.)* I want my gifts back.

Isaac. Here's your ring.

Isabel. Tell me. What did you do with my precious gifts, my dear?
(She puts on her ring.) Did you display them under the light of
the moon and recite strange words? Did you perform kabbalistic
rituals? And what happened? Didn't the amulets have any effect,
Isaac? Am I too strong for the Kabbalah?

Isaac. (Overwhelmed by a profound melancholy) I'm a desperate man . . .

Isabel. A man who has suddenly turned into a child. *(She goes to him with tenderness.)* You see, Isaac, I am open to your weaknesses, but you don't open yourself to the cross! *(Silence. She claps her hands.)* To the hall! Everyone is waiting for me. *(She exits quickly, followed by her entourage.* ISAAC *covers his face. He is very upset.* DEVOTO *appears from behind a pillar, and walks over to him on tiptoes.)*

Devoto. She found out about your magic tricks! In these cases the kabbalists recommend, above all, fasting, asceticism and much prayer.

Isaac. You find my situation amusing . . .

Devoto. I'm trying to figure out how to help you!

Isaac. When they expel us it won't be better for you! *(Crushed)* There hasn't been an edict like this since Babylonian times. God, when did our exile begin? When Adam disobeyed you in paradise?

Devoto. At the palace they think you're going to convert, like all the intelligent people. *(He points to himself as he bows.)*

Isaac. I am not going to convert!

Devoto. Isaac, we know what's going to happen afterwards!

Isaac. That's right. No one will dare to be different, no one will criticize, write, investigate . . .

Devoto. Careful . . . the archbishop is pointing at you . . . the Inquisition is naming you and sharpening its knives.

Isaac. We have lived here for a thousand years! A thousand years, and one day . . . they signed an edict that . . .

Devoto. Isaac, that's not the way for a serious doctor to talk! *(He laughs, maliciously.)* What you need now is a Christian doctor by your side. *(He points to himself, as he bows again.)* But you never appreciated me . . .

Isaac. Come on, Devoto. I remind you of a past that's difficult to accept. *(Two important court officials draped in impressive garments that cover them completely, look at* ISAAC *from the corner of their eyes.* DEVOTO *bows deeply to them, but they ignore him.)*

Devoto. Farewell, Your Excellency. And how are you, most distinguished lord? At your service! Eternally at your service. Whatever you need, you may count on me . . . for a cold or a toothache. *(He turns to* ISAAC.*)* Have you noticed that all the cardinals have flat feet? That's why they have backaches. What you need is to build up a clientele. *(While he speaks, an imposing*

*figure with a piercing stare emerges silently from the wings. He
is dressed in black from head to toe and wears an enormous
crucifix.)*

Isaac. Tomás de Torquemada. *(The* QUEEN *reappears followed by
her entourage. She extends her hand and he takes it as they
proceed to the hall where the court dignitaries are awaiting
them.* ISAAC *leans over to watch. Then he goes to a water fountain and drinks in great gulps.* DEVOTO *follows him.)*

Devoto. I recently returned from a long trip. *(He walks around,
pretending to be an important doctor.)* I'm up to date on the
latest findings of the Arabs. In Egypt they've discovered rare
herbs . . .

Isaac. (Grabs him, suddenly interested) . . . What do they cure?

Devoto. New illnesses that the wind brings in this direction. Why?

Isaac. I need one that will change the way people think!

Devoto. Only the Kabbalah can take care of that! *(Pulling away)* I
barely managed to obtain an ointment to ease skin eruptions . . .

Isaac. Perhaps you had one of my patients in mind?

Devoto. You guessed right! *(He laughs, while* ISAAC *wanders
distractedly.)*

Isaac. Medicine no longer brings me peace . . . Alchemy will not
stop the expulsion . . . What's left? *(His face darkens.)* I must
go deeper into the world of the occult. *(Slowly the lights dim.)*

Scene 9. Torquemada.

Strident court music is heard. The QUEEN *is sitting on her throne
with a rigid expression.* TORQUEMADA, *who has accompanied her
to the hall, sits at her side. The court officials take their ceremonial places.*

Isabel. Let the representatives of the Jewish community enter!
*(Her tone is different from the one we have come to know. She
speaks and breathes authority. A high ranking official exits to
carry out her order. Three nervous people cross the corridor
that leads to the hall. For an instant their gazes meet* ISAAC'S,
who lowers his head. They enter the hall and bow.)

Leader 1. Your Majesty . . .

Isabel. I receive you with the same deference with which we have
always received you, because the Jews have lived here for centuries under royal protection. I myself have always kept my doors
open and my ears ready to listen to your concerns. Isn't that so?

Leader 2. Yes, Your Majesty. *(She turns her head to be sure that they are following her. But the man who is seated next to her has his gaze fixed on a distant spot. He looks like a statue.)*

Isabel. But we have not been treated with the same respect. *(The Jewish leaders exchange tense looks. One of them steps forward and asks permission to say something.)*

Leader 3. Excuse me, but . . . *(The* QUEEN *stops him short.)*

Isabel. You have come to listen, not to speak. *(Silence. She turns towards* TORQUEMADA. *Her tone changes.)* We have asked our Inquisitor General, Tomás de Torquemada, whose intelligence is proverbial, to explain the attitude that we intend to assume. *(Silence.* TORQUEMADA *is the center of attention. He seems absent, his mind deep in his own thoughts. He speaks very softly at the beginning. As soon as* TORQUEMADA *begins,* ISAAC *hurriedly exits.)*

Torquemada. Your Majesty, any of your servants could do it better than I, but I am here at your command. *(He bows, then advances. His steps are deliberately slow. At times he seems like a sick man.)* I shall resume your thought, Your Majesty. You . . . the Jews . . . have offended us.

Leader 1. We have?

Torquemada. For trying to distance the Christians from the Church.

Leader 2. That's not true . . . *(Silence.* TORQUEMADA *slowly turns to the* QUEEN.)

Torquemada. I know them. Now they're going to say that I am lying.

Isabel. Go on, Monseñor . . .

Torquemada. They always get their way. They are stronger than we are.

Isabel. Calm down, they have come to listen, not to plead their case. *(Silence.* TORQUEMADA *looks at them with malice.)*

Torquemada. Haven't you tried to initiate Christians into your rites and religious customs? Didn't you give them books to recite your prayers, so that they would know the dates of your festivals and celebrate them with you? Didn't you show them how to prepare your foods, and when to fast so that they would do the same? *(He stands behind the throne.)* We have proof! The Inquisition has confessions from Jews . . . and from those who were corrupted by the likes of you . . .

Leader 3. We are being accused with lies!

Torquemada. *(To* ISABEL*)* I told you, Your Majesty, that they would deny everything.

Isabel. Conclude, Monseñor! *(She stands up. Her authoritarian tone makes the Jewish leaders back away.* TORQUEMADA *breathes deeply, as if searching for strength.)*

Torquemada. Our decisions were thought out very carefully.

Isabel. I can attest to that. Before deciding, we consulted with the men of the Church, the nobility, the scientists. No one can say that we proceeded hastily! *(Silence)* Monseñor, are you feeling better? *(He leans on her.)* I am going to make them listen now to what we have prepared. (ISABEL *sits on her throne once again. Deadly silence.)* Gentlemen, we have decided on the expulsion of all the Jews from these lands. *(Murmuring)* Everyone must leave with their sons, their daughters and their relatives, young and old.

Leader 1. (To LEADER 2*)* But . . .

Leader 2. (Whispering to him) Where to?

Torquemada. You'll be given time to sell your land, your belongings, your furniture . . .

Leader 3. (To LEADER 1*)* It's a death sentence.

Leader 1. (To LEADER 2*)* What are we going to do?

Torquemada. . . . And when you leave you may take your belongings as long as you do not remove gold, silver or money from the country.

Leader 2. But then . . .

Torquemada. You will have a merciful protection of the Crown until the last day. But if you return, death will be waiting for you. And those who protect you will suffer the same punishment. (DEVOTO *paces among the pillars in a daze.)*

Devoto. Finally! Finally!

Isabel. (To TORQUEMADA*)* They need to hear exactly what the Edict says, to know what they can and what they can't do.

Torquemada. They will have it as soon as you sign it. And then it will be known in the cities, the towns, and the villages, as is the custom. *(Pause)* Your Majesty, I feel weak. May I withdraw? *(The* LEADERS, *greatly disturbed, approach the* QUEEN *and desperately beseech her.)*

Leader 3. Please, Your Majesty, do not sign that Edict.

Leader 2. It will cause enormous harm.

Leader 1. By what you hold most dear . . .

Leader 2. We belong to this land . . .

Leader 3. To this people . . .

Leader 2. We promise to . . . *(Exchanging glances with each other)* raise a large amount of money.

Leader 1. (Agreeing) We understand the difficult times that the Crown is going through . . .

Leader 2. . . . It is the motherland of our children, too.

Leader 3. Thirty thousand crowns! We offer thirty thousand crowns to your coffers!

Leader 2. Thirty thousand crowns . . . *(Lowering his head. It is an enormous sum.)*

Leader 1. Thirty thousand crowns! Is that good, Your Majesty? Please, think over your decision . . . We are all part of one big family . . . Do not tear us away from this land!

Leader 2. We will never be the same away from this country where we were born. *(The* QUEEN *hesitates. Amid the silence, she looks all around for* TORQUEMADA.*)*

Isabel. Monseñor . . .

Torquemada. They look at me with terror. I can't stand it. I can't face them.

Isabel. (Stands up and goes to him) But I need your opinion!

Torquemada. So many hours of work . . . I'm at the end of my strength.

Isabel. You are my advisor, my confessor . . .

Torquemada. My enemies are killing me. I am carried away by my passions.

Isabel. Father, please! *(Silence)*

Torquemada. Your Majesty, my intuition tells me that we must strive for a strong fatherland, united by a single idea and a single faith . . . *(Murmurs. He raises his voice.)* Only then shall we be invincible!

Leader 3. (Steps forward) We too want a strong fatherland . . .

Leader 2. . . . even though we don't share the same faith. Why should that be so important?

Torquemada. (Taking a step backwards. He feels attacked. The exchange has been exacerbating.) Yes, I heard . . . you have just offered a huge amount of money . . .

Leader 1. Thirty thousand crowns!

Torquemada. It is a significant amount.

Isabel. We do need it.

Torquemada. Take it . . . I do not disapprove.

Isabel. You accept it then?

Torquemada. Yes. *(The* QUEEN *observes the bewilderment around her.)*

Leader 1. But then . . .

Leader 2. Then you're not going to sign the Edict?

Isabel. Monseñor, what is this? Are we going backwards? *(Suddenly* TORQUEMADA *becomes frantic.)*

Torquemada. Why shouldn't you accept such a fortune? Who op-

poses it, Your Majesty? *(Smiling sarcastically)* Is honor worth
less than social position? Is lineage less important than wealth?

Isabel. Explain yourself! (TORQUEMADA *lifts the crucifix in front
of everyone.*)

Torquemada. Judas sold Christ for thirty coins . . . We do it for
thirty thousand! Who will stop us from selling him? Everything
has its price! We'll save the coffers, but we can't save the souls.
Someone just said that thirty thousand crowns is a huge amount,
and he knows what he's saying. Do we know what we are con-
demning ourselves to? To hell! Then let us sell Christ and let us
all be damned! (ISABEL *agonizes with uncertainty.* TORQUEMADA
*knows that his moment has come. Perhaps for that reason he
moans and squirms, about to suffer a nervous attack.*) Your
Majesty, I had a different image of my Spain. But let me die and
you'll see how horror reigns . . .

Isabel. Monseñor . . . What should I do?

*Torquemada. (Holding the crucifix in one hand and lifting the pen
in the other)* Sign the expulsion, Isabel! Let's be done with this
damned community . . . Let's eradicate them from our land . . .
Then we shall grow healthy roots, because our blood will be
pure . . .

Isabel. The King . . . did he sign?

Torquemada. He signed!

Isabel. Then . . . I shall sign too. *(Takes the pen and signs. The
LEADERS become hopeless with despair, while TORQUEMADA triumphantly rolls up the parchment.)*

Leaders. No, Your Majesty . . . Listen to us . . .

Isabel. (Shouting) From this moment on, the Edict takes effect!
*(The Jewish LEADERS bang their heads together in desperation.
Music is heard. The royal retinue takes its place behind ISABEL.
TORQUEMADA positions himself next to ISABEL, and loudly
declares)*

Torquemada. The three pillars on which the New Order stands
are: one crown, one people, one religion! *(He leaves shouting
through the corridors. A patriotic march muffles his voice.
Lights go down.)*

Scene 10. *At the Village Square.*

Lights go up on the plaza in ISAAC'S *village. Crowds of poor peasants run through the streets, desperately looking for ways to satisfy
their hunger. Some carry bags with their belongings.*

Male peasant 1. There is nothing! Nothing left!

Male peasant 2. Doesn't anyone throw out any garbage in this town?

Female peasant 1. (Looking through a heap of scraps) The dogs don't leave even the bones . . .

Male peasant 1. Why did God give me a belly if he doesn't help me fill it up? (RODRIGO *walks to the Town Hall clicking his boots.* FEMALE PEASANT I *approaches him with her hand out.)*

Female peasant 1. Please sir, you must be a pious and generous man . . . (RODRIGO *brusquely pushes her away.)* Not pious . . . nor generous.

Female peasant 2. Sir, the harvest is over. We have no place to go!

Rodrigo. Pray that the mayor doesn't find you here begging, or he'll give you a good beating . . . ! *(As he leaves, one of the* MALE PEASANTS *makes an obscene gesture.)*

Male peasant 1. (Shouting) We want to eat! *(The* PRIEST *passes them on his way to the church. They start badgering him.)*

Female peasant 1. Father, let us enter the church . . .

Female peasant 2. Let us sleep inside . . .

Juan. The last time I let peasants like you enter, they stole everything.

Male peasant 1. Then there's nothing for us in the church?

Juan. You go to church to pray! (JUAN *exits.* EZRA *enters, with a distracted look. They all surround him.)*

Female peasant 1. (Elbowing MALE PEASANT I*)* And that old man? What's that old man doing in the square?

Female peasant 2. (Smiling at him) Did you come for some fresh air?

Ezra. No, my brother disappeared . . . *(Lifts up his* tallith, *questioning them)* Do you know him? Do you know Moisés? (MALE PEASANT I *and* FEMALE PEASANT I *look at each other and wink.)*

Female peasant 2. (Approaching EZRA*)* Yes, I know him . . . come, come.

Male peasant 1. Come with us, Grandfather . . . *(Attempts to take him away.* FEMALE PEASANT 2 *elbows him.)*

Female peasant 1. Wait a minute, I saw the old man first. *(Meanwhile,* MALE PEASANT 2 *grabs* EZRA's *tallith.)*

Male peasant 2. What's this? I saw this somewhere . . . *(They check* EZRA *out to see if they can rob him of something else.)*

Female peasant 2. Grandfather, don't you have anything for us?

Ezra. What could I have?

Male peasant 2. He has nothing!

Female peasant 2. Not even a miserable coin . . . ! (SANCHO *goes to the entrance of the Town Hall, followed by* RODRIGO, *who is brandishing a whip.* FEMALE PEASANT 1 *shouts at them.)*

Female peasant 1. Listen, they're robbing an old man . . .

Female peasant 2. I'm going to kill you!

Male peasant 1. (Holding his torn hat in his hand) Good afternoon, Señor Mayor . . .

Male peasant 2. Good afternoon, Señor Constable . . .

Rodrigo. Starving peasants again . . .

Sancho. (Beating them) Go on, and I better not find you here again or I'll kill you!

Female peasant 1. (Defending herself) We're peasants . . .

Female peasant 2. The harvest is over!

Female peasant 1. They throw us out of everywhere!

Sancho. I don't want to see them here ever again!

Rodrigo. What were you doing to the old man? *(To* EZRA*)* You're outside of the Jewish quarter, Grandfather.

Male peasant 1. He's a Jew . . . He can't take anything out of Spain . . .

Female peasant 1. (Grabbing the tallith *from the* PEASANT*)* Give me that! We can sell it . . .

Female peasant 2. We're hungry.

Rodrigo. (He chases them away with the whip.) Get out of this town! *(*JUAN *enters.* SANCHO *keeps watching old* EZRA, *as he gets up with great difficulty. The* PEASANTS *return slowly.)*

Sancho. He is Isaac's father.

Rodrigo. He must be lost. He's a bit . . .

Male peasant 2. Father, do you have something to eat?

Juan. (Furious, clapping his hands) Go on home!

Female peasant 2. Look Father, I can't walk.

Male peasant 1. We're asking for a coin to buy food!

Female peasant 1. Not to go to the market, like everyone else is doing, to buy what the Jews are selling!

Juan. I don't want to hear another word about that . . .

Rodrigo. You're in front of a church, you animals!

Sancho. Get out of here! *(The* PEASANTS *leave once again.* SARA *enters, followed by* RAQUEL. *They remain on the sidelines.* RODRIGO *pays special attention to* RAQUEL.*)*

Raquel. (Finding EZRA*)* There he is! Grandfather, Grandfather! *(When the* PEASANTS *spot the two women they run to them.)*

Sara. Be careful, Raquel.

Male peasant 1. I took care of the old man! Give me something . . .

Male peasant 2. Me too, for the love of God! *(Shamelessly, the* PEASANTS *look them over and push them to the ground.)*

Raquel. That's enough! *(She turns to the* CONSTABLE *in desperation.)* Rodrigo . . . please, Rodrigo!

Sara. Let me go . . .

Sancho. These people never learn. *(*RODRIGO *exchanges a meaningful look with* RAQUEL. *Then he proceeds to crack his whip, hitting the* PEASANTS *right and left.)*

Rodrigo. Get out of here or I'll beat you to death!

Sancho. Go on! Find yourselves another country!

Female peasant 2. For us there's never anything . . .

Female peasant 1. They always tell you, "The royal coffers are empty."

Sancho. And don't let me see your face in town anymore! *(The* PEASANTS *leave grumbling.* FATHER JUAN *walks away shaking his head.)*

Juan. Why do I leave the church open? No one ever comes looking for God . . . *(He raises his eyes.)* What should I do? I ask your forgiveness. I've treated them badly . . . Lord, let me hear your voice. I need your help. *(Meanwhile, in the plaza,* EZRA *approaches* SANCHO.*)*

Ezra. Sancho . . . And my brother?

Sancho. *(Callously)* He's with God. I told you already, the last time you asked me.

Ezra. With God? *(He grabs his head.)* Then they killed him . . .

Raquel. Come on, Grandfather . . . *(She pulls him aside and they both sit down.)*

Sara. *(To* SANCHO*)* Forgive us for being outside of the Jewish quarter.

Sancho. Don't treat me like a stranger, Sara!

Sara. I have something to tell you . . .

Ezra. *(To* RAQUEL*)* Did she go over there to ask about my brother?

Raquel. Yes, Grandfather. Just calm down. *(*RODRIGO *approaches both of them, smiling at* RAQUEL. *She returns the smile, somewhat intimidated.)*

Rodrigo. Raquel . . .

Raquel. Thank you for what you just did.

Ezra. Raquel, where's Isaac? . . . They don't want us here. *(*SARA *looks at* RODRIGO, *who frowns and walks away from* RAQUEL.*)*

Sancho. Sara . . . Let me tell you something . . . *(Uncomfortable)* Why don't you convert, like everyone else, and stop causing so much trouble? I don't care if you're not religious. I'm not going to inspect your house to see what you're doing . . .

Ezra. They killed him. What will become of us now?

Sara. (Lowering her head in silence) We're leaving this country, Sancho.

Sancho. (Looking away) Then, have a good trip.

Sara. It's not so easy to leave, knowing that we'll never come back.

Devoto. (Suddenly appearing, as he always does) Is Isaac going with you?

Sara. (To the MAYOR*)* I need your help . . .

Sancho. I can lend you a cart. *(Exchanging looks with* FATHER JUAN, *who is listening from the church door.* SARA *looks at* EZRA.*)*

Sara. The problem is, I don't know what to do with Grandfather. Since his brother disappeared, he doesn't eat or sleep. *(Pauses. To the* MAYOR.*)* He won't survive the trip.

Devoto. So you want to leave Isaac's father behind, Sara? Old Ezra! How many times did he slap us around when we were kids, coming back from playing in the street! *(To* SANCHO*)* He was a good friend of your father's.

Sancho. You don't have to remind me about that, you fool.

Devoto. (Frightened, he turns to JUAN.*)* May I confess, Father? *(The two of them walk away slowly.)*

Ezra. (To RAQUEL*)* Promise me that you're going to take care of yourself. And that you'll take care of your brother.

Sancho. Isaac is a doctor. Did he examine him?

Sara. It's going to be long trip, a difficult one. No one knows who will survive. And he deserves to live his last days in peace.

Sancho. If I do my part . . . what will you do, Sara?

Sara. And you . . . what are you asking for?

Sancho. (Taking a few steps) Who's going to take care of your house until you return? Who'll look after it for you? *(Silence)* No one better than we.

Sara. (Lowering her head, resigned) It's true . . . *(*RODRIGO *approaches slowly, listening.)*

Sancho. Of course you'll return, Sara! And then you'll find everything clean and tidy, just like you left it.

Sara. (Silent, inquiring) And Grandfather . . . Where would he go? *(*RODRIGO *and* SANCHO *look at each other not knowing what to say.* RAQUEL *walks over to them to listen.)*

Sancho. That's a difficult question.

Rodrigo. He could stay in the convent . . . and the nuns could take care of him.

Sancho. Yes, but . . . the sisters do charity . . . Christian charity.

(The four of them exchange glances, and then turn their heads towards EZRA.*)*

Scene 11. *The Holy Place.*

The shofar *is heard. Lights up on the holy place. The* TEACHER *is blowing the* shofar. *At his side a* DISCIPLE *is praying.* ISAAC *approaches him, consumed with anxiety, as he nervously puts on the prayer shawl. Suddenly, the* DISCIPLE *begins to sing.*

Teacher. Merciful God . . . Omnipotent God . . .
Here where we threw the letters of your name into the air . . .
so that you'd show us the way . . .
(The mournful sound of the shofar *is heard.)*
Here, where we sowed and reaped,
where our animals multiplied,
our children grew,
we entoned our prayers
and composed songs in your honor . . .
(The shofar *is heard. The* TEACHER *begins once again.)*
Here, where we threw the letters of your name . . .

Isaac. Today we will throw the words of the Edict into the air! We want to know if it is your will that we leave! *(The* DISCIPLE *throws the words into the air. The three of them watch the fantastic designs as they fly and then slowly fall. All this time the* TEACHER *never stops playing the* shofar. *When all the words have fallen to the ground, the* TEACHER *pushes the* DISCIPLE *to one side.)*

Teacher. No, let Isaac read them.

Isaac. (He leans over and examines them.) "Men" . . . "Women" . . . "nights" . . . "days" . . . "fields" . . . "children" . . . "parents" . . . there are no more beautiful words than these . . . because they speak of this land, its seasons and the people who inhabit it . . . But when put together in this way . . . they become the Edict.

Teacher. (He strokes his beard, pensively.) The words of the Edict become the Edict. Then it must be that God wants us to go.

Isaac. No!

Teacher. (He looks at him, surprised.) It is God's will.

Isaac. But why, teacher, why?

Teacher. (He sighs deeply. His eyes survey the sky as if they were looking for a sign.) Isaac, after thinking seriously about the ways of the Lord, I have arrived at the conclusion that it is because the coming of the Messiah is closer everyday . . . *(He lifts his thin arms.)* And so the Lord will close the Book of Life, the dead will be reborn, the Divine Tribunal will be formed, the just will be rewarded and . . .

Isaac. Teacher, Teacher! Why must His divine plan be realized at the expense of our death and destruction, when we are still able to live and think, and create?

Teacher. It will be our reward to be forever at the side of the Lord.

Isaac. (His trembling hands play with the papers that flew through the air.) But behind each one of these words there are men who struggled their whole life to build a family, a flock and a heritage . . . How can God be so cold? How can He be so unmoved before the eyes of a child, before his mother who wonders where to go? *(His hands open and close around the letters.)* He asks us to renounce everything. In the end, was our life a dream? I demand another answer!

Teacher. We must greet His arrival . . . the world will be filled with glory. In His sight our cries will turn into songs . . .

Isaac. (Rebellious) You're wrong! This is not the message of these words! You cannot love God without loving man first! I alone am going to receive His light! I no longer have a teacher! I deny you as my teacher . . . ! *(Silence. The* DISCIPLE, *just a child, begins to cry. The* TEACHER *strokes his head and comforts him.)*

Teacher. Isaac, if there's another answer, it's in your hands. *(In the background another young* DISCIPLE *appears, lifts the* shofar, *and plays it in long, melodious tones.* ISAAC *looks at his hands, intrigued. He walks away, pensively, while the* TEACHER *looks at the sky.)* God! Your people have been your bride for so long. Hasn't the moment arrived for you to wed them?

Scene 12. *Conversion at the Church.*

EZRA'S *laments can be heard in the darkness.*

Ezra. Isaac! Where's my son? I don't want to be here. What will they do to me? . . . Isaac! *(Liturgical music is heard. As the lights go up* EZRA *is seen in the church, supported by* SARA *and* RAQUEL. *He is still wearing his brother's* tallith.)

Juan. (Putting on the ritual garments) Maybe we should look for another solution.

Raquel. Calm yourself, Grandfather . . .

Sara. We brought him because we want him to convert.

Juan. But, have you considered him? Does he want to?

Sara. He doesn't have much time left. There are no more decisions for him to make.

Ezra. (Anxious) That's Juan. He always used to tell me, "This isn't your place."

Sara. No, it wasn't he.

Ezra. They don't love us here.

Raquel. But he loves you, Grandfather.

Ezra. (To JUAN, *suddenly lifting the* tallith*)* Did you see my brother?

Devoto. (Enters, crossing himself) Excuse me, Father.

Juan. I need you as a witness. I need one more . . .

Ezra. Abraham! *(He embraces him.)* How is your father?

Devoto. (To JUAN*)* I'm going to get him.

Ezra. Yes, I want to see him! (DEVOTO *leaves.* SARA *pats* EZRA *to calm him, but he continues with his obsessions.)* I want to know what happened to my brother.

Juan. I knew your brother well. We spoke about him often.

Ezra. (To SARA, *not understanding him)* Did he see you?

Sara. (She straightens his clothing.) Afterwards you can talk to him about anything you want, Grandfather.

Ezra. After what . . . ? *(He pauses, full of anguish.)* What's going to happen? Why doesn't anyone answer me, Sara? (ISAAC *enters. What he sees moves him.)*

Ezra. (He is very upset and tries to get up.) Isaac! That's Isaac. My dear son.

Juan. Calm yourself, please . . . (EZRA *wants to get away. The women restrain him.)*

Ezra. Isaac is an important person! The Queen's physician. He is very intelligent. Nothing escapes him. *(They force him to sit down. Silence.)*

Juan. We cannot go on like this! (ISAAC *goes towards* SARA, *who looks intently into his eyes.)*

Isaac. I went home . . . there was nobody there . . . *(Silence)* I'm shaking. What are you doing inside here?

Sara. Isaac, your father will never survive the trip.

Isaac. What trip!

Sara. (Sighing) Since you weren't here, I had to decide alone.

Isaac. What are you talking about? He's my father . . .

Sara. Don't raise your voice. This is very hard for me too.

Isaac. (Making a fist) I've been thinking about all of you, day and night, trying to stop this wave of evil that is beating us down.

Sara. If we don't see you, we don't know what you're doing, Isaac.

Isaac. I am here! Let's leave this place! What humiliation, my God . . .

Sara. We're not leaving, and we're not giving up. *(She gently puts her hand on his arm.)* We're going to continue and I need your help.

Isaac. (He holds his face and weeps.) You're giving me orders . . . What is my place in this family?

Sara. The best one there is, in my heart. But it's not right that you complain now . . . At this time Grandfather needs all our love.

Isaac. What am I going to say to him? I can't bear to face him!

Sara. What we say to ourselves: If things change . . . we will all sit together around the table again. And if they don't . . . we will try to be very strong, to keep hope alive. *(Silence.* ISAAC'S *and* EZRA'S *eyes meet.)*

Isaac. Papá! Papá!

Ezra. What . . . *(He takes him by the arm and leads him away.* EZRA *becomes quiet.)*

Isaac. Once again the tragedy of our people is upon us. We're surrounded by hatred.

Ezra. What do you mean?

Isaac. That we are forced to unite. *(He looks at him with a sad smile.)* Including us, who have been fighting each other our entire lives. *(He strokes his father's cheek with affection.)* And now, the son must decide for the father.

Ezra. I don't understand . . .

Isaac. Papá, don't make this more difficult . . .

Ezra. You never believed me when I told you they don't love us here, that this is not our country.

Isaac. (Stands and shouts) Juan! Is everything ready?

Ezra. Isaac! *(He grabs his arm.)* Why am I here?

Isaac. Hold him up! Let's do this quickly. *(SARA and RAQUEL subdue* EZRA *while JUAN prepares everything for the baptism.* ISAAC *approaches and watches JUAN.)*

Juan. So you're leaving. We'll never go to the banks of the river again to talk?

Isaac. (Sits at the side of the stage and wipes his brow) God will say . . .

Ezra. (Intuiting what is going to happen) Isaac . . .

Isaac. What!

Ezra. You have to tell him!

Isaac. What . . .

Ezra. That I belong to the synagogue, not to the church!

Juan. Grandfather, why don't you sit down?

Ezra. (To FATHER JUAN) Sara, Raquel . . . I belong to the synagogue, not to the church.

Juan. You don't want to convert?

Ezra. What did he say?

Raquel. Nothing, Grandfather! Nothing.

Sara. Yes, he wants to convert. *(Pause. The two women hold him up.* JUAN *prays and then crosses himself. Liturgical music is heard once again. The lights go down.)*

Isaac. He will not be Ezra anymore . . . He will be Benedicto.

Juan. Ah! He chose to call himself Benedicto.

Isaac. No. I chose it for him. It just occurred to me. *(He exchanges a glance with* EZRA *while* JUAN *prepares the holy water.)* Benedicto, blessed and ben-edict . . . Son of the Edict . . . Papa, your baptism announces a new era . . .

Juan. "Benedictus" *(He prays, dipping his fingers in the water and making the blessing.)*

Ezra. Sara, Raquel, why do you call me that, if I'm leaving this place?

Raquel. Benedictus is a nice name, Grandfather.

Ezra. You must speak to the Queen, Isaac . . . *(*DEVOTO *returns with* FEMALE PEASANT I*.)*

Devoto. I found another witness, father. *(To* ISAAC*)* You have to pay her. *(*ISAAC *gives her a few coins.)*

Juan. Lord, the things we do in your name!

Ezra. *(Noticing him)* Abraham has returned. Where is your father?

Sara. Calm down, Grandfather . . .

Ezra. *(Struggling)* No! Him, no.

Devoto. I can be a witness.

Ezra. Not him . . .

Sara. They just wet your forehead and then you can go on playing chess . . .

Ezra. Not him! *(He spits at* DEVOTO. RODRIGO *appears and observes what is happening.* RAQUEL *sees him.)*

Raquel. All right, he won't be a witness. Rodrigo!

Rodrigo. Yes?

Raquel. Please . . . I need you as a witness.

Rodrigo. Whatever you want, Raquel. *(Silence.* ISAAC *lowers his head and exits.* FATHER JUAN *looks at* FEMALE PEASANT I. *The music grows louder.)*

Juan. Come closer. *(Anointing* EZRA'S *forehead)* "In the name of the Father, the Son, and the Holy Ghost . . . I baptize you Benedictus . . . Amen."

Ezra. *(He sinks his head into his brother's tallith, trying to protect himself with it, as he weeps silently.)* I'm falling, Isaac! I'm falling! I'm falling . . . *(They hold him up until the end. The stage lights go out.)*

Scene 13. Isaac *and* Devoto *in the Holy Place.*

ISAAC *wanders alone in the mountain where he used to meet with his* KABBALAH TEACHER.

Isaac. Teacher, where are you? It's me . . . (*A distant fluttering of birds can be heard.*) I'm desperate! I sacrificed my old father . . . (*Ironically*) And God didn't send an angel to stop me. (*Suddenly* DEVOTO *appears, as calm as ever.*) What are you doing here?

Devoto. You look upset.

Isaac. I'm looking for my teacher.

Devoto. Your teacher?

Isaac. Idiot! (*He pushes him out of the way.* DEVOTO *laughs instead of defending himself.* ISAAC *looks around him, exasperated.*) He used to live here! He would fast here, and see his students here. This was his place . . .

Devoto. His place! They destroyed it and they burned it.

Isaac. What?

Devoto. Yes! Ibn Pérez, the one who used to blow the *shofar*, they found him and they took him away. He disappeared!

Isaac. Ibn Pérez?

Devoto. Didn't you know that that was the teacher's name? I'm going to miss him! Always making arrangements for the coming of the Messiah . . .

Isaac. Then, you used to visit him?

Devoto. Ibn Pérez, the Kabbalah teacher? Of course. We used to have long conversations . . . they were fantastic.

Isaac. (*Pointing at him*) A man like you . . . devoted to the cross, came to see him? I can't believe it.

Devoto. I used to come . . . as a former Jew. As a curious man. As a spectator to the events that stir our times. I know that the last time you threw the words of the Edict into the air and they fell, you got angry because they didn't come out as you wanted. Are you convinced God wants you to go?

Isaac. God . . . (*Lifts up his eyes. His tone becomes strange.*) has not pronounced his last word. (DEVOTO *looks at him and becomes angry.*)

Devoto. You're doing something forbidden! You're not qualified to call Him! You have to leave! You've tried everything here. Enough! (*Long silence.* ISAAC *wipes off his perspiring face with his hand.* DEVOTO *turns his back to him, realizing that he has talked too much.*)

Isaac. Devoto . . .

Devoto. Yes?

Isaac. I want to know . . . How was it that you converted? (DE-VOTO *moves back a step. He feels strangely trapped.*)

Devoto. One night . . . Jesus appeared to me.

Isaac. What are you saying?

Devoto. Jewish books no longer had anything to say to me.

Isaac. Jesus used to read the Old Testament.

Devoto. But he also preached, "Love thy neighbor as thyself."

Isaac. And what men follow that? (*Silence. He approaches him.*) Now I understand everything! You sent me Kabbalah books so that I'd remove myself from reality . . . and leave you my place next to the Queen. You nursed my desperation, my insecurity. You discovered that I couldn't rebel, that I didn't have the strength. Then, you pushed me to come here.

Devoto. There's no proof of any of that!

Isaac. How many did you betray, pretending to be a submissive "former Jew," concerned with the "events that stir our times"?

Devoto. (*Beside himself*) Ibn Pérez used to blow the *shofar*. Toooo! That crazy man would climb the mountain and played with all his might! Tooo . . . Tooo! Calling the Messiah! You could hear him everywhere! . . . He alone led them here . . .

Isaac. You wanted to take my place at the court.

Devoto. Yes I did!

Isaac. Become the Queen's doctor.

Devoto. Why not? Did you intend to keep that position for the rest of your life?

Isaac. No! (*He laughs bitterly and takes a few steps.*) I wanted to be one of the just. Yes, a just man! It is written in Proverbs . . . "Thirty six just men are required to sustain the world," and I wanted to be one of them . . .

Devoto. (*Laughing*) Isaac the Just . . . Look at you now, a victim of the greatest injustice of your life! I want to see what proverbs sustain you now! (*His laughter resounds as he leaves.* ISAAC, *in a hurry, looks for signs in the sky.*)

Isaac. My God, now I don't have anyone to lean on. Then . . . you've decided . . . I have to do it all alone. And for that, I first need to be myself! (*Lights dim on the holy place.*)

Scene 14. Rodrigo *and* Raquel.

Suddenly the lights change. A clinking sound is heard. It is made by the metal parts of the wheel of torture banging by themselves in the Town Hall. RAQUEL *appears running and laughing.* RODRIGO *playfully tries to catch her.*

Raquel. No, Rodrigo!

Rodrigo. Yes!

Raquel. No! *(She bumps against the wheel. She has no strength left. Finally* RODRIGO *embraces her.)*

Rodrigo. Why not? Eh . . . Raquel? I've never kissed a Jewess . . .

Raquel. So . . .

Rodrigo. Is it true what they say? That they are very passionate?

Raquel. You have to find that out.

Rodrigo. I want to begin now . . .

Raquel. (Touching him) Hm, your arms are so strong.

Rodrigo. (Looks at her and laughs) Did you ever think of what I can lift with these arms? I'll show you. *(He lifts her up, holding her over his head.)*

Raquel. Enough . . .

Rodrigo. Do you see? *(Walking)* Do you see?

Raquel. Put me down . . . *(He puts her down, pressing her against his body. When she touches the ground she hides behind the wheel.)*

Rodrigo. Raquel!

Raquel. Please don't touch me! *(They look at each other across the wheel. He moves it, teasing her.)*

Rodrigo. Come in and see, ladies and gentlemen! The machine of truth, the machine that softens hearts . . . *(She laughs, bewitched. He takes advantage of the moment to grab her and kiss her.)*

Raquel. No, not on the mouth.

Rodrigo. Yes . . .

Raquel. Rodrigo . . . I'm engaged.

Rodrigo. Your fiancé . . . You think I don't know he's left?

Raquel. (Freeing herself abruptly) Halil . . . always loved me. Halil is coming back for me!

Rodrigo. I bet he doesn't come . . . And if he does, I won't let him take you. I won't even let him come near you! *(He kisses her passionately. Silence)*

Raquel. Your kisses hurt . . . like this machine. *(She strokes the wheel behind her. The sound seems strange in the night.* ISAAC, *who has arrived unexpectedly and has watched the scene, separates them.*

Isaac. Enough!

Raquel. Papá . . . *(She wants to leave, but with a defiant gesture Rodrigo pulls her to his side, as if she belonged to him.)*

Rodrigo. You're not leaving! (ISAAC *looks at him. He prefers to address himself to his daughter.)*

Isaac. How painful . . . to see you with him . . . how painful, Raquel . . .

Raquel. Why, Papá? Tell me why!

Isaac. You should have had the best man . . . the man who would swear to make you happy . . .

Raquel. Oh! *(She manages to free herself and run away.* RODRIGO *and* ISAAC *look at each other intently.)*

Rodrigo. What's the matter, Doctor? Am I not a good candidate? Can't I win your daughter?

Isaac. There are many things I can't do either, Constable. *(Lowers his head and leaves in the same way as his daughter did.* RO-DRIGO'S *voice pursues him.)*

Rodrigo. Chief Constable, since yesterday! And don't you forget it! In charge of anyone suspected of heresy! *(Pause. After* ISAAC *exits,* RODRIGO *furiously kicks the wheel of torture and leaves. The wheel continues to turn crazily on its own.)*

Scene 15. Yehuda's *Farewell.*

At his house, YEHUDA *is filling a sack with great care. He already has the look and the gestures of a man who lives with the suspicion that he is being watched or followed. His mother approaches him.*

Sara. Yehuda . . .

Yehuda. Mamá?

Sara. (Looking at his bag) Your departure . . . does it have to be today?

Yehuda. Yes. *(They give each other a prolonged look.* SARA *removes a piece of clothing from another bag.)*

Sara. I've knitted this with my own hands, for when you're far away and it's cold, and I can't keep you warm.

Yehuda. That's fine . . . *(He holds her close to him.)* It will be good . . . for when I miss you. *(He hugs her.* RAQUEL *runs in.* ISAAC *comes in behind her and looks at the bag.)*

Isaac. Yehuda, what does this mean?

Yehuda. Papá . . . *(SARA and* YEHUDA *separate.* ISAAC *takes the bag and pushes it away.)*

Isaac. I'm not going to let you go away!

Yehuda. I'm not a child anymore.

Isaac. I'm still your father! I'm the head of this family . . .

Sara. Isaac, you're not going to make him stay if you talk to him that way . . .

Isaac. Ah, you're on his side! And on her side too? *(He takes* RAQUEL *by the arm and pushes her in front of* SARA.*)* Look at her . . .

Sara. What happened, Raquel?

Raquel. (Weeping) Let me go . . .

Isaac. I found her . . . rubbing up against the constable! And we all know who he is . . .

Raquel. Yes! And what of it? I like Rodrigo! What are you going to do? Are you going to make the wheel of time turn back? Make everything the way it was before?

Sara. Raquel!

Raquel. Papá! The only wheel that turns here is the wheel of torture! I'm tired of being pointed at and told "You can't be here, you can't do that." I'm fed up with being afraid, with not knowing if tomorrow I'll be here or somewhere else, or even under the ground! Everyone is scared! No one knows if they should change their name, or their religion, or their country. That's why I like Rodrigo! He knows what has to be done! He shouts "We need a New Order!" and he shouts it at the top of his lungs because he knows that it's coming, because he knows that you can't wait for signs from heaven for it to come. The wheel of torture, Papá, keeps moving forward . . . and Rodrigo is turning it!

Isaac. Enough!

Raquel. I'm young, I'm beautiful. I have the right to be loved, to be protected, to be happy *(*ISAAC *slaps her.* RAQUEL *holds her face and weeps.)*

Sara. What are you doing, Isaac? I don't know you . . .

Isaac. I don't want to hear anymore! *(He wants to raise his hand to her too, but he stops himself.)*

Sara. We are a family. Why can't we be united in times of grief as we were in times of happiness? Now we have to decide together what we're going to do!

Yehuda. Papá can't decide anything anymore. *(*ISAAC *clenches his fists and beats them against his chest.)*

Isaac. You've always hated me, Yehuda! Whatever I did was always wrong to you . . . What do you hold against me? That I devoted myself to science, more than to you? That I preferred life at court, serving the Queen? But can't you see that I loved you just the same?

Yehuda. Mamá always defended you here.

Isaac. You don't understand me.

Yehuda. But what you did to Grandfather . . . I'll never forgive you for that.

Isaac. I wanted to go far in life! I wanted to have prestige, power, that worthless, invisible power we achieve, which, when the moment comes, is swept away from us in a puff.

Yehuda. I'm sorry, but now the time has come to do something with my life. *(He lifts up his bag, putting an end to the discussion. They all look at him in silence.)*

Isaac. Yehuda! I don't know if I'll be able to live without seeing you! *(His voice breaks and becomes conspiratorial.)* I have been studying the secrets of the Kabbalah for a long time and I've finally succeeded in getting the attention of the Lord. Today a miracle will happen before midnight.

Yehuda. I hope your magic works. All the Jews of Spain are throwing numbers and letters into the air. They not only want to stay here, but now they want Spain to become their Promised Land!

Isaac. God will abolish the Edict! Those who left will return.

Yehuda. If that happens, I'll be the first to celebrate.

Isaac. And what a celebration it will be, Yehuda! *(Laughing)* What a celebration!

Yehuda. That won't be so easy. Things have happened that can never be forgotten. I prefer to trust in what I feel now. And at this moment I want to fight. Papá, destiny is in my hands.

Isaac. *(Silence. To* SARA*)* What did he say?

Sara. That destiny is in his hands.

Isaac. Did he really say that destiny is in his hands?

Sara. Yes . . .

Isaac. That's what my teacher told me the last time I saw him! *(Looking at his hands.* SARA, RAQUEL *and* YEHUDA *do not understand.* ISAAC *furiously beats himself.)* And like an idiot, I spent days looking at my fingers, studying the lines of my hand, when he was telling me something as simple as "act," and that has nothing to do with magic!

Yehuda. You see, Papá, you have to look very deeply to understand great teachers. *(Carrying his bag)* It's late! Those with money have left already. The Kabbalah scholars, the true ones, will try to reach Palestine. The only ones left are the poor, like always. And I, who in the end never went to the university, and won't become a doctor, choose to stay behind with them. We'll hide in the mountains. We'll resist. *(He hugs* ISAAC, *then he kisses his mother and his sister. Two men silently appear, and remain outside.)*

Isaac. Yehuda! "Act," he said to me, "Act!" Tonight I will act . . .

Sara. Don't listen to Papá. He's crazy. God be with you.

Raquel. *(Suddenly going to him and hugging him)* Poor Papá!

(They look at him with pity, while YEHUDA *leaves silently. He stops to take with him the last image of his family, then lowers his head and exits. The figures that were waiting in the dark reveal themselves.)*

Man. Don't move! *(*YEHUDA *pushes them aside and runs away. They follow him.* ISAAC *goes to the door when he hears them.)*

Isaac. Don't let them catch you, Yehuda! Don't let them catch you. Don't turn back. *(The women hold their breath.)*

Sara. Did he get away?

Isaac. Yes, but for how long?

Sara. Isaac, I'm afraid for us!

Isaac. (Looking at them, a strange expression spreads over his face.) Pack your bags, as if we were going away. I'll come for you.

Sara. I really want to leave! Didn't you see what happened?

Raquel. (Covering her face) The worst is yet to come.

Isaac. Be quiet, all of you! Tonight I'll lead a ceremony, and God's will be done. *(He leaves the illuminated space of the house. The women hold each other.)*

Scene 16. *Farewell at the Tavern.*

A familiar song is heard once again. In the tavern, SANCHO, RO-DRIGO *and* DEVOTO *are singing, along with other neighbors. Their movements are accompanied by clapping, dancing and shouting.*

All. What are you taking, Isaac?
   What are you leaving, Isaac?
   Today you're here,
   Tomorrow there,
   Isaac, oh Isaac,
   You won't forget us . . .

*(*ISAAC *stops tumbling, and slowly gets up from the ground. His reverie ends. The time to remember is over. He understands that he is once again at the farewell table, and that his time is limited.)*

Isaac. I have to go to the cemetery.

Sancho. Isaac! *(They surround him and shake him. Only* JUAN *remains at the table, drinking alone.)*

Devoto. More wine, Isaac?

Isaac. I have to go.

Rodrigo. He got angry because in the little chair game we threw him out of the country . . .

Sancho. I know another game *(He takes out the* tallith *belonging to the grandfather's brother, and begins to blindfold* ISAAC.*)*

Isaac. You kept my uncle's *tallith* . . .

Sancho. Let's play blind man's bluff, like when we were children.

Juan. (*Getting up*) Leave him alone. He has to leave before midnight.

Sancho. (*Tries to sit* JUAN *down, but he resists*) Where are you going, Father?

Juan. It's getting late for him!

Devoto. Then aren't we going to take him to town, so he can say goodbye to his beloved places?

Rodrigo. The synagogue is closed, isn't it, Father Juan? (*With a violent gesture* JUAN *knocks the* tallith *out of* SANCHO'S *hand.*)

Juan. You have no right to do this to him!

Sancho. It's just a game. (*Picking up the* tallith *again*)

Devoto. Father, you were doing just fine over there at the table!

Rodrigo. That's right, (*He sits him down.*) with your jug, and your wine . . .

Juan. This was supposed to be the farewell gathering for a friend!

Isaac. Let me go . . . (*With his eyes blindfolded,* ISAAC *reels.* SAN-CHO *turns him around in circles.*)

Devoto. What do you see, Isaac? Didn't you always say one has to look inside oneself?

Sancho. Isaac, let's get blind man's bluff started!

Isaac. (*Bumping into them*) I have to go!

Sancho. Who am I?

Rodrigo. Who am I?

Devoto. Who am I? (ISAAC *stumbles in front of the three of them, who pretend to be statues.*)

Sancho. I am the Great Inquisitor.

Rodrigo. I am the Hangman.

Devoto. I am the Devil!

Juan. (*Getting up and separating them*) I'm sick of all this! (*Silence. A hostile atmosphere develops.*)

Sancho. Why, Father? When you converted old Ezra, did anyone bother you?

Juan. I did it to save his life!

Rodrigo. You locked him up in a convent!

Devoto. With nuns. (ISAAC *stumbles, straightens up and takes off the blindfold.*)

Juan. What are you trying to tell me by that, hypocrites? (*He points to them, one by one.*) You kept all his possessions . . . You tried to win his daughter . . . You became a Christian to live better . . .

Sancho. Ah, no! I will not allow you to say that! My house is full of crosses and scapularies, not of Isaac's belongings!

Devoto. *(Pushing him)* So, you're trying to discredit me in front of everyone?

Rodrigo. *(To* JUAN, *and then to* DEVOTO, *in a menacing tone)* Soon the Holy Office will straighten up everyone's life.

Juan. I know who the sinners are. *(He overturns everything on the table.)* Sinners are always the same! *(He looks at them.)* I've known them my whole life! *(Suddenly* ISAAC *slips away.)*

Devoto. Look, we were arguing and he disappeared!

Sancho. Isaac, it was a joke!

Rodrigo. The game is not over yet. *(They look disappointedly towards where* ISAAC *left. Behind them* JUAN *puts his hat on, looks them up and down with contempt, and leaves.)*

Scene 17. *Ceremony at the Cemetery.*

The shofar *is heard. Lights on the cemetery.* ISAAC *arrives out of breath. He notices that only his wife and his daughter* RAQUEL *are there, surrounded by a few bundles.*

Isaac. Where are the others?

Sara. They left already . . .

Raquel. We're the last ones, Papá! *(The somber tolling of a bell can be heard.)*

Isaac. That bell . . . is it midnight?

Raquel. Yes, it's midnight . . .

Sara. Let's go, please. I don't want to die here.

Isaac. Leave me alone! *(Makes a tremendous effort and manages to concentrate)* God, here where our dead are resting, I ask for your help! *(His feet move by themselves on the soft earth. His lips murmur a chant.)* God, what can I tell you about me that you don't already know? I tried to live by your precepts. I had weaknesses, that's why I never became a wise man. But with this head and these hands, I cured the sick for your glory! Now I am lost, but I know the way is here, on this earth. *(He stumbles. His wife and daughter look at each other in despair, but he continues. His feet begin to dance.)* Where can I be happy, if not here, where I was born and where I lived? I learned that a man who is at peace with himself radiates light and can help others. God, I want you to help me be well and to radiate light! *(His feet dance faster and faster, in a frenzy.)*

Raquel. Papá . . .

Sara. You'll fall . . .

Isaac. Sara, Raquel, I need your hands! I can't receive his word alone . . . *(He leans on them. His feet move by themselves in the sand.* RAQUEL *is frightened.)*

Raquel. What's happening to you, Papá!

Isaac. Schss! Read . . .

Sara. What?

Isaac. On the ground, look.

Raquel. He wants us to decipher the drawings he's making with his feet.

Isaac. Look, please. *(He dances as if possessed, with his eyes closed, until he falls exhausted, face down. The two women examine the ground.)*

Sara. These stripes don't say anything.

Raquel. I'm afraid.

Sara. They're just marks from his footsteps. *(She pulls her shawl closer.)* If only Yehuda was here to help us . . . *(Silence. All of a sudden a murmur is heard. It is the humming of a Jewish liturgical theme, sung by three figures who slowly approach, wrapped in ritual shawls. Frightened, she brings her hand to her breast.)* Who are they? *(*ISAAC *quickly lifts his head.)*

Raquel. *(Holding onto* SARA*)* Mamá, I'm afraid.

Isaac. But, don't you see?

Sara. Isaac, what is it?

Isaac. Our brothers are coming back.

Raquel. I don't know . . .

Isaac. Yes! Look, faithless woman, who made fun of what I was doing. Look! The Edict was ripped up in a thousand pieces. They're coming to tell me that.

Raquel. *(Pulling him away)* Let's go, Papá.

Isaac. God decrees that today is a festive day! Where there were tears, there will be joy. Where there was fear, there will be rejoicing. Thousands of men and women will return to their homes.

Sara. But . . . why are they all covered up? *(*RAQUEL *looks at the patterns on the ground in confusion, unable to associate them with the ghostly figures that are approaching.)*

Raquel. I'm afraid.

Isaac. *(Grabs her by the arm and shakes her)* Blind, isn't this enough for you? *(He points to the three figures who are already upon them. Suddenly they stop chanting. The women are distrustful, suspecting something.* ISAAC *goes towards them, as they suddenly lower their shawls. They are* RODRIGO, SANCHO *and* DEVOTO.*)*

Devoto. Congratulations!

Rodrigo. (He bows ironically.) You've just entered the country where the New Order reigns.

Sancho. We were the ones who heard you! *(They laugh heartily.* ISAAC *looks at them, confused.)*

Isaac. Was it another game?

Sancho. The best of all! *(*ISAAC *shouts with pain and begins to hit them. They finally subdue him, without hitting back.* ISAAC *looks at them, breathing heavily. All of a sudden he begins to laugh.)*

Isaac. You really tricked me! I felt like a fool. *(Silence. His expression changes.)* What a need I have to believe, God . . . Poor me . . . Your ways are so mysterious . . . *(He blinks, looks up and then looks at his wife and daughter, who have nothing to say to him.)*

Sancho. Did you hear the bells?

Isaac. Yes.

Sancho. What a pity! They found you here.

Devoto. It is twelve midnight of July 31, 1492.

Rodrigo. As of this moment no Jew can remain alive in Spain. *(He unsheathes his sword slowly.* SARA *screams.)*

Raquel. Rodrigo . . . no! *(She goes to him, as if surrendering herself. He grabs her with his left hand and pushes her behind him.)*

Rodrigo. Your place is here from now on!

Isaac. You'll have to take my life, because I'm not giving it to you. *(*RODRIGO *advances towards him without letting go of the girl.)*

Raquel. Don't hurt him!

Rodrigo. On guard!

Isaac. Here I am . . .

Raquel. Let them go. Let both of them go. *(In an uneven combat,* ISAAC, *unarmed, attacks the* CONSTABLE. SARA *covers her eyes.* SANCHO *and* DEVOTO *move aside to avoid being stabbed by accident. At that endless moment the voice of a* COURT OFFICIAL *is heard.)*

Court official. One moment! *(There is something impressive about him. They all look in his direction, disconcerted.)* On your knees, vassals! *(The combat ceases. An* OFFICER *enters followed by his* SOLDIERS. *They all obey.)* Doctor Levy must appear before Her Majesty! *(Everyone is astonished as they take* ISAAC *by the arms and carry him off. Those who remain, react slowly.)*

Sancho. The Queen is summoning him!

Rodrigo. What's going on? Did we make a mistake?

Sara. Isaac! She wants to trap you again! *(She runs after him.)*

Don't leave me! Don't forget me . . . *(She falls to the ground as the lights go down.)*

Scene 18. *At the Queen's Palace.*

A hall in the palace. Royal music is heard. Her Majesty, QUEEN ISABEL *is seated on her throne, accompanied by high ranking uniformed officers. The atmosphere is austere. The military guard brings* ISAAC *to her and withdraws a respectful distance away.*

Isabel. The last Jew! To think that once you were the first Jew for me. *(She stands up. Now she is all nobility, lineage, paleness, arrogance, coldness, harshness, distance. Her stare is terrifying.* ISAAC *lowers his head.)* Let me tell you! The new Spain is on the march, with its plumes, banners, and faith. Will you become part of it? *(She drums her fingers impatiently on her arm.)* I am listening to what you have to tell me. *(Silence)*

Isaac. No, Your Majesty. (ISABEL *looks behind her. The* OFFICIALS *don't move. She turns to the* GUARDS.)

Isabel. All right. But let's not waste any more time. Doctor Levy is going to convert. *(Two guards hit him to make him kneel. A sword pointing downward serves as a cross.)*

Isaac. (Kneeling and forced to look at the cross) And what will you convert me to, gracious Queen? Into a toad? A snake? A hangman? Into a knight? *(He stands up and frees himself.)* I am Isaac! If I got this far, it is because I'm not going to masquerade as what I'm not. *(They threaten him with their weapons. The* QUEEN *intervenes.)*

Isabel. Leave him alone! He's out of his mind. He doesn't know what he's doing. *(She walks to the side of the hall. He follows her. The dignitaries move away so as not to hear.)* To think that once I granted you all my favors . . .

Isaac. Isabel . . .

Isabel. Your Majesty! *(Pause. He bows, paying homage to her.)*

Isaac. Your Majesty.

Isabel. Idiot! If you would only pronounce one word! You would set an example, which is what I want. *(She offers her hand. Slowly, she touches him and he feels the contact.)* Together, we could return to those places where we liked so much to wander . . . the hills of Toledo, the banks of the Guadalquivir . . .

Isaac. What will I find in those places now? Desperate Jews exchanging a house for a donkey, Jews like me, who stayed, waiting for the Messiah to come . . .

Isabel. Ahh . . . *(Scratching herself furiously)* I listen to you and I'm horrified! I live plagued by horror! All right. It's over! *(She returns to the throne.)* The decision is made! The Doctor is leaving our land.

Isaac. No!

Isabel. I decide your fate!

Isaac. No . . .

Isabel. The parchment! *(An* OFFICIAL *brings her a parchment. Sitting erect on her throne* ISABEL *unrolls it.)* I issued an order! The Edict has been postponed for two days.

Isaac. Why?

Isabel. Because there are thousands of Jews who haven't reached the borders yet. And I'm including you among them. As you can see, I'm merciful. And also because a boat is leaving in two days. *(She reads the parchment while she scratches her skin.)* From Puerto de Palos. Friends of yours *(smiles ironically)* who have now become Christians, are financing this undertaking. They are my partners, of course. This is a letter in my own handwriting for the captain of the caravel *(running her eyes over the parchment)* which isn't one, but three . . . *(She gives it to an* OFFICIAL *who immediately hands it to* ISAAC.*)*

Isaac. (Grabs the envelope and looks at it) And what am I supposed to do on that boat?

Isabel. Go far away! *(Ironically)* Have a good trip, Isaac! I hope that you never come back.

Isaac. (Slowly ripping up the letter) No. *(*ISABEL *becomes furious.)*

Isabel. Why this insistence on staying!

Isaac. Because I am a Jew, a Spanish Jew . . .

Isabel. (Walking away from him) I don't want to listen to you anymore. *(*ISAAC *turns to everyone present in the hall.)*

Isaac. I have a respected name and a recognized profession. I have always been devoted to science and have disciples who follow me. Why should I submit to you, and give up everything? I have earned a place in this land that I love. *(*TORQUEMADA, *who has just entered the hall, overhears his last words. He is followed by many* PRIESTS. *He steps forward and bows to the* QUEEN. *His entourage remains with the* OFFICIALS.*)*

Torquemada. Your Majesty, I have heard that the Jew refuses to leave.

Isabel. He also refuses to convert. I tried everything.

Torquemada. He won't convert either? Deplorable!

Isabel. He claims he is an important doctor.

Torquemada. But I ask, a doctor who dances in cemeteries . . .

What can he teach his disciples? A doctor who summons the dead for help, who goes into a trance, hoping that God will dictate words to him that he can trace with his feet . . . that isn't very scientific.

Isaac. (Surprised) You had me followed . . .

Torquemada. You waited for Her Majesty on the terrace of the castle to seduce her with your magic. *(Silence. He goes towards her. The three of them are almost alone.)*

Isaac. Then they were spying on us! And you informed him about us.

Isabel. He's my confessor! *(To* TORQUEMADA*)* Don't let him come near me. He still confuses me! *(*TORQUEMADA *steps in between them.)*

Torquemada. You are a diabolical man. You are dangerous to the Crown. *(*ISAAC *wants to leave at once, but the* PRIESTS *and the* OFFICIALS *stop him.)*

Isaac. You are the Devil! You are Evil . . .

Torquemada. We act in the name of God . . .

Isaac. Don't bring God into this!

Torquemada. And in the name of Jesus, our Lord . . . *(He takes the cross that hangs from his neck and raises it.)*

Isaac. Don't bring Jesus into this either! He is not present in the torture chambers, nor at the stakes. You are not Christians! You only own the power, not the truth!

Torquemada. The Inquisition is very interested in your practices, Doctor Levy.

Isaac. You can sacrifice us, but you cannot erase all that we've done!

Isabel. Silence him!

Isaac. You won't be able to make us disappear either! Because there are many, just like myself, who become stronger in the face of hate and persecution. *(*YEHUDA *suddenly appears on top of the mountain and waves to him.* SARA *appears from another area, waiting anxiously.* RAQUEL *watches from another point, cradling her face with her hands.)*

Yehuda. Papá!

Sara. Isaac . . . *(*ISAAC *falters for a moment and falls on his knees.)*

Isaac. My dear ones, where will I meet you all again . . . *(A very moving melody is heard. In the background brilliant flames can be seen.)*

Isabel. It was a mistake to bring him here. Take him away!

Torquemada. Seize that bearer of celestial messages. *(On another part of the stage—also phantasmagorical—the* TEACHER *appears blowing the* shofar. ISAAC *turns towards him. It now becomes evident that the flames are stakes.*)

Isaac. Enough, Teacher! I don't want to hear you anymore! I have understood. God is not going to come to our aid, nor to anybody else's. He grants his favors to no one. He has left everything in our hands. He wants to see what we do with our fate! I reject the annihilation of the innocent. I put my strength with those who choose to live. Love is as strong as death! (*Two* PRIESTS *approach* ISAAC, *who resists them. Nevertheless, they take him away. Now behind the stakes, like a huge fresco, we see a caravan of people leaving. They carry bundles on their backs and children in their arms. They are the ones who have chosen the path of exile.*)

The End

Osvaldo Dragún: *Onward, Corazón!*

OSVALDO DRAGÚN (ENTRE RÍOS, 1929)

Dragún began his career by writing realistic theatre and has experimented with naturalistic, mythical, absurdist, and symbolic theatre forms. From his early period comes *La peste viene de Melos* (The plague comes from Melos) (1956) about the invasion of Guatemala, *Tupac Amaru* (1957) and *El jardín del infierno* (The garden of hell) (1962). He is responsible for the Yiddish version of Alejandro Berruti's play *Madre Tierra* (Mother Earth). Influenced by Bertolt Brecht, whom he helped introduce into Latin America, and concerned mostly with the social content of Brecht's plays, Dragún has always created well-defined proletarian characters. His style changed with *Historias para ser contadas* (Stories to be told) (1957). One of these *historias* was made into a film entitled *Los de la mesa diez* (The people from table number ten). In 1958 he wrote a musical *Los del 80* (The people from 1980) in collaboration with Andrés Lizarraga, and in 1959 he wrote *Historias de mi esquina* (Stories of my corner). Between 1961 and 1963 Dragún headed the Seminario de Autores Dramáticos de La Habana. In 1962 he was awarded the Theatre Prize from Casa de las Américas for *Milagro en el Mercado Viejo* (Miracle at the old market) and in 1966 he received the same prize for *Heroica de Buenos Aires* (Heroica of Buenos Aires). Dragún's activity has been continuous and prolific.[1] He has also written extensively for television and cinema. His project, Teatro Abierto (Open theatre), which took place in 1981 during the military repression, was highly innovative.

¡*Arriba, Corazón!* (*Onward, Corazón!*) (1987), originally entitled "Hijos del Terremoto" (Children of the earthquake), is Dragún's oblique version of the Wandering Jew. The play's central character, Corazón, is revealed on three levels: the child, the young man, and the older man in his fifties, who is always present on stage, observing and commenting on the scenes that are enacted from his life. These moments are disjointed memories, hopes, dreams, and conflicts that constitute Corazón's world. The play is overtly political

Osvaldo Dragún

with its implicit denunciation of fascism, dictatorship, and war, using the character of Canfunfa, a grotesque type who transforms himself into all the sleazy characters in the play: the dictator, the military man, the deceitful politician, and the jailer.

The play can also be read primarily as a biographical drama, born as a reaction to the years of repression in Argentina from 1976–82. Upon his return to Buenos Aires in 1976, after being abroad for a number of years, Dragún talked about looking for a life-line that would connect him to his homeland. What he found instead was that everything had burst "in an earthquake of instability and precariousness."[2] He tried to withdraw into a "labyrinth" of his own creation, but "even the labyrinth burst." *Onward, Corazón!* was conceived out of Dragún's feelings of desolation, having realized he had lost his home. His imperative need was to make contact with the world he left behind and feared lost. Dragún's own recounting of how the first images came to him offer the clearest analysis of the play:

> I felt myself floating in space, unconnected. And I returned to Buenos Aires, looking for my life-line to earth. My sound. What I found enveloped us for seven years. (My god, was it only seven?) It was the sound of terror. Terror has its own sound. Whoever hasn't lived through it will never know what it's like. It is untransferable. A group of us became internal and external exiles. Buried in black lists, threatened, expelled, scattered. If going outside was an act of aggression, we had to shut ourselves in our homes, create the religion of the family, make believe that "the whole world is this home," close all doors and windows, and survive. While the majority of my countrymen jumped with joy celebrating the World Cup of 1978 . . . (the American Dream: to finally be number one), they were turning their fear, their cowardice, their renunciation, into philosophy in order to be able to shave without cutting their faces with shame. And they shouted "crazy women" at that small group of women who circled the Plaza de Mayo, their heads covered with white kerchiefs, with the names of their disappeared children written on them.

This was Dragún's spiritual earthquake. After forty years in a city "without earthquakes," he suddenly felt that he had always lived on ground shaken by metaphorical earthquakes. In *Onward, Corazón!* Dragún attempts to convey the sense of instability felt by his countrymen:

> When I sat down to write, or rather, when I sat down to wait for those ghosts to have time to come and visit me, or rather, for me to have the courage to accept them, I discovered that for the first time in my life

I had begun to write a letter to myself. The letter took seven years to write. . . . You can open the envelope. Perhaps, who knows? It's possible (even precarious) that we can share this feeling of inhabiting a land that is forever moving under our feet. . . . Immigrants who will never reach paradise.

Dragún emphasizes that sense of precariousness that he shares with his ancestors. His grandparents were Russian merchants who escaped pogroms in search of paradise, but never found it because an absurd earthquake dragged them from Buenos Aires, their port of arrival, to unbearable conditions in the interior, where they had to work the arid land.

Like Eichelbaum's *Aarón the Jew,* where words take precedence over action, *Onward, Corazón!* is an interior play. The characters are taken from Dragún's past: an idealistic father, a fighter and a loser, noble and naive, unable to earn money; an accommodating, ambitious uncle, "protector" of a wandering family, searching for its daily bread; a mother whose love for her son is her only purpose for being alive; a farmer friend, simple and clever; another uncle, adventurous and idealistic.[3] *Onward, Corazón!* poses a series of moral questions that prompt its characters to define themselves and to plumb their deeper consciousness.

NOTES

1. Other plays include: *Y nos dijeron que éramos inmortales* (And they told us we were immortal) (1963); *Amoretta* (1964); *El amasijo* (The trashing) (1967); *Historias con cárcel* (Stories with jail) (1972); *Y por casa, ¿cómo andamos?* (And how are things at home?) (1979); in collaboration with Ismael Hasse, *Mi obelisco y yo* (My obelisk and I) (1981); the trilogy written between 1982 and 1983, *Al violador* (To the rapist), *Al perdedor* (To the loser), and *Al vencedor* (To the winner); *Hoy se comen al flaco* (Today they're eating skinny) and *Como Pancho por San Telmo* (Like Pancho in San Telmo) (1986). See bibliography.

2. This quote and the following ones, translated by the editors, are from the program notes to *¡Arriba, Corazón!* which premiered at the Teatro Municipal General San Martín in 1987.

3. Frank Dauster analyzes an earlier version of this play in "'Los hijos del terremoto': Imágenes del recuerdo," *Latin American Theatre Review* (Fall, 1988): 5–11. Here Dauster establishes a parallel between the *sainete orillero* and Brechtian theatre, both of which had a large influence on Dragún.

Onward, Corazón!

List of Characters
Corazón-man
Corazón-youth
Corazón-child
Mother
Father
Uncle Juan
Uncle Manuel
Canfunfa
El Negro
María-Wanda
Fiddler
Drummer

A Play in Three Acts

Act 1

An empty stage with a few props lending dream-like quality to the set. A table is ready for a birthday party; an old, broken down rocking-chair made up like a throne; another smaller chair, exactly like the first one, placed at another angle.

CORAZÓN, *about fifty years old, enters and walks around the stage slowly. When he reaches the table, a* FIDDLER *appears from the darkness and begins to play a very beautiful, sad and luminous Jewish melody. As the music plays, a ten-year-old child arrives carrying a tablecloth. Smiling, he hands it to the older man, who spreads it on the table. The child leaves, returning with a birthday cake with a single candle on it. The older man lights it. The boy tries to blow it out unsuccessfully. He tries again, but he still can't do it. He looks at the older man, asking for help. The man shrugs his shoulders as if to say "It's your problem." He opens his arms helplessly. Then the boy blows even harder and the candle goes out. The music becomes softer. As the rhythm changes,* CORAZÓN'S MOTHER *and* FATHER *appear. Their steps suggest a dance. They move towards the table and light the birthday candle again. The man and the child sit in their respective chairs. The man lets the child sit down first. Then he begins to rock himself with a smile. Suddenly, the* FIDDLER *starts to play "The Fifth Regiment," a song from the Spanish Civil War. The man looks at the* FIDDLER, *then he moves his hand through the air, as if looking for something.*

Corazón-man. There he goes again! It must mean something . . . Why do my first memories begin that July 17, 1936, with Franco's rebellion against the Spanish government?

Father. No pasarán![1]

Mother. It's better to die on your feet than to live on your knees.

Corazón-man. Why should we, if we live in a small city in Argentina?

Mother. (After placing a tray of empanadas[2] *on the table, she walks over to the child.)* Happy birthday, Corazón! *(She kisses him.)*

Corazón-man. Thank you, Mamá.

Father. Arriba, Corazón![3] Onward and upward!

Corazón-man. I'll try, Papá. (MOTHER *puts a second-hand jacket around* FATHER'S *shoulders.)*

Mother. I'm sorry. I had to dress him in the little suit that his cousin gave him. . . .

Father. Look, at his age the only thing I had was a pair of balloon pants tied at the ankles, and a pair of *alpargatas*.[4] (CANFUNFA *enters from the right in a wheel chair and stops. The* MOTHER *senses his presence and turns to him. She shields her son with her body, as if he were being threatened.)*

Canfunfa. Sugar.

Mother. Yes, Señor Canfunfa. *(The* MOTHER *runs to the table, looks for the sugar, finds a large package and walks towards to* CANFUNFA.) Did you bring a. . . ? *(She was going to say "sugarbowl," but* CANFUNFA *brutishly grabs the whole package and leaves. The* MOTHER *watches him leave. She pauses as if she wished to forget. She hums a Jewish melody, and with her hands and her expressive Jewish gestures, she beckons the* FIDDLER *to play the same melody very softly. She begins to set the table. The* FATHER *walks towards the little boy.)*

Corazón-man. Papá . . . *(The* FATHER *turns around and looks at him. He sits on the floor next to him while the man continues to rock himself.)*

Father. Balloon trousers, Corazón, and a pair of *alpargatas*. That's all. Hard times! There are things you must know. They'll become your history. You're at the right age for them to sink into your brain, even if you don't realize it now: certain ideas, messages, prejudices, a sense of the heroic, fear of everything, courage, resistance, survival, future, nothing, everything . . . everything . . . everything. . . . Luckily you were born into a family that

can teach you those things. Important things, Corazón! *(He turns and looks at the* MOTHER, *who is setting the table and humming, while next to her the* FIDDLER *tentatively plays the same Jewish melody as before. The two of them seem like old, contented friends.)* Your Mother, for instance. She was so beautiful! . . . We used to plant seeds together. And I can tell you that planting is very difficult. The most difficult thing. Because you can't see anything. The land and the worms swallow it all up. And the black color of the earth, like dirty water, confuses you. You think that that seed is important, but it disappears. Everything disappears. Yet your Mother and I planted seeds. She was so beautiful, Corazón . . . and so sad! *(He bows his head, crying silently.)* I used to play the guitar and sing to her. I used to wear my hair like Gardel.[5] (CORAZÓN-MAN *looks at him.)* In the field, Corazón, eh? With brilliantine, I looked a lot like Gardel! (CORAZÓN-MAN *rests his hand on his* FATHER'S *head.)* I used to sing to her . . . (CORAZÓN-MAN *messes his* FATHER'S *hair roughly. The* FATHER, *looking at him sadly, sings.)*
This little sorrow of mine,
   vidalitá[6]
I give it to you with my soul
   vidalitá. . . .
(Taking out a comb and quickly combing his hair, he sings.)
I give it to you, it's all yours.
It's all yours, *vidalitá.*
(As the song ends, he finishes combing his hair. He looks at the comb and blows on it.) Until they threw us out of the field because we couldn't keep up our payments. We made you that night. Our last night there. As we were leaving, I saw in front of me that black land full of worms. I saw the horses that I had broken in . . . and I cursed it all. But you were coming with us, Corazón, in your mother's belly . . . and I was afraid of the worms, even the silk worms, that—as we all know—are hard workers and turn into butterflies. And I told you, do you remember?

Corazón-man. *(Loudly)* You'll never go through that! Never! The future has to be yours! *Arriba, Corazón!*

Mother. *(Turning towards the* FATHER*)* Speak quietly! You'll wake up the neighbors.

Father. I wasn't talking loudly! It's always me, always me! *(Moving towards the boy and taking off one of his own shoes)*

Mother. What are you doing?

Father. My birthday present! *(Giving his shoe to the boy, he looks at him and ruffles his hair.)*

Corazón-man. On July 18, 1936, over there in Spain, Franco's general, Queipo del Llano, was fighting against the Spanish Republic. And over here, my father gave me his shoe as a present.

Mother. The candle went out and I don't have any matches . . .

Father. Let me light it. *(Moving to the table while the* MOTHER *walks towards the boy)*

Mother. Did you mess his hair?

Father. (Looking at her with surprise) Me? I don't know . . .

Mother. Yes, you, you. . . . Give me your comb. *(He hands her the comb. She walks to the child and combs his hair.)* Your Father is nervous, Corazón, because my family is coming. You see, they studied and he never did. . . . *(Moving to* CORAZÓN-MAN, *and combing his hair)* We were seven children, Corazón, and all five brothers studied! The two girls didn't, because we were women! But of course the five boys did! *(The boy has messed up his hair. Seeing him this way, she combs it again.)* You have to study, Corazón! You have to study!

Father. What are you whispering in his ear?

Mother. That he has to study! *(The boy messes up his hair again with a wild gesture.)*

Father. (Observing him) He's not even listening to you. He's always somewhere else! When is your family coming? It's late!

Mother. Birthdays never begin on time, except for the one whose birthday it is. *(Moving towards* CORAZÓN-MAN) He's nervous, you see! Since he couldn't study, when he sees my brothers, he gets nervous . . . And sad. He was always sad. In the field. . . .

Corazón-man. It seemed as if the land were on top of him, instead of him being on top of the land. . . .

Mother. Luckily I'm here, Corazón! *(Combing his hair)* Clean and groomed! *(She looks at the* FATHER. *He takes off his shoe and gives it to* CORAZÓN-MAN. *Then he moves to the child. He takes off the other shoe and gives it to him. He combs his hair.)* Clean and groomed! You're going to live better than we ever did! I'll take care of that, Corazón! Even if I have to tear out part of my body! *(*CORAZÓN-MAN, *and* CORAZÓN-CHILD, *show their shoes to each other.* UNCLE MANUEL, *the mother's brother, enters, bringing three books. He moves to* CORAZÓN-CHILD.)*

Manuel. The first grade history book! *(Giving it to him)* The second grade history book! *(Giving it to him)* The third grade history book! I want a nephew who knows what he's about! *(Going to*

CORAZÓN-MAN) Happy Birthday! *Arriba, Corazón! (Kissing the* MOTHER) How are you?

Mother. Very well! I'm happy . . . *(Looking at the* FATHER *and correcting herself)* We're happy that you could come, Manuel!

Manuel. I was at a political meeting, but I managed to get away. After all, it's my favorite nephew's birthday!

Mother. (Confidentially, knowing that he likes them) I made you *empanadas!*

Manuel. (Voraciously) Oh yes? *(He moves to the table and tastes an* empanada. *The* FATHER *looks at him from a distance.* MANUEL *sees him and greets him with his mouth full.)* Hello!

Father. (Always intimidated by his wife's family) Hello . . .

Manuel. Did you see the Governor with the letter I gave you?

Father. Yesterday. *(Pause)* He gave me a job. The one you asked for.

Manuel. The Governor and I are pals!

Father. I hadn't opened the letter. I didn't know you asked him for a job as a janitor.

Manuel. We're *landsman,* compatriots. I didn't want to take advantage. Besides, you're just here from the countryside. You're the poetic type. You have to get rid of that first. Then . . . we'll see. *(Going to the* MOTHER *who is next to* CORAZÓN, *he eats some more. Alluding to the* FATHER*)* Watch him. Be sure he makes me look good. *(Alluding to* CORAZÓN*)* Did he learn something new in school?

Mother. Everyday! He'll be carrying the flag soon! Corazón, recite what they taught you for your Uncle Manuel! (CORAZÓN *looks at his uncle sadly.)*

Manuel. What's the matter with him? Is he afraid of me?

Mother. He's not afraid of anything! Come on, Corazón! Recite for your Uncle! *(The* FIDDLER *plays a solo, while* CORAZÓN-MAN *rocks himself in his chair, smiling. The violin solo begins to falter. Suddenly there is silence.)*

Manuel. Bravo! A real macho voice! *Arriba, Corazón!* Recite for your Uncle! *(The violin is heard again, but even more quietly.* MANUEL, *acting as if he were starving, goes to the table and takes another* empanada.)

Father. (This is his only possible revenge.) There are only seven left!

Manuel. (Looking at him, surprised, about to take a bite of the empanada*)* What? Excuse me! *(Leaving the* empanada *on the tray. To* CORAZÓN*)* I want him to study law! Then he'll be my partner! (CANFUNFA *enters in his wheelchair.)*

Canfunfa. Flour! *(Running to the table, the* MOTHER *gives him a package of flour. Grabbing it roughly,* CANFUNFA *leaves.)*

Father. If he comes back, I'll kick him the hell out! *(*CANFUNFA *returns.)*

Canfunfa. Bread! *(The* FATHER *threatens* CANFUNFA *with a violent gesture.)*

Mother. *(Screaming at him)* Think of your son! *(Looking at her and pausing, the* FATHER *takes an enormous loaf of bread and gives it to* CANFUNFA, *who takes it and leaves in his wheelchair.)*

Manuel. *(Patting the* MOTHER's *shoulder)* Luckily, you've adjusted better than he has!

Father. If he keeps taking everything, there'll be nothing left for Corazón!

Mother. Don't you worry about that. If I have to, I'll nurse him again!

Manuel. A worthy heiress of Remedios Escalada, of Mariquita Sánchez,[7] of . . .

Father. Don't waste your breath on speeches, because I don't intend to vote for you anyway!

Manuel. Oh, no?

Father. No!

Manuel. Why not? Don't you like being a janitor? Are you thinking of going back to the country? Where? Where they threw you out because you couldn't pay?

Mother. *(Taking* MANUEL *by the arm)* Of course he'll vote for you! We don't know anything about politics! You're the only politician in the family . . . Well, Juan too, but it's different. . . . Of course he'll vote for you! Come, have another *empanada*! *(Leading him to the table)*

Manuel. He said there were only seven left!

Mother. So only six will be left! If we have to, we'll cut them in half! *(Giving* MANUEL *an* empanada*)* Hasn't Juan written to you?

Manuel. No. And he's not going to. My brother knows that I opposed his fighting in Spain. Why Spain? Aren't there enough civil wars here, where he could prove to himself he's a man? I stayed! Here! *(Choking and coughing as he eats. The* MOTHER *slaps his back. The* FATHER *goes to* CORAZÓN-MAN.*)*

Father. Corazón, your Uncle Juan is in Spain, fighting for the freedom of the world. Do you remember?

Corazón-man. *(Covering his* FATHER's *mouth)* You . . . Mamá . . . the port . . . the ship . . . and there on top . . . Juan! Above everyone . . . *(*JUAN *appears. The* FIDDLER *plays the first chords of "The Fifth Regiment.")*

Juan. Happy Birthday, Corazón! I'm in the middle of the battle-field, operating in a hospital full of blood. And suddenly, under the bombs, I remembered that today is your birthday. I also remembered that last year on this day, I gave you a pair of foot-ball shoes. They must be small on you by now. . . . People, Corazón, people! Only in war one learns to know them profoundly! I'm a doctor, and here, under the bombs, I've felt for the first time that my profession is good for something! We're fighting for the freedom of all of us, of all of you far away in Argentina . . . and this will help people live better, in a better world . . . I hope that this letter reaches you some day, Corazón, so you can understand that those people and that world are your legacy . . . yours and all of the children whose birthday it is anywhere . . . in any city. . . . Don't forget it, Corazón! *(The music of "The Fifth Regiment" becomes more intense. It matches the* MOTHER'S *euphoria as she runs to* CORAZÓN. *Both she and the* FATHER *struggle to get hold of* JUAN'S *letter.)*

Mother. Let me have it, he's my brother! *(To* CORAZÓN*)* We received a letter from your Uncle Juan from Spain! He remembered your birthday and he congratulates you! Right there on the battlefield, and he remembered! Do you realize this, Corazón? Everyone came to my little boy's birthday to bring him some-thing. *(Kissing him as if she were biting him, then pulling back)* Forgive me, Corazón, I almost chewed off your cheek! *(Standing up)* Luckily, you're going to live in a better world than ours. There are many people fighting for that! Many people! I'd like to be much older already, to see you living in that world! Tomor-row! The future! What beautiful words! What a marvelous thing the human language is! *(Takes off her woolen jacket and wraps it around* CORAZÓN. *The violin music becomes somber. The* MOTHER *looks at the* FIDDLER *in anguish. She shakes her head in denial, taking refuge in the* FATHER. *The music reaches its climax, and ceases.)*

Corazón-man. Franco was fifty kilometers from Madrid. The pa-pers published the news along with the football scores. It hardly mattered . . . to anyone . . . to only one. *(Slowly,* JUAN *enters. He has been taken prisoner.)*

Mother. It's better to die on your feet than live on your knees!

Father. No pasarán!

Corazón-man. It wasn't the same for them either, but here they were . . . while he . . . *(*JUAN *is standing next to the chair of* CORAZÓN-MAN. CANFUNFA *enters without his wheelchair. He is* *a pro-Franco general. He places himself opposite* CORAZÓN's *chair. The child observes the whole scene with fear.)*

Canfunfa. (To JUAN) Are you Argentinian?

Juan. Yes.

Canfunfa. What are you doing in my country? I was in yours five years ago, invited by General Uriburu. But I didn't come to fight. Why did you come to make war in my country? All of you . . . what are you doing in my country? Answer me. You know I'm going to shoot you. *(The* CHILD *runs and takes refuge in his* MOTHER's *arms.)* Why did you come? Don't you know why you came?

Juan. No, well, maybe . . . I could tell you that sometimes a person goes, and goes . . . and keeps going. . . . He has to. It's written. It's destiny . . . From the time you're a child it's destined . . . It's a color . . . a sound . . . a space that belongs to you . . . and you keep going . . .

Canfunfa. That's no answer.

Juan. No. *(A short pause)* I could tell you that my creditors ran me out. *(He laughs.)*

Canfunfa. (Laughing) That's no answer!

Juan. No . . . I could tell you that I ran away from my wife because she was cheating on me with my own friends . . .

Canfunfa. That's no answer!

Juan. No . . . Oh, yes . . . I remember now . . . I came to fight for freedom. And we will all be wiped out, destroyed, forgotten. That's why we came. To be erased, destroyed, forgotten.

Canfunfa. The only thing that will outlive us is this situation, stranger. A man with the power to shoot and another man destined to be shot. You didn't have to travel so far to prove it. It's the same in your country. You don't have an answer to my question. *(Short pause)* Shoot him. (CORAZÓN-CHILD, *cries inconsolably in his* MOTHER's *arms.* JUAN *leaves slowly, and so does* CANFUNFA. *As* JUAN *leaves, the* FIDDLER *follows him playing what sounds like a funeral march. During* JUAN's *march to his death, the* MOTHER *embraces the child.)*

Mother. It's better to die on your feet than to live on your knees . . .

Manuel. (Shouting as he waves a letter) No!, No! *(The* FIDDLER *stops, surprised.* JUAN *continues his march and leaves.* MANUEL *quickly approaches the* FATHER *and* MOTHER.) A letter from the Argentine Ambassador to Spain . . . About Juan! *(Everybody is in anguish.)* He's in a concentration camp. The Argentine

Ambassador saved him from being shot. He's a great friend of Franco!

Corazón-man. On April 13, 1939, Franco's troops entered Madrid.

Mother. (Taking the child to his chair) He was saved, Corazón! He was saved!

Father. (Moving towards her) Now you can calm down . . . Everything is all right . . . Let's enjoy the birthday . . . It's not his fault! *(Referring to* CORAZÓN-CHILD. EL NEGRO, *a friend of the* FATHER'S *enters.)*

Manuel. Luckily the Ambassador of Spain is a friend! *(Going to the table, and helping himself to an* empanada. *The* FATHER *goes over to him and takes it away.)*

Father. Leave something for the others! *(He is about to take it to* EL NEGRO *when the* MOTHER *stops him and takes away the* empanada. *Then she calls him aside.)*

Mother. What's that friend of yours doing here?

Father. He's my friend! I invited him!

Mother. He has no business here! Especially today! Tell him to . . . to come back another day! *(Looking at her with hatred, the* FATHER *pauses and then walks quickly toward* EL NEGRO.*)*

Father. Let's go, Negro!

El Negro. (Surprised) Where?

Father. I don't know . . . to the river!

El Negro. I want to eat *empanadas,* not fish! *(But the* FATHER *takes him to the river. The violin is heard again.)*

Corazón-man. It's true . . . the river! We were a family of poor Jews. When they were thrown off the farm, my parents went to live in Paraná. Later I became a swimmer. But until that time, the river was for me a far-off sound that helped me to sleep. That night when my father came home sick and drunk, and went to my bed to hug me, I discovered in his hands, for the first time, the smell of the river . . . *(Pause)* The smell of the river . . . the smell of the river . . . *(The* FATHER *tenderly runs his hand through the water.* EL NEGRO *watches him.)*

El Negro. It's water . . .

Father. Yes *(to the water),* adiós.

El Negro. Who are you talking to?

Father. I know who. Didn't I ever tell you about myself?

El Negro. (Defensively) No, but I never told you about myself either!

Father. A horsebreaker. I used to break in horses. Didn't I tell you? A thousand horses, Negro, I broke in a thousand horses between my thighs. Here, Negro, here! *(He slaps his thighs.)*

El Negro. You don't look it . . .

Father. No. Not now. Horses of every color, Negro! And when I saw a plane passing overhead, I would choke with laughter! What good are planes? When you are breaking in a horse, Negro, the horse's legs tie you to the center of the earth . . . and the mane, wet with sweat, flies in the wind . . . and the body, the body, Negro! . . . When you break in a horse, you feel in your body the galloping of the whole world! All the sounds of the world . . . all the resounding of the world! What good are planes?

Corazón-man. (*Watching the scene*) You were a horsebreaker, Papá? What were you, and what weren't you? If I didn't know you then, how could I be sure that this memory has to do with you, and not just some wish of mine . . . a wish to have a history . . . or something that I read in a book? How to know it, with so much fog and so much drizzle, Papá? So many nights I dreamt about a field of flax . . . Tell me! (*His* FATHER'S *voice interrupts him.*)

Father. Did I tell you when I planted a small field of flax?

El Negro. No, but I never told you everything I did either!

Father. It was blue, Negro, . . . a little blue sea . . . like this water.

El Negro. It's not blue, it's black.

Father. You're black, too.

El Negro. I'm black, and so is the water.

Father. The water is always blue, Negro, always . . . I felt like swimming in my sea of blue flax . . . That's what I felt like. (*Crying silently*)

El Negro. You're drunk, *Moishe.*[8]

Father. No. I can't get drunk. . . . It's my liver!

El Negro. Then why are you crying?

Father. Because of the locusts. . . .

El Negro. What did the locusts do to you?

Father. They ate up everything, Negro. They ate all the flax. Do you know what I'm saying? First, I took off my shirt, then my undershirt, then my pants. I even took off my shorts to see if I could scare them off! Nude in the middle of the field! Nude! (*Short pause*) Negro . . . what's the point of so much flax, for the locusts to destroy later? (*Running his hand through the water*) Adiós!

El Negro. Who are you talking to?

Father. To myself.

El Negro. You're here.

Father. No. You might think so, but I'm not. I'm in Corazón already. That's my legacy to him!

El Negro. All right, that's what parents are for. That's what children are for.

Father. Let's go home. We have to cut the cake.

El Negro. You go. I'm staying by the river.

Father. What for?

El Negro. I want to swim to the island. They say there are partridges there. I'll tell you about it tomorrow in the office. Ciao. (EL NEGRO *walks away. The humming of Jewish music returns. The* MOTHER *and* MANUEL *dance in a twilight of memories. The* FATHER *hums the music very softly. Marking the rhythm, he half dances, as if he were walking to the chair of* CORAZÓN-CHILD. *He looks at him, pauses, takes off his shirt and drapes it over the child.*)

Father. Arriba, Corazón! (*The* CHILD *looks at him. Suddenly afraid, he runs to take refuge in the arms of* CORAZÓN-MAN. *Until the end of the act, both* Corazóns *appear fused in a single character.*)

Mother. You're going to wake him up.

Father. It's his birthday! He has to be awake!

Mother. He's just a child! He's not used to running around like you until all hours of the night. And your friend?

Father. I threw him out . . . He's one of those people who eats everything if they stay! Just like your brother! He always finishes the *empanadas.*

Mother. He's my brother! He helped you, didn't he?

Father. To become a janitor!

Mother. You're no longer a janitor! Now you work in an office, thanks to his recommendation. (*She looks at him, surprised, and touches him.*) You're wet! Where were you?

Father. All over . . . (*Looking at her and suddenly taking her hand*) Let's go to the river!

Mother. Where?

Father. To the river!

Mother. What for?

Father. To find out where it flows!

Mother. What?

Father. The river!

Mother. Don't be silly! I know where it flows!

Father. Where? (*Anxiously awaiting the answer*)

Mother. Nowhere!

Father. (*Looking at her, furious*) Goddamn you! What have you done to me, what have you done to me? (*The* CHILD *wants to look.* CORAZÓN-MAN *gently prevents him from looking.*)

Mother. Don't shout! He's going to wake up!

Father. He never wakes up when he's sleeping. You know that. What have you turned me into? *(The* FATHER *speaks in a low but furious tone, biting his words.)*

Mother. (In the same tone as the FATHER*)* Into my husband. And you've turned me into your wife. That's what we were born for, no? And don't shout, because he's going to wake up. You know that as soon as he hears the slightest sound, he wakes up.

Father. Let him wake up! He knows that I love him! *(Going towards the two* CORAZÓNS*)* He knows that everything I have will be his. *(Taking off his undershirt and draping it over both of them)*

Mother. Don't behave as if you were Corazón! When you act that way I feel like asking you, "What are you going to be when you grow up?"

Father. A businessman!

Mother. (Laughing quietly) You already are a businessman! We have a store. It's small, but it's a store. *(Taking off her skirt and draping it over the two* CORAZÓNS*)*

Father. It's not for me! Each time a customer comes in to buy sugar, bread, vinegar or oil, I die of shame. What I'd really like to sell is . . .

Mother. (Smiling) What?

Father. I don't know . . . Or I do! I'd like to sell . . . rivers! And lakes! And streams! And our youth! . . . And horses!

Mother. (Laughing) They don't use horses in the city, my love! And the rest . . . is free!

Father. Is it?

Mother. (Laughing) Isn't it?

Father. But I don't have it!

Mother. (With possessive, and at the same time, disparaging love) Oh . . . you!

Father. (Taking her hand with the intention of bringing her with him) Let's go to the country!

Mother. (Resisting, she begs him) No, please, not that, my love! Not that . . . You can't die so many times and keep on living . . . Please!

Father. (Pausing) No, you're right, you can't. *(Pulling her to him)* You were so beautiful! So very beautiful! *(Singing)* This little sorrow of mine, *vidalitá.*

Father & Mother. (Singing softly)
 I give it to you with my soul
  vidalitá. . . .

I give it to you, it's all yours.

It's all yours.

(They look at each other and embrace. He slowly places her on her back, facing the public. He is kneeling on top of her.)

Mother. Manuel is here. . . .

Father. When he's eating he doesn't notice anything. *(Caressing her)*

Mother. It's useless . . . I don't feel anything.

Father. Why?

Mother. My flesh is asleep . . . Before, you only had to touch me and my flesh awakened, crying for you . . . It must be asleep now . . .

Father. Yes, mine too. Why?

Mother. The weather . . . Fall, winter, spring, summer, fall, winter, spring, summer. And this endless birthday! I'm tired. *(He helps her stand up, slowly.)*

Father. It's late now. It will be over soon. I'll help you sweep the garbage and wash the plates.

Mother. And you'll never speak about the country again. Promise me!

Father. *(Pausing)* I promise you.

Mother. *(Smiling)* You see? Now everything is just fine, my love! We have the store . . . *(She approaches both* CORAZÓNS.*)* We have him and he has us! Everything we have is his! Everything, everything! *(Taking* CORAZÓN-CHILD *in her arms. To the* FATHER.*)* Is there anything left?

Father. What do you mean, is there anything left? Everything I have is for him! *(Taking the* CHILD *from the* MOTHER's *arms and squeezing him, almost suffocating him)* Everything I have! Everything!

Mother. My dearest little boy! Look how nicely he sleeps!

Father. Arriba, Corazón! *(*CORAZÓN-MAN *feels suffocated, as if he were the child.* CANFUNFA *enters in his wheelchair. The parents see him, and cling to the child.* CANFUNFA *does not ask for anything. He laughs very softly, and crosses the stage as he leaves. The silence is broken by* MANUEL.*)*

Manuel. *(Laughing very loudly, as if responding to a joke)* I ate the last *empanada!* *(The* FATHER *and the* MOTHER *approach* MANUEL.*)*

Mother. You could have left one. We could have shared it among all of us . . .

Manuel. *(Laughing)* When I eat, I eat! That's the way I am!

Father. You're a pig! *(While this dialogue is taking place,*

CORAZÓN-CHILD *is in his* FATHER'S *arms. He looks at the adult, as if asking for help.)*

Mother. Shut up. He's my brother!

Father. He's a pig!

Mother. He's my brother!

Father. He's a pig!

Manuel. (Laughing) When I eat, I eat! That's the way I am!

Father. You're a pig! Now I can say it to you!

Mother. Please . . . It's very late for Corazón. Let's blow out the candle, all right? (CORAZÓN-MAN *gets up from his chair and walks towards the cake. He looks at the* CHILD, *smiles at him and gestures as if inviting him to blow out the candle. The* CHILD *looks at him, and turns his head. The* MAN *smiles and the* CHILD *blows out the candle.* CORAZÓN-YOUTH *appears. He is about twenty years old. He carries a rifle in his hands. He moves to the center of the stage and takes his post as a guard.)*

Corazón-man. I had discovered the rivers . . . and that day I discovered the circle . . . *(Makes a circle with both hands, as if it were a telescope, and examines everything around him)* It was the first of September, 1939. The German troops invaded Poland. The Second World War had begun. *(A very short pause)*

Father. (Shouting) No pasarán!

Mother. It's better to die on your feet than to live on your knees!

Corazón-man. (Focusing the circle of the imaginary telescope on his parents) The end is transformed into a beginning. (CORAZÓN-CHILD *looks at him. He stretches his arms towards him. But the* MAN *opens his, in a gesture of helplessness. The* CHILD *looks at the youth, asking for help. But the* YOUTH, *on guard duty, keeps staring ahead. The* CHILD *is alone.)*

Corazón-child. (Very softly) He . . . e . . . lp! *(Louder)* He . . . e . . . lp! *(Violin music begins, a martial melody, played softly, then louder . . .)* He . . . e . . . lp! *(The shouting and the music grow louder still.)* He . . . e . . . lp! He . . . e . . . lp! He . . . e . . . lp! He . . . e . . . lp! *(The music reaches a crescendo and suddenly ceases.)*

Father. (Rocking the child in his arms) Don't cry, Corazón! Don't cry! You'll wake up the neighbors! (CORAZÓN-MAN *covers his eyes with his hands.* CORAZÓN-YOUTH *continues looking straight ahead, his eyes wide open. The spotlight finds him. A short pause.* CORAZÓN-MAN *barely enters the circle of light. From the edge of the circle, he looks at* CORAZÓN-YOUTH. *The light begins to fade and the sound of a* bombo[9] *is heard in the distance.)*

Act II

CORAZÓN-CHILD *has left the stage by the time the lights go up. The circle of light has shifted, but* CORAZÓN-YOUTH *is still in its center, and at the border is* CORAZÓN-MAN, *looking at him.* CORAZÓN-YOUTH *wears a soldier's uniform and other pieces of clothing that his* MOTHER *and* FATHER *gave him in the first act. The other characters appear scattered in the background, wrapped in the semidarkness of the fog where* CORAZÓN'S *memories live.*

When the other characters speak with CORAZÓN *during this act, they address both the* YOUNG *and* OLD CORAZÓN.

There are two MUSICIANS *in this act: The* FIDDLER, *bearing the weight of melancholy from the past, and the* DRUMMER, *whom we already heard, although from afar, at the end of Act I.*

As this act begins, both musicians share the stage, but gradually the FIDDLER *takes over. At the same time, the lighting on the* FATHER *becomes more intense, not as intense as on* CORAZÓN-YOUTH, *but enough to remove him from the atmosphere that envelopes the other characters.*

A sentry box is dropped in the circle of light where CORAZÓN-YOUTH *is, and he stands guard in front of it. When the violin prevails over the drum, and the lighting around the* FATHER *is stronger,* CORAZÓN-MAN *seems to sense his* FATHER'S *presence. He turns to him. In his memory he sees his* FATHER *earnestly going through the contents of a large suitcase full of nuts, bolts, screws, etc. that is lying on the floor and that somehow threatens and upsets him.* CORAZÓN-MAN *is moved by this image. He goes towards his* FATHER *and tries to cheer him up, there, in the past.*

Corazón-man. Hey, you big clown! (*The* FATHER *looks at him, without reacting. He looks at the suitcase again.*) Come on, Mr. Clown! (*The* FATHER *turns to him with a clownish voice and smile.*)

Father. Do you want to hear a joke, little clown?

Corazón-man. That's what we're here for!

Father. I used to have a friend.

Corazón-man. What a rich man you are!

Father. He had a bar. He had arrived!

Corazón-man. Where was he going?

Father. Nobody knew! He sold it and he opened a factory in Buenos Aires, where they made scrubbing boards.

Corazón-man. So what's the joke, Mr. Clown?

Father. (*Now in his own voice*) That, my friend, is me. (*The*

MOTHER *cuts off the conversation in a loud voice. She is sitting and mending as she watches the sentry box.)*

Mother. That's not true! I didn't insult him! *(In a normal tone)* I never insulted your father, Corazón. But when he told me that they had tricked him with that scrubbing board factory, and he burst out crying, I thought it was a little late to have another son! I comforted him, yes, because he expected that of me, that I comfort him. But I closed my eyes and I thought about you. I always thought about you. (CORAZÓN-MAN *goes to her.)* It was so beautiful to close my eyes and think about you . . . so beautiful to watch you grow, Corazón! You were so bright! The brightest, by far! I don't even remember what your father was like anymore, but you . . . Oh, my god, if I could be young again! I'm sure you would fall in love with me, Corazón. *(Changing)* But it's not true. I never insulted him, poor man . . . *(Standing up)* And I hope that you never insult anyone either, Corazón! That's what I expect of you! *(Going towards* CORAZÓN-YOUTH*)* I don't like people who offend others just for the sake of it! One should know how to respect people! *(As she reaches* YOUNG CORAZÓN, *he reflexively crouches and adopts a firing position with one knee on the ground, pointing his rifle at her.)*

Corazón-youth. The password!

Mother. (Stopping, taken aback) I'm your mother, dear . . . I came to bring you . . .

Corazón-youth. (Stopping her) Nothing doing! The password!

Mother. (Shouting) I'm your mother, dear!

Corazón-youth. Nothing doing! The password . . . or I'll shoot!

Mother. (Shouting desperately) I'm Mamá! (CORAZÓN-YOUTH *gets ready to shoot. The* MOTHER *runs away. She reaches the* FATHER *who is struggling with his suitcase.)* It's your fault! Why do you let him smoke?

Father. Don't ever insult me again . . .

Mother. I never insulted you!

Father. You told me to go to hell, you useless slob . . .

Mother. I never insulted you!

Father. You told me to go . . .

Mother. Not me! It was . . . Manuel!

Father. (Looking at her) Your brother? Your brother? . . . when I find him, I'm gonna kill him.

Corazón-man. Were you a horsebreaker, Papá? Did you ever kill anyone? Did you?

Father. I'm gonna kill him!

Mother. (Loud and insulting) Don't be so stupid! *(Short pause)*

Please! How do you think we survive? With the lousy little nothing that you earn selling nuts and bolts and junk? With that? Do you think that gives us our food and clothing, you and me and Corazón? Really! Just be thankful that my brother helps us . . . and you want to kill him!

Corazón-man. You never killed anyone?

Father. (Looks sadly at CORAZÓN-MAN *and then at the* MOTHER.) But I have to hit somebody . . . just let me hit somebody!

Mother. Me? I'll let you! But choose well . . . *(The* FATHER *looks at her, pauses, looks around him, and doesn't find anyone. Suddenly he slaps himself. He enjoys it. He smiles and slaps himself again. He laughs. Amused, the* MOTHER *also laughs.* CORAZÓN-MAN *goes to the sentry box and sits there. His* FATHER, *baffled, watches him as he leaves. He pauses and immediately starts slapping himself again. He and the* MOTHER *laugh and look at each other happily. The* MOTHER *straightens his jacket and his tie.)* I'm so glad that you finally found something to amuse yourself with. It's no good for you to go around sad all the time. Seriously, my love! Let's see if from now on . . .

Father. I promise you! Don't worry about me anymore! Finally I know what I have to know! *(He starts slapping himself again. They both laugh.)*

Mother. My love! *(He turns around, smiling. She smiles too.)* Go to hell, you useless slob! *(He laughs and so does she.)* Go to hell, you useless son of a bitch! *(Both laugh loudly. She screams, still louder.)* Go to hell, you useless son of a bitch! *(They both laugh uproariously.)* You see, you see, my love?

Father. Yes, my love! It's very clear!

Mother. You must guide Corazón! YOU—ARE—THE—MAN—

Father. Don't worry! Leave it to me! *(He goes to the sentry box, slouching as he walks, as if the suitcase were getting heavier and heavier. He finally reaches the sentry box, overwhelmed by the weight of the case. He looks at* CORAZÓN *and begins to circle the sentry box. The* bombo *is heard.)*

Corazón-man. (From inside the sentry box) In Paraná during Carnival we used to dry the tripe that the butcher gave us to make the drums for the *murga.*[10] The drum was a fiesta in 1945 . . . the drum was a far off sound, unreachable, and my family read it as a threatening sign, coming from a mysterious camp, a stampede that advanced over us, a thunder against which we closed the window. Or was it the sound of the Russian cannons over Berlin, as we celebrated the end of the Second World War in the streets of Buenos Aires? Or was it just your heart, Papá, the heaviness of your heart? *(The* FATHER *stops moving and interrupts* CORAZÓN'S *reveries.)*

Father. Is everything all right in school? I'm glad! *Arriba, Corazón!* You have to study! The future is yours! You can count on me! Any help, any advice . . . I'm your father. Besides, you have your mother, your uncles. Ours is a very close family, thank God! Not like others. You're not alone, Corazón! Never stop asking whatever you feel like! I'm your father . . . (CORAZÓN *looks at him. The* FATHER *tries to move the case that appears to be stuck to the ground, in an attempt to draw closer to his son.)*

Corazón-youth. The password . . .

Father. (Looking at him, trying to avoid the answer) Why do you smoke, my son? In the end, it's no good for you. I'm your father and . . .

Corazón-man. (To CORAZÓN-YOUTH*)* Let him come in.

Corazón-youth. (Pausing, to the FATHER*)* The password or I'll shoot.

Father. (Looks at him, weak and confused) You shouldn't smoke. Listen to Papá because Papá knows best.

Corazón-man. (To CORAZÓN-YOUTH*)* If you don't let him come in now, it will be too late for both of you. . . .

Corazón-youth. (Resolutely, to the FATHER*)* The password, or I'll shoot! *(The young man is kneeling, aiming at his* FATHER, *and gets ready to shoot. The* FATHER *runs away, crossing the stage and dragging the heavy suitcase full of nuts and bolts.* CORAZÓN *continues to aim at his* FATHER *as he runs.* CORAZÓN-MAN *rests his hand on the young man's shoulder. The latter finds himself face to face with* CANFUNFA *as he follows his* FATHER'S *flight through the sight of the gun. He stiffens and stands at attention.)*

Canfunfa. (In a dry, military tone) Good evening!

Corazón-man. (Clicking his heels) Good evening, Sir!

Canfunfa. It's damn cold out there.

Corazón-man. It is very cold, S-i-i-r!

Canfunfa. Or is it hot?

Corazón-man. It is hot, S-i-i-r!

Canfunfa. Bravo! You have to learn not to make mistakes. That's why you're here.

Corazón-man. That's why I'm here, S-i-i-r!

Canfunfa. First command: Kill, whatever the price! (CORAZÓN-MAN, *looks at* CORAZÓN-YOUTH. *He pauses and hesitates.)*

Corazón-youth. Yes, S-i-i-r!

Canfunfa. Second command: Avoid being killed, whatever the price!

Corazón-youth. Yes, S-i-i-r!

Canfunfa. Third command: Don't pay the price!

Corazón-youth. Yes, S-i-i-r!

Canfunfa. Fourth command: Figure out how the June sun can protect our rearguard, while the frontline and the constitution still rule those who know how to religiously preserve a rigid morality, in spite of the fact that the frogs croak in the lake and bring our country seeds of rue to confound us with. It follows that only the eternal clarity of our aims, beyond the pitiful screams of the children, will make us victorious, strong, humble yet proud, and always, always . . . ARGENTINES!

Corazón-man. *(Softly)* Yes, S-i-i-r . . . yes, S-i-i-r . . .

Canfunfa. Have we taught you how to see yet?

Corazón-youth. Sight in order, S-i-i-r.

Canfunfa. Look behind you.

Corazón-youth. I can't S-i-i-r! I'm on duty!

Canfunfa. I'll take over your post!

Corazón-youth. I can't S-i-i-r! I'm the guard!

Canfunfa. Bravo! Do you have a mirror?

Corazón-youth. I have a mirror, S-i-i-r! *(He produces a little mirror.)*

Canfunfa. Look in the little mirror!

Corazón-youth. I'm looking in the mirror, S-i-i-r!

Canfunfa. What do you see?

Corazón-man. *(Looking at the audience)* I see . . . windmills, S-i-i-r.

Canfunfa. Continue that way, and there will always be water in your mill! You may smoke! And while you're at it, why don't you give me a cigarette . . . *(He goes towards* CORAZÓN, *who crouches and takes aim at him.)*

Corazón-youth. The password, S-i-i-r . . .

Canfunfa. *(Stops and pauses)* Windmills . . .

Corazón-youth. The password or I'll shoot, S-i-i-r!

Canfunfa. Argentines!

Corazón-man. The password or I'll shoot! *(The young man aims, ready to shoot.)*

Canfunfa. He'll change his mind soon! (CANFUNFA *leaves in his wheelchair.* CORAZÓN-YOUTH *maintains his position for a moment. The drums begin.* CORAZÓN-YOUTH *suddenly stands up. He presents arms and clicks his heels, all very mechanically. Looks right, looks left, until the violin is heard. We see the* FID-DLER *following* JUAN *very closely.* CORAZÓN-YOUTH *stands at ease, sliding down along his rifle to a crouching position.* CORAZÓN-MAN *takes a few steps toward* JUAN. *The drums stop.)*

Corazón-youth. Dear Uncle Juan: I don't know why I'm writing to you. You're like a shadow to me since that day when we came to Buenos Aires to say goodbye to you and you boarded a ship and sailed away to Spain. Maybe for that very reason, because you are a shadow who's not like anyone near me . . .

Corazón-man. You never spoke to me . . . you never wrote to me . . . Uncle . . . Uncle Juan . . . what is the password? *(Pause)* I would like it so much if you returned!

Juan. Dear Nephew: This is the other letter that I am writing to you and not sending to you. I'm in Mexico, working in the mines with the Indians, as a doctor. I feel better . . . recuperated, but I still don't have it in me to write you. I know from the papers that your country is going through special times. Everyone here is talking about Peronism. Some okay, some badly. I'm afraid of it. I know that it's a popular movement, yes. But . . . do any of them know it is a revolution? Did any of them die in Spain? Do they know Marx, Engels, *Das Kapital,* La Pasionaria? I don't know . . . a popular movement without class consciousness, without political education, doesn't inspire confidence in me. I have learned a great deal and I would like to teach you something of what life has taught me . . . I . . . *(JUAN interrupts himself when the* FIDDLER *begins to play very near him, as if it were a signal for him to leave.* JUAN *looks at the* FIDDLER.*)* I . . . *(The* FIDDLER *insists with a smile and* JUAN *starts to leave.)*

Corazón-man. Juan . . . *(JUAN keeps walking away.)* Juan . . .

Corazón-youth. Juan! *(He speaks just as* EL NEGRO *comes running in.* EL NEGRO *is the same friend of his* FATHER, *who now appears as if he were young again. He is carrying a chicken.)*

El Negro. And why should I be called Juan? Can I come in? I . . . *(Smiling)* I found a chicken . . . *(He shows it to him.)* For you and for me. Well, can I come in?

Corazón-youth. (Hesitating) Do you know the password?

El Negro. I just arrived from *El Chaco,*[11] compañero! The only thing I know is that I found this chicken! Well?

Corazón-youth. (Pausing) Come in. Inside the little house there's a stove. But pluck the feathers!

El Negro. (Laughing) So, here you eat them without feathers! Dammit! You're so refined around here! *(EL* NEGRO *enters the little house,* CORAZÓN-MAN *walks to the sentry box and leans on it. He hums the* FIDDLER'S *melody, as if conjuring it up.)* How do you want it done?

Corazón-youth. Tender. (CORAZÓN-MAN *is still looking for* JUAN.)

El Negro. So particular, aren't you? I bet it's hard. I had to chase it for a hundred blocks!

Corazón-youth. Didn't they see you? (*Also looking for* JUAN *while he talks to* EL NEGRO)

El Negro. Yes, but they thought I was in training! (*He laughs heartily.*)

Corazón-youth. Who taught you how to do it?

El Negro. You're born with it. It was the chicken or me. This time I won. (*Looking at him. Short pause.*) They told me that you're a Jew . . .

Corazón-youth. They told me too.

El Negro. What do you feel?

Corazón-youth. At times, at night, you wake up . . . and you feel something.

El Negro. I don't like Jews.

Corazón-youth. And I don't like Blacks.

El Negro. Why did you let me come in if I didn't know the password?

Corazón-youth. (*Pausing and shrugging his shoulders*) I was alone. . . . (CORAZÓN-MAN *has continued to invoke* UNCLE JUAN *with his humming. The violin music is heard. The man searches for its source, but can't identify it. The* FIDDLER *enters playing the violin and smiling.* JUAN *has still not appeared.*)

Corazón-man. (*Searching for the memory of* JUAN) I want you to return. (*He goes to another corner.*) The family says that you're in Mexico, that you got married. (*Suddenly changing tone*) Mara . . . Mara . . . Why, Mara? . . . Why? (*He stops himself, surprised at his own flashback, and resumes his conversational tone.*) When they speak of you, Uncle Juan, they do it in hushed voices, as if it were mystery. I know you were in Spain, in the Civil War, and I'd like to ask you, what was your password? I'd like to ask you . . . Juan, Juan, I need to ask you! (JUAN *appears from the corner where the* FIDDLER *is waiting for him. The* FIDDLER *leads him across the stage with his playing.*)

Juan. I prefer not to send you this letter. I remember you in the port waving goodbye to me, but so much time has passed, and you've become a mystery to me. And I can't tell you that! Just as I can't confess to myself that I am living among the Indians, I'm sick with malaria, no salary, while they keep on speaking their dialects as soon as they see me, and I don't understand them . . . because they don't want me to understand them. (*Short pause*) If I could only see you again! (JUAN *rips up the*

letter. The FIDDLER *leads him to the exit. Just before leaving,*
MARA *appears. She is waiting for* JUAN.)

Corazón-man. Mara! (JUAN *reaches* MARA. *They kiss and leave.
The drums are heard off stage.* EL NEGRO *comes in with the
roast chicken. He and* CORAZÓN-YOUTH *begin to eat it.*
CORAZÓN-YOUTH *moves his hand through the water. Now they
are in El Tigre.*[12])

Corazón-youth. It's the first time I've come to El Tigre.

El Negro. I always come! For the trees . . .

Corazón-youth. What trees? I only smell the stench!

El Negro. A smell is a smell. Don't think about it, Moishe!

Corazón-youth. How can I not think about it?

El Negro. Just don't think about it? (CORAZÓN *lies down and leans
on* EL NEGRO'S *shoulder, satisfied and content after their meal.*
EL NEGRO *looks at him and pauses. He strokes his hair,
tenderly.)*

Corazón-man. My family is waiting for me. . . .

El Negro. It's our last day. Go!

Corazón-youth. I can't . . . I don't know if I'm going to miss
you, Negro.

El Negro. Neither do I. I don't like Jews.

Corazón-man. And I don't like Blacks.

El Negro. (*Looking at the sky*) We have to go back. Get into the
boat. (*They get into the boat and both of them row.*)

Corazón-youth. (*Looking at the river*) What a putrid river! Look
. . . a dead dog. It comes and goes . . . comes and goes. . . .

El Negro. (*Looking at the sky as he rows*) Look at the clouds!
They come and go . . . come and go. . . .

Corazón-youth. What are you going to do now, Negro? Will you
return to El Chaco?

El Negro. No. My whole family came to Buenos Aires. I'll look
for Mom. I'll get a wife. I'll have children. I'll make a home. I'll
have grandchildren. I'll plant lettuce, tomatoes, onions, some
fruit . . . And what about you?

Corazón-man. My family is waiting for me. (CANFUNFA *appears.
The two men move towards him. When* CORAZÓN *sees him, he
freezes.)*

El Negro. (*To* CANFUNFA) Thanks for the boat, Señor. (*To* CORA-
ZÓN) Ciao, Moishe.

Corazón-youth. Ciao, Negro. Will we see each other again?

Corazón-man. Yes, we'll see each other. We'll see each other! (EL
NEGRO *shrugs his shoulders and walks away.)*

Corazón-youth. Negro! *(*EL NEGRO *turns to him.)* You didn't give me the password.

El Negro. I'm not going anywhere. *(*EL NEGRO *leaves.* CORAZÓN-MAN *remains next to* CANFUNFA, *who is now an elegant professor.)*

Canfunfa. *(Referring to* EL NEGRO*)* Who is he?

Corazón-man. We met in the army.

Canfunfa. Cannon fodder. Zoological allusion. A monkey at Tiffany's. Do you know what Tiffany's is?

Corazón-youth. A woman, I think.

Canfunfa. You only think about women. You have a one track mind. I see you in class, you know. You only look at the girls.

Corazón-youth. I study, sir.

Canfunfa. Study, study! It's a bad time to be studying. What you know, it's better not to know. *(Looking at the audience, he points at something.)* What's that?

Corazón-youth. *(Looking at them)* Windmills, sir.

Canfunfa. That's what I thought . . . Let's take a walk. *(*CORAZÓN and CANFUNFA *walk back and forth across the stage.)* This is what Aristotle did with his students. Like you and me. Only they were lucky enough to be in Athens. Here, we've been invaded by slaves. *(Drums are heard.)* Do you know what the Athenians used to do when the slaves wouldn't stop giving birth to more slaves?

Corazón-youth. No, sir.

Canfunfa. You see? You know what's useless and you don't know what's really worth knowing. War! That's what they did! War! War is the art of eliminating unnecessary slaves. There are necessary slaves and there are unnecessary slaves. Is that clear?

Corazón-man. I have an uncle who was in the war.

Canfunfa. Which war?

Corazón-man. In Spain . . .

Canfunfa. Did the Communists kill him?

Corazón-youth. He's in Mexico now.

Canfunfa. Mexico! Mexico! Great Señor Maximiliano! I assume you know what history is, right?

Corazón-man. It's an hour a day, before recess.

Canfunfa. That's it, an hour a day! Just an hour a day! The rest doesn't count. History, my dear, is that long, clear, limpid, straight line that stretches for only an hour a day! The meeting of the ethical and the aesthetic. Do you know what Ethics and Aesthetics are?

Corazón-man. No, sir. I'm taking them next year.

Canfunfa. Ethics, my dear, is a treasure chest full of memories . . . a certain way of being with a friend . . . like statues you recognize, like inherited hats. And Aesthetics, my dear, the straight line is aesthetic, and a certain color, and a smell that becomes ours.

Corazón-youth. Isn't a smell, a smell?

Canfunfa. A smell is like a person! It has a first and last name! It has fingerprints! It has a police record! It has a family album! Each smell is separated from the next by barbed wire! A smell is like a concentration camp, and only death can free us from it! Where are we?

Corazón-youth. At the Plaza de Mayo, sir. (*Pointing to the sentry box*) There's the *Casa Rosada.*[13]

Canfunfa. And you . . . what are you doing here?

Corazón-man. I don't know . . . I'm still waiting for the password.

Canfunfa. Don't be such a Jew and try to get off the hook!

Corazón-man. I am a Jew, Sir . . .

Canfunfa. (*Looking at him with excitement*) Listen to me . . . And you too . . . are you missing the . . . the little piece?

Corazón-youth. Yes, Sir, thank you. (*He shows him his penis.* CAN-FUNFA *looks at it, first from afar, scientifically. Then he pulls on it.* CORAZÓN-YOUTH *screams with pain. He examines himself between his legs.*)

Canfunfa. What are you looking for?

Corazón-youth. The password, Sir.

Canfunfa. I already told you all the ones I know! Can I come in?

Corazón-youth. It's better if you don't today, Sir. I have orders to shoot to kill.

Canfunfa. Not today . . . but what about tomorrow? You'll return tomorrow, won't you?

Corazón-man. No, Sir. Today I finished high school.

Canfunfa. (*Looking at him, anguished*) You finished . . . They all finished . . . Will anyone return next year? Tell me . . . Each day I feel more lonely . . . (*Looking at the sentry box*) So that's the *Casa Rosada* . . . Once I was at a reception there . . . now it looks to me like a parade in *Mataderos!*[14] It's cold . . . Don't forget to do your homework . . . (*Remembering*) Oh, yes, you finished! (*Looking around him*) I don't even recognize the pigeons! (*Starts moving away*)

Corazón-youth. Sir!

Canfunfa. What do you want?

Corazón-man. Give me back what you stole from me!

Canfunfa. Oh, yes . . . (*Returning his penis*) I thought I was young

again . . . too bad . . . Why isn't that catching? Why? (CAN-
FUNFA *leaves.* CORAZÓN-YOUTH *takes the rifle. Kneeling, he puts
it on his knees and rows slowly. The* FIDDLER *and the* DRUMMER
*appear from opposite sides of the stage, facing each other as
they play.* JUAN *and* MARA, *his young wife, also appear.)*

Corazón-youth. (Rowing as if he were towing a boat to shore) Dear
Uncle Juan: Please, come back! I don't know what to do. I think
I changed the orders. The first was to kill, no matter what it
took, and I only tried not to be killed. I guess now I should start
to kill, but who? Why? Did you kill anyone in the war, Uncle
Juan? Who? Why?

Corazón-man. It's Christmas today. Everybody is inside their
houses, and I'm still on duty. I really would have liked to send
you this letter, but I don't have any paper or pencil. So . . .
that's that!

Mara. There's so much fog, Juan!

Juan. That's the way the Río de la Plata is. There it is, right in
front of you! Well, we're finally back!

Mara. You are, not me.

Juan. You're coming with me. You're the only thing I'm bringing!
Don't leave me alone, Mara. I don't know why I have these fears.
Maybe it was a mistake. I'm too old to go back anywhere. Maybe
I should have kept on floating . . .

Mara. Don't say that. Your family is waiting for you. Do you see
them?

Juan. (Looking around) I only see seagulls.

Mother. (To MANUEL*)* Do you see them?

Manuel. Fog. Pure fog!

Mara. (To JUAN*)* Do you see them?

Juan. Only seagulls.

Mother. (To FATHER*)* Do you see them?

*Father. (Struggling with the suitcase that has him hunched over.
Looking at the ground.)* No . . . !

Mara. Do you see them?

Juan. Only seagulls . . . Please don't leave me alone! (CORAZÓN-
YOUTH *stops rowing. The boat has arrived.* CANFUNFA *approaches* JUAN *and* MARA.)

Canfunfa. Doctor . . .

Juan. Yes?

Canfunfa. You have to come with me.

Juan. My family is waiting for me . . . *(The family waves to him.)*

Canfunfa. It will only be for a moment. (JUAN *hesitates. Pauses.*

Moves forward a few steps. Stops and goes toward MARA. *He looks at her with anguish and fear. She goes with* JUAN.)

Canfunfa. The lady?

Juan. She's my wife.

Canfunfa. From what I know, she's your lover. I don't want to offend you, but if you call a spade a spade, everything will be clear.

Juan. (Excited) She's my . . .

Mara. (Trying to soften the situation) I am his lover. *(Throughout this interchange* CORAZÓN-YOUTH *remains on guard.* CORAZÓN-MAN *takes the suitcases and watches them lovingly.)*

Canfunfa. Are you Mexican?

Mara. I'm Polish.

Canfunfa. And half French.

Mara. Yes.

Canfunfa. And you live in Mexico.

Mara. Yes.

Canfunfa. And you're Jewish.

Mara. Yes.

Canfunfa. My God! What a mixture! You're confusing me! And in my job, confusion is bad! *(Pointing somewhere)* The fingerprints are there. *(*MARA *is about to leave.)*

Juan. (Restless) Mara!

Mara. (Trying to calm him down. Smiling) It's all right . . . *(To* CANFUNFA*)* Is it far?

Canfunfa. No.

Mara. (To JUAN*)* Don't be afraid. *(*MARA *exits. The family waits.)*

Canfunfa. Do you remember me, Doctor?

Juan. (Looking at him attentively) Yes . . . I don't know . . . Was it in Spain?

Canfunfa. How well travelled you are! Why would I go to Spain? This is my country! No, it wasn't in Spain. It was at a hospital in Entre Ríos, a long time ago . . . You saved me from a yararᡠ[15] bite. Why did you come back?

Juan. This is my country.

Canfunfa. No. It's my country. I held on. I started off a farmhand. And I held on. They paid me badly. And I held on. I'm like him. You're not. What did you go to Spain for?

Juan. I was asked that question a long time ago and I didn't know how to answer it.

Canfunfa. And now you know?

Juan. Yes, now I do. *(Pause)* I think I went . . . to die.

Canfunfa. (Pausing, dryly) Do you see what I'm talking about?

You're a misfit. You shouldn't have returned. You should have remained to die in the air . . . or at sea. Not here. You don't come here to die. You come here to live. The ones who come here to live, adapt themselves. They learn to believe in what we believe. They grow like everyone else. They look like everyone else. You know who you're dealing with. You know how to deal with the situation because fear is the salt of life, not of death. *(Pause)* You're a problem, Doctor. A misfit. But I'm going to let you go. A favor I owed you. We're even now.

Juan. And my papers?

Canfunfa. No. Starting today you don't belong. You don't count. No one will have to pay attention to you. You don't exist. Be careful, Doctor. This is my advice for having saved my life a long time ago. It's dangerous to live in a country where we're all trying to live at any price. *(Pause)* Merry Christmas. (JUAN *looks at him, nods his head and goes to* MARA.)

Mara. What did he tell you?

Juan. Merry Christmas!

Mara. *(Looking at him, happy to find out)* Today is Christmas, Juan! Like the day we met! I want you to teach me to love your city, to live in your city, to walk through your city! *(Exultantly)*

Juan. *(Smiling)* It's not my city, I was born in the country.

Mara. *(Laughing happily)* No one can be born in the country, with a city like this! It's not like Paris, Juan . . .

Juan. It's not like anything else.

Mother. *(Seeing him, she shouts.)* Juan!

Manuel. Juan!

Juan. *(To* MARA*)* Don't say anything to them about what happened when you arrived.

Mara. But they're your . . .

Juan. Don't tell them anything!

Mother. Juan! *(To the* FATHER*)* There he is! Do you see him?

Father. *(Always struggling with his suitcase, staring at the floor)* No . . . I'm busy. (JUAN *and* MARA *reach the family. They look at each other. Pause. The* MOTHER, *dramatically, falls to her knees and bursts out in tears.* JUAN *looks at her, at his brother* MANUEL *and at his* FATHER. *They greet each other. Their gestures are meant to be slow, suspended in the air, but showing strength rather than weakness. The* MOTHER *cries as* JUAN *looks on. Then he turns and points to* MARA *as his way of introducing her to his family.* CORAZÓN-YOUTH *remains kneeling in front of the sentry box, with the rifle between his legs, while* CORAZÓN-MAN *removes* JUAN'S *jacket and the shawl* MARA *wore on her shoulders. The* MOTHER *starts weeping again. The* FATHER, *leaning over his suitcase, looks at* JUAN.)

Juan. *(To the* MOTHER, *as if he were guilty of something)* Forgive me!

Manuel. It doesn't matter. You'll get used to it. We never had a war. Everything is very different here. Much better. You'll be able to start all over again. *(The drums become louder, like an Indian drum. The family is startled.* MANUEL *moves towards the sound.)*

Corazón-man. Then my Uncle Manuel closed the window, and the thunder disappeared. *(*MANUEL *pantomimes closing a window.* EL NEGRO *enters playing the drum with a funereal rhythm. When* CORAZÓN-MAN *sees him, he starts laughing at him.)*

El Negro. Don't laugh, Moishe! She's . . . dead!

Corazón-man. Who's dead, Negro? Your wife? *(*EL NEGRO *starts to leave, playing the drum lugubriously.)* Who, Negro, who?

Manuel. Luckily, she died. There's only one left! *(To* JUAN*)* They've invaded us, Juan. But when they leave, it will all be rebuilt, starting with us. That's why the family should stick together, now more than ever!

Juan. You and I don't have the same ideas.

Manuel. Around here, it's not a question of ideas! When they eat you alive, what good are your ideas!

Juan. I appreciate everything you did for me. Before, in Spain, when you saved me from being shot, and now for your financial help. But don't tell me how I should think. *(*CORAZÓN-YOUTH *stands up and looks at* JUAN. CORAZÓN-MAN *does the same.)*

Manuel. But, the family . . .

Juan. *(Pointing to* MARA*)* She's my family! I don't want to offend you. . . .

Manuel. I'd like to go on talking about this. . . .

Juan. Why not? *(Turning to* MARA*)* Mara, my brother Manuel is coming for lunch. *(*MARA *turns, walks across the stage.* JUAN *turns slowly. He sees* CORAZÓN-YOUTH *near him, and they look at each other closely.* CORAZÓN-YOUTH *is carrying the rifle in his hands. To* CORAZÓN-YOUTH, *aggressively, in spite of himself)* You're skinny, you have freckles, a scrawny moustache, a lousy shave, you look like a madman. Why don't you take vitamins? Are you sick? I had to operate in Spain while bombs were exploding. I had to amputate limbs in a concentration camp in France . . . I had to help Indians give birth in Mexico. Tell me if you're sick! I'm a doctor! *(*CORAZÓN-MAN *has been listening to the speech standing next to* CORAZÓN-YOUTH. *They are like* *one person, both facing* JUAN, *in silence.* JUAN *reaches out to* CORAZÓN-YOUTH *attempting to touch him, embrace him, pull him close, but something in* JUAN *stops him from expressing his feelings. He crosses the set quickly and goes to* MARA, *who is kneeling. He looks around.*) Is anyone here?

Mara. No. (*After making sure no one is looking, he lies on the floor and rests his head on* MARA'S *lap.*)

Juan. What am I doing here? I'm a stranger, just a stranger!

Mara. Please Juan, help me! I don't want to be a stranger. I want to belong to something, once and for all! This is your country, your family, your friends! Help me, Juan!

Juan. I can't, Mara. I can't. Forgive me.

Mara. (*Looking at him and getting up*) Why did we ever come, Juan?

Juan. I thought you realized. (*Pause*) To die.

Mara. (*Looking at him and rejecting the idea*) No! No! Not me! I don't want to die. I'm young. (*Running across the stage to the sentry box. Also running,* CORAZÓN-YOUTH *meets her there. She grabs the rifle. Both of them hold on to it as they look at each other.* CORAZÓN-MAN *stares at* JUAN.) You are Corazón!

Corazón-youth. Yes.

Mara. Your uncle is busy. He's taking care of a patient.

Corazón-youth. Oh . . .

Mara. (*Looking at the sentry box*) Can I come in?

Corazón-youth. I don't know . . .

Mara. (*Laughing*) Why does everyone say "I don't know" around here? Is Perón any good? "I don't know". Why?

Corazón-youth. I don't know.

Mara. (*Laughing. Short pause*) Do you know how to row?

Corazón-youth. (*Kneeling down. Pretending to row.* MARA *is standing behind him.*) So so. An army friend taught me.

Mara. What does your friend do?

Corazón-youth. He works in a factory. He got married. He bought a house. He has a child. He planted lettuce and tomatoes . . . Soon he's going to have grandchildren. (*The beat of the* bombo *is heard in the background. While* CORAZÓN-MAN *searches for* EL NEGRO, *following the sound of the drum,* CORAZÓN-YOUTH *stares at* MARA. EL NEGRO *enters playing the drum.*) Did you get married, Negro? Did you plant tomatoes? Did you have grandchildren?

El Negro. (*Walking as he plays the drum*) They're killing us, Moishe, they're killing us . . . Oy! (*Now he beats the drum creat-*

ing the sound of bombs, like the bombs that fell on the Plaza de Mayo. He exits.)

Mara. (To CORAZÓN-YOUTH*)* What's happening? Why are you looking at me like that?

Corazón-youth. Why can't I call you Aunt?

Mara. (Smiling) Why?

Corazón-youth. I don't know.

Mara. How old are you?

Corazón-youth. Twenty one.

Corazón-man. Fifty.

Corazón-youth. And you?

Mara. Twenty-five. Do you want to die? *(Both* CORAZÓNS *look at each other. The older one hesitates for a moment while the younger responds passionately.)*

Corazón-youth. No.

Mara. (Embracing him, happy that he does not want to die. Laughing as she says) Me neither! Me neither! Me neither!

Corazón-youth. You're going to fall in the water.

Mara. You'll save me. Your uncle told me in Mexico that you're a great swimmer. Let's swim. *(Taking off her clothes until she is naked, she jumps into the water and begins to drown.)* Corazón . . . I'm drowning!

Corazón-youth. (Surprised and frightened) Don't you know how to swim?

Mara. No . . . But you do! CORAZÓN-MAN *laughs as he remembers the absurd scene. He walks over to them.* CORAZÓN-YOUTH, *after a moment's hesitation, throws himself into the water and grabs* MARA *without looking at her.)*

Corazón-man. (To MARA*)* Now do what I tell you . . .

Mara. I will. Are you married?

Corazón-youth. No.

Corazón-man. Move your feet as if you were a frog. *(*MARA *obeys first moving one foot, then the other.)*

Mara. Why aren't you married?

Corazón-youth. I don't know . . . *(He always avoids looking at her.)*

Corazón-man. Now move your hands, as if you were a puppy. *(*MARA *follows his instructions.)*

Mara. Do you like women?

Corazón-youth. They drive me crazy.

Corazón-man. (To MARA*)* Keep going! Frog, puppy! Frog, puppy! Let's go! *(*CORAZÓN-YOUTH *embraces her again. The rifle is between them. He looks up to avoid seeing her naked.)*

Corazón-youth. Mara: I won't send this letter either. I don't know where you are after so many years, or if you even remember that day in El Tigre when I taught you to swim. *(Smiling)* Or you taught me, I don't know . . . *(Laughing)* And always that "I don't know." Like you used to say! Until that day, water from the rivers had been like railroad tracks for me, taking you from here to there, towards somewhere. But that afternoon, at your side, I found that water penetrated me and would never leave me. Was that true freedom, all within oneself? How I would like to ask you this, Mara! If I only knew where you are, what you're doing, after so many years without seeing you! *(Young* CORAZÓN *takes in* MARA'S *scent. He turns towards her, but with his eyes closed.)*

Mara. (Surprised. Smiling) What are you doing?

Corazón-youth. I'm smelling. *(Intensely)* I'm smelling! I'm smelling you! I'm smelling you! *(They spin around until they slowly stop. They are euphoric.* CORAZÓN-MAN *guiltily walks over to* JUAN *and* MANUEL. JUAN *looks at his revolver.)*

Corazón-man. Nothing else happened, Uncle Juan . . . air . . . smells . . . water . . . freedom . . . nothing else. *(JUAN starts cleaning the revolver.)* Even though I believe you wouldn't have cared then anyway . . . but I didn't know it!

Manuel. (Cutting in with his characteristically coarse, strident and heavy voice) The meal was good. A little spicy for my taste.

Juan. Mexican food. A little spicy.

Manuel. (Looking at him, uneasily) What are you doing?

Juan. I'm cleaning my revolver.

Manuel. Why? Listen. We're not in Spain here! It's another time . . . There are ways to . . . Our party doesn't approve of violence.

Juan. I was never in your party.

Manuel. I know that! But even your Communists abandoned you! And they know why! They're watching you!

Juan. Is that why you come every day? Don't worry! I never killed anyone!

Manuel. Then what do you want the gun for?

Juan. I have no one to talk to . . .

Manuel. They're afraid of you! That's why! *(He pauses, somewhat surprised.)* And your wife? *(JUAN turns towards* CORAZÓN-YOUTH *and* MARA.)

Mara. (Looking at CORAZÓN-MAN, *who is very close to* JUAN) I would like to send you this letter, Corazón, but I'm traveling on the Paris Metro. Many years have passed since that afternoon.

If you hadn't expected so much of me . . . who knows. . . . Why expect so much? Why? Besides, exactly what is it that you expected, Corazón? Did you find it. Tell me. Did you find it? I'm almost there. A beautiful Metro station in Paris! *(To* CORAZÓN-YOUTH*)* You made me swallow water! *(She moves away and coughs. He hands her her clothes without looking at her.* MARA *gets dressed.)*

Corazón-man. Nothing else happened, Uncle Juan. Air, smells, water, freedom! Nothing else!

Juan. (Interrupting) My wife is going back to Mexico. She didn't tell you yesterday.

Manuel. And you?

Juan. (Cleaning the revolver) I'm back already. *(Short pause)* Ciao.

Manuel. (Surprised) Aren't you going to give me a check-up?

Juan. What for? I don't have to give you a check-up to know that your stomach is getting bigger.

Manuel. Why do you always make fun of me?

Juan. It's your color.

Manuel. What color?

Juan. Yellow, like an old newspaper.

Manuel. And what's your color, Juan? Mine walks calmly through the streets and no one says anything. No one is afraid! Everyone knows what they are! What's yours?

Juan. (Staring at the revolver) He knows it. *(*JUAN *continues cleaning the gun.* MANUEL *leaves.* MARA, *dressed by now, walks over to* JUAN. CORAZÓN-YOUTH *returns to his post as a sentry guard.)*

Mara. (To JUAN*)* You want me to leave!

Juan. (Without looking at her, continues cleaning his gun) Yes, my love.

Mara. Why, Juan? Why?

Juan. Because I'm a doctor, and I can't allow a sick person to die.

Mara. Juan!

Juan. Go, my love! Go!

Mara. (Pausing) I owe you everything I am.

Juan. (Pausing, without looking at her) Forgive me, then.

Mara. (Anguished) Juan!

Juan. (Screaming at her) Go! *(*MARA *looks at him, turns around and goes to* CORAZÓN-YOUTH. *She looks at him and tousles his hair. She goes to the* MOTHER *and* FATHER. CORAZÓN-YOUTH *fixes his hair with hand.* MARA *formally nods to the* FATHER *and* MOTHER *then exits.)* Are you there, Corazón?

Corazón-youth. Yes, Uncle Juan.

Juan. You were waiting for me . . .

Corazón-youth. Yes, Uncle Juan.

Juan. Finally, the two of us alone . . . What do you want? Hurry up! I don't have much time! What do you want?

Corazón-man. The password, Uncle Juan! I'm on duty!

Juan. (*Softly, without looking at him*) Let them come in. It's not worth it.

Corazón-man. Did you let them?

Juan. (*Shouting*) Let them come in!

Corazón-youth. (*Digging his heels in and aiming*) The password or I'll shoot!

Juan. (*Looking at him*) No . . . don't let them in . . . (*Raving*) Don't let them contaminate us . . . We, the martyrs, the gods, the heroes, the masters of the future! The future, the future, Corazón! That's what I meant to tell you since I came back! The future, Corazón. When we get to the year 2000, it will find us at the head of . . . (*beginning to lose track of what he is saying*) at the head of . . . (*Bursting into tears*) God! My God! Is this the Word? Is this it? (*JUAN looks at his gun. He slowly falls to his knees. He puts the gun to his temple. EL NEGRO appears, beating a deliberate rhythm on the drum. CORAZÓN-MAN sees him. He looks at JUAN and goes to EL NEGRO who walks across the set.*)

El Negro. They're killing us, Moishe! They're killing us! (*A shot is heard before EL NEGRO exits, with the final beat of the drum. CORAZÓN-YOUTH, who was kneeling before the sentry box, stands up. The FATHER approaches him, dragging the heavy suit-case. CORAZÓN-MAN looks at JUAN's body.*)

Father. (*To CORAZÓN-YOUTH*) What did he tell you?

Corazón-man. (*Turning to the FATHER*) "The future," he said!

Father. Ah, yes! (*Looking at the MOTHER*) Your poor mother! She loved him so much! (*MANUEL goes to the MOTHER and puts his hand on her shoulder.*)

Manuel. It was better for him.

Mother. Yes . . .

Manuel. It was better for everyone.

Mother. Yes . . .

Manuel. And Corazón?

Mother. He's on duty.

Manuel. When does he finish?

Mother. He doesn't know.

Manuel. When he's finished, tell him to come to me. I want him to work with me in my office.

Mother. Thank you. (CORAZÓN-MAN *goes to the* FATHER.)

Corazón-man. Papá . . .

Father. (*Struggling with his suitcase*) What?

Corazón-man. It's cold. Do you want to come in? (*Taking pity on the* FATHER, *he offers him the sentry box. The* FATHER *looks at it, pauses, then shakes his head.*)

Father. No, no, no . . . (*Slapping his cheek and laughing. The* MOTHER *and* UNCLE MANUEL *also laugh. The* FATHER *slaps himself again and they all laugh even harder. He slaps himself once more and they continue laughing.*) No, no, no . . . (*The same action is repeated. The* FATHER *looks at* CORAZÓN.) No! It's all yours, and if you offer it to me again, I'll spit on you, son of a bitch! Or was it all for nothing, eh? (*Slapping himself and laughing*) All for nothing, eh? (*The drums beat very loudly, like circus music in crescendo. The* FATHER *speaks to* CORAZÓN-YOUTH *in a clown's voice.*) Should I tell you a joke, *Payasín?*[16]

Corazón-youth. That's what we make a living from, *Payasota!*[17] (*The* FATHER *looks at him and begins to cry, quietly. Old* CORAZÓN *goes to the side of the stage towards the audience. A circle of light closes in on him while* CORAZÓN-YOUTH *and the* FATHER *remain in semidarkness. The memory fades away and the drums begin to beat softly, yet threateningly.*)

Corazón-man. Uncle Juan left me his books and I began to read. I was twenty-three and Perón had just fallen.

Act III

When the lights come up, CORAZÓN-MAN *is in the same spotlight as he was at the conclusion of the second act.* CORAZÓN *is in semidarkness. The drumming continues. The* FIDDLER *enters, playing soundlessly. He goes to* CORAZÓN-YOUTH *and leads him offstage. Then he returns to* CORAZÓN-MAN.

Corazón-man. July 17, 1976. Dear Mama: Today is my birthday, and although I'm very far away, I can't forget you. (*Interrupting himself, looking around, searching for the* FATHER *and* MOTHER. *He doesn't see them. The* FIDDLER *plays faster, although the music is inaudible. Martial drumming however, can be heard. In the back of his mind,* CORAZÓN-MAN *tries to find a memory which he claims he still owns. But it is more distant than he thought. The* FIDDLER *encourages* CORAZÓN-MAN *to follow him, and he does. A ladder is brought to the back of the stage. It can serve as the gangway of a ship or possibly the ramp of a plane.* WANDA *is walking down the ramp. She is the same actress who played* MARA. *The* FIDDLER *leads* CORAZÓN-MAN *to the foot of the ramp.* CORAZÓN-MAN *climbs up until he reaches* WANDA. *From one side of the stage, a man with a sandwich board appears and remains there. From the other, the* FATHER *enters carrying a cot and also stays there. They all seem to be waiting for someone who will arrive accompanied by military drumming: it is* CANFUNFA *in his wheelchair. He goes to one side of the ramp and stays there. He looks at* CORAZÓN-MAN. *When* CANFUNFA *has settled in, the* FATHER *and the man with the sandwich board—who is really* EL NEGRO, CORAZÓN'S *friend—get to work: the* FATHER *assembles the cot and lies on it;* EL NEGRO *kneels between both boards and remains there, like a prisoner, his face towards the ground.* CORAZÓN-MAN *and* WANDA *reach the top of the gangway. He is carrying a small suitcase.* MANUEL *appears and joins* CANFUNFA *on his side of the stage.)*

Wanda. (To CORAZÓN-MAN*)* Do you see anyone?

Corazón-man. No, only seagulls. Do you think something happened to Papá?

Wanda. Don't think that, my love! Maybe the boat was early!

Corazón-man. Yes. *(Looking around)* Seagulls. It's been so long!

Wanda. Let's wait for them, all right? *(*CORAZÓN-MAN *agrees, worried about his* FATHER.*)*

Manuel. (To CANFUNFA*)* Señor, he's only here to . . .

Canfunfa. Don't say anything to me, Doctor. Your nephew will tell me everything. Bring him to me.

Manuel. He doesn't . . .

Canfunfa. Bring him to me. *(*MANUEL *looks at him. He walks briskly to the foot of the gangway, waving his hand, happily.)*

Manuel. Corazón! Corazón! Here I am! Welcome! *(He quickly climbs up the ramp and embraces* CORAZÓN-MAN.*)* Welcome to Buenos Aires, Corazón! You look great!

Corazón-man. You too, Uncle. And Papá, how is he?

Manuel. You'll see for yourself. *(Changing his tone, fearful, with an edge in his voice)* Don't talk.

Corazón-man. What?

Manuel. Don't talk. *(Looking at* WANDA, *changing his tone again, jovial)* Is she?

Corazón-man. Yes. She's Wanda.

Manuel. (Kissing and hugging WANDA*)* Welcome to Buenos Aires, Wanda! *(Changing tone again)* Don't talk. *(Jovial)* Someone wants to see you, Corazón.

Corazón-man. Where is Papá?

Manuel. In the sanatorium. You're going to see him! You're going to see him! *(Resuming the other tone)* Don't talk.

Canfunfa. (The others surround him.) Who's the lady?

Corazón-man. Pardon me, but first I want to know who . . . *(He is about to say "You are", when* MANUEL *cuts him off.)*

Manuel. Don't talk.

Canfunfa. She's your mistress, right, Architect?

Corazón-man. I won't allow you!

Manuel. (To WANDA*)* Don't let him talk!

Wanda. He's right. I'm his mistress. *(To* CORAZÓN-MAN*)* It's all right, my love.

Canfunfa. (To MANUEL*)* Doctor, stay with the lady for a moment. Come with me, Architect.

Corazón-man. Where?

Canfunfa. (Calming him) For a walk . . . (CORAZÓN-MAN *hesitates, still pleasant.)* Let's go! (CORAZÓN-MAN *looks at him, then at* WANDA, *who nods her head. He starts to push* CAN-FUNFA'S *wheelchair.)*

Wanda. (To MANUEL*)* What's going on?

Manuel. Don't talk. I don't want them to think that we're talking.

Wanda. What's going on here? Since we arrived you've been telling us "Don't talk, don't talk!" Who is that man?

Manuel. Haven't you realized yet? What kind of a world do you live in?

Wanda. Corazón and I came from France, Señor!

Manuel. Please, don't start in with French culture now! Everywhere, there are people like him. Even if they disguise themselves as Frenchmen. That's why I've been telling you "Don't talk."

Wanda. (Looking at him) And you?

Manuel. Me? *(Short pause)* Before, it was the other one. Now it's these. I wait and I stay alive! Between the *bombo* and the trumpet, some day a Strauss waltz will turn up.

Wanda. (Surprised at the possibility) A waltz?

Corazón-man. (To CANFUNFA, *uneasily)* Why did you call me? What do you want to know?

Canfunfa. Nothing. I just wanted to know your smell. Do you remember our conversations about smells? You don't? Well I do, Architect. And I needed to know what you smell like now. *(He sniffs him and smiles.)* It doesn't matter. You'll have a smell soon! *(Pointing to a place in the distance)* There it is! The *Casa Rosada!*Do you see how nicely we painted it? *(Moving forward* *in his wheelchair.* CORAZÓN-MAN *is about to follow him when he hears* EL NEGRO *scream.)*

El Negro. What do you want from me? (CORAZÓN-MAN *is surprised. He turns around and goes to* EL NEGRO.)

Corazón-man. Excuse me, are you talking to me?

El Negro. (Looking at him) Are you going to get me out of here?

Corazón-man. Me? No! I don't even know why I'm here! I just arrived . . . I came to see my father and . . . *(He seems to recognize him. He looks at him closely.* EL NEGRO *tries to avoid his glance, out of fear.)* Negro?

El Negro. (Looking up and pausing) Moishe?

Corazón-man. (Happily) Negro!

El Negro. So, you're a cop now, Moishe?

Corazón-man. I'm an architect!

El Negro. (Doubtfully) Oh yes? And what are you doing here, dressed up so fancy?

Corazón-man. I'm an architect and I don't know what I'm doing here! I just got back and they brought me here! And you, what are you doing here?

El Negro. (Elusively) I don't know either . . . *(Changing his tone)* Did they ask you if you knew me?

Corazón-man. They didn't ask me anything. If you just got back, keep going. But leave me your cigarettes.

Corazón-man. (Hesitating) I don't smoke . . .

El Negro. Then you can't help me. Just get going.

Corazón-man. Listen, Negro . . .

El Negro. Get out of here. They'll be coming any second. (CORAZÓN-MAN *stands up.* EL NEGRO *shouts and weeps, so they can hear him outside.)* Please, what do you want from me? I didn't do anything Señor, nothing! (CANFUNFA *arrives. He looks at them.)*

Canfunfa. (To CORAZÓN) Do you know him?

Corazón-man. (Pauses, softly) No.

Canfunfa. (Shouting) Take him away! His father wants to see him!

El Negro. My old man is already dead! *(The two sandwich boards close in on him as if they were two guards pressing him together.* CORAZÓN-CHILD *and* CORAZÓN-YOUTH *enter. They look at* CORAZÓN-MAN. EL NEGRO *crosses the set, squeezed in by the two sandwich boards.* CORAZÓN-MAN *watches him leave. He looks at all three* CORAZÓNS. *In order to avoid their eyes, he goes to* WANDA *and leads her by the arm, showing his nervousness.)*

Corazón-man. What did they do to you?

Wanda. Nothing . . .

Manuel. Why do you ask her that? We're not in . . .

Corazón-man. (*Cutting him off in an outburst*) I knew him. Why did I tell them I didn't, when I did know him?

Manuel. Don't talk. You're both all right. No one did you any harm. Why talk?

Corazón-man. I should have told them that I knew him! I could have helped him!

Manuel. How, if you don't smoke?

Wanda. (*Surprised, to* CORAZÓN-MAN) You told him that you didn't smoke? (CORAZÓN-MAN *looks at her, at the other two* CORAZÓNS, *and feels ashamed for his lie.*) Why? (CANFUNFA *laughs softly.* CORAZÓN-MAN *looks at him.* CANFUNFA *holds his nose.*) It's the stench. (*Exits*)

Corazón-man. (*Abruptly*) I want to see Papá. (*He looks at his* FATHER. *As if on cue, the* FATHER *sits up in his bed and shouts out the shout of the Lone Ranger.*)

Father. Hi-i-i-i-o-o-oh, Silver! (*He flings an imaginary lasso and hurls it toward* CORAZÓN, MANUEL *and* WANDA. *He pulls them to him.*) Hands up!

Corazón-man. Papá . . .

Father. So, you're thinking about holding up the Wells Fargo Express! I told that to Mamá! I told it to her! (*He looks up the ramp.*) Mamá . . . Mamá . . . (*The* MOTHER *appears at the top of the gangway.*)

Corazón-man. Mamá is no longer here. Papá . . .

Father. (*Looking at him and pausing. Firmly*) Don't drop your hands or I'll kill you! (*Looking at his shoes*) Did you rob my boots?

Corazón-man. Yes, Papá . . . Papá, she's Wanda, my wife . . .

Father. (*Looking at* WANDA *and at* CORAZÓN-MAN) Right now I'm going to collect the reward! (*The* FATHER *hides under the sheets.*)

Manuel. He's crazy.

Corazón-man. He's alone, ever since Mamá died. I wasn't there with him . . .

Manuel. But I was! We all feel alone, but what can you do? You have to know how to handle it with dignity!

Wanda. Corazón, let's go to the hotel, please! I need to take a bath.

Corazón-man. Uncle, will you take Wanda? I'm going to stay with Papá for a while.

Wanda. (*Protesting*) Corazón!

Corazón-man. Please. (*She looks at him.* CORAZÓN *sits on the floor, staring at his* FATHER. *She turns around and leaves, followed by* MANUEL. CORAZÓN-MAN, *absorbed in thought, looks at his* FATHER. *He is still hiding under the sheets. The* MOTHER *walks slowly down the ship's gangway to* CORAZÓN-MAN. CORAZÓN-YOUTH *and* CORAZÓN-CHILD *seek shelter from* CORAZÓN-MAN. *The three of them listen to the* MOTHER'S *monologue. The* MOTHER *whispers in her son's ear, bridging the gap of time.)*

Mother. My dear child, we miss you very much. *(*CORAZÓN-MAN *keeps looking at his* FATHER.*)* You made us very happy with your letter and those clippings from Spanish newspapers where they talk about you. Your father didn't say anything, but, well . . . you know how he is. I showed them to your Uncle Manuel, to see if he would get over the anger he feels over your studying architecture, and not law. *(She laughs a little.)* I hardly ever go out. There are so many problems out there. Besides, I've been having chest pains. And think of it, I never even smoked! Maybe I should start now, right? *(She laughs quietly.)* I'll finish this letter tomorrow . . . I don't feel too well now . . . it's that pain again . . . *(She stops. It was the day of her death. She runs her hands over her face, as if obliterating herself. The* FATHER *moans under the sheets.)*

Father. Mamá . . . Mamá . . . *(No answer)* Mamá! *(The* MOTHER *caresses* CORAZÓN'S *head. The* FATHER *sticks his head out.)* Mamá. *(Smiling at him and pointing to* CORAZÓN-MAN*)* Who is it? Who is that?

Mother. Corazón . . . our little boy!

Father. It's my son. That's what Mamá says. But I . . . I don't know him. I don't know him. I don't know him.

Mother. (Shaking her head, laughing) Oh you, you, you!

Father. It's all right if you say so, it's all right, but . . . I must know him from somewhere, sometime . . . What should I do? Should I hit him to see what he would do? No, no, maybe I should just ignore him. He'll have to say something. *(Looking at* CORAZÓN-MAN, *who looks back at him.* CORAZÓN-MAN *tilts his head.)* He doesn't say anything. He doesn't say a word. Everybody keeps everything to himself. I don't believe he's my son. Everything has gone wrong, distant. I don't know him. Only Mamá is Mamá! *(He cuts himself off. His body tenses as he perceives something threatening approaching.)* The locusts! Stop the locusts, Mamá. They said that there weren't any! That you could plant . . . But there are locusts! *(He attempts to drive the locusts away. Smiling, the* MOTHER *helps him with condescending, mechanical movements.)* Was that all, Mamá? The locusts?

Mother. (Stroking his head) Take it easy, Old Man, rest . . . We didn't lose a son, we gained a daughter.

Father. (Shaking his head) I never gained anything! Never . . . never . . . never . . . I never gained anything . . . *(He hangs his head. The* MOTHER *caresses him as if he were her child, not her husband.* CORAZÓN-MAN *looks up. Pauses. He straightens up and leaves, taking his suitcase with him. He bends over in the middle of the stage, opens the suitcase and takes out a large construction set. He is about to start building blocks when the* MOTHER *gets up, walks across the stage and goes up the ramp. When she reaches the top, the* FATHER *shouts.)* H-i-i-i o-o-o-h, Sil-ver! *(The* MOTHER *turns around to look at him and laughs. The* FATHER *laughs too. He gets up and begins to imitate breaking in a colt, with great skill and beauty. When he is finished he is full of dignity. The* MOTHER *applauds him in silence. Then she disappears at the top of the ramp. The* FATHER *maintains his dignified stance for a moment, then he lies down again.*CORAZÓN-YOUTH *and* CORAZÓN-CHILD *are listening to their* MOTHER *as old* CORAZÓN-MAN *did before. They are like two leaves in the midst of a storm.* CORAZÓN-MAN *tries feverishly to build blocks. His* UNCLE MANUEL *goes over to him.)*

Corazón-man. How long is it since anyone brought flowers to Juan?

Manuel. I brought him flowers a couple of weeks ago. All that seems so long ago . . . as if it never happened . . . Besides, I don't like cemeteries. I came to keep you company, that's all.

Corazón-man. Did you notice?

Manuel. What?

Corazón-man. Since we're here . . . no funerals. What is it, nobody is dying, or are people burying their dead in the river?

Manuel. Don't pay attention to what others say! Everything is just the same!

Corazón-man. Too quiet.

Manuel. What's there to say? Besides, that's the way we are . . . an introverted race!

Corazón-man. Who are you talking about, the Jews?

Manuel. I'm Argentine!

Corazón-man. What's the difference? We become more and more alike, without knowing if we're coming or going, whether we've arrived or are still trying to get there.

Manuel. Why did you come back, Corazón? Why? When you've been away so long, you forget . . . you don't understand . . .

Corazón-man. I only came to see Papá!

Manuel. He doesn't recognize you! He's crazy! And I don't believe you. . . . You spend all your time going to the cemetery! When you abandoned law, I thought you were going to become a doctor, like him.

Corazón-man. I'm not Juan!

Manuel. Each day you're more and more like him . . . you even look to me the way he used to. But if you want to find him, it won't be with my help. You'll have to bury yourself there with him, because that's where he is. You'd be better off worrying about your wife! (CORAZÓN-MAN *looks at him, surprised. As* MANUEL *leaves he meets* WANDA *on her way in.*)

Wanda. Always silence. "Don't talk, don't talk, don't talk." And you told your friend that you didn't smoke. Silence, my love. Is that what you came looking for?

Corazón-man. No! I came home because Papá needs me . . .

Wanda. It's not true.

Corazón-man. (Looking at her, pausing) All right. But there's something I must find!

Wanda. In the cemetery?

Corazón-man. I don't know where! When I find it, I'll know!

Wanda. And what about me?

Corazón-man. (Looking at her and taking her hand) Look! *(Taking her where he has begun to build blocks)* I've started to build, Wanda! We can stay . . .

Wanda. What will it be?

Corazón-man. Well, it's just the beginning. You never know . . .

Wanda. Don't you ever know? I told you once, in Paris, remember? Here buildings last forever. Even time doesn't destroy them. But you've always built for a country of earthquakes, an unstable country. Why did you bring me here?

Corazón-man. Because I love you.

Wanda. I love you too. So? *(She starts walking towards the gangway.)*

Corazón-man. Are you leaving?

Wanda. Yes. *(Walking up two steps and turning to him)* I would have liked to have met your mother.

Corazón-man. Why?

Wanda. To hate her to her face. It's sick to hate a ghost. (WANDA *continues climbing up the ramp. She comes across the* MOTHER *and looks at her. The* MOTHER *does not return the glance.* CORAZÓN-MAN *looks at* WANDA *who is leaving, and at his* MOTHER *who is staying.* CORAZÓN-YOUTH *and* CORAZÓN-CHILD *quickly turn to embrace the* MOTHER. CANFUNFA *approaches* CORAZÓN.)

Canfunfa. I'm sorry to have brought you the news of your mother's death, Architect. (CORAZÓN-MAN *lowers his head and cries.* CORAZÓN-YOUTH *and* CORAZÓN-CHILD *cling to the* MOTHER *even more.*) But your uncle thought that since I was already going to Europe . . . We're not friends, but . . . but we get along. This letter is proof that we get along, don't you think so? Don't forget it, Architect. I try to get along with everyone. That's why I agreed to bring you the letter. Today I do something for you, tomorrow you do something for me. We live in the same country.

Corazón-man. I don't live in the same country as you! Because of you I had to leave! Because of you I wasn't here when Mamá . . .

Canfunfa. (*Cutting him off*) Are you sure? Come back, Architect. Come back. You have to learn to get along. And you can only get along once you know what you are. This is what we are. You and I. Come back. Things have changed . . . (*Looking at him*) Or you still don't know who you are? I like Spain! (*Looking at the construction set*) What are you building, a waterfall? God made them already, and very well. (*Canfunfa exits.* CORAZÓN-YOUTH *has left with his* MOTHER. CORAZÓN-CHILD *exits too. At the head of the ramp* MARA *appears wearing a native Mexican dress. Her hair is white.*)

Mara. What did you come to build in Mexico? Montezuma's tomb, his summer palace, or the Pyramid of the Eclipses?

Corazón-man. (*Looking at her, surprised*) Mara . . .

Mara. (*Going down the stairs swiftly*) I found out through the newspapers that you had arrived.

Corazón-man. (*Putting his hand on her shoulder and spinning around like they did years before in El Tigre*) Did you recognize me?

Mara. (*Playfully*) Of course! (*Pausing, earnestly*) No! They pointed you out. Did you recognize me?

Corazón-man. (*Equally earnest*) No. The hotel clerk told me who you were.

Mara. Better! Let's begin! (*Spinning around*) Hey, don't move around so much! You'll fall into the lake!

Corazón-man. It doesn't matter, I was a swimmer.

Mara. I already know it, silly. Don't you remember that you taught me to swim?

Corazón-man. I taught you?

Mara. Frog, puppy, frog . . . You've forgotten!

Corazón-man. It's just that . . . I'm sorry . . . I mix everything up.

Mara. (Looking at him, she suddenly starts laughing.) You're going to be just fine in Mexico! It's the ideal place for mixtures . . . Just look around. *(Pointing)* Everyone's Indian. The porter and the manager! The señora and the maid! It attracts mixtures! Everyone comes here to be purified!

Corazón-man. You too? You used to be in Paris.

Mara. (Smiling absently) Will you stay in Mexico?

Corazón-man. Maybe, I don't know. It depends . . .

Mara. What are you going to build?

Corazón-man. I don't know . . . I think that . . .

Mara. (Laughing) I don't know, I don't know, I don't know! Argentine to the very end.

Corazón-man. (Interrupting her) Mamá is dead.

Mara. (Looking at him, neutral) Ah!

Corazón-man. You never loved her.

Mara. I didn't know her. I never even came close enough to touch her. I went through your country like a rainless cloud, not even a drizzle. *(Laughing)* Hell . . . I don't think I ever left a drizzle anywhere! Will you come to my house tonight? *(He looks at her.)* I'm inviting you to dinner. Authentic Mexican food. *(She pauses, becoming more intense.)* Please . . . *(He smiles. She also smiles and gently strokes his face.)* What a child you are! Did you ever have children, Corazón?

Corazón-man. No.

Mara. Oh! I thought . . . because of the toy. *(She points to the construction set. She leaves.* CORAZÓN-MAN *looks at the set, bends over and continues building blocks. A drum is heard in the background.* CORAZÓN-MAN *is startled. He looks around and doesn't say anything. The drum becomes louder and stronger.* CORAZÓN *touches his eyes.* EL NEGRO *appears at the top of the ramp playing the drum.* CORAZÓN-MAN *sees him and goes to the foot of the ramp.* EL NEGRO *descends, playing the drum. He reaches* CORAZÓN-MAN *but does not look at him.* CORAZÓN-MAN *is very moved, as he recognizes him.)*

Corazón-man. Negro?

El Negro. (Playing, without looking at him) I'll accept anything you can spare, mister. But if it's dollars, my children will be very grateful.

Corazón-man. Negro! Don't you recognize me? *(EL NEGRO looks at him. He stops playing for a moment.)*

El Negro. You people are everywhere, Moishe! *(He starts playing again.)*

Corazón-man. (Happily) I thought they had killed you, Negro! Do you know how much I thought about you . . . about that day in Buenos Aires?

El Negro. I made it. The only job I could get was in a circus. And here I am! (CORAZÓN-MAN *and* EL NEGRO *march through the scene as* EL NEGRO *continues playing the drum.*)

Corazón-man. What are you doing with this in Mexico?

El Negro. I'm making a living. I'm the most folkloric man in the most folkloric country in the world. And they pay for it! Do you have a dollar? (CORAZÓN-MAN *looks at him, surprised. He takes a dollar out of his pocket.*) In my left side pocket, please. (CORAZÓN-MAN *laughs and puts the dollar in his pocket.*) My children thank you, mister.

Corazón-man. Negro . . . *(With difficulty)* You know . . . I spent a lot of time thinking about you . . . listening to you. That day in Buenos Aires I lied you to . . . (EL NEGRO *looks at him.*) I told you that I didn't smoke. It was a lie. I didn't even want to leave you my cigarettes! And that thing . . . that fear I had, I spent nights without sleeping. I would have wanted to take your place . . .

El Negro. That was easy. All you had to do was take off your suit, your tie, put on overalls, and send them all to hell.

Corazón-man. Can't you stop playing that thing?

El Negro. Talk! I'm rehearsing. *(He touches his ear, as if asking him to listen.)*

Corazón-man. What I want to tell you is that I . . . *(He is at a loss for words.)* The important thing is that you're alive, Negro . . . that you escaped!

El Negro. You were always so complicated, Moishe! Why do you always go round in circles? Things are the way they are. Grab them and swallow them before someone else swallows them for you.

Corazón-man. I don't understand you.

El Negro. You'll never understand me. I didn't escape. They freed me. They wanted the names of three guys. I gave the names to them. Fear was there and I swallowed it. I couldn't take it anymore . . . I had to see my wife, and the kids. I swallowed the fear Moishe, and I gave them the names. Things are the way they are. That's why when I got home and I discovered that the one who had returned was someone else, I split. Things are the way they are. And here I am cleaning elephant dung in Mexico. Boom! Boom! *(After making those sounds, he beats the drum twice.)* I'm throwing this in as a little extra. Boom! Boom! *(Beating the drum twice.* CORAZÓN-MAN *is devastated.)*

Corazón-man. You're a son of a bitch, Negro, that's what you are!

El Negro. Why? Because now you'll be able to sleep? You're lucky! I haven't been able to sleep for ages. Boom! Boom! *(Beating the drum twice)* Do you have a dollar, mister? (CORAZÓN-MAN *looks at him, pauses, takes out a dollar and hands it to him. Putting the dollar away)* My children thank you, kind sir. *(He beats the drum repeatedly as he leaves.)* Boom! Boom! *(Two more beats and he leaves.* MARA, *seated on the floor, takes off her white wig, but her real black hair underneath looks more like a wig than the wig itself.)*

Mara. I put on this wig because I don't want you to see me with white hair! So if you're thinking of dragging me through the streets of Mexico, it better not be by the hair! Let's keep the illusion, shall we? (CORAZÓN-MAN *goes to her, but his eyes are fixed on the spot from which* EL NEGRO *exited.)*

Corazón-man. If . . .

Mara. You can drag me by my legs! *(She shows off her beautiful legs.)* In Buenos Aires they just loved my legs . . . *(He looks at her. It takes him a moment to move his eyes from* EL NEGRO *and to look at her. He smiles.)*

Corazón-man. I still like your legs!

Mara. (Pausing) Did you ever think about me?

Corazón-man. About you . . . ? I did think about the water, though . . .

Mara. (Surprised) The water?

Corazón-man. About the water all around you . . . that day in El Tigre.

Mara. I saw pictures of your buildings all over the world. They looked as if they weren't finished, as if they were flattened by an earthquake.

Corazón-man. (Smiling stiffly) It's my style. Earthquake style!

Mara. (Smiling) If . . .

Corazón-man. Maybe I'll change my style in Mexico and finish this. Maybe, who can tell . . . This is where I belong, *(Short pause, as if he wanted to take it all as a joke)* Among the Indians!

Mara. (Quickly) Just like him.

Corazón-man. (Reacting immediately, brusquely) I'm not him. (MARA *looks at him, pauses and suddenly laughs. He does not understand why, but he makes an attempt to smile.)* You're laughing at me . . .

Mara. I'm laughing at you and at myself!

Corazón-man. As you wish. Your laugh makes you even more beautiful . . .

Mara. Oh no, Corazón, please! *(Showing him a mirror)* There's nothing here any longer, not beautiful, not ugly! Nothing! Come, take a look! *(He walks over to her. They look at themselves in the mirror.)* Do you see? You and I . . . Nothing! We are children of the air . . . of the earthquakes. Like your unfinished buildings. There's not even a mirror left for us! I lived in Paris, in *my* Paris! With my philosophy classes . . . I know all that philosophy by heart, all the Metro stations, all the neighborhoods of Paris, all the people in the neighborhoods of Paris . . . and suddenly . . . what am I doing here? What am I looking for? What are you looking for? There's no place for us, Corazón. *(She throws away the mirror.)*

Corazón-man. Speak for yourself! We are the way we are! I have my place! I live in Buenos Aires. Not now, because, well . . . I don't like the way it is nowadays. But I'm not looking for anything . . . I'm only traveling . . . They hire me . . . and I build . . .

Mara. What are you going to build for the Indians?

Corazón-man. *(Looking at her, surprised)* How did you know that I'm going to. . .

Mara. I did the same thing. As soon as I returned to Mexico I went to live with the Indians in the same place where he said he had lived.

Corazón-man. You still hold a grudge against him, even after so many years. He didn't just say it, he did it.

Mara. No. No one remembers him, Corazón! No one. Do you realize the truth now? He cured them for free, he taught them to read Marx, Engels, the speeches of La Pasionaria . . . But no one remembers him! He lied to us. He didn't live there really, because they never gave him a place! And you and I, all these years. . . Why didn't we make love that afternoon in El Tigre? Why can't we even touch each other now? *(Picking up the mirror quickly and putting it in front of his face)* Look at us! Just look at us!

Corazón-man. *(Avoiding the mirror by turning his head away)* Speak for yourself. *(Walking towards the ramp)* I'm not you, Mara. I'm only traveling . . . They hire me . . . and I build . . .

Mara. You're going to leave.

Corazón-man. Yes. *(He has reached the top of the ramp. The spotlight finds him. He turns around.)* I didn't go. I was afraid because there's something I didn't tell you. As soon as I got to

Madrid I went looking for the Hotel Nacional that he had told us so much about . . . I met an old survivor of the Spanish Civil War. He didn't remember Juan . . . He introduced me to others. I know it mattered a lot to him that someone remembered him . . . He worked with bombs exploding around him . . . they almost shot him . . . but nobody remembered him! You'll never know it Mara, because I'm writing this letter on board the ship, on my way back to Buenos Aires. (CANFUNFA *comes in and waits for* CORAZÓN-MAN *at the foot of the ramp. The* FATHER, *feeling upset, looks at* CORAZÓN-MAN *and sits up in his bed.* CORAZÓN-MAN *climbs down the gangway and stops in front of* CANFUNFA.)

Canfunfa. Help yourself, Architect. (*He hands him an identity card.*)

Corazón-man. What is this?

Canfunfa. Your uncle's passport. He left it in my office many years ago. I figured that you would like to keep it.

Corazón-man. Do you remember him?

Canfunfa. It depends. At times I remember him one way . . . at times another. Age does it!

Corazón-man. (*Looking at him intently*) Don't we know each other?

Canfunfa. Who knows.

Corazón-man. They wrote me that everything had changed.

Canfunfa. Everything did change. But what do you want me to do? Have plastic surgery?

Corazón-man. Why did you come looking for me?

Canfunfa. I didn't come looking for you. I came to welcome you on behalf of your uncle.

Father. Mamá! Mamá! (*The* MOTHER *appears dressed as a nurse. She goes to the* FATHER *and caresses him.*) He's back! Will he come to see me?

Mother. It's possible. But calm down. It's not good for you to get upset.

Father. What am I going to say to him, Mamá?

Mother. Calm down. Everything is all right!

Father. But what am I going to say to him?

Mother. There's always something to say!

Corazón-man. My uncle? (UNCLE MANUEL *appears, very upset.*)

Manuel. Corazón! (*Waving his arms to welcome him*) Welcome to Buenos Aires! (*Going to* CORAZÓN-MAN *and embracing him*) Sorry to have come late, but . . . we're so busy! We were very happy to know you were coming home! So many people are returning . . .

Corazón-man. I realized that. The boat was full. But *(referring to* CANFUNFA*)* what's he doing here?

Manuel. What do you mean by that? He's Argentine! Let's go home. Your aunt prepared a stew.

Father. I hope he doesn't show up. I don't know what to say to him!

Mother. (Caressing him) There's always something to say . . .

Corazón-man. How's Papá?

Manuel. Fine! *(Pause)* I think.

Corazón-man. (Looking at him) Don't you see him?

Manuel. Yes . . . sometimes. We're very busy, Corazón! We have to rebuild everything! But we got him a woman, a reliable woman! She takes care of him. Let's go! *(He is about to take his arm, but* CORAZÓN *goes to his* FATHER *and leaves* MANUEL *abruptly. The* FATHER *is upset. The* MOTHER *caresses him.)*

Mother. Calm down! (CORAZÓN-MAN *goes to his* FATHER'S *side, unaware of his* MOTHER'S *presence. He sits on the floor in front of his* FATHER. *The* MOTHER-NURSE *continues caressing the* FATHER.*)*

Canfunfa. Ah, you people!

Manuel. We? What people?

Canfunfa. Your whole family, Doctor. They don't even know what's going on!

Manuel. (Offended) You don't have any right to. . . (CANFUNFA *exits in his wheelchair, leaving* MANUEL *dumbstruck.* MANUEL *pauses, looks at his watch, and shouts.)* Hurry up, Corazón! There are a lot of people waiting for you at home!

Corazón-man. How are you, Papá?

Father. (Looking at him, upset) Eat . . . Eat . . .

Corazón-man. No, thank you. I have to go to Uncle Manuel's and . . .

Father. Have a *mate.*

Corazón-man. Thanks.

Father. Have a coffee.

Corazón-man. Thanks.

Father. Remember, Corazón! Moses led the Jews out of slavery, he led them through the desert and they all followed him. But in the middle of the desert Moses vanished and a part of him entered everyone of them. And the Jews reached the Promised Land because each one carried a part of Moses inside of them. Remember, Corazón!

Corazón-man. Yes, thank you.

Father. Eat, eat.

Corazón-man. Thank you.

Father. Remember, Corazón. San Martín led his soldiers through the Cordillera. And they all followed him! But up there high in the mountains, San Martín vanished and became a part of each and everyone of them! And if those people gave us our freedom it was because each one of them carried a part of San Martín inside them. Remember, Corazón!

Corazón-man. Yes, thank you.

Father. *(To the* MOTHER*)* Doesn't he look thin?

Mother. No, no.

Father. He looks thin to me.

Mother. Calm down, now! You see how you did have things to tell him?

Father. *(To* CORAZÓN-MAN, *sententiously)* You look so-o thin, Corazón! So-o thin. Eat. There are cookies, cheese, salami. It's all for you. Mamá and I, we . . . *(Makes a vague gesture, as if to say "We don't need anything anymore")* It's all for you, Corazón.

Corazón-man. Thanks.

Manuel. *(Shouting)* Corazón, hurry up! *(Hearing him,* CORAZÓN-MAN *makes an effort to get up, but he cannot. He is distraught.)*

Corazón-man. I came to look for you, Papá! Not the parts of you that are inside me! You, you! We are not the sand in the desert, we are not an army of soldiers. We are you and me! I came looking for you, Papá . . . because if I find you, I will have found myself. There must be something of yours, something that I haven't been dragging all over the world . . . something that I haven't stolen from you . . . that you haven't let me steal from you . . . something of yours, unknown, that if I discover . . . I came back to find that, Papá! Don't you understand? *(At the same time as* CORAZÓN *speaks, his* FATHER *speaks in an ever-increasing rhythm. He finally utters the scream that silences* CORAZÓN-MAN.*)*

Father. Eat, eat! There are crackers, cheese, salami. Eat! Eat! Eat! Eat! Crackers! Cheese! Salami! EAT! EAT! EAT! *(Silence.* CORAZÓN-MAN *gets up.)*

Corazón-man. I understand you. I understand you, Papá. I don't know you, but I understand you. *(Pause)* There must be another way of loving. There must be. This one seems like martyrdom . . . *(Leaving quickly,* CORAZÓN-MAN *walks over to* MANUEL, *who takes him by the arm and leads him to the plank of the ship. They climb three steps.* MANUEL *makes him turn back, always holding his arm. He introduces him. The* MOTHER *looks in his direction and softly hums a waltz.)*

Manuel. *(To* CORAZÓN-MAN) Do you hear the waltz? *Arriba, Corazón!* Friends, it is with great pride that I present to you my nephew, the Architect! Everyone's read about him! Here he is, in person! He has come to work with us! *(*MANUEL *applauds, so does the* MOTHER. CANFUNFA *enters in his wheelchair and applauds. The* MOTHER *takes the* FATHER'S *hands and makes him applaud.)*

Mother. Come on, applaud!

Father. I don't know who it is . . .

Mother. It doesn't matter! Applaud, applaud! *(She makes him applaud. Suddenly the* FATHER *bends over).*

Father. I feel cold!

Mother. I'm going to bring the bedpan. *(She starts to leave.)*

Father. Mamá, don't leave me alone!

Mother. Don't be afraid! I'm going to bring you the bedpan so that you can pee, like a good little boy!

Father. Please, Mamá. Don't leave!

Mother. But I'm coming right back. What a little boy you are! Let's see. Sing me that pretty little song that I like so much!

Father. *(Pause. He shouts.)* Hi-y-o-o-o Sil-ver!

Mother. You're a real treasure! *(She leaves.* UNCLE MANUEL *and* CANFUNFA *continue applauding* CORAZÓN-MAN, *while he looks at them, at the audience, and takes a paper out of his pocket.)*

Corazón-man. I don't want to improvise. *(To the audience)* Ladies and gentlemen: I remember my childhood. We were all heroic in the face of death. Other people's death. Other people's death wiped out all differences. And they got together to sing. *(He sings a song from the Spanish Civil War.)* "Con el quinto, quinto, quinto, con el Quinto Regimiento! Con el quinto, quinto, quinto, con el quinto Regimiento!" And the others kept on dying. And they kept on singing. *(He sings.)* "Questa matina, mi sono alzato, bella ciao, bella ciao, bella ciao, ciao, ciao. Questa matina!" And the others kept on dying, and dying, and here, everyone was heroic while they let themselves be stepped on, and manhandled and destroyed, and they let it happen, they just let it happen! They were my parents, and I live trying to hide that . . . and I do hide it . . . But I know . . . I feel it . . . like an open wound inside me. *(*MANUEL *and* CANFUNFA *applaud him enthusiastically.)*

Manuel. Very good, Corazón! Very good! These are the things we need to hear now.

Corazón-man. (Surprised) Why are you applauding?

Canfunfa. Bravo, Architect, bravo!

Corazón-man. (Anguished) Why are you applauding? (EL NEGRO *appears at the top of the stairs, wearing a woolen cap closely drawn around his head, and carrying a bucket.* CORAZÓN *runs to the top of the stairs and bumps into* EL NEGRO, *who is cleaning the staircase with his back towards him.)* Excuse me.

El Negro. (Without looking at him) You can't go through. We're cleaning the boat. (CORAZÓN-MAN *turns around and runs down the stairs. They continue applauding him. He stops in front of* CANFUNFA.)

Canfunfa. A very nice speech, Architect!

Corazón-man. You mustn't applaud! You can't!

Canfunfa. Why not? It's the same speech your uncle made when he became a lawyer. I gave him his final exam. Your uncle is very much respected among us! That's why we're applauding! You know, I thought that you had borrowed the speech.

Manuel. You'll never leave again, Corazón. I've brought you your new appointment here! We have to build, Corazón. And this is the right time! The country has changed.

Corazón-man. (Looking at him) Oh yes? Has it changed? Has it really changed? Then tell me, where am I? What kind of ground am I walking on? Water, earth, stone, air? What ground am I on? What kind of land am I supposed to build on?

Manuel. You won't find the answer in the cemetery!

Corazón-man. I know that. Here I've only found questions . . . but I don't know why I feel more secure on the land of the dead. Maybe I'm dead too? Couldn't I be dead? Juan! Let's play "Twenty Questions" . . . but bring the gun!

Manuel. (Hurries to CANFUNFA) He's asking for a gun!

Canfunfa. Try to stop him, just to be safe.

Manuel. What can I do? He's my sister's son.

Canfunfa. He didn't say he wanted to leave.

Manuel. Yes . . . but . . .

Canfunfa. Let him go, Doctor. Really . . . he has such an awful smell. He stinks . . .

Corazón-man. Come on . . . I know you've always been there, dancing around me. Come on, Juan! (JUAN *appears at the top of the stairs.)*

Juan. What do you want? (CORAZÓN'S *hand turns into a gun. He raises it slowly and looks at it, happily.)*

Corazón-man. Here you are, finally!

Juan. What's the matter with you? Are you sick? You look very thin!

Corazón. You're not my father! Don't protect me! I don't want your protection. I want you to hurt me! (CORAZÓN-YOUTH *takes off his shirt, like he did in the scene with* MARA, *in the second act.* CORAZÓN-CHILD *swings himself in the same way that* CORAZÓN-MAN *did in the first act.)*

Juan. All right. Ask!

Corazón. What am I doing here?

Juan. Here? Here doesn't exist! It's an error in calculation. An absurdity. You're just like me. You have to find a place that fits you.

Corazón. I was born here! Why?

Juan. Sometimes we live absurd lives. Keep searching, as I did. I should have stayed in Paris, in Madrid, in Mexico. Those were real places!

Corazón. Juan, don't lie to me!

Juan. I'm not lying to you!

Corazón. Then don't lie to yourself! I searched for you in all these places . . . you were always five yards ahead of me . . . I used to start buildings that I thought I would finish when I found you, but I never found you! You weren't there! You were never there! Nobody remembered you!

Juan. It's not true! There are many women who . . .

Corazón. Not even one! I also had many, and yet not one, not one! We never got one of them pregnant, we never hurt one of them, we never murdered one of them. What did we do then? Did we sit around drawing pictures of them?

Juan. What's wrong with drawing what one loves? A perfect picture to fit our dream . . . I lived in a time when you could draw your dreams. Nowadays . . . Yes, it's true, all these years I was there, dancing around you, watching you grow. I thought that you would be just like me.

Corazón. Everyone says I'm just like you.

Juan. No, of course you're not like me! It's not the right time for that! In my day one could understand history . . . explain it . . . one could. . . .

Corazón. Make a drawing of that! (JUAN *looks at him. He looks toward the top of the stairs.)*

Juan. The ship will sail soon . . .

Corazón. *(Looking at the gun)* Juan . . . please!

Juan. *(Shouting at him)* What do you mean? There are no answers, Corazón! Haven't you realized that yet? There are no answers.

Corazón. But I'm full of questions . . .

Juan. Because there are only questions! You're a question your-self. On the other hand, an answer is always a drawing, made by you, by others, a beautiful and perfect drawing, but nothing more than a drawing!

Corazón. Why did you come back, then?

Juan. What an idiot you are! A poor guy like your father, couldn't produce anything but an idiot! I came back because hell was here . . . witches . . . sorcerers . . . an absurd world . . . and because I hadn't found a place there in the paradise of my draw-ings where I left my dreams behind . . . maybe I would find it here. But no. Not even here! Not even a trace of my blood was left! Yesterday I passed by the house where I used to live. It's now a dressmaker's shop. Not a drop of my blood. Nothing! No one.

Corazón. There is me.

Juan. Do you see? You're drawing in the quicksand of this country, trying to fight against a swamp. What do you see?

Corazón. Your blood is my blood, Juan.

Juan. It's invisible. No one can see it!

Corazón. Do you want someone to see it?

Juan. (Surprised) What?

Corazón. Do you want others to see your blood, to know your blood through mine? (CORAZÓN-CHILD *covers his eyes.* CORAZÓN-YOUTH *aims, as if to shoot someone.* CORAZÓN-MAN *points the gun at his forehead. Pause.* JUAN *turns, looks at the* FATHER *and the* MOTHER. *The* MOTHER *opens her arms to* JUAN, *as if begging him to help* CORAZÓN. *The* FATHER *mutters.*)

Father. Hi-i-i-o-o-o-o Sil-ver . . . (JUAN *looks at* MANUEL *and* CANFUNFA.)

Manuel. (Looking at CORAZÓN) He's got a gun. What should we do?

Canfunfa. Leave him alone. It's all the same. He's leaving anyway. (JUAN *looks at* CORAZÓN *again.*)

Juan. You know something? It's your problem! (*He starts to climb the steps. When he reaches the top, he turns to* CORAZÓN.) You asked me to hurt you. I don't know how. I prefer to kill you. (*He leaves.* CORAZÓN *points the gun at his forehead.* EL NEGRO *enters.*)

El Negro. Stop, Moishe! Stop! Not that . . . ! (*He walks toward* CORAZÓN *and he yanks his hand away from the gun.*) Here's the partridge!

Corazón. (Surprised) What?

El Negro. The partridge! Go ahead . . . aim . . . now. The trigger
. . . pull the trigger! That's it! The trigger! (EL NEGRO *directs*
CORAZÓN'S *hand as he shoots, but* CORAZÓN *moves his hand
and shoots into the air.* EL NEGRO *looks at him, mocking and
incredulous.*) You missed! At five yards!

Corazón. I never even killed a fly . . .

El Negro. Why would you want to kill a fly? You don't eat flies,
you eat partridges! Go ahead, row! (*He sits next to* CORAZÓN.
*Now the mechanical building block serves as a paddle. They
row.*)

Corazón. When did you come back?

El Negro. Two months ago. I'm working in the port, but we're
on strike now, so I came to El Tigre. And you? What are you
doing here?

Corazón. Hunting.

El Negro. (In disbelief) You'll starve to death!

Corazón. It's not for food . . .

El Negro. (Looking at him) You're all so screwed up!

Corazón. You don't like Jews . . .

El Negro. And you don't like Blacks . . .

Corazón. I thought you were in Mexico.

El Negro. So did I. Lots of money!

Corazón. Why did you come back?

El Negro. Gardel.

Corazón. (Surprised) Who?

El Negro. Gardel, Moishe, Gardel! Besides . . . my brother-in-law
wrote me that the pig had piglets . . . I wanted to see the piglets.

Corazón. And you ate them!

El Negro. Are you crazy? *(Short pause)* Not all of them.

Corazón. What happened with your friends after what you did
to them?

El Negro. They didn't know anything. The only one who knew
was you.

Corazón. Oh . . .

El Negro. But I told them . . . *(Simply)* I had to, didn't I?

Corazón. And didn't they kill you?

El Negro. They gave me some beating! They broke my head.
Look. *(He shows him.)* And look at this nose. What can I tell
you! *(He shows him the scar.)* But I'm here . . .

Corazón. And have you seen your wife and your children?

El Negro. From a distance. She got together with someone else,
the poor thing. So much is going on! I'm involved with someone
too, a girl from Entre Ríos. I need to find a woman. I need to

find myself. What a situation! You know I can hardly recognize myself after what happened. It's hard for me, but . . . this is my place, Moishe . . . Besides, I was tired of cleaning elephant dung! So many elephants, so much shit! Lay off! Row, Moishe, row . . . don't start with me. I'm black, but I'm not a dummy! *(They row.* EL NEGRO *breathes in the air.)* Smell that!

Corazón. What?

El Negro. That smell.

Corazón. Like something rotten!

El Negro. That's your garlic smell, Moishe! Why don't you leave the country, and give your nose a treat.

Corazón. I'm leaving soon. *(*EL NEGRO *looks at him, apologetically.)* They hired me in . . . *(He looks at him, unable to continue speaking. He breaks down and rests his head on* EL NEGRO'S *chest.)* Why do you have a place and not me? Why can you be a coward, and return home, and have your head and your nose smashed, and wind up alone without a wife, and find your children with another father, and eat your brother-in-law's pigs, and smell this putrid smell and it's like perfume to you? And it's still your place . . . and I need to rest my head on your chest so that I don't fall completely apart. Why, Negro, why?

El Negro. Why don't you knock it off, Moishe, you're sinking the boat . . .

Corazón. *(Pauses, looking at him)* Do you like me a little, Negro?

El Negro. *(Mocking)* With so much traveling around, you learn bad habits. My old man was right . . .

Corazón. Do you like me, Negro?

El Negro. Does it really matter to you?

Corazón. Yes.

El Negro. Then go screw yourself! I'm not going to tell you a thing! *(He stands up.)*

Corazón. Are you getting off here?

El Negro. Yeah. The girl from Entre Ríos I told you about, works as a cook in that amusement park. I help her out a little and . . .

Corazón. *(Teasing)* You were always a pimp!

El Negro. Yes. I was born for that. It's a shame I had to work so hard and never had time for it. Are you coming? Help me wait on the tables and I'll invite you to dinner.

Corazón. No. I have to keep going.

El Negro. Alone? You don't even know how to row.

Corazón. You have to start sometime.

El Negro. You were born for numbers, not for rowing, Moishe.

Corazón. You're lucky. You know what you were born for and what I was born for. Everyone has his place.

El Negro. Are you making fun of me?

Corazón. No. At times . . . I envy you.

El Negro. You must learn!

Corazón. It's a difficult job.

El Negro. Go screw yourself.

Corazón. You still haven't answered me.

El Negro. What do you want me to do? Throw you a kiss? *(He gets out of the boat.* CORAZÓN *begins to row with difficulty.* EL NEGRO *turns around and looks at him.)* Moishe! *(*CORAZÓN *turns and looks at. him.* EL NEGRO *blows him a kiss and laughs.* CORAZÓN *laughs too.* EL NEGRO *exits.* CORAZÓN *keeps rowing with more and more difficulty. He is short of breath. The* FIDDLER *appears. As he plays, both* CORAZÓN-YOUTH, AND CHILD *step into the boat. The* CHILD *caresses the water, just as his* FATHER *did in the first scene. Suddenly the boat carrying the three* CORAZÓNS *is caught in a whirlpool and begins to spin. The silhouettes of the other characters emerge from the shadows.)*

Corazón. The whirlpool! How could I have forgotten? Everything would have been clearer . . . the whirlpool . . . like there in Paraná. So many drowned, but I kept spinning and I let myself be dragged, until I pushed myself up from the bottom . . . covered in mud . . . and reached the surface! *(To everyone)* Ladies . . . gentlemen . . . colleagues . . . guests . . .

Canfunfa. The speech! He's going to give his speech! *(To* MANUEL*)* Give it to me, doctor. You have it! *(*MANUEL *hands it to him.* CANFUNFA *hands it over to* CORAZÓN.*)* Here is the speech, Architect! You can still read it!

Corazón. (Rejecting it) No . . . No! They left the port . . . The water enveloped them . . . The water was the path . . . and it brought them here . . . They were told they were sailing to nowhere . . . but the water brought them here . . . the caravels . . . My grandfather, singing the Psalms, trying to decipher a black and unknown land . . . My father! The locusts that followed them from the time they left, and met them when they arrived, because they had lost and they met other losers . . . And the water! Only the water! . . . And they were told they were sailing to nowhere . . . and they believed it . . . because they had lost everything. . . . But the water laughed at them and at us . . . It always laughed at us! Because it knew what nothing was—a sound . . . a new color . . . a smell . . . a new miracle— That's it . . . a new miracle . . . different from others . . . made

from the scraps of losers! Maybe that's all there is! The water
. . . a new miracle . . . and nothing else! Nothing else! Nothing
else! *(The boat has made it out of the whirlpool. They slowly
stop spinning.)*
Mother. *(Her silhouette in the fog, almost begging him)* Arriba,
Corazón . . .
Father. *(The same)* Arriba, Corazón . . .
Mother. *(Imploringly)* Arriba, Corazón!
Father. Arriba, Corazón! *(The three* CORAZÓNS *embrace and be-
come one.)*
Corazón-man. My scraps! My miracle! Such a poor little thing, so
rickety, so consumptive. What else can you expect from this, but
a survivor? *(The three row harder and harder.)* Arriba, Corazón!
Arriba, Corazón!
Canfunfa. *(He comes closer than the others.)* You're leaving, Ar-
chitect, right? *(He wants him to leave.)*
Corazón-man. No . . . I've just arrived. *(Short pause)* I believe.

The End

NOTES

1. *No pasarán:* They shall not pass. The rallying cry coined by "La Pasionaria," Dolores Ibarruri, in defense of Madrid during the Spanish Civil War
(1936–1939).
2. *Empanadas:* meat patties.
3. *Arriba, Corazón:* Onward, Corazón! That's it! Courage! Corazón, the name
of the protagonist, means "heart."
4. *Alpargatas:* espadrilles, sandals made of hemp.
5. *Carlos Gardel* (1890–1935): French-born composer and singer who popular-
ized Argentine tango in the 1920s.
6. *Vidalitá:* popular Argentine love song, generally sad, played with guitar
accompaniment.
7. *Remedios Escalada de San Martín* (1797–1823): wife of General José de
San Martín and active supporter of the independence movement in her own right;
Mariquita Sánchez (1786–1868): a social and community leader in Buenos Aires.
8. *Moishe:* Yiddish for Moses; colloquial term, referring to Jews in Argentina.
It can be endearing or pejorative, depending on the speaker's intention.
9. *Bombo:* a bass drum.
10. *Murga:* a company of amateur musicians who use the pretext of holidays
and birthdays to knock on the doors of wealthy families, expecting some payment
for their performance.
11. *El Chaco:* province in the north of Argentina.
12. *El Tigre:* an area of small islands on the delta of the River Plate in Buenos Aires.
13. *Casa Rosada:* the President's residence in Buenos Aires.

14. *Mataderos:* the neighborhood that once housed the major slaughterhouse in Buenos Aires.

15. *Yarará:* a poisonous viper.

16. *Payasín:* little clown.

17. *Payasota:* big clown.

Diana Raznovich: *Lost Belongings*

DIANA RAZNOVICH (BUENOS AIRES, 1943)

Poet, television scriptwriter, and cartoonist, Raznovich is best known for her plays, translated into several languages and performed internationally. Best known are "Plaza hay una sola" (There's only one plaza) (1969); "El guardagente" (The peoplekeeper) (1971); *Desconcierto* (Dis-concert) (1981); *Jardín de otoño* (Autumn garden) (1983); "Objetos perdidos" *(Lost Belongings)* (1988); and *Casa matriz* (Matrix house) (1988). Born and raised in Argentina, Raznovich resided in Spain for lengthy periods in the 70s and 80s. Although she was not persecuted by the military dictatorship, thousands of persons had already disappeared, and a bomb had been placed at a theatre where one of her plays was being performed. In spite of her need for Spanish as a language for expression, in spite of feeling at home in Spain because of her cultural ties with that country, her emotional and intellectual ties are with Russia, Germany, and Austria, lands from which her grandparents emigrated. Raznovich identifies with the theatre of Dostoyevsky, Chekhov, Mayakovsky, and Tolstoy. She also feels much closer to Kafka than to the gauchesque literature she studied during her school years in Buenos Aires.

Europe is the place to which Raznovich returns, rather than a new place to which she immigrates. The image of "return" is best illustrated in the luggage that surrounds the protagonist of her play *Lost Belongings,* which premiered in Sydney, Australia in 1989. Although this image may be common to every traveler and wanderer, the act of having one's suitcases always ready for any eventuality is particularly appropriate to the Jew. A parallel can be drawn between this play and the abrupt orders the Nazis gave the Jews to prepare themselves within a few hours to leave their homes. Raznovich also alludes to the repeated warnings that passengers hear when getting off an airplane, not to forget their personal belongings. In her urgent search for a place that "calls" her back to her past, the protagonist leaves behind items that later

325

Diana Raznovich

become essential, while she takes along others that prove useless to her. What then are the important things one should take along, and what are the unnecessary things?

Raznovich considers *Lost Belongings* a Jewish play. There is only one character in it, Casalia Beltrop, not her actual name, but rather a combination of two real estate agencies in Buenos Aires. Symbolically, the name is the result of many migrations and changes of names, where original names are often lost. Like all immigrant names, it is misspelled or mispronounced at every step.

The set is crowded with suitcases. This landscape is the true country of the Jews. It is a mythical stage that has served the protagonist's grandparents and great-grandparents, and will serve her children and grandchildren. Being surrounded by suitcases gives them the feeling that they can either adopt or move on if they have to. Always present is the knowledge that they never fully belong to any country. They only know they are a number and have to guard their number well. Casalia Beltrop loses her suitcases and tries to find them, but she is confused and unable to remember what color they are or what they look like.

The space of *Lost Belongings* is subjective; although it may seem like a nightmare or a surrealist dream, Raznovich conceived it as a real experience. Casalia will not wake up and find herself in a different place; she is condemned to remain there, crowded among suitcases for the rest of her life. In this sense, Raznovich identifies with Kafka, who deals with Jewish themes, although his characters are not Jewish. Casalia Beltrop does not know if she is coming or going, if she is in Latin America, Europe, Russia, or Japan. Her sense of disorientation leads her to question what she left behind and what she lost.

Lost Belongings was inspired by Beckett's theatre of the absurd. Such a moment occurs when Casalia opens her suitcases and finds one of them is filled with human bones. The bones represent her past, centuries of ancestors transplanted from one place to another. Black humor is also present when the protagonist recognizes her grandmother's coccyx and later the scaphoid of the man she once loved. The bones are her memories.

And there is always the threatening voice that warns her over the loudspeakers: "Beware, Casalia Beltrop, beware, your number is 46, watch your number at all times." Her obsessive thinking does not help her, but she is always trying to protect herself and be prepared for any eventuality—a Jewish characteristic. An absurdist example of this is when Casalia finds herself with a suitcase filled with sardine cans, but without a can opener.

Chameleonic, like a "safe" Jew, Casalia finally decides to get inside a suitcase, that is, to "become" a suitcase. She recalls the slogan: "Wherever you go, do what you see others do." If there are suitcases surrounding her, the best thing for her is to become a suitcase, to seem as much like the objects around her as possible, not to call attention to herself, not to differ from the rest. Like some Jews in the concentration camps, who even in that extreme circumstance resisted the idea of genocide and mass murder, and held on to the hope that things would get better, Casalia fears for her life and yet refuses to accept the worst.

Raznovich's style is suggestive. She does not reveal; she merely hints, so her plays can be read in various ways. She is not interested in explaining ideas in her plays. When her character Casalia contemplates the possibility of having reached Russia, she makes a satirical comment about communism:

My name is Casalia Beltrop but my friends call me Diva . . . I couldn't have chosen a less communist name. What a problem! Exacerbated individualism, addicted to Marlboro, to Coca Cola, sophisticated clothing; a victim of fashion. I'll change my name. Where is the Soviet Supreme? It's an honor to be in such an admirably guarded place. Even the suitcases have been socialized here. They expropriated my red crocodile set. How do you say "red" in Russian? They're mad about that color, like bulls are. My name is not Diva any longer. I don't care about fashion any longer. I wear the same clothing as everyone else. But doesn't wearing the same clothing mean to be in fashion? I will always wear grey, it will always rain, they'll always suspect me. . . ." (pp. 337).

Her confession shows the ironic relationship between the individual and the system as she tries to decodify it: what she should or should not wear, do or say in order to be accepted. Yet she realizes that "they'll always suspect me." This is central to Raznovich's world view. Casalia will be regarded suspiciously no matter in what system she lives, simply because she is a human being.

Characteristically Jewish in Raznovich's writing is the possibility of abstraction: her search for metaphysical ideas and for universal metaphors. Her Jewish world is not evident in her descriptions of situations, nor in her anecdotes. Much like the Kafkaesque labyrinths, it is to be found in moments of anguish, laughter, and humor. Her plays do not identify Jewish protagonists by name, but rather by the situations they find themselves trapped in. Raznovich's *Weltanschauung* is distinctly Jewish, in her writing, her drawings, and her thinking.

Lost Belongings

List of Characters:
Casalia Beltrop, also called Diva, or the Actress. A middle-aged
woman. Exotic, beautiful, extravagant.

A One-act play

*Stage completely filled with suitcases, trunks, packages, wrapped
boxes, backpacks, and all sorts of luggage. It looks like a check
room, since the suitcases are all numbered with tickets. Some are
modern, others are old, and covered with dust. Piled up, they fill
the whole stage, so that the actress will have to maneuver her way
around them. The light, initially absolutely unreal, allows the
viewer to make out the suitcases. Like a specter,* CASALIA, *wrapped
in a grey raincoat, is holding her ticket and looking for her luggage.
She carries a grey, wet umbrella in her hand. She appears busy,
trying to find her belongings, without success. Her searching inten-
sifies. The light gradually increases. She is visibly upset. In order
to control her anxiety, she keeps checking her ticket against the
different groups of suitcases. They never match.*
Her recorded voice, offstage.
Three. Fifteen. Seven hundred ninety-four. Zero. One thousand,
five hundred and eleven. Fifty thousand eight hundred twenty-six.
One million seven hundred seventy-three. Fourteen million three
hundred, ninety thousand and one. Forty-four. Five. Fifty-five. Five
hundred fifty-five. Five thousand five hundred fifty-five. Fifty five
thousand five hundred fifty-five. Five million five hundred thousand
five hundred fifty-five.
Casalia. (Speaks aloud for the first time) This is unbearable!
    *(Kicks a suitcase furiously. It seems to be made of stone. Her
    foot bounces back. She screams and grabs her ankle. She jumps
    on one foot, yelling in pain. Meanwhile, she continues searching
    on one foot, and in pain.)*
Her recorded voice, offstage. Forty. Forty-one. Forty-two. Forty-
    three. Forty-four. Forty-five. Forty-five twice. Forty-five trice.
    Forty-five and a half. Forty-five and three quarters. Forty-six.
    Forty-six, Casalia! Forty-six!
Casalia. (Relieved) Forty-six! *(Waving her ticket)* Here's my num-
    ber! *(She holds it out, hoping that someone will take it. Impa-
    tient. Her voice shrieking)* What's going on? Is there a strike?

Where's the one responsible for this disgusting place? Listen, who's in charge of all this? *(Looks significantly at her watch)* These are working hours! *(To herself)* People have been waiting for me for a long time. I can't fail because of circumstances. I am never late for my important appointments. *(Once again in a very loud voice)* People! Come on! I need my luggage! I need it!

Her recorded voice, offstage. I have number forty-six. No doubt about it. And here are the suitcases with number forty-six. Of course mine were green. Or were they mauve? Well, the way I'm dressed, leads me to think I sent the white ones. It's natural. Or at least it's quite logical. Forty-six coincides with forty-six. And I'm forty-six.

Casalia. *(Superimposing her complaint over the last part of her recorded voice, starting from "It's natural")* Where is the general manager? *(Talking to herself, with a gesture of displeasure)* It's been too long since I've changed my clothes. *(She walks clapping her hands. She looks for a handkerchief in her pocket and waves it to attract attention. She walks over the suitcases, quite crazed.)* It's not right to keep passengers tied up here without knowing if we're coming or going! *(Talking to herself)* If I only knew that, I would personally adopt another attitude! Of someone about to meet a loved one. Or the classic farewell attitude. *(She puts her handkerchief away. She obsessively checks her number. She examines the suitcases labeled forty-six. Rather worried)* Is it a national holiday? Is the staff having a day off? Or maybe it's the country's birthday? *(Anxious, feeling guilty)* If that's the case, they should have warned me! I would have worn my Scottish suit, and pinned a large rosette on my chest with the colors of the right country. That way, at least I'd know what country they'd sent me to. What's more, I would happily wave that country's flag. What's it to me to make a gesture of solidarity to the country that I hope will take me in? *(Her recorded voice, offstage, is heard superimposed with her last words on the stage, beginning with: "I would happily wave . . ." While we hear her voice offstage, CASALIA decides to search actively. She moves a group of suitcases from the right to the left of the stage. Behind the suitcases is a moveable luggage rack with suitcases on it. She walks around with it, finally placing it in the center of the stage. Not liking this location, she moves it to one side. Still not satisfied, she walks around the stage without finding the right place for the rack.)*

Her recorded voice, offstage. Forty-six is my number, but it doesn't match. Probably during the arduous trip, the appearance, the contents and the circumstances of my suitcases have all changed. They were made of black crocodile. I can remember perfectly the shape, the size, even the pleasure I felt when I touched them. Crocodile is an unmistakable type of lizard. I acquired mine right after they were hatched. The female had laid forty-six little eggs. I got the last one. My brother preferred the thirty-eighth. Much more voracious. My sister preferred the seventh, a treacherous fighter. Mine was destined to become luggage. And that's the way it looks when it's with me. *(She speaks aloud, along with the last part of her recorded speech, while she takes out a bunch of keys that she finds in the side pocket of her rather ragged backpack. She repeats the same words as those heard offstage.)*

Casalia. Mine was destined to become luggage and that's the way it looks when it's with me.

Her recorded voice, offstage. It's what befits someone of my class.

Casalia. These are made of painted cardboard. Even if they say number forty-six.

Her recorded voice, offstage. Now it's clearer. It's an intentional accident. They exchange crocodile for painted cardboard.

Casalia. *(She positions herself center stage and strikes the pose of a* Vogue *model.)* So this is the way this country welcomes Casalia Beltrop? *(Changes her pose, but in the same style)* Where are my hosts? *(She changes poses once again, this time holding a worn out suitcase in her hand.)* Did they forget that they promised to send photographers? *(She takes out a hairbrush from a kind of sailor's duffle bag and combs her hair, annoyed, while her recorded voice is heard.)*

Offstage. These could have been mine. Somehow they remind me of a crocodile. But unfortunately they're number six hundred and nine.

Casalia. *(While she combs her hair)* What kind of a world are we living in? What can we expect from the rest of the country if there isn't even any luggage control?

Her recorded voice, offstage. And what if they imprison me for taking someone else's personal belongings? Who'll be the judge and who'll be the accused? *(Afraid of being arrested, she picks one key from the bunch. She tries to open the suitcases that have her number. They won't open. She picks another key and this time it works.)*

Casalia. I'm opening this suitcase, Mr. Boss, simply because it has my number, forty-six. *(When the suitcase opens, a large number of human bones fall out. Some are whole skeletons of people. She gives a loud, terrified shriek as she recognizes the bones.)* Pedro!! Catherina!! Francis!! Hans!! Isabel!! Alex!! *(Shocked, she examines the bones.)* My dear Miss Herminia! That idiot! Humberto! *(Each bone belongs to a particular person.)* Rita's maxillary! Grandma Gertrudis's coccyx! *(Extremely upset)* Victor's famous scaphoid! *(Weeping)* Victor, what a handsome scaphoid . . . What moments we shared there at the border! Our love, our hopes, our sorrows have not died . . . Fallen angel with moonlit wings. So unexpectedly young, and so irreverent! I didn't know how to say it in time, Victor. But I waited for you like a little girl behind the wall, suddenly blurred by the rain. . . . Victor, you'll never be alone again. Your familiar and unmistakable scaphoid makes me understand what my voice is saying. *(Holding Victor's scaphoid and some other bones, she speaks to an imaginary police inspector.)* You can imagine, Mr. Inspector, I couldn't have brought this bunch of bones here from the other end of the planet! Even if they match my number, I assure you that carrying Sonia's palatine is very different from running hand-in-hand with Sonia along the wide beaches of Santa Teresita!

Her recorded voice, offstage. This is your ticket, Diva, be very careful. The tests are conclusive. It's Victor's scaphoid. You didn't expect this mastermove. They did everything to perfection. Granted, they're backed by a powerful organization. You sent out people, and bony substances arrived instead. *(Somewhat lost on the stage. Kicking suitcases that fall, and with a bone in her hand,* CASALIA *addresses an invisible boss.)*

Casalia. Look here, Mr. Boss of the luggage depot: this is not my beloved Horatio's coccyx. I would have recognized it, because in our last encounters he was extremely thin. *(She removes a complete human skeleton from another suitcase.)* Ivan. Exposed to every damnation. Betting on other people's needs. With your strange, desperate messages. Laughing, Ivan, laughing to erase the tell-tale signs of the mirror. You, too, had to wait today in this sinister joke. Ivan, it isn't difficult to feel Hamlet's puff of smoke when I see you. *(She takes him in her arms, like a son.)* "And therefore as a stranger give it welcome.
There are more things in heaven and earth, Horatio,
Than are dreamt of in your philosophy.
But come—
Here as before, never, so help you mercy
(How strange or odd some'er I bear myself,
As I perchance hereafter shall think meet

To put an antic disposition on)
That you at such times seeing me, never shall
With arms encumbered thus, or this head-shake,
Or by pronouncing of some doubtful phrase,
As 'Well, well, we know,' or 'We could an if we would,'
Or 'If we list to speak,' or 'There be an if they might,'
Or such ambiguous giving out, to note
That you know aught of mine—this do swear,
So grace and mercy at your most need help you!"
(She puts the skeleton away. Then she starts to put the other bones away.)
Her recorded voice offstage.
"That you at such times seeing me, never shall
With arms encumbered thus, or this head-shake,
Or by pronouncing of some doubtful phrase . . .
(Fearfully and hurriedly she goes about putting the bones back in the suitcase. Some fall, and she quickly packs them up.)
As 'Well, well, we know,' or 'We could an if we would,'
Or 'If we list to speak,' or 'There be an if they might,'
Or such ambiguous giving out, to note
That you know aught of me—this do swear,
So grace and mercy at your most need help you!"
(Once she has put all the bones back in the suitcase she hides it among the others. The intimate atmosphere changes completely. She takes off her raincoat. She places it ritualistically over a bundle. Underneath she is wearing an identical raincoat. She searches her pockets and takes out a little piece of colored paper.)
Her recorded voice offstage. (Amused) Forty-six, Casalia. You're lucky! *(She takes off this raincoat, too. Underneath she is wearing an identical one. She searches her pockets.)* Everything seems to indicate that the circumstances are in your favor. Forty-six too, but light blue.
Casalia. (Aloud) The other one was yellow! *(She jumps for joy. It is an exaggerated excitement.)* Gentlemen, you're making fun of my color blindness! I have several forty-sixes in beautiful colors! Who wants them? *(Laughing)* The one who put them in my pockets is a big joker, and deserves a promotion. Congratulations.
Her recorded voice, offstage. I thought that Europe was more organized!
Casalia. Where is the one responsible for this old continent? *(Defiantly)* A continent that keeps the *Mona Lisa* in a small room,

doesn't even have a uniformed guard at the entrance hall? And what if I came to rob the *Mona Lisa?* Answer! What if I had already stolen it? *(She adopts a resolute attitude. Energetically, she singles out a trunk and puts it in the middle of the stage. The trunk is illuminated by strong light. The rest of the stage is in darkness. Without using a key, and like a magician who takes a rabbit out of a hat,* CASALIA *opens the trunk. Inside is the* Mona Lisa *by Leonardo Da Vinci. No one should doubt that it is the original.)* That's right. I stole the *Mona Lisa.* I took the famous Neapolitan lady, the wife of Zenobio del Giocondo. You tell me, Mr. Inspector. How could she pull off this spectacular robbery in front of the whole world? How could she have taken it out of the Louvre in broad daylight and walked through Paris carrying the most famous masterpiece in the world, without anyone stopping her to ask her: "What are you doing with the *Mona Lisa?* Where do you think you're taking her?" Well, Inspector, I was so obvious that no one thought for a moment that the picture was anything but a forgery! I'm very sorry. Now the forgery is hanging in the Louvre and the tourists go crazy over it, while the real *Gioconda* is with Casalia Beltrop. I always wanted to have *La Gioconda* at home. It goes with twelve of my major pieces of furniture. *(Shouting)* And not even now, does an official show up? No one confronts this suspicious woman who is confessing. *(She waves* La Gioconda *as if it were a flag. She ostentatiously shows it to the public. Shouting)* Europe, listen to me! What will be left in this continent if you let me run away with *La Gioconda?* All of Europe rests on this painting. At night they sleep peacefully, because the wife of Zenobio del Giocondo assures them a lasting past and allows them to enter the future with confidence. *(Smiling like* La Gioconda*)* This thoroughly studied enigmatic smile protects Europe from an incurable depression. *(Defiantly)* And now what? What will they do without her? I say this out of guilt, a moral condition that endangers my perfect robbery. I am trying to get the attention of the Queen of England, but she will probably say, "At last the French have lost a battle!" Then I address the King of Spain: "Sir, I have left Europe bereft of its *Gioconda.*" "My dear, for years they excluded Spain from Europe and now that we're back, who cares about *La Gioconda.* If you had stolen *Las Meninas,* that would be a scandal, but it's impossible to compare Velázquez's light with anything but divine light. Besides, *La Gioconda* was painted in Italy. Talk to the Pope!" (CASALIA *noisily claps her hands).* Europe, is it all the same to you, the forgery that I left and the precious original I stole? Europe remains silent! Africa prowls about! North America takes care of the future! We will eventually make space-age *Giocondas* and Leonardo will paint again using computers. *(Suddenly scared)* Am I in South America?

Her recorded voice, offstage. Where is South America?

Casalia. Am I smuggling *La Gioconda* into Paraguay?

Her recorded voice, offstage. Perhaps this is Brazil. Did you bring your Carnival costume? Do they still celebrate Carnival on these white beaches?

Casalia. And if I am in Argentina . . . *(Very concerned)* To the person responsible for this continent, or this country . . . or more modestly, this check room: I need my things, my personal belongings! *(Pause)*

Casalia, together with her recorded voice, offstage. If indeed I have arrived in South America.

Casalia. If I have arrived in Argentina, or if they are deporting me from there—I must have done something! Maybe there's a new dictator, and he's writing his speech before becoming President of the Nation.

Her recorded voice offstage. A coup d'etat! They're sending away the ones who think, Casalia.

Casalia. To claim. What can I claim? To declaim. What can I declaim? To clamor? What can I clamor for? I've got my number! But my things still don't show up. *(She walks among the suitcases. Arrogant)* What's the use of having stolen the *Mona Lisa* if my house has been taken over by an infantry battalion? And won't Victor's famous scaphoid be evidence against me?

Her recorded voice, offstage. If the supposed country is in a supposed war and tomorrow we have a President who can shoot you, or who might have already shot you, it would be a good idea to find your documents, my dear! *(She takes off two identical grey raincoats, but first she goes through the pockets, turning them inside out, looking for her documents. She finds the number forty-six in various colors in each garment. She ends up wearing a raincoat identical to the ones she took off.)* I'm exhausted! Orders and counter-orders! To have to hold my head straight! To sing hymns of praise to their victory! *(She is getting worried.)*

Her recorded voice, offstage. What victory? Whose victory? By what means?

Casalia. And the one who will lead the people to victory hasn't even shown up yet!

Casalia together with her recorded voice, offstage. To have arrived in Argentina the very day of the coup d'etat, and not to find the way to show who I am!

Casalia. Besides, everything implicates me!! My umbrella is all wet. *(She opens it and water pours down.)* The water indicates that I was somewhere else before, in a rainy place, where there were stormy clouds.

Casalia together with her recorded voice, offstage. I have to leave fast! (CASALIA, *looks lost on the stage, but moves very quickly, searching and kicking bundles around. She walks over some suitcases on her haunches and moves others from one place to another. She picks up a very heavy suitcase which falls on top of her and crushes her. Only her waving hands and feet can be seen. As this happens, her recorded voice is heard, offstage. Furious)* General, order them to remove this weight from me! I know nothing, I assure you.

Casalia. (Shouting from under the suitcase, superimposing her shouts with those of the recording. Threatening) By the time I count to ten, somebody better get this weight off my back. One, two, three, four . . . otherwise I'll report this to the International Press. Every country in the world will defend me. Every human being in the planet will support Casalia Beltrop . . . five, six, seven, eight, nine, ten, eleven. *(She continues counting along with her recorded voice.)*

Her recorded voice, offstage. While she keeps on kicking under the suitcases) I am a thrush in the mist calling to a deaf man buried in the darkness! *(She tries with all her might to move the suitcase, but it is very heavy. Finally it gives.)* I won the first battle. But it could well be an excuse. Don't forget the future. Keep up your capacity for surprise. As long as you can be surprised, you'll never grow old. And don't lose your forty-six.

Casalia. (Showing her forty-six) This oppressive suitcase contains a small June cloud and another small September cloud. No doubt about it! *(She opens it and from the same suitcase that crushed her, thick white smoke fills the space.)* When the clouds crash against each other, it will rain. And the rainwater will have the same chemical composition as the water that constantly falls from my umbrella. I am terribly committed. That's why it weighed on me. *(Resigned)* Well then, it's high time you let me know what place this is. What seas surround it? What animals wander at dream time? What greenness waves in the golden woods? *(She falls on her knees with her umbrella open.)* Are my butterflies alive? Does Blanca, Peter's cat, still breathe? Have the palm trees of my Botanical Garden grown bigger? Do they still dance in some street? Does anyone fall madly in love, and sing in a state of grace in the vast night? When the clouds crash against each other the flood will come. Everything implicates me. Even if I have an excellent garden full of safe suitcases. *(She closes the suitcase from which the smoke has continued to leak.)* They're even suspicious of the water. It's contaminated. You're drinking transparent radioactivity. *(She gets rid of the suitcase with smoke.)* Everything seems to indicate that they're intentionally concealing my whereabouts. *(She finds a whistle inside a suitcase and blows it.)* And what if I were in Russia? To have arrived in the Union of Soviet Socialist Republics could be quite an event. *(She blows the whistle.)* My name is Casalia Beltrop. But my friends call me Diva.

Her recorded voice, offstage. Diva! What a problem! I couldn't possibly have a less communist name! Exacerbated individualism. Addicted to Marlboros.

Casalia. I consume a lot of Coca Cola.

Her recorded voice, offstage. And what's worse, my clothes are sophisticated.

Casalia. I'm a victim of fashion!

Her recorded voice, offstage. I'll change my name!

Casalia. Where is the Supreme Soviet? *(She blows the whistle.)* It's an honor to be in such a well-guarded place! They have even socialized the suitcases! And they've expropriated my set of red crocodile luggage. How would you say "red" in Russian? It's a color they adore, just like the bulls do! *(She opens a suitcase full of raincoats identical to the ones she's been using. Rejoicing)* God is on my side! Can you talk about God in this paradise? *(She happily waves the raincoats and cheerfully throws them in the air.)* My days of individualism are over.

Her recorded voice, offstage. My name is no longer Diva. I have left fashion behind. I wear the same clothes as everybody else.

Casalia. (Her last phrase is superimposed over her recorded voice.) I wear the same clothes as everybody else. But doesn't wearing the same clothes as everyone else actually mean to be in fashion? I shall always wear grey. It will always rain. They will always suspect me. *(She opens a suitcase which is full of sardine cans.)* They won't let me die either. *(She tries to open a can by biting it. She can't find a way to open it.)* I'm hungry. What time is it? Day or night? Early or late? Before or after? *(She walks around impatiently with the can in her hand. She takes out other cans. She throws them furiously against the suit-*

cases as if they were grenades. One of them explodes. It was, in fact, a grenade.) I want to lodge a complaint!
Her recorded voice, offstage. I'm involved in a public scandal!
Casalia. Horrible things are happening!
Her recorded voice, offstage. Before or after?
Casalia. Smuggling explosives! Piles of bones! They've stolen *La Gioconda* from the Louvre and nobody reacts! I wonder if I'm in Japan. How do you say forty-six in Japanese? *(She throws another can that explodes. The explosion scares her. She makes up her mind, opens a suitcase and gets inside it. She sticks her head out of the suitcase.)*
Her recorded voice, offstage. If they'd at least tell me if I'm coming or going! *(She gets into the suitcase once and for all. Section by section the stage becomes dimmer. The only remaining light is on* CASALIA *in her suitcase. Pause. Blackout.)*

Selected Bibliography

General Background and Criticism

Books

Avni, Haim. *Argentina y la historia de la inmigración judía: (1811–1950).* Universidad Hebrea de Jerusalén, 1983.

Casadevall, Domingo. *La evolución de la Argentina vista por el teatro nacional.* Buenos Aires: Ediciones Culturales Argentinas, 1965 (Serie Cuadernos Culturales).

Castagnino, Raúl H. *Sociología del teatro argentino.* Buenos Aires: Editorial Nova, 1963.

Dujovne, Miriam S., Ana Brecz, Abraham Miller, and Jaime Barylko. *Los judíos en la Argentina.* Buenos Aires: Betenu, 1986.

Elkin, Judith Laikin. *Jews of the Latin American Republics.* Chapel Hill: University of North Carolina Press, 1980.

Foppa, Tito Livio. *Diccionario teatral del Río de la Plata.* Buenos Aires: Argentores, Ediciones del Carro de Tespis, 1961.

Glickman, Nora. "The Jewish Image in Argentine and Brazilian Literature," Ph.D. diss., New York University, 1977.

Itzigsohn, Sara, et al. *Integración y marginalidad: historia de vidas de inmigrantes judíos en la Argentina.* Buenos Aires: Pardés, 1985.

Kleiner, Alberto. *La temática judía en el teatro argentino.* Buenos Aires: Polígono Sur, 1983.

Lewin, Boleslao. *La colectividad judía en la Argentina.* Buenos Aires: Alzamor Editores, 1974.

———. *Cómo fue la inmigración judía en la Argentina.* Buenos Aires: Plus Ultra, 1971.

Marco, Susana, et. al. *Teoría del género chico criollo.* Buenos Aires: Eudeba, 1974.

Onega, Gladys. *La inmigración en la literatura argentina (1900–1910).* Cuadernos del Instituto de Letras. Universidad del Litoral, 1965.

Ordaz, Luis. *El teatro en el Río de la Plata. Desde sus orígenes hasta nuestros días.* Buenos Aires: Leviatán, 1957.

———. *El teatro argentino.* Buenos Aires: Centro Editor de América Latina, 1982.

Orgambide, Pedro and Yahni, Roberto, eds. *Enciclopedia de la literatura argentina.* Buenos Aires: Editorial Sudamericana, 1970.

Perales, Rosalina. *Teatro hispanoamericano contemporáneo (1967–1987).* México: Grupo Editorial Gaceta, 1989.

Saldías, José Antonio. *La inolvidable bohemia porteña. Radiografía ciudadana del primer cuarto de siglo.* Buenos Aires: Freeland, 1968.

Sebreli, Juan José. *La cuestión judía en la Argentina.* Buenos Aires: Editorial Tiempo Contemporáneo, 1968.

Senkman, Leonardo. *La identidad judía en la literatura argentina.* Buenos Aires: Ediciones Pardés, 1983.

Tirri, Néstor. *Realismo y teatro argentino.* Buenos Aires: Ediciones La Bastilla, 1971.

Weisbrot, Robert. *The Jews of Argentina: From the Inquisition to Perón.* Philadelphia: Jewish Publication Society of America, 1979.

Zayas de Lima, Perla. *Diccionario de autores teatrales argentinos (1950–1980).* Buenos Aires: Rodolfo Alonso, 1981.

Articles

Dauster, Frank. "Los hijos del terremoto: Imágenes del recuerdo." *Latin American Theatre Review* (Fall 1988): 5–11.

Foster, David W. "César Tiempo y el teatro argentino-judío." In *El Cono Sur: Dinámica y dimensiones de su literatura,* ed. Rose Minc. Montclair: Montclair State College Publications, 1985, 43–48.

Gambaro, Griselda. "Teatro de vanguardia en la Argentina de hoy." *Universidad* 81 (1970): 301–31.

Glickman, Nora. "Desarraigo contemporáneo en la narrativa de Germán Rozenmacher." *Latin American Fiction Today* (1980): 109–17.

―――. "The Jewish White Slave Trade in Latin American Writings." *American Jewish Archives* 34, no. 2 (1982): 178–89.

Halac, Ricardo. "Recuerdo de Germán." Program Notes to *Simón, caballero de Indias.* Teatro Tabaris, Buenos Aires, July 1982.

Karduner, Luis. "Carta abierta a César Tiempo." *Judaica* 4, no. 45 (1937): 99–194.

Lyon, Ted. "The Argentinian Theatre and the Problem of Identity." *Latin American Theatre Review* (1972): 5–18.

Orgambide, Pedro. "César Tiempo." In *Enciclopedia de la literatura argentina,* by Pedro Orgambide and Roberto Yahni. Buenos Aires: Editorial Sudamericana, 1970.

Pelletieri, Osvaldo. "El realismo en el teatro argentino de los años sesenta." *Espacio* 1, no. 1 (1986): 70.

―――. "Ricardo Halac y sus veinticinco años de realismo." *Latin American Literary Review* (1987): 85–89.

Pogoriles, Eduardo. "Una generación fracturada." *Teatro* 4, no. 12 (1983): 43.

Schalom, Myrta. "Teatro judío en la Argentina." In *Judíos argentinos: Homenaje al centenario de la inmigración judía a la Argentina 1889–1989.* Buenos Aires: M. Zago Ediciones, 1988.

Sosnowski, Saúl. "Germán Rozenmacher: Tradiciones, rupturas y desencuentros." *Revista de Crítica Literaria Latinoamericana* 3, no. 6 (1977): 93–110.

Trastoy, Beatriz. "El teatro argentino de los últimos años: del parricidio al filicidio." *Espacio* 2, no. 2 (1987).

Zayas de Lima, Perla. "Los inmigrantes judíos: personajes del teatro nacional." In *Jornadas de la Historia de la Ciudad de Buenos Aires*. Buenos Aires: Municipalidad de la ciudad de Buenos Aires, 1993.

PERIODICAL SOURCES ON LATIN AMERICAN JEWISH LITERATURE

Folio 17, special issue (1987). *Latin American Jewish Writers*. Ed. Judith Morganroth Schneider. SUNY/Brockport.

Latin American Theatre Review, Ed. George W. Woodyard. University of Kansas, Center of Latin American Studies.

Noaj 1987. Ed. Leonardo Senkman. *Revista de la Asociación Internacional de Escritores Judíos en Lengua Hispana y Portuguesa*. Jerusalem.

WORKS BY AUTHORS INCLUDED IN THIS ANTHOLOGY

Date in parenthesis immediately following the title of the play indicates when it premiered in Argentina.

Dragún, Osvaldo. *La peste viene de Melos* (1956). *Ariadna* (1956).

———. *Historias para ser contadas: 4 tragicomedias de la vida cotidiana* (1957). *Revista Talía* (1957).

———. *Tupac Amarú* (1957). *Losange* (1957).

———. *Los de la mesa diez* (1958). Buenos Aires: G. Dávalos y G. Hernández, 1965.

———. "Los del 80" (1959).

———. *Historia de mi esquina* (1961). Buenos Aires: G. Dávalos y G. Hernández, 1965.

———. *El jardín del infierno* (1962). Centro Editor de América Latina (1966) 73–112.

———. *Milagro en el mercado viejo* (1962). La Habana: Casa de las Américas, 1963.

———. *Y nos dijeron que éramos inmortales* (1962). (with *Los de la mesa 10* and *Historias para ser contadas*). Xalapa: Universidad Veracruzana, 1962.

———. *Amoretta* (1964). Buenos Aires: Carro de Tespis, 1965.

———. *Heroica de Buenos Aires* (1966). La Habana: Casa de las Américas, 1966.

———. *El amasijo* (1967). Calatayud. 1968. (Reedited under the title: ¡*Un maldito domingo!*).

———. *Historia del hombre que se convirtió en perro.* In *Teatro breve hispanoamericano contemporáneo*. Madrid: Aguilar, 1967.

———. *¡Un maldito domingo!* (with *Y nos dijeron que éramos inmortales* and *Milagro en el mercado viejo*) Madrid: Taurus, 1968.

———. "Pedrito el grande" (1973).

———. *Historias con cárcel.* In *Caminos del teatro latinoamericano.* La Habana: Casa de las Américas, 1973.

———. *El amasijo.* In *9 dramaturgos hispanoamericanos. Antología de teatro hispanoamericano del siglo XX.* Ottawa: Girol Books, 1979.

———. "Y por casa, ¿cómo andamos?" (1979).

———. *Hoy se comen al flaco* (with *Al violador*). Ottawa: Girol Books, 1981.

———. *Al violador.* Ottawa: Girol Books, 1981.

———. *Mi obelisco y yo.* In *Teatro abierto 1981: 21 estrenos argentinos.* Buenos Aires: Editorial Teatro Abierto, 1981. 49–61.

———. "Al vencedor" (1982).

———. *Al perdedor.* Rosario: Paralelo 32, 1982.

———. *Hijos del terremoto* (previous title *¡Arriba, Corazón!*). *Gestos* no. 2 (1986).

———. "Como Pancho por San Telmo" (1986).

Eichelbaum, Samuel. *Intimidades. Juventud:* Centro Juventud Israelita Argentina 29 (1913) 18–19.

———. *La mala sed.* Buenos Aires: Selectas América. 1920.

———. *Un romance turco* (with Pedro E. Pico). *La Escena.* suppl. 9 (1920) 1–13.

———. *La Juana Figueroa* (with Pedro E. Pico). *El Teatro Argentino* no. 47 (1921) 1–16.

———. *La cáscara de nuez* (1921) (with Pedro E. Pico). *Teatro popular* no. 133 (1921).

———. *El dogma* (with *El camino de fuego*). *Bambalinas* no. 236 (1922).

———. *El gato y su selva* (1922). (with *Un guapo del 900, Pájaro de barro* and *Dos brasas*). Buenos Aires: Editorial Sudamericana, 1952.

———. *Un hogar* (1922). *Bambalinas* no. 361 (1925) 1–32.

———. *Doctor* (with Pedro E. Pico). *Bambalinas* no. 254 (1923) 1–21.

———. *El ruedo de las almas* (1923). *La Escena* no. 259 (1923) 1–24.

———. *La hermana terca* (1924). Buenos Aires: Argentores, Ediciones del Carro de Tespis.

———. *Sed de amor. Mundo Israelita* 51. no. 2 (1924).

———. *Instinto (narración escénica).* Buenos Aires: M. Gleizer. 1925.

———. *El judío Aarón* (1926). *Revista Talía* 32 no. 6 (1967) 2–17.

———. *Nadie la conoció nunca* (1926). Buenos Aires: Argentores, Ediciones del Carro de Tespis, 1956.

———. *N.N. Homicida* (1927). Buenos Aires: Ediciones del Carro de Tespis, 1965.

———. *Señorita* (1930). *Comoedia para todos.* no. 63 (1930).

———. *Cuando tengas un hijo* (with *Señorita*). Buenos Aires: Argentores, Ediciones del Carro de Tespis.

————. *Soledad es tu nombre* (1932) (with *La mala sed*). Buenos Aires: Argentores, Ediciones del Carro de Tespis.

————. *Ricardo de Gales, príncipe criollo*. Buenos Aires: Sociedad Amigos del Libro Rioplatense, 1933, 136–212.

————. *Destino. Contrapunto* 2 (1945).

————. *En tu vida estoy yo* (1934). Buenos Aires: Argentores, Ediciones del Carro de Tespis, 1966.

————. *Tejido de madre* (1936) (with *Nadie la conoció nunca*). Buenos Aires: Ediciones del Carro de Tespis, 1956.

————. *El gato y su selva* (1940). Buenos Aires: Editorial Sudamericana, 1952.

————. *Un guapo del 900* (1940). Buenos Aires: Editorial Sudamericana, 1952.

————. *Pájaro de barro* (1940). Buenos Aires: Talleres Gráficos Celina, 1971.

————. *Divorcio nupcial* (1941). Buenos Aires: Ediciones Conducta.

————. *Verguenza de querer* (1941). Buenos Aires: Talleres Gráficos Celina, 1971.

————. *Un tal Servando Gómez* (1942) (with *Verguenza de querer* and *Divorcio nupcial*). Buenos Aires: Ediciones Conducta, 1942.

————. *Un patricio del 80* (1949) (with Ulyses Petit de Murat). *Revista Talía,* 1969.

————. *Rostro perdido* (1952). Buenos Aires: Editorial Universitaria, 1966.

————. *Dos brasas* (1955). Buenos Aires: Editorial Universitaria, 1952.

————. *Las aguas del mundo* (1957). Buenos Aires: Ediciones del Carro de Tespis, 1959.

————. *Un cuervo sobre el imperio* (1967). Buenos Aires: Editorial Universitaria, 1966.

————. *Gabriel, el olvidado* (1967). Buenos Aires: Editorial Universitaria, 1966.

————. *Subsuelo* (1967). Buenos Aires: Editorial Universitaria, 1966.

Goldenberg, Jorge. "Argentine Quebracho Company" (1972).

————. *Relevo 1923*. La Habana: Casa de las Américas, 1975.

————. "Fifty-fifty" (1976).

————. *Krinksy* (1977). Buenos Aires: Ediciones de Arte Gaglianone, 1984.

————. *Rajemos, marqués, rajemos*. In *El arca de Noé. Antología de teatro para niños*. Méjico: Mejicanos Unidos, S.A., 1979. 15–54.

————. "Yo estoy bien" (1983).

————. *Knepp*. Buenos Aires: Ediciones de Arte Gaglianone, 1984.

————. *Poniendo la casa en orden. Hispamérica,* no. 42 (1985) 100–121.

————. *Argentino*. Buenos Aires: Ediciones Colihue, 1986.

————. *Cartas a Moreno. Variaciones de una carta de María G. Cuenca de Moreno*. Buenos Aires: Teatro Municipal General San Martín, 1987.

Halac, Ricardo. *Soledad para cuatro* (1961). In *Teatro completo*. Buenos Aires: Corregidor, 1987.

————. *Fin de diciembre* (1965). (with *Estela de madrugada*). *The Angel Press* (1965).

————. *Estela de madrugada* (1965). *The Angel Press* (1965).

———. *Tentempié I y II* (1968). *Tentempié I.* In *Teatro breve contemporáneo argentino.* Buenos Aires: Colihue, 1986.

———. *Segundo tiempo* (1976). In *Teatro completo.* Buenos Aires: Corregidor, 1987.

———. *El destete: un trabajo fabuloso* (1978). Rosario: Ediciones Paralelo 32, 1984.

———. *Lejana tierra prometida.* In *Teatro Abierto 1981.* Buenos Aires: Editorial Teatro Abierto, 1981.

———. *Ruido de rotas cadenas* (1983). In *Teatro completo.* Buenos Aires: Corregidor, 1987.

———. "¡Viva la anarquía!" 1982.

———. *El dúo Sosa-Echague* (1986). In *Teatro completo.* Buenos Aires: Corregidor, 1987.

———. *Teatro completo: Soledad para cuatro, El dúo Sosa-Echague, Segundo tiempo, Ruido de rotas cadenas.* Buenos Aires: Corregidor, 1987.

———. *Mil años, un día* (1986). (originally "La cabala y la cruz"). Buenos Aires: Corregidor, 1993.

———. "La Perla del Plata" (1986).

Novión, Alberto. "Los primeros fríos"

———. *El cambalache de Petroff.* In *La Escena* 4, no. 36 (1921).

———. "Jacinta" (1904).

———. "La tapera" (1905).

———. "Tierra adentro" (1904).

———. "La cantina" (1907).

———. "Mandinga" (1911).

———. "La chusma" (1913).

———. "Don Chicho" (1933).

Raznovich, Diana. "Buscapiés" (1968).

———. "Plaza hay una sola" (1969).

———. "El guardagente" (1971).

———. "El contratiempo" (1972).

———. *Plumas blancas.* Buenos Aires: Ediciones Dédalos, 1974.

———. *Casa matriz.* In *Salirse de madre.* Buenos Aires: Ediciones Croquiñol, 1981.

———. *Desconcierto.* In *Teatro Abierto.* Buenos Aires: Editorial Teatro Abierto, 1981.

———. "Marcelo el Mecánico" (1978). Original version of *Jardín de otoño* (1982).

———. "Autógrafos" (1983).

———. *Jardín de otoño.* Buenos Aires: Edición del Ministerio de Cultura de la Provincia de Buenos Aires, 1983.

———. "Cables pelados" (1987).

———. "Objetos perdidos" (1989).

Rozenmacher, Germán. "Los ojos del tigre" (1967).

———. *Réquiem para un viernes a la noche: drama en un réquiem y un acto.* *Revista Talía (1964).*

———. *El avión negro* (with Roberto Cossa, Ricardo Talesnik and Carlos Somigliana). *Revista Talía* (1970).

———. *El lazarillo de Tormes. Versión teatral de la obra anónima* (1969). *Revista Talía* (1971).

———. *Simón Brumelstein, el caballero de Indias* (1982) (originally, "Simón, caballero de Indias"). Buenos Aires: Argentores, 1987.

Tiempo, César, *El teatro soy yo; farsa romántica en tres actos.* Buenos Aires: Anaconda, 1933.

———. *Pan criollo.* Buenos Aires: Talleres Gráficos Porter Hermanos, 1937.

———. *La alfarda.* Buenos Aires: Talleres Gráficos Porter Hermanos, 1938.

———. *Quiero vivir. Drama increíble en tiempo de fuga: un prólogo, cuatro actos y un epílogo superpuesto.* Buenos Aires: Talleres Gráficos Porter Hermanos, 1941.

———. *El lustrador de manzanas.* Buenos Aires: Argentores, 1958.

———. *La dama de las comedias.* Buenos Aires: Argentores, 1971.

SELECTED ARGENTINE PLAYS ON JEWISH SUBJECTS

Aliber, Alicia and Bernardo. *Mis abuelos campesinos.* Buenos Aires: Ediciones Maicel, 1985.

Aquino, Benjamín. *El yacaré. El Teatro Argentino, Revista Teatral* año 1, no. 7 (19 Nov. 1919).

Beltrán, Oscar R. *El judío Blum. Nuestro Teatro, Revista Teatral* 4, no. 48 (11 March 1937).

Bortnik, Aída. *Soldados y soldaditos.* Buenos Aires, 1972.

———. *De a uno.* In *Teatro Abierto 1982.* Buenos Aires: Argentores, 1982.

———. *Primaveras.* Buenos Aires: Teatro Municipal General San Martín, 1985.

———. *Papá Querido.* In *Teatro breve contemporáneo argentino.* Buenos Aires: Ediciones Colihue, 1986.

———. Domesticados. Buenos Aires: Argentores, 1988.

Capdevilla, Arturo. *La Sulamita.* Buenos Aires: Ed. Agencia General de Librerías y Publicaciones, 1922.

Defilippis Novoa. *Hermanos nuestros. Bambalinas* 4, no. 293 (1923).

Di Yorio, Rafael. "La librería de Abramoff."

Etchegoin y Caselli. "Cuando menos se piensa, salta la liebre" (1914).

Ferri, Oscar [Abraham Zadumaiky]. *La Santería del judío Abraham.* 1932.

Graiver, Bernardo. *El hijo del rabino* (1932). *Argentores, Revista Teatral* (1936).

Kantor, Moisés. *"Leyendas dramáticas"* (1924).

Karduner, Luis. *"David y Betsabé"* (1902).

López de Gomara, Jesús. *"Las biznietas del Virrey o La túnica de Neso,"* (1918).

Malach, Leib. *Regeneración*. Translated by Nora Glickman and Rosalía Rosembuj. Buenos Aires: Pardés, 1984.

Muello y Segré, *Usurero. La Escena* 14, no. 681 (1931).

Muñoz, Alicia. *"Pichincha."* n.d.

Pacheco, Carlos. *De hombre a hombre. El Teatro Nacional* 133, no. 3 (1920).

———. *El caminito de la gloria.* Buenos Aires: Sociedad Argentina de Autores, 1921.

———. *El patio de don Simón.* Buenos Aires: Sociedad Argentina de Autores, 1921.

———. *Compra y venta* (with Pedro E. Pico) Buenos Aires: Sociedad Argentina de Autores, 1921.

———. *Cuadros porteños.* Buenos Aires: Sociedad Argentina de Autores, 1922.

———. *Ropa vieja. La Escena* (1923).

———. *La bandada.* Buenos Aires: Sociedad Argentina de Autores, 1924.

———. *La patota.* In *Los disfrazados y otros sainetes.* Buenos Aires: Eudeba, 1964.

Pelay, Ivo. *Judío.* Buenos Aires: Editorial Argentores, 1926.

———. *Semilla de mirasol. Argentores, Revista Teatral* 10, no. 218 (1943).

———. *Panorama Nacional* (with Rafael Romero) *La Escena* 4, no. 32 (1921).

Rada, Alberto y Mario. *Criollos, gringos y judíos. La Escena* 4, no. 36 (1921).

Romeu, Carlos. *"Hijos de Israel"* (1920).

Roxlo, Conrado Nalé. *"Judith"* (1956).

Schaeffer Gallo, Carlos. *El gaucho judío. La Escena* (1920).

———. With Luis Bayón Herrera. *Los tenebrosos.* 1915.

Sciurano Castañeda, Adolfo, and Lamarque, Víctor. *Un domingo en el suburbio. Bambalinas* 9, no. 458 (1927).

Serebrinsky, Hebe. *Don Elías, campeón.* Buenos Aires: Sociedad Argentina de Autores, 1915.

Vacarezza, Alberto. *Remedios caseros.* Buenos Aires: Sociedad Argentina de Autores, 1915.

———. *La ley palacios.* Buenos Aires: Sociedad Argentina de Autores, 1922.

———. *Casa de juego.* Buenos Aires: Sociedad Argentina de Autores, 1917.

———. *El barrio de los judíos. Revista Teatro Nacional.* 1919.

Villalba, Juan, and Bragam, Hermidio. *Ensalada Rusa. La Escena* 13, no. 619 (1930).

Ziclis, Germán. *Don Jacobo.* Buenos Aires: Editorial Argentores, 1958.